D0768801

Friends and Apostles

Friends and Apostles

The Correspondence of Rupert Brooke and James Strachey,
1905–1914

Edited by Keith Hale

Yale University Press
New Haven and London

PE
6003
.R4
Z483
1998

All material written by Rupert Brooke and James Strachey copyright © 1998 the Trustees of the Rupert Brooke and Strachey Trusts respectively. All editorial matter, appendices and annotations copyright © 1998 Keith Hale.

All rights reserved. This book may not be reproduced in whole or in part, in any form (beyond that copying permitted by Sections 107 and 108 of the U.S. Copyright Law and except by reviewers for the public press) without written permission from the publishers.

Set in Meridien by MATS Typographic Services
Printed in Great Britain by Redwood Books, Wiltshire

Library of Congress Cataloging-in-Publication Data

Brooke, Rupert, 1887–1915.
    [Correspondence.   Selections]
    Rupert Brooke and James Strachey: the hidden correspondence.
  1905–1915/edited by Keith Hale.
    Includes bibliographical references and index.
    ISBN 0–300–07004–7
    1. Brooke, Rupert, 1887–1915—Correspondence.   2. Poets.
English—20th century—Correspondence.   3. Strachey, James—
Correspondence.   4. Translators—Correspondence.   5. Cambridge
Apostles (Society)   6. Bloomsbury group.   I. Strachey, James.
II. Hale, Keith.   III. Title.
PE6003.R4Z483   1998
821'.912
[B]—DC21   98–7353
                                                                          CIP

A catalogue record for this book is available from the British Library.

10 9 8 7 6 5 4 3 2 1

Contents

CONCORDIA UNIVERSITY LIBRARY
PORTLAND, OR 97211

Illustrations

Preface

The Berg Collection of the New York Public Library purchased the complete set of correspondence between the English poet Rupert Brooke (1887–1915) and his close friend, the primary English translator of Freud, James Strachey (1887–1967), in November 1967 from Alix Strachey, James's widow. The collection also included a small number of letters from Brooke to James's brother Lytton.

The letters were obtained on condition that no one would have access to them for ten years without Alix Strachey's permission. In addition, the Brooke Trust sent a letter to Berg curator Lola L. Szladits on 19 December 1969 to say that after the ten-year period the Brooke Estate would be unlikely to grant permission for publication. Although Paul Levy, James Strachey's literary trustee, was subsequently given permission to edit the correspondence (he later abandoned the project), the letters have remained unpublished for more than eighty years.

When Brooke died of blood poisoning on his way to fight the Turkish forces at Gallipoli, his friends in England were quick to turn him into a national hero – a patriotic symbol of the many young men of England who were going to war. That Brooke had recently published five sonnets glorifying patriotic sacrifice did much to promote his legend. That his friends included Winston Churchill, Anthony Asquith and General Ian Hamilton did even more. Churchill capitalized on Brooke's 'most precious' and 'most freely proffered' sacrifice, painting a portrait of Brooke as an eager defender of nation and honour willing to give up his life for England.

Brooke has since been known as a 'war poet', although he saw no action during the war and completed only five poems on the subject. This classification has done his reputation serious injury, for his war sonnets seem misguided and maudlin when compared with the verse of his fellow soldier poets. Although Siegfried Sassoon and others were writing the same type of sentimental poetry as Brooke in the early days of the war, they were fortunate to live long enough to provide a more realistic correction to their early verse. Brooke never had that chance.

His war poems have often been used by critics as a foil against which Owen and Sassoon's later war poems are favourably compared.

Whatever one thinks of Brooke's poetry, it is difficult to dispute Bernard Bergonzi's claim that 'of all the myths which dominated the English consciousness during the Great War the greatest, and the most enduring, is that which enshrines the name and memory of Rupert Brooke' (36). Bergonzi says Brooke's life 'will never lack some kind of archetypal quality, if only because he was such a perfect symbol of the doomed aspirations of Liberal England: a figure from an unwritten, or suppressed, novel by his friend, E. M. Forster' (37). Samuel Hynes has echoed Bergonzi, saying the story of Brooke's life and death 'becomes an obituary of a class and a generation that was destroyed in the war' (*Occasions* 151). He is correct: Rupert Brooke was a man of his time – just not the man they thought he was.

Indeed, to maintain the patriotic legend during and after the war, Brooke's biography had to be altered beyond recognition. And it was. When Brooke Trustee Geoffrey Keynes edited and published his collection of Brooke's letters, he deleted much of the evidence that would have proven that Brooke the man was not the same as Brooke the legend. Keynes edited the letters heavily. More than 300 excisions are indicated in his edition, but actually the number is higher, for he made many deletions silently. The correspondence from his editor at Faber and Faber is full of exasperated enquiries of 'Why delete?' and 'Why bowdlerize this?' To give but one example, Keynes deleted this passage from Brooke's 30 November 1908 letter to Erica Cotterill: 'Do you understand about loving people of the same sex? It is the question people here discuss most, in all its aspects. And of course most of the sensible people would permit it.' In selecting the letters to be published, Keynes in particular refused to includes those between Brooke and James Strachey, saying they would appear in print 'over my dead body' (Rogers, *Brooke* 6). Keynes's refusal to allow the Brooke–Strachey letters into print was undoubtedly due to the strong homosexual current running through the correspondence. Even at Rugby, Keynes had tried to moderate that side of Brooke, complaining of his 'decadent' posings, and expressing his disapproval of Brooke's flirtation with Michael Sadleir. To his credit, Keynes did publish, with few omissions, many of Brooke's letters to him about the poet's adolescent romances. But he was reluctant to print anything the adult Brooke had to say on the subject, and he tried to prevent others from writing on the subject as well.

While working on his 1948 biography of Brooke, *Red Wine of Youth*, Arthur Stringer advanced the view that Brooke was homosexual. When Keynes received word of Stringer's conclusion, he wrote to him to rebut the idea, adding that he hoped Stringer would not allow his book 'to be even remotely coloured by the idea that Rupert was in any way abnormal' (10 June 1947). But the idea of Brooke being homosexual became an increasingly touchy subject for Keynes from this time forward. Robin Skelton added to Keynes's concern by writing to him some time later: 'my generation and all succeeding generations will continue to regard Rupert as a plaster-cast Apollo with homosexual tendencies, as an effete and decadent boy with a gift for sentimentalising reality: that is what my colleagues and my students think' (4 December 1955). Skelton blamed Edward Marsh's *Memoir* of Brooke for this perception and went on to suggest that Keynes's forthcoming edition of Brooke's letters would certainly correct it. Just a month after receiving Skelton's letter, Keynes wrote to Cathleen Nesbitt: 'The letters should effectively dispose of the widespread belief (particularly, I believe, in America) that Rupert was "queer"' (14 January 1956).

Keynes was not the only friend of Brooke who had been upset by Marsh's memoir. James Strachey and many others were concerned that the book had damaged Brooke's reputation. To a large extent, Marsh presents Brooke through Brooke's own words, often by quoting from his letters. Unfortunately, when he is not quoting, Marsh is gushing. Critics also felt that Marsh's quotations from Brooke and his friends did not tell the whole story. Virginia Woolf, herself a longtime friend of Brooke, reviewed the *Memoir* anonymously for the *Times Literary Supplement*, noting that 'it is evident that his friends have not cared to publish the more intimate passages in his letters to them. Inevitably, too, they have not been willing to tell the public the informal things by which they remember him best' (*TLS* 8 August 1918). She was more to the point in a letter to Brooke's friend Katherine Cox written five days after the review appeared:

> It seemed useless to pitch into Eddy [Marsh]. James [Strachey] meant to try, but gave it up. I think it was one of the most repulsive biographies I've ever read [...] He contrived to make the letters as superficial and affected as his own account of Rupert. We're now suggesting that James should write something for us to print. He's sending us the letters to look at. (*Question* 267–8)

The letters Woolf refers to in her letter to Cox, obviously, are those Brooke had written to Strachey. It is unclear whether she ever saw them, but Strachey did approach C. K. Ogden, editor of the *Cambridge Magazine*, in July 1918 about the possibility of reviewing Marsh's *Memoir*. 'I knew him better than many people,' Strachey writes, 'and it would give me a good deal of pleasure to try and explain what he was really like [...] If I wrote it would be something rather scandalous.' Whatever Ogden's response, Strachey did not write a review.

Years later, in 1948, Leonard Woolf addressed the problem when discussing his wife's letters with Vita Sackville-West: 'The difficulty is that the really personal letters are unpublishable and it seems to me that if one publishes only the impersonal ones, one gives a totally false

impression of the character. This was certainly the case with the first
volume of Rupert Brooke's letters which were published' (L. Woolf,
Letters 488).

Geoffrey Keynes called Marsh's *Memoir* 'an elegantly written trifle'
(*Gates* 164) and complained that

> Brooke's unmanly physical beauty was often taken as an indication
> that he was probably a homosexual and therefore to be despised. [...]
> It had, of course, been far from Marsh's intention to produce any such
> impression. He had been deeply attached to Rupert, as he was to
> many young men, but lived himself in a sexual no-man's-land whose
> equivocal aura pervaded the memoir and contributed to the Brooke
> 'legend'. Mrs. Brooke had probably sensed this even though she might
> not have been able to put it into words, and was quite right to feel
> that the pretty sketch should never have been printed. (165)

It is noted elsewhere in this volume (see footnote, p. 47) that the *Memoir*
never had a chance because of the constraints placed on Marsh by Mrs.
Brooke. She is at least partially responsible for the two omissions David
Garnett complained of in a letter to his mother:

> James – who knew him better than anyone else … is silent – he is
> mentioned once as having been on a walking tour with him – Noel
> [Olivier] is of course not mentioned. [...] I am amazed at the
> underlying assumption of the authors.
>   That is: We like our boys to wear their hair rather long – to dabble
> in Socialism, to dabble in 'decadence' … to fancy they really care
> about ethics – but all the time we know they are SOUND: SOUND
> TO THE CORE.
>   When the time comes they'll go off heroically and forget their wild
> oats and die in a Greek island and then we can wallow in sentiment
> … but the wild oats of Mr Marsh are really the important things in
> life. Rupert even though he did go to the bad some time before his
> death at one time cared about the important things and was able to
> understand them. (quoted in *SOL* 282)

Strachey eventually approached a Cambridge publisher concerning
the possibility of writing something – which would have included
publishing some of Brooke's letters to him – to 'set the record straight'.
His reasons for eventually abandoning the idea no doubt included the
realization that the Brooke Trustees, not he, owned the rights to
Brooke's half of the correspondence, and Geoffrey Keynes had made it
quite clear that he would never allow publication. Strachey may have
decided as well that the letters should eventually be published in their
entirety, after those individuals mentioned unfavourably within them

were no longer alive to be wounded by their appearance in print. The letters themselves testify, in any case, that both Brooke and Strachey, while writing them, fully expected them one day to be published.

Now, more than eighty years following Brooke's death, the publication of the letters between Brooke and Strachey provides one of the final pieces of the puzzle of Brooke's life. It is an important piece, for Strachey was Brooke's best friend for longer than any other person, and of Brooke's surviving letters more were addressed to Strachey than to any correspondent other than his own mother. The letters to Strachey cannot provide a completely accurate portrait of Brooke – since he was so intent on showing different sides of himself to different people, none of his letters can. But these letters are among Brooke's most important precisely because they more than any others show the side of Brooke that his early executors tried so hard to suppress.

A Note on the Text

Because so much of the previously published Brooke correspondence was heavily edited or censored, the temptation to publish every last sentence that he and James Strachey exchanged was strong. In the end, however, the decision was made to omit the least interesting one-third of the 400 letters, postcards and telegrams so that readers would not have so much to wade through. The editor's dissertation at Purdue University (1994) does, however, contain all the letters (and a much lengthier introduction), should any reader wish to consult that document.

Nothing has been omitted or changed in the letters printed in this volume, with the exceptions that Brooke's irregular spacing between words, irregular length of dashes and haphazard paragraphing styles (he sometimes incorporates a variety of indentations within the same letter) have all been standardized. Also, whenever a word has been underlined by either writer to indicate italics, that word appears here in italics. Errors in grammar, spelling and punctuation have not been silently corrected and, to preserve the flow of the letters, are not indicated with '[sic]' except when confusion is otherwise apt to occur.

Because James and Lytton Strachey kept the envelopes of letters they received from Brooke, the headings of Brooke's letters bear information on both sender and receiver. Because Brooke generally did not keep envelopes, the letters from Strachey usually do not contain information on the receiver (that is, Brooke's address).

After the initials of the sender and receiver, all words in the heading not in brackets are either written by the sender or appear on the stationery (both Brooke and Strachey were careful to mark through the printed addresses when they were using the letterhead of one place in another). Thus, the heading 'RB, Tuesday late afternoon [22 April 1910],

School Field, Rugby' indicates that Brooke wrote 'Tuesday late afternoon' as the heading for his letter, and the editor has supplied the date. 'School Field, Rugby' is either written by Brooke or is printed on the letterhead. If any uncertainty exists about the date a letter was written, a question mark follows the part of the date in question. Thus, '[22? April 1912]' indicates that the letter was written in April 1912, probably on the 22nd.

Throughout, square brackets are used for editorial insertions. In the infrequent cases in which Brooke or Strachey uses square brackets, a footnote calls attention to the fact. All ellipses and lines appearing in the letters were put there by Brooke and Strachey. When the editor has omitted material from quotations appearing in editorial sections of the book, an ellipsis appears inside square brackets.

Brooke's letters to Lytton Strachey are included in their chronological order in relation to the other letters. The index provides page numbers for all letters written to Lytton.

Christopher Hassall's *Rupert Brooke: A Biography*, the Geoffrey Keynes edition of *The Letters of Rupert Brooke*, and *Song of Love: The Letters of Rupert Brooke and Noel Olivier* edited by Pippa Harris are the sources for many citations in this volume; they have been given the abbreviations *RBB*, *LRB* and *SOL*, respectively. Otherwise, citations are by page number where the author has only one work listed in Works Consulted or by abbreviated title and page where several works are listed; author, title and page are given where clarity requires.

Incorporated throughout the editorial apparatus of the book is a large amount of unpublished material from Brooke's notebooks, manuscripts and letters to friends other than Strachey. Most of this material is located in the King's College Modern Archives at Cambridge. Quotations also appear from unpublished letters relating to Brooke written and/or received by Maynard Keynes, Virginia Woolf, Duncan Grant, David Garnett, Edward Marsh, Jon Stallworthy, Cathleen Nesbitt, Walter de la Mare, Wilfrid Gibson, Geoffrey Keynes, Hugh Dalton, Katherine Cox, Michael Sadleir, Lascelles Abercrombie, Frances Cornford, Dudley Ward, Violet Asquith, Christopher Hassall, George Mallory, Brooke's mother and others. Geoffrey Keynes's papers are located in the University Library, Cambridge. Most of the correspondence involving Mrs Brooke, Edward Marsh, Christopher Hassall, Walter de la Mare, Frances Cornford and Dudley Ward is located in either the Geoffrey Keynes collection or the Brooke collection. Other letters such as those between James and Lytton Strachey, Duncan Grant, Harry Norton, Maynard Keynes and George Mallory are housed in the British Library, London. Additionally, some privately held, uncatalogued material has been supplied by descendants of Brooke's school friends. With previously published letters, the original manuscripts have been consulted whenever possible and any inaccuracies corrected here.

Acknowledgements

I wish most of all to thank Wendy Stallard Flory for her considerable efforts on my behalf while I was working on this project at Purdue University. These efforts included providing exceptional guidance and helping me decipher handwriting, translate foreign terms, identify references and obtain research grants. I am fortunate to have worked with someone so generous and knowledgeable.

Many individuals provided assistance at various stages of this endeavour. Greg Humpa, Andy Hale, James A. McDonald (S.J.) and John Walsh assisted with foreign translations. Raymond-Jean Frontain and Stuart Steltzer provided useful information during the research phase of the project. Roy Russell-Smith, Rupert Russell-Smith and Joan Dunne generously provided information on Hugh and Denham Russell-Smith and the family connection with Brooke. Michael Hartford, Ed Rendell, Terrance Kearns and Lorna Fitzsimmons helped identify certain references in the letters that eluded me. Paul Delany and Michael Hasting shared useful information they obtained while writing their biographies of Brooke. Margaret Moan Rowe, Robert Paul Lamb, G. R. Thompson and Jeff Henderson provided guidance. Berg curator Francis O. Mattson was helpful during my research in New York, as were Jacqueline Cox and Elizabeth Street while I consulted the Brooke Papers in the Modern Archive Centre at King's College Library, Cambridge. Postmaster Tony Johnson of Brockenhurst generously made his collection of historical photographs available to me during my field research in the New Forest. Charles Harvey assisted me in New York. My sincere thanks to all.

I also wish to thank the staffs of University Library (Cambridge), the British Library Manuscript Reading Room and the British Archives. Additional thanks go to Philip N. Cronenwett (Curator, Dartmouth College Library) and Jennifer B. Patterson (Harry Ransom Humanities Research Center, University of Texas at Austin). My gratitude, as well, to the staff of Yale University Press, London: Kevin Brown, Julia Chamberlain, Candida Brazil, Sheila Lee, my copy editor Peter James, and Robert Baldock.

This project could not have been undertaken without the necessary permissions from the Brooke and Strachey Trusts and the New York Public Library. For those permissions, my appreciation to Paul Levy and Michael Holroyd of the Strachey Trust; Jon Stallworthy and Andrew Motion of the Brooke Trust; and Wayne Furman, Office of Special Collections, Henry W. and Albert A. Berg Collection, The New York Public Library (Astor, Lenox and Tilden Foundations). My thanks as well to E. E. Jones who helped with obtaining permission from the Brooke Trust.

I also owe much gratitude to Jim Hright, who first brought the Brooke–Strachey letters to my attention. And I thank the Purdue Research Foundation and the University of Guam (especially Robert Burns and Mary Spencer) for support.

Finally, on a personal note, I want to thank my wonderful mother, Carolyn (Harrell) Hale (who also helped with deciphering Brooke's handwriting); my partner, José Cubol Porcioncula; my Brazilian son, Rogerio dos Santos; and my longtime friend, Anderson McLay Simmons. *Mahal ko kayong lahat. Eu amo todos voces.*

Introduction

Although most readers will be better acquainted with Rupert Brooke than with James Strachey, James comes from the more famous family. The Stracheys have, for more than 400 years, played an important, if often quiet and frequently behind-the-scenes, role in English arts and letters and public affairs. Indeed, even Shakespeare is believed to be indebted to a Strachey: in the early seventeenth century, William Strachey, secretary of the Virginia Company, wrote an account of his journey aboard the *Sea Venture* (one of several ships leaving England destined for Virginia colony) in which a storm caused the ship to be grounded off Bermuda. *The Tempest* appears to contain elements of Strachey's narrative.

James is not the only Strachey to befriend an English writer. William's grandson, John, was a friend of Locke, and James's paternal grandparents, Edward and Julia Strachey, were close friends of Carlyle.

James's father, Richard Strachey, distinguished himself first in military campaigns in India and then, after illness had forced him into convalescing in the Himalayas, in the field of botany. He and a friend by the name of Winterbottom together collected 2,000 botanical specimens in and around Tibet. Richard later returned to India and served in public administration, but he also made significant contributions in meteorology, biology, geology and geography (Holroyd, *Unknown* 14–15). He found time too to paint and to father thirteen children, ten of whom survived into adulthood.

Jane Maria Grant, James's mother, met Richard Strachey in India, and on 4 January 1859 became his second wife (Richard's first wife had died in 1855). When they married, Richard was forty-two and Jane was nineteen. James Beaumont Strachey was the youngest of their thirteen children. Indeed, his eldest sister was so much older than he – twenty-seven years – that her children sometimes referred to James as 'Uncle Baby'.

James and his more famous brother Lytton were by no means the only Strachey children to leave their mark. The eldest son, Richard John

(1861–1935), fought in Burma and served in the War Office during the First World War. The second child, Dorothea, who married French artist Simon Bussy, was a writer and translator. Her best-known original work is probably *Eugène Delacroix* (1907); her most important translations include eleven titles by her friend André Gide. Dorothea also published anonymously a fictionalized autobiography titled *Olivia*. She was an important figure in the French Resistance during the Second World War and she was a friend of Eleanor Roosevelt.

Ralph, who followed Dorothea, became Chief Engineer for the East Indian Railway. Philippa (or 'Pippa'), the next child, was Secretary of the National Society for Women's Suffrage. She published a treatise in 1935 titled *Memorandum on the Position of English Women in Relation to that of English Men*.

Lytton Strachey's accomplishments are well known, thanks in part to the critical success of his *Eminent Victorians*, but thanks also to his eccentric personality and his influence in Bloomsbury. The sister between Lytton and James, Marjorie, was, like Lytton, an accomplished writer, publishing many articles and five books, among which are an account of David (*David the Son of Jesse*, 1921) and a life of Chopin (*The Nightingale*, 1925).

The last of this illustrious group was James, or 'Jembeau'. James early on developed a love of literature. His mother had picked up a keen appreciation of French literature and Elizabethan drama from her father – an appreciation which she passed on to all her children both in the privacy of their home and in her frequent public readings. Charles Richard Sanders, who chronicled several centuries of Stracheys in his book *The Strachey Family*, says, 'It was not unusual for a group made up of some of [Mrs Strachey's] children and their friends to sit around the fire after supper and listen intently while she read the whole of such a play as *Volpone* straight through' (251). She had been raised in Scotland: the Grant family had owned Rothiemurchus, a 25,000-acre estate in the Scottish Highlands to which James repeatedly and persistently invited Brooke (who never went), since the time of the first Queen Elizabeth. Scottish history, songs, dances and folklore made a huge impression on all the Strachey children, who were sent north every summer to stay with their grandparents.

Like most of his siblings, James was a precocious child. When he was five, his mother read to him a letter from the twelve-year-old Lytton, and reported James's response in her return letter to Lytton: 'When I read James the superscription of your letter, he said, "I know that's from Lytton, he's always so absurd"; and when he had heard the contents he exclaimed, "He *is* a funny little creature!"' (15 November 1892, quoted in Sanders 266).

Just as it was natural that James should be closer to his mother than his father – who was seventy when James was born – it was natural as well that James was closest to the two siblings nearest his own age: Marjorie, five years older, and especially Lytton, seven years older.

Michael Holroyd says in his two-volume biography of Lytton:

> the superannuated Victorian family of which [Lytton] was a very junior member must have appeared to him like some faded, splendidly old-fashioned illustration from a schoolroom history book, depicting a social phenomenon already extinct. The new literary idols of the undergraduate, Ibsen and Shaw, Samuel Butler and H. G. Wells, were flying in the face of Victorianism and much that the last three generations of Stracheys had upheld. (*Unknown* 10)

But Holroyd says that Lytton's temperament was not audacious enough for him to break completely free of such a 'potent influence' (10). James was far less audacious even than Lytton, but because he was under the influence of both Lytton and Brooke, another rebel, many of the same opposing forces can be observed at work in him. Ironically, in the end it was James who managed to establish an intellectual life apart from his Victorian heritage, while Brooke was in many ways reclaimed by his.

Virginia Woolf once wrote of the Strachey family in her diary:

> There are three words knocking about in my brain to use of Stracheys, – a prosaic race, lacking magnanimity, shorn of atmosphere. As these words have occurred automatically, & will tease me till written down, I daresay there is some truth in them. All the unpleasantness that I wish to introduce into my portrait of Lytton is contained in them, as if in deep wells. I shall only need one drop of this gall for his portrait, but I fancy a tinge of the kind is perceptible in him too – far more in James, Oliver & Marjorie. Roger's version is that all, except Lady S., lack generosity. It is an air, a vapour, an indescribable taste of dust in the throat, something tickling & irritating as well as tingling & stimulating. But then one must combine with this a great variety of mental gifts, & gifts of character – honesty, loyalty, intelligence of a spiritual order. [...] But when I think of a Strachey, I think of someone infinitely cautious, elusive & unadventurous. (*Diary* vol. 1, 235–6)

David Garnett, a mutual friend of Brooke and the Stracheys, painted much the same picture:

> James was the first of his family I got to know and I was immediately struck in him by what I later discovered was a very marked characteristic of the whole family: an astonishing inelasticity of values, a rigid adherence to certain limitations which they have imposed upon themselves. [...] To know Stracheys well, one has to be ready to accept the atmosphere in which they live. (*Echo* 257–8)

Garnett tells how once, when he was camping with the Olivier sisters and everyone was having a wild time outdoors, James's appearance suddenly transformed the mood of the girls:

> By tea-time, my careless companions were scarcely recognisable: the body was forgotten, the mind supreme.
>   [...] This domination of the ruthless Valkyries of my childhood by James Strachey proved there was some strange virtue, some source of power, in him which made him unlike the rest of us. I gathered, however, that he would have been astonished at the possibility of such a view, but that he regarded his elder brother Lytton rather as we regarded him. (*Echo* 257)

Still, it is difficult to think of a man like James Strachey – who revolted against public opinion in his opposition to the war, in his support of Women's Suffrage, in his acceptance of homosexuality, in his championing of the theories of Freud – as a man with an 'inelasticity of values'. Even in his old age, Strachey certainly could not be called a prude. He objected, for instance, to Holroyd's handling of Lytton's university poems, writing to the biographer:

> I have been positively staggered by some of your ethical judgements on the subject of sex and religion. Your remarks about Lytton's poems astound me. I can quite understand your saying that they're very poor poems and also that you can't quote them. But the impression you give of holding up your hands in shocked horror at their fearful obscenity makes me wonder whether you've ever come across a young human being. . . . When I read these passages I wonder why on earth you ever set out to write this book – and I feel inclined to want the whole thing thrown out of the window. The whole of Lytton's life was entirely directed to stopping critical attitudes of the sort that you seem to be expressing. (quoted in *Unknown* 138n)

Both sides of James Strachey emerge in his letters to Brooke. He is certainly no prude. Yet there is a certain mindset, a product of pedigree, perhaps, that lends itself to exactly the kind of descriptions Woolf and Garnett provided. Strachey possesses an open-mindedness grounded not in the emotions, but in science and reason. Ironically, throughout their correspondence, Brooke accuses Strachey of being the more emotional and sentimental of the two.

Rupert Brooke once wrote to Katherine Cox:

> I am here because at Fettes, in the seventies, Willie Brooke and May Cotterill got thrown together. And then they had a son and a

daughter, and the daughter died, and while the mother was thinking of the daughter another child was born, and it was a son, but in consequence of all this very female in parts – [...] me. (April 1912)

Rupert, the middle one of three boys, was born on 3 August 1887, at Rugby to William Parker and Ruth Mary Brooke. Mrs Brooke had lost her second child, a girl, and was hoping for another daughter when Rupert was born. The awareness of this situation is, as the above passage indicates, one reason Brooke believed himself equipped with what he called his 'feminine intuition'. He once remarked – after the photographer Eugene Hutchinson mistakenly sent him photographs of one Mrs Funk instead of his own – that the soul of a poet was hermaphroditic by nature (Brooke added that 'the modern photographer seems to an old-fashioned person like myself to retouch almost *too* much') (Stringer 204).

As in the case of James Strachey, Brooke was closer to his mother than to his father. In both households, the father was generally removed from the circle of family affairs, while the mother was at the centre of that circle. In Strachey's house, this was mostly because his father had become too old to run the household himself, but also because Mrs Strachey had a magnetism that drew people to her, whether they were family members or persons among her very large circle of friends. If, in Strachey's letters to Brooke, the Strachey household always appears to be overflowing with guests, it was because Mrs Strachey liked people and liked entertaining people. Indeed, she objected to family members marrying cousins not because of moral scruples, but because such marriages limited the growth of the family.

In Brooke's case, Parker Brooke, a housemaster at Rugby, had little choice than to be subservient to his domineering wife. Mrs Brooke ran the family because it was in her nature to control those around her. Of her three sons, it seems that Rupert had a particularly difficult time breaking free from her overbearance.

Unlike James Strachey, who developed a close relationship with Lytton, Rupert does not appear to have been especially close to his elder brother by six years, Richard. Rupert was considerably closer to his younger brother Alfred, who was only three years his junior.

Brooke's diaries reveal a contented boyhood spent playing games, training in the Rugby Rifles (a uniformed militia company), attending plays in London and joining his mother's campaigns for Liberal Party politicians. His diaries also reveal an active academic competition between himself and Strachey. The boys were both ten when they met at Hillbrow School, which Brooke attended as a day pupil. Brooke's June 1900 diary entries include: 'I got 10 less than Strachey for Latin grammar,' 'I got 14 for Ex and Strachey 15½. We had to do some more this morning for which I got 4 an[d] Strachey 0,' and 'I have beaten

Strachey by one mark in Latin Ex.' Another page contains Strachey's address in Stevenage.

Brooke must have taken pleasure in occasionally faring better in Latin exercises than Strachey, for, in truth, Brooke always hated Latin. But he took to Greek, and his fascination with literature began early. By the age of seven he was reading constantly and writing simple rhymes. He wrote his own magazine at the age of ten and made numerous contributions to both official and unofficial magazines of Rugby School. Early notebooks, particularly one he kept from 1904 to 1907 (and dedicated 'To those who understand'), indicate that Housman and Wilde were the writers who most impressed him. Housman was a particular favourite. Brooke wrote at least two poems for Housman – 'Letter to a Live Poet' (January 1911) and 'Letter to A Shropshire Lad' (February 1911) – and he imitated Housman's poetic form, though rather poorly, in 'Lines Written in the Belief that the Ancient Roman Festival of the Dead was called Ambarvalia' (1910) and several unpublished poems. In an address to Rugby's literary society, the Eranos, Brooke said that one should read Housman's *A Shropshire Lad* 'on an autumn morning when there is a brave nip of frost in the air and the year is sliding quietly toward death' (*RBB* 95) – and he wrote to Geoffrey Fry in July 1907: 'I met Laurence Housman the other day. His brother is the only poet in England' (*LRB* 90).

After Hillbrow, Brooke and Strachey parted company for a time, Strachey going to St Paul's and Brooke attending school at Rugby, where his father's position of housemaster assured him of always having a room of his own. In fact, except for a night or two, Brooke never shared a room with anyone for the entirety of his life.

Geoffrey Keynes and Hugh Russell-Smith became Brooke's best friends at Rugby. Both later observed that many of Brooke's Rugby schoolmates regarded him as unorthodox, primarily because of the extravagant length of his hair, but that he won their respect by distinguishing himself at sports.

At the age of seventeen Brooke became friends with the poet St John Welles Lucas-Lucas, a follower of Ernest Dowson and of Oscar Wilde (whose trial had taken place only nine years before). Lucas, then aged twenty-five and, in Paul Delany's words, 'a homosexual aesthete' (*Neo-pagans* 8), was for a while Brooke's mentor and, as such, the most frequent recipient of his poetry. Brooke wrote to Lucas that he wanted 'to complete my set of the three great decadent writers – Oscar Wilde, St. John Lucas, and Rupert Brooke' (*LRB* 65). It is not surprising, then, that Brooke began copying the style of both Lucas and Wilde in his poems and letters. Wilde's *De Profundis* seems to have made a particularly strong impact. Brooke ordered the book even before its release, and it followed him to Italy. He read it on the train going back to England, then re-read it, making notes to himself in the margins. He also copied maxims from Wilde into his notebooks, and on one page simply wrote Wilde's name.

Second only, perhaps, to his interest in literature was his interest in politics. His disdain for both the Conservative Party and the Church of England can be seen in a 1907 letter to Hugh Russell-Smith:

> As for the Church of England Young Lady, I wasn't cynical. I used to be cynical about the C. of E. when I went every Sunday. [...] Now I'm no longer cynical about it. I hate it; and work against it. [...] Also I think it has a bad influence. A very small part of this may be seen, very clearly, if you and the other Liberal members of your family will get a book and see exactly how the Bishops in the House of Lords have voted for the last twenty years. It's amusing reading: but indignation-stirring in a quite serious minded person.

Romance did not escape the young Brooke's attention, either. During his Rugby years, he fell in love with a boy named Charles Lascelles. Virtually everything we know about this relationship is gleaned from Brooke's letters to Katherine Cox and James Strachey. In an undated letter to Cox, Brooke wrote that once when he was listening to music in chapel, 'the last part was rather drowned by the steady clump of young boots up the aisle . . . And by then, no doubt, I was all eyes, & straining, for Charlie's brunette radiance among them all – & he'd look up towards me a fraction of a second as he passed.' Brooke wrote to Strachey on 10 July 1912, that during his summer holidays of 1906 and 1907 he and Denham Russell-Smith, Hugh's brother, would often 'lie entwined' in a hammock at the Russell-Smith summer home in Brockenhurst, 'But I lay always thinking Charlie.' Paul Delany reports that Brooke still kept Lascelles's photograph in his room while he was at Cambridge in 1908 (*Neo-pagans* 239 n.9), and Brooke's letters to Strachey show him still interested in Lascelles and trying to arrange meetings with him in London until fairly late in his life. There is also an April 1913 letter to Geoffrey Keynes asking Keynes to return a favour by providing Brooke with Lascelles's London address.

Brooke's romance with Lascelles seems to have been one of the most intense relationships of his life. It appears that in Brooke's mind none of his subsequent loves approached the innocent, pure beauty of this first romance. Adrian Caesar says, 'it is the "innocence" of his love for Charles Lascelles that seems to be the template for all his other relationships' (34). It is therefore likely that Lascelles was the object of some of Brooke's early poems of love and loss.

However, it was not with Lascelles but with Denham Russell-Smith, two years his junior, that Brooke had his first sexual experience. Brooke's long, graphic description of the event can be found in this volume in a letter to James Strachey. It is in many ways the most fascinating letter written by Brooke. Denham, who died at twenty-three, had been sixteen and Rupert eighteen when they first began 'kissing and hugging' at Rugby and Brockenhurst; Russell-Smith was twenty when Brooke seduced him at Grantchester.

More is known of Brooke's third flirtation with a young male friend, Michael Sadleir, thanks to Rupert's detailing the developments in a series of letters to Geoffrey Keynes. Although Brooke's early tone implies that he entered the relationship out of a desire for adventure and perhaps a good laugh, it soon changes. By the end of the summer term, when he and Sadleir were forced to part, Brooke was in despair. Sadleir, the famous book collector and author, was at that time still Michael Sadler – he later added the 'i' to his surname to distinguish himself from his father, Sir Michael Sadler. His involvement with Brooke began in early 1906 when he asked the school photographer for Rupert's photo. On 23 February, Brooke sent Keynes – who was spending the term with a family in Germany – his first letter describing the situation:

> It began by Dean catching me one day & informing me that 'a gentleman' in another House, had been trying to buy a photo of me: Dean was willing, but my leave was necessary. My enormous conceit was swelled even more – and I gave leave. [...] I secretly made inquiries and found it was one I knew of old – one with the form of a Greek God, the face of Hyacinthus, the mouth of Antinous, eyes like a sunset, a smile like dawn. . . . Sadler. It appears that the madman worships me at a pale distance: which is embarrassing but purple. . . . So I wander around, taking a huge aesthetic delight in the whole mad situation.

This letter is quoted in Keynes's *The Letters of Rupert Brooke*, though Keynes silently omits Sadleir's name (see *LRB* 41).

Brooke began calling his new love 'Antinous' in reference to the young lover of Hadrian who was known throughout the Roman world for his beauty, and whose posthumous cult had rivalled for a time the growing popularity of Christ. Although Hassall insists that Brooke merely adopted the name from a figure in one of Simeon Solomon's paintings (*RBB* 83), the fact that Brooke knew something about Hadrian's Antinoüs is evident in his referring to 'Antinous, the fair Bithynian' (*RBB* 131). Bithynia is, indeed, where Antinoüs was born and where Hadrian met the young man. The motif of dangerously beautiful boys was popular among many poets of the Decadent movement – and the name of Antinoüs was commonly invoked (John Addington Symonds, for example, wrote 'The Lotos-Garland of Antinous' and Montague Summers published *Antinous and Other Poems* in 1907 – and it is worth mentioning that Brooke's poems from this period show a marked similarity to those of Summers).

Brooke was a disciple, telling Keynes on 4 June 1906 that he had in his room 'a framed picture of the Roman Antinous (the prototype, of course. The reincarnation's likeness is within a cupboard)'.

Brooke continued to mention Sadleir in his letters to Keynes, though Keynes was less than receptive. On 23 March, Brooke reported that 'Antinous' was ill 'and so left the paths of men. [...] This will allay your fear of my "doing something rash" during this term. But next term you must be prepared for the worst. An English summer (and my last term) really invites one to all that is "rash"' (23 March). This letter is followed on 31 March with:

I have obtained Antinous's – I mean Sadler's – photograph from him; and I employ my spare time in sending & receiving letters. [...] His letters are quaint and a little sad. They are filled with little halting sentences, faintly expressive. [...] 'X said he met you going out a walk. *I* never seem to be able to do so for all my efforts' [...] It is all rather sweet and rather unusual: and he really looks very nice.

Again, Keynes quotes the letter but silently deletes 'I mean Sadler's' (see *LRB* 46). At the time, Keynes must have written back questioning either the verity or the sincerity of Rupert's reports. Brooke replied, 'You wonder how much of my affaire is true. So do I. (So, no doubt, does he!) It does not do to inquire too closely. It is now very pleasant. Some day perhaps we shall grow old and "wise", and forget. But now we are young, and he is very beautiful' (15 April 1906). Brooke goes on to say that 'At present he – the adorable, rose-crowned – is at Rome: and I receive affectionate pale letters from him whenever the Gods, and the Italian posts, permit.' Brooke wrote to Keynes a month later:

Antinous has got – the mumps! This is so horribly incongruous that it sounds like a line from one of Heine's most bitter lyrics. He will be back in a week or two. I am a little sorry. For though I love to look upon him – as a supreme work of art – yet he is something of a *tertium quid* [...]

I am writing nothing, not even a Hymn to Antinous. I am content to exist. I know now whither the Greek Gods have vanished now-a-days. They are to be found in public schools. Always, in the sunshine, and the Spring, I see them, thinly disguised, rushing over the grass, supple of limb & keen-eyed, young and beautiful. Here is Olympus, and now. I feed on the nectar of Life, from Ganymede's hands, and from amidst my young unconscious gods, write to you now, ecstatically. (10 May 1906)

The reference to Sadleir as a third party must mean that Brooke was still involved with – and more serious about – Lascelles. Whatever the

case, it is clear from Brooke's letters to Keynes that Brooke was hurt
when the 'affaire' with Sadleir ended. It is not clear whether Sadleir
actually broke off with Brooke, or if the completion of term at Rugby
ended it for them, since Brooke was bound for Cambridge and Sadleir
for Oxford. Lascelles was going to Oxford as well, and the sudden
departure of both young men left Brooke downhearted. He had written
to James Strachey the previous year that it was a pity Strachey was going
to Cambridge 'since I am for Oxford'. Christopher Hassall remarks that 'It
is curious that the fitness of his father's college at Cambridge should ever
have been in question' (*RBB* 67). The obvious explanation is that Brooke
wanted to be with Lascelles and Sadleir. But it was not to be, and he
wrote again to Keynes on 22 June that 'Beauty and light have fled on
tumultuous wings, and walk in lonely unlit places beyond the stars.
Rugby is full of the dreary ghosts of dead hopes and remembered joys.'
This year the summer did not mean vacation, it meant the end of his
days at Rugby: 'That gay witch, the Summer, who charmed me three
weeks ago! I have looked into her face, and seen behind the rouge & the
smile, the old, mocking visage of an harlot.'

Near the end of the summer, on 5 August, he wrote again to Keynes:

> I am a little grieved that my conduct at the end of last term was
> strange. You must have found me absent & very frigid, at Rugby and
> at Lord's. I suppose I seemed, as I felt, to be existing rather
> perfunctorily, my attention fixed upon things many millions of miles
> away. I had warned you so of course you understood, in part. You
> realize that I considered myself *in profundis*; that, to my puerile
> imagination, my heart was being slightly fractured [...] in future, my
> Scheme of Things will never be quite as real and home-like as in
> recent, dead days when I, with one other, imagined heaven, and
> found it real, for a time. . . . But my self-pity must be as nauseous to
> you as it is to me. It is not fashionable to feel these things deeply. But
> this deserted Rugby is Hell, and I am a pale ghost who has lived, and
> can now only dream.

The sentence 'It is not fashionable to feel these things deeply' reveals
that Brooke did, in fact, feel the loss of Lascelles and/or Sadleir deeply.
Exactly one month later, when Keynes was planning a trip to the part of
England where Sadleir lived, Brooke wrote again: 'In or about an house
in that town, named Eastwood, you may happen upon a beautiful youth
named Michael Sadler. Smile on him for I loved him – once.'

1905–1907

B rooke spent a few weeks in Italy at the beginning of 1905, but it is clear from his letters that he was homesick and unimpressed. He wrote to Geoffrey Keynes from Rapallo: 'Half the night perhaps I lie awake thinking [...] all the time I am profoundly bored. At intervals they drag me up to Genoa and round a picture gallery; which is wasted on me. I say "How Beautiful!" at every fourth picture, and yawn' (*LRB* 15).

In the summer of 1905 Brooke made the first of several consecutive summer visits to the Russell-Smith home in Brockenhurst. In October he became Head of his House at School Field, Rugby. And in December he sat, along with Geoffrey Keynes and Hugh Russell-Smith, for University scholarships at Cambridge. Brooke received a classical scholarship from King's College, while his friends were accepted at Pembroke and St John's respectively. It was at Cambridge that Brooke was reunited with James Strachey.

After leaving Hillbrow, Strachey had attended St Paul's School and then made his plans for Trinity College, Cambridge. Once Strachey heard that Brooke was bound for Cambridge, too, and once he relayed the information to his brother Lytton, Brooke became an 'embryo' – a possible candidate for election to the secret Cambridge Conversazione Society, more commonly known as the 'Society' or the 'Apostles', to which Lytton belonged and to which James would be elected once he himself got to Cambridge. Meanwhile, Geoffrey Keynes's constant words of praise for Brooke while at Rugby had drawn the attention of another Apostle – Geoffrey's elder brother Maynard. James, writing in 1906, probably to his cousin Duncan Grant, explains the events:

> To begin at the beginning. Lytton, as you know, went to spend a week-end at Cambridge in the end of July. He stayed with Mister Keynes who said 'I've just been down to Rugby to see my young brother who's at school there in Brooke's house.' Wall [sic], Lytton just says if he's heard of Rupert. 'Of pretty well nothing else.' So between them they guessed he'd better go to Cambridge.

In order to evaluate the new embryo, Lytton asked James to prepare a 'catechism' for Brooke to answer. James obliged, but Brooke did not take it seriously, providing frivolous answers. Lytton then suggested that Brooke be asked to visit so that he could be examined in person; thus Brooke came to be a guest at the Strachey residence in September. James's letter, quoted above, continues:

> There was, then, great excitement when he was to arrive. For Giles [Lytton] had arranged to become intimate with him &, if necessary, start a correspondence.
>   When he came he was merely, as it seemed to me, uninteresting.
>   The visit went off with a smoothness that was, for an epistolary description, fatal.

For his part, Brooke wrote to Geoffrey Keynes after the visit: 'Lytton Strachey I found most amusing, especially his voice.'

Brooke was unhappy during his first term at Cambridge. He longed for Rugby and spent his time mostly with his former Rugby friends, Keynes and Russell-Smith. Jonathan Gathorne-Hardy, in his study of the British public schools, noticed this phenomenon among many of the boys leaving the schools, and leaving the boy they loved (see *Old School Tie* 179). But Brooke did make one important new friend during his first term: Edward Hugh John Neale 'Daddy' Dalton (1887–1962), who would go on to become a prominent figure in the Labour Party. Hugh Dalton had attended Eton and was now studying economics at King's. Dalton and Brooke formed a bond due to their mutual love of Swinburne and of Housman's *A Shropshire Lad*, which they often read to each other (Dalton 39). Before the term ended they had founded a club known as the Carbonari, a name taken from an early-nineteenth-century revolutionary society in Italy. The Carbonari (or the 'charcoal-burners') met once a week to discuss poetry and read papers to each other. Other members of the group included Gerald Shove, Francis Birrell, Arthur Schloss and Steuart Wilson; all were students of King's College.

Brooke and Dalton were together invited to join another society during their first year: G. Lowes Dickinson's discussion group of a half-dozen undergraduates and a half-dozen dons, which met in his rooms and was known simply as Dickinson's Society.

Throughout the term (indeed, throughout the next year and a half), Brooke continued to be privately evaluated by the Apostles. When Strachey wrote to Duncan Grant on 18 October 1906, inviting him to a series of parties for possible embryos, he noted in parenthesis: 'The most important guest at the parties is Rupert Brooke.' Among those questioning Brooke at one such party was Harry Norton, who sent off a report on 'the Rajah' to Lytton in London: 'He also thought one shouldn't commit sodomy "since in physical things one should obey the dictates of Nature".' Maynard and Lytton had begun the practice of calling Brooke alternatively 'Rajah' and 'Sarawak', after hearing erroneous rumours that Sir Charles Johnson Brooke, the second Rajah of Sarawak, was a distant relative of Brooke. When Brooke heard of his nickname, he began calling his mother – though not to her face – 'the Ranee' (after the Rajah's wife, Margaret de Windt), a practice he maintained until his death.

James, meanwhile, was involved in brief liaisons with Walter Lamb and Duncan Grant (who was also being courted by Lytton). James mentions ending his affair with Lamb in a letter to Grant in late January 1906. He wrote to Grant the following autumn, on 3 October:

> I really believe I was speaking the truth when I said I wasn't in love with you. But at the same time when you're not here its simply awful. [. . .] The truth is simply that I thought you and Lytton (even in my most passionate moments) worthy of one another: I was not angry nor jealous. [. . .] But I still went on thinking I was in love with you till you came back – with a moustache. [. . .] I suppose the explanation is that I have a great affection for you and a lust for you and yet I'm not in love with you.

Strachey wrote to Grant again on 8 November 1906, from Cambridge: 'This is a dreary hole; where one divides one's time between buggering the senior dean's sons and hearing Donald Tovey massacre The Appasionata [sic]. [...] I suppose you'll be coming to see the Rajah in his tights and spangles.'

As Strachey's letters suggest, Brooke by this time had grown into the handsome young man whose looks became the stuff of legend. He was just under six feet tall, had small ears, a long neck, a mix of auburn, blond and golden-brown hair (which was very thick, worn quite long, and which he frequently had to toss back off his forehead), deep-set eyes and an attractive mouth. W. B. Yeats's appraisal of Brooke as the 'handsomest man in England' and Frances Cornford's poem calling him 'A young Apollo, golden haired' have been too often quoted. But they had considerable company in commenting on Brooke's beauty. Indeed, it sometimes seems that every person who ever met Brooke, and certainly every person who ever wrote about him, felt compelled to write down their impressions of his appearance. A complete compilation of these descriptions would probably make a book, and doubtless a cloying one. Still, it seems worth while to look at just a small selection of the comments here in order better to understand Strachey's adulation of Brooke, and to show the extent to which even otherwise dispassionate males fell under the spell of his physical presence.

Leonard Woolf, on the first time he saw Brooke: 'That is exactly what Adonis must have looked like in the eyes of Aphrodite. [...] It was the sexual dream face not only for every goddess, but for every sea-girl wreathed with seaweed red and brown.'

Cambridge under-librarian Charles Sayle, who became a friend of Brooke, writing in his diary: 'Standing in my hall in the dark, thinking of other things, I looked towards my dining-room, and there, seated in my chair, in a strong light, he sat, with his head turned towards me, radiant. It was another unforgettable moment. A dramatic touch. A Rembrandt picture. Life' (quoted in Lehmann, *Strange* 28–9).

The photographer Eugene Hutchinson, on taking Brooke's photo:

I had found myself confronted by an unbelievably beautiful young man. There was nothing effeminate about that beauty. He was man-size and masculine, from his rough tweeds to his thick-soled English boots. He gave me the impression of being water-loving and well-washed. Perhaps this was due to the freshness of his sun-tanned face and the odd smoothness of his skin, a smoothness you see more in women than in men. [...] He submitted to my manipulations without protest, though he broke into a laugh when with my own hands I removed his neck-tie and opened up the throat of his soft-collared shirt. (Stringer 203).

George Dangerfield, in his epilogue to *The Strange Death of Liberal England*:

All his life he stood out from his surroundings. . . . that beautiful head, the wild blond hair threaded with metallic gold, the incredibly clean features, the wide eyes. Brooke's was a face which could, with perfect plausibility, be compared to a young god's: it was at once pure and sensual and sensitive. (427)

Maurice Browne, describing Brooke walking through Chicago after returning from the South Pacific: 'Every woman who passes – and every other man – stops, turns round, to look at that lithe and radiant figure' (16–17).

General Ian Hamilton, writing in his diary after offering Brooke a staff position that was refused: 'He looked extraordinarily handsome, quite a knightly presence, stretched out there on the sand with the only world that counts at his feet' (quoted in *RBB* 496).

Atlantic Monthly's Ellery Sedgwick, on first meeting Brooke: 'A young man more beautiful than he I had never seen. [...] His complexion was as ruddy as a young David's. [...] Man's beauty is much more rare than woman's. I went home under the spell of it and at the foot of the stairs cried aloud to my wife, "I have seen Shelley plain!"' (328–9).

In *Memories and Friends*, A. C. Benson provides what may be the least emotional and most complete physical description of Brooke – the type of description that one cannot glean from black-and-white photographs:

> It was the colouring of face and hair which gave a special character to his look. The hair rose very thickly from his forehead, and fell in rather stiff arched locks on either side – he grew it full and over-long; it was of a beautiful dark auburn tint inclining to red, but with an underlying golden gleam in it. His complexion was richly coloured, as though the blood were plentiful and near the surface; his face much tanned, with the tinge of a sun-ripened fruit. [...] his voice was far from beautiful, monotonous in tone, husky and somewhat hampered in his throat. (327)

Brooke's mother did not approve of people openly admiring his appearance. It greatly distressed her when she first learned that he was being called 'the handsomest man in England' (she wrote to one of his friends, 'He wasn't, was he?'), and the would-be biographer Richard Halliburton, for one, found that 'any reference to Rupert's physical attractiveness invariably awakened her anger' (Stringer 17).

All of the emphasis on Brooke as a physical entity is important to remember when discussing the friendship between Strachey and Brooke, for Strachey admitted that his Cambridge friendship with Brooke developed out of carnal attraction. As early as 30 November 1906, James was letting Rupert know he was in love with him. And in a letter to Duncan Grant written on 25 February 1907 Strachey tells of the agony of waiting for Brooke to return to Cambridge (unknown to Strachey, Brooke had been delayed by the death of his elder brother Richard). James looked more than once each day for a light in Brooke's window. After finally meeting up with him, Strachey then waited in his room every evening for six weeks in case Brooke should stop by. After the third week he approached Brooke and asked, 'Are you ever coming to see me?' Brooke replied, 'Perhaps I may, some day.' Strachey continued to wait, meanwhile writing to Grant: 'Will he ever come? [...] But the worst of all is that every one else can see him as much as they like [...] everyone but me: – and I love him. [...] By the way, the whole thing's public now.' Not long afterwards, Strachey was writing to Grant again, admitting that his feelings for Brooke were creating problems:

> I have spoken to Rupert again. Nowadays three sentences in the street seem incredibly heavenlike. [...] The whole of my behaviour must have seemed to indicate that I wanted to bugger him. [...] I merely said I was in love with him. [...] But naturally he doesn't want to go and have a tête-à-tête with a person who may at any moment try to rape him. [...] *Do* believe in him. (11 March 1907)

Grant was trying to believe in Brooke, but confessed to Lytton in an early March letter: 'I cannot understand Rupert; the absolute vagueness of his behaviour to James is so inexplicable.' But it was James's behaviour that was bothering his brother. Lytton wrote to Grant:

> I am dreadfully shattered about James. [...] he takes no interest whatever in anything but the few people whom he happens to admire or be in love with – which of course is simple Death. The poor thing seems to be unable to think or to read or to work *at all*. He spends his time dreaming of Rupert over a solitary fire [...] I now think that Rupert is certainly the best person going about; but I don't see how to renew acquaintance, for I don't feel at all inclined to be snubbed. (6 March 1907)

A 9 April letter to Grant finds James making detailed calculations as to when Brooke will answer his last letter, even delaying plans to join Lytton on holiday in case Brooke's letter should arrive.

During May Term 1907, Brooke teamed up with a new friend, Justin Brooke, to found the Marlowe Dramatic Society, which performed Marlowe's *Faustus* in November with Brooke cast as the Chorus.

Brooke spent part of the summer with Hugh Russell-Smith at Lulworth Cove and Brockenhurst. He wrote to St John Lucas-Lucas from the Russell-Smiths on 4 August: 'Now I am staying with this foolish family again till about next Saturday. They are delightful, and exactly as they were last year.'

By August rumours were spreading that Brooke was having an affair with Arthur Hobhouse, an Apostle who had been elected primarily because of his good looks. Virginia Woolf was aware of the rumour, and recorded it:

> 'Norton tells me', Vanessa [Bell] would say, 'that James is in utter despair. Rupert has been twice to bed with Hobhouse' and I would cap her stories with some equally thrilling piece of gossip; about a divine undergraduate with a head like a Greek God – but alas his teeth were bad – called George Mallory. (*Moments* 174)

The Hobhouse rumours did indeed have Strachey in despair, but by the end of term he was reassured. He told Grant that when he and Brooke shook hands upon parting, 'the only thing that mattered was the love [...] he meant me to understand from it that in some wonderful way he sympathised, he really cared. And so I too became different and miraculously expressed to him how much I loved him' (December 1907).

At Christmas, Brooke joined a skiing party in Switzerland.

JS, July 4, 1905, 69 Lancaster Gate, London

Dear Brooke,

Do you remember my name? I deserve that you should have forgotten it, considering that it's entirely my fault if you have. I shall always admire your courageously spasmodic attempts at a correspondence – which have long since (alas!) been crushed by my stolid silence. But Conscience and Hope for better things have finally defeated Idleness; and I hereby vow that I will write you a letter once a week, on condition that you (but I'm afraid you'll refuse to have any dealings with me) will do the same. I haven't the faintest notion what there will be to write – but all the same I'll do my best.

And eventually perhaps you may be able to accept what is at present a perfectly indefinite invitation to stay with me in the summer (somewhere?) as you did at Ardeley Bury in the year – but it would be too horrible to write down the date in cold ink.[1]

I hope you won't think me rude or mad; but I want to try once more to be

Your friend

James B. Strachey.

RB, July 7th [1905], Rugby Station
to JS, 69 Lancaster Gate, London

Dear Strachey,

I refuse to vow anything. I know myself too well. My resolves are continually being shattered (in 1905 as in 1895 – or whatever that prehistoric Hill-brovian date may be) especially in the matter of letters. However, I promise to do my best, and if at any time my resolution lapses, pen me a few fierce vitriolic words and you shall receive by the next post a lachrymose & abject apology in my most emotional hand writing. Of you I have had fairly recent information. It is a long story for my diffuse pen to explain how I came by it; but I will strive to be concise. 'Twas thus: – Last winter holidays – Dec. 24th to be exact – I fell ill, – a habit of mine.[2] So for a fortnight I dwelt in realms of drugs & thermometers & convalescence, until one day my credulous mother & my maniac doctor persuaded themselves that I was 'pulled-down' and 'done-up' and other such things, & so needed rest. In time they ordered me to absent myself from Rugby School for a term & 'recover' in Italy.

1 Brooke had visited the Stracheys at Ardeley Bury, a country house near Stevenage, Hertfordshire, in 1898.
2 Brooke suffered from recurring bouts of conjunctivitis, which he said came from 'gazing too often on Butterfield's architecture'. The chapel and New Quad at Rugby School were designed by Butterfield.

At this I was very wroth, for I knew that I was really quite well & I did not desire exile. However, the Fates & the hare-brained doctor were too stubborn, and at length they packed me off, sadeyed & solitary to the South. There I abode for about the space of two months, during which I spent a week at Florence. At Florence on Carnival night I quite remarkably met Duncan Grant,[1] who gave me the latest information about you. He contradicted himself every three minutes, so the information was probably wrong; but it was very interesting, and I have entirely forgotten it all. The one thing I can remember is that you are destined for Cambridge, which is unsatisfactory, as I am for Oxford. Pray explain all these things and tell me who you have become since I knew you last. For myself I am as ever, – dividing my time between playing cricket badly, and dreaming.

Why at the end of your epistle do you express a hope that I shall think you "neither rude nor mad"? Obviously I should not think you rude. Anyhow I very rarely think anyone rude. And equally obviously I think you mad. You always were; and I hope you are still. I always endeavour to be as mad as possible in this sane grey world; and I shall not insult you by calling you sane.   Yours ever

Rupert Brooke

Please ignore this vast [ink] blot. It is very ugly and I can't imagine how it got there.   RCB

JS, July 12 [1905], 69 Lancaster Gate, London

Dear Brooke,

I suppose this letter must be mainly biographical. I have been at St. Paul's for six years, during which many things have happened which at the

---

1   Duncan James Corrowr Grant (1885–1978), the painter, and Strachey's elder cousin by two years. Like Strachey, he met Brooke at Hillbrow School. His lovers included David Garnett, Maynard Keynes, Arthur Lee Hobhouse, both James and Lytton Strachey, George Mallory, Vanessa Bell and Adrian Stephen. Grant lived with David Garnett and Vanessa Bell after the war, first trying to be lover to them both, but finally opting for Garnett. He told Paul Roche that the first time he made love to Bell, her husband Clive 'burst into the room while we were at it and went straight through to the next room', saying as he passed through, 'Oh, don't stop. Please go on' (Roche 19). Grant was the one Bloomsbury figure Brooke never broke with, perhaps because Grant was also a member of Eddie Marsh's social circle. Brooke wrote to Katherine Cox from Germany in March 1912: 'Give Duncan my love'. He also kept paintings by Grant in his Old Vicarage rooms. Even at the height of his anti-Bloomsbury tirades, Brooke dined with Grant, Marsh and George Mallory in Soho on 17 September 1912. And, while in America, Brooke wrote to Marsh that he missed him, Harry Norton and Grant – and that he thought about all three devotedly and tearfully. Paul Roche's engaging travelogue, *With Duncan Grant in Southern Turkey* (1982), provides many delightful anecdotes involving Grant.

time seemed cosmic, but which are now at the best amusing. For instance, for the first three years I was a 'weekly boarder'; for certain definite reasons, I am now a 'day boy'. And so on, quite irrelevantly. I made the acquaintance of many people – Jews and Gentiles – all more or less wanting in intelligence and (what, I suppose – for I agree with you – is the same thing) in insanity. I wrote Latin Prose moderately, and played cricket not at all; I went to the Gaiety,[1] and was considered vulgar by the cultured; I read poetry, and was thought a fool by the athletic. (I hope all this sounds dark – it's meant to: perhaps it'ld sound darker if recited in a monotone.) But it was all very soothing, and of late quite amusing.

My infamous cousin deluded me with false hopes, and told me with circumstantial details that you too were going to Cambridge. I go to Trinity in October. I'm then supposed to go into the Home Civil Service; but it's horribly dull. He also told me (but I've no more faith in him) that you were going to be a journalist. I suppose that's merely a step towards becoming Prime Minister. I am bound thither myself (or to the Vatican).

I think letters are disgusting – because I find it impossible to write what I mean, to give any delicate shades, or even the atmosphere; – it's difficult enough in conversation: perhaps if one were supreme one might?

And I think this letter is the most disgusting of all. So I cease.

Yours ever,
James Strachey.

*RB, [postcard, postmarked 9.30 p.m., 14 July 1905]Barby Road[2]
[Rugby] to JBS, Great Oakley Hall, Kettering, Northamptonshire*

I have just received your letter. I am in work till 1.p.m. and for the honour of my house have to play at 3.p.m. Can you come to lunch to this address at 1.30? I shall be waiting for you any time after 1. Or if you are going to Hillbrow for lunch, drop in on the way & leave a message, & then come round after lunch at two. You know our house I suppose.   R.C.B

*RB, July 30 [1905], School Field, Rugby
[The writing paper and envelope bear a watermark reading
'Orando Laborando 1567'[3] to JBS, Great Oakley Hall, Kettering*

Dear Strachey,

Many apologies & thanks. The certificate exams are extremely worrying just now. But they will soon – thank heaven! – be over. I

1 A theatre in central London. Its most popular shows between 1900 and 1905 were *The Messenger Boy, The Wicked Uncle, The Toreador, The Linkman* and *The Orchid.*
2 School Field, Rugby, where Brooke lived and where his father was housemaster, is located on Barby Road.
3 The motto and foundation year of Rugby School. Presumably, this was Parker Brooke's stationery.

have consulted – various authorities – the greater Intelligences who understand such things – and find that my next holidays are fairly full. I come back here about the 10th (Aug.) recover from Camp life for about 5 days & then go to some vague unwholesome place called the Sea, for the rest of August. About 5 days after that a Tutor appears on the scene for a fortnight or so – in prospect of a hypothethical [sic] scholarship next December.[1] Then for the remaining week of the holidays I slowly recover from the effect of Tutor life. Such, as the Gods be willing, are the plans. I fear I haven't a whole week any where, but, if you are still at Kettering then, I should be very delighted to snatch three days at the beginning of September. Would that be possible? 1st to the 4th perhaps, or thereabouts.

In two days the Summer Term will be over, & already people are going about bidding sad farewells. All of which is highly mournful, & may account for the pessimistic tone of this letter.

My time is at present divided between playing cricket with gigantic vigour, reading Swinburne on a grassy bank, and toying with mildly foolish examination papers. The first duty of an examinee is to irritate the examiner. Last year in the Certificate Exams I failed to get a History Certif. entirely on one question. It was about Roman chronicles; & I defined them as being as dull, useless, untrue, & far from Literature as the average Roman History. I afterward discovered that the examiner was a wretch who had written four Roman Histories, & two "Skeleton Outlines", & held an entirely new & original view as to which eye Hannibal was blinded in.

Hinc illae lacrimae.[2]

I have just discovered I am supposed to go to Chapel in about nine minutes, which must be done though it is against my conscience. I am a Wesleyan, an Anabaptist, & several other things. They would not let me become a Roman Catholic, so I did the next best thing & joined the Salvation Army.   Yrs ever
                                                                   Rupert Brooke

JS, August 2 [1905], Great Oakley Hall, Kettering

Dear Brooke,

The dates you mention are quite convenient.

Are you allowed to read letters in Camp? At least, certainly not, I suppose, to write them?

---

1 Specifically, the holiday plans included an army camp for cadets at Aldershot, a trip to Brockenhurst to visit the Russell-Smiths, a visit to his elder brother Richard who had just obtained a job in Southsea, and then a return to Rugby to study classics under the tutelage of his godfather, Robert Whitelaw.
2 'Hence these tears'.

The disadvantages of this Fine Old Elizabethan Mansion grow on one.[1] Why should innumerable ugly plates be hung on the walls? Why should Chelsea candlesticks crowd the tables? The result is, of course, that there is no copy of Shakespeare in the house. But perhaps the worst feature is that the church is on the croquet-lawn. My only mild amusement is therefore banned between the hours of eleven and one on Sundays.

I notice that the clergy behave in the same way towards the saved and the damned: The Revd. Mr. Clarke had observed no one in the family pew. He came to luncheon afterwards, and found eighteen people grouped around the table. He didn't even cross himself on entering the room . . . But perhaps as a member of the Wesleyan Army, you are insulted – or rather (for you say you can't be) pained.

I am going to sleep now; or rather to finish reading Swinburne's novel: as far as I've got it's merely amusing. Have you read it?[2]

You'ld hate me to mention the Bastille: but may I ask if the Pyramids are obtainable?[3] If they are I must have a copy, even if only lent.   Yours,

James Strachey.

RB, Thursday [10 August 1905, Rugby station]
to JS, Great Oakley Hall, Kettering

Dear Strachey,

My lateness in response this time was somewhat inevitable. As you surmised to write letters from Camp is very impossible. A hasty & smudged post-card is occasionally feasible; that is all. I cannot fix the dates with perfect accuracy yet; but you know to within a day or two, & I hope that will suffice. If not I will try to discover the exact date.

It is very strenuous of you to attack the "Pyramids" after trudging through the Bastille. I have a Pyramid or two left somewhere and I vow to dig it up & send it along in a day or two, if you have not yet repented of your rash request.[4]

Only yesterday I returned, weary, very healthy, with sore feet & a sun-blistered nose from a week of the Strenuous – exceedingly Strenuous –

---

1   The Strachey family had moved from their home at 69 Lancaster Gate – a Victorian house near Kensington Gardens where James had spent all but the first year of his life – to a large Tudor country house six miles from Kettering called Great Oakley Hall. They were renting the house for the summer.
2   *The Children of the Chapel* (London: J. Masters, 1864).
3   Brooke entered the school poetry prize in 1904 for a poem on 'The Pyramids', for which he received a *proxime accessit*. In 1905, he won the prize for a long poem on 'The Bastille'.
4   Brooke refused a request for the poem from his cousin, Erica Cotterill, claiming his mother had taken it from him and 'stowed it away in the family archives', and that in any case he had 'disowned it long ago' (*LRB* 6).

Life. It is a quaint & comforting return from Camp's alternation of eating &
walking enormously, to moderation in food & no exercise at all. For of
that are my Summer holidays constituted. I hope you have finished
A[lgernon].C[harles].S[winburne]'[s] novel. I have not attempted it yet,
being fearful that it might be as verbose as his usual prose, which
overwhelms & stuns me. I imagine that by now you have been galled to
desperation; that you have quite smoothly one day recently run amok
through your Old Mansion with a poker, smashing the ugly plates hung
on the walls, annihilating the crowding Chelsea candlesticks & with a keg
of dynamite relieving for ever your beloved croquet lawn from its
ecclesiastical encumbrance. In fact I trust to find Great Oakley Hall a
reformed and enlightened place when I arrive. Your account of the Revd.
Mr. Clarke greatly shocked me. But you will doubtless receive a Bull of
Excommunication ere the month is out; or perhaps he was only too
thankful that you did not insist on playing croquet in spite of the services.

It is 8.53., and the post is at 9. Farewell.   Rupert Brooke

JS, August 18 [1905], Great Oakley Hall, Kettering

Dear Brooke,

Pyramids to hand with many thanks.

I find that these letters are becoming distinctly painful in the writing.
To fill these four clean pages is a desperate future. I think the only plan
will be to institute some argument on the lines of the "Daily Mail"
correspondence columns. (You read that dear journal?)

But some people might proceed with descriptions of scenery, vapid
but voluminous. [The history of the last sentence is: I wrote the first five
words (on the other page) with one end in view, but then changed my
mind – with the above inconsequent result.][1] I append some questions.
You may either (1) answer them in the form of a catechism – or (2)
select one or more as the basis of an elaborate discussion.

Do you approve of the Royal Academy?

What are your views on Wagner, Mr. Chamberlain, and Christ?

Are you in favour of War at any Price?

Why are you going to Oxford?

Does Jackson play such a good all round game as Fry?

I think these questions embrace all the Important in this life, and I
warn you that you will be judged by your answers to them. I shall be
most happy to answer in my turn any similar 'quaere's.

And now . . . by the help of spacings and gas I have reached the last
page and harbour is in sight.

You might perhaps mention the day of your visit eventually?

1   These brackets are Strachey's.

Lor – the (Last) Post   JBStrachey.

RB, [20] August [1905], Southsea (but write to Rugby)

Dear Strachey,

This is an exceeding low place, where we are staying for a fortnight, – not because we like the town, but because we wish to see something of my brother, who is working down here. Southsea is a loathsome place, full of ugly houses, and trippers, and noises. I solemnly curse it.

After a studious examination of calendar of various *data* referring to tutors and other immovable arrangements, I should suggest Monday Sept. 4th (I think the number is right) for two or three days – till Wednesday afternoon or Thursday morning. On the Thursday I find that I am supposed to begin work.

With regard to the Catechism: – The Royal Academy – Yes: I approve of all forms of charitable institutions. Also my religious soul commends their case in keeping the 2nd Commandment. 'Thou shalt not make any image of anything that is in heaven . . . or earth . . . or the sea . . . . .'

In RE *Oxford*. Because they tell me to, – that is, if I am going. At present it is undecided which University I shall grace: some of my masters advise one, some the other; and my father is torn asunder. Anyhow I don't much mind which.

Thirdly

Certainly I approve of War at any Price. It kills off the unnecessary.

As for Mr. Chamberlain – I detest him. He is a modern politician, and I hate modern politicians; he comes from Birmingham, and I abhor Birmingham; he makes a noise, and I loathe noises; he is utterly materialistic, and . . . . !

About Wagner I have no views. I am very sorry, but I can't help it. I have tried very hard for years, but I *cannot* appreciate music. I recognize that it is a fault in me, and am duly ashamed. In Literature, and a little even in Painting, I humbly believe I can feel the Beautiful, but I am born deaf.

This is a Tragedy.

For Christ – I am so obsessed by [Wilde's] De Profundis that I have no other views on this subject than those expressed therein. The Perfect Artistic Temperament. – !

You demanded a return catechism. Here it is. As yours "embraced all the Important in Life"; so mine, I hope, embraces all the Unimportant in Life – a much more essential thing.

1. What are the two greatest tragedies in Life?
2. Shew the comic side of both.
3. What is the most beautiful adjective in English?

4. When did you give up reading Tennyson?
5. What *is* the World coming to?
Good-night.   Rupert Brooke.

RB, Sunday Sept 24 [1905], School Field, Rugby
to JS, Great Oakley Hall, Kettering

Dear Strachey,

I am utterly evil not to have kept up my end of this correspondence for three weeks, especially when I should have written to thank you for sheltering my weary soul from all classics, tutors, & labours for three placid days. I might allege several excuses; – that I was so humiliated & crushed by my overwhelming defeat at billiards (& after my conceit had offered you 30 in a hundred!) that I could not raise by [sic] bowed head to address you; or that the wonderful & beautiful novel by Marie Corelli,[1] which I read in those three days, reduced me too [sic] such a pulpy stupefaction that I am only now beginning to recover. As a matter of unimportant fact directly I returned from you I plunged headlong into a wild confusion of Demosthenes, Horace & such; and that lasted two weeks; wherein my brain was full of nothing but grammar & horrible matters, and I could not have written a letter for the life of me. After Purgatory was over I snatched a few hurried hours in London (seeing among other things 'John Bull's Other Island', a perfectly delightful play.), & now in my first calm moments for weeks I write. Such is my obviously inadequate excuse; beyond which there is nothing, – almost nothing, – to write about. One piece of personal news there is. The Fates have issued a decree, which I take to be final, that, after all, I am to go to King's Cambridge a year hence, D.V.[2] So we shall meet there some day. I hope you are, or are about to, or have enjoyed the society of the elder Keynes, of whose visit to you I hear from other sources. (The grammar of the last sentence will *not* bear investigation.) If he is staying with you at Great Oakley Hall, pray do not allow him to read the 'Sorrows of Satan', it may affect him as it affected me.

I hear from an authority that almost all the rooms in that mansion are haunted. Please let me know if the room I occupied was; I trust it was. I hope Lady Strachey is better.   yours ever
                                                          Rupert Brooke

---

1 Corelli (1855–1924) was a popular English novelist. The novel referred to, as indicated later in the letter, is *The Sorrows of Satan*.
2 *Deo volente* ('God willing').

RB, [30 December 1905], Rugby
to JS, 69 Lancaster Gate, London

Dear Strachey,

Many thanks for your telegram. I fear I am somewhat late in acknowledging it. I hope you passed that exam in "English Literature" as exemplified by Walter Scott (or was it Dickens?). On the Friday afternoon I came round to have tea with you, but found your door inexorably barred, and therefore came away after three-quarters-of-an-hour's banging.

I suppose you know a play called Peter Pan? I saw it last year & fell so much in love with it that I am going up to see its revival again in a few days.[1] I found it enchanting, adorable, and entirely beautiful. In reality, no doubt, it is very ridiculous. I am very aged & this mania for children's

---

1   Brooke has sometimes been compared with the title character of Barrie's *Peter Pan*, the boy who refused to grow up. When Kenneth Millard compares Henry Newbolt with Brooke, he says Newbolt 'chafes at having to grow up. Like a petulant Peter Pan he wants to remain a lad forever. Again there is a comparison with Rupert Brooke, who bitterly regretted the exigencies of sexual relationships, which threatened his innocent pubescent friendships' (25). Another critic, Graham Chainey, notes Brooke's 'Peter Pan humour' (181). *Peter Pan* may have been Brooke's favourite play. He saw it at least ten times, and after one of those performances wrote to his friend Lucas, 'I have gone about as one in a dream, quoting to myself all the gorgeous fragments of *Peter Pan* that I can remember.' Brooke was not a Rugby schoolboy but a university man when he wrote this letter. He continued, 'As I stroll through Cambridge, Trinity Street fades and I find myself walking by the shore of the Mermaid's Lagoon. King's Chapel often shrinks before my eyes, and rises, and is suddenly the House in the Tree-tops' (*RBB* 117).

    Brooke's desire never to grow up is well chronicled. He once wrote to his friend Ernst Goldschmidt, 'Is there a greater tragedy than for a boy to die, except for him to grow old, to live!' Virtually every critic has had something to say regarding Brooke's failure to mature, most echoing Frank Field's observation that Brooke 'behaved like an adolescent' in matters of love and sex 'until his death' (110). In any case, Brooke was certainly not alone in adoring the play. Prior to the war, *Peter Pan* was the best-attended play in England, and thousands of Englishmen identified with Peter. In a chapter of *The Road to Armageddon* titled 'Peter Pan's England', Cecil Degrotte Eby discusses J. M. Barrie's relationship with the Davies boys – his collective model for Peter – and attempts to explain Barrie and his play using Cyril Connolly's 'theory of arrested development'. This theory held that 'the experience undergone by boys at the great public schools, their triumphs and disappointments, are so intense as to dominate their lives and to arrest their development. From these it results that the greater part of the ruling class remains adolescent, school-minded, self-conscious, cowardly, sentimental and in the last analysis homosexual' (quoted in Gathorne-Hardy, *Old School Tie* 210). Among Eby's insights using this theory: 'Homophilic protocol is as rigidly enforced in *Peter Pan* as in an English public school. Mermaids, traditionally creatures associated with destructive female sexuality, become the object of jolly hunting expeditions – but they are dangerous game because they pull boys into the water and drown them. Peter Pan restructures the ideal world according to a parthenogenetic model of women as mothers but never wives or lovers' (132).

    Of course, not every Englishman liked the play. Brooke's friend David Garnett says, 'I disliked *Peter Pan* as a child and when I grew up it seemed to me morbid

plays is a token of advanced senility. At Keynes' rooms one night while I was up, I met a delightful man named Norton[1] (I think) who said he knew you & your kitten (*apropos*, how *is* the kitten?), and talked incessantly & brilliantly for six hours.

I am at present reading the Elizabethan dramatists at the rate of four a week.   Yours always

Rupert Brooke

JS, (After the Eumenides)[2] Friday Evening [30 November 1906], Trinity College, Cambridge[3]

Dear Rupert,

In the excitement of the moment, I must just write to tell you (a truism) that you were very beautiful tonight. How sorry I shall be tomorrow morning that I sent you this! How angry you will be when you read it! Vogue la galère.[4]   Yours in admiration,

James.

JS, April 2nd, 1907, 69 Lancaster Gate, London

Dear Rupert,

I can't let everything go without a struggle: and I believe that things cannot be worse for me than they are now. But there is really only one thing that I want you to tell me. Why mayn't I go on knowing you? Why did you never come to see me last term? I don't suppose that if I stopped at this you'ld answer me at all; so may I tell you what I believe is the answer?

First, however, let me say that, if you are what I know you are, and if

and unhealthy in a particularly unpleasant way. The sexual instinct which in a healthy normal man is aroused by the women painted by Rubens or Renoir, or in a homosexual by a beautiful adult of the same sex, emerges in Barrie as a baby's bedtime sexuality which revolts me. This watery perversion has come to be a national institution' (*Flowers* 84).

1 Henry Tertius (Harry) Norton (1886–1937), Apostle no.246, mathematician and lifelong friend of Lytton Strachey, who dedicated *Eminent Victorians* to him. Virginia Woolf, in *Moments of Being*, describes Norton as the essence of Cambridge – 'so able, so honest, so ugly, so dry'. Having never attained the fame of others in the Bloomsbury circle, Norton suffered a nervous collapse in 1920 and welcomed an early retirement.

2 Brooke performed as a herald in a performance of *Eumenides* on this date. In the audience, 'packed with Edwardian hellenists and paedophiles', was A. C. Benson, who wrote, 'A herald made a pretty figure' (Chainey 182).

3 James was now living in Lytton's old rooms on Staircase K of the Great Court of Trinity College.

4 'Let's chance it.'

you understood my state of mind, you would have come to see me. Therefore as you did not come to see me, either you are not what I know you are, or you do not understand my state of mind. But you *are* what I know you are; and so, by an irrefutable logical train, I reach my first conclusion: that you do not understand my state of mind.

Being, then, what you are, what must you think of me in order to treat me as you have? You told me you were quite indifferent about me; if that were so, you would not have changed, but would have continued as before, willing, at least, to speak to me sometimes. And I do not think your feeling towards me can be one of mere dislike. Do you remember when we met face to face outside the Union gate; I mean when you walked down the passage from the street to the doors just two yards in front of me? You wouldn't have done that even to Cunningham major. (Do you still hate Cunningham major as much as I do?) I believe then that you must regard me with a violent hatred;[1] and that the hatred began on the ninth of December, though no doubt you despised me before then. In what way then did you misconstrue my feelings so as to develop a sudden hatred for them? I'm frightened of this part of the letter, and everything depends on it. Be kind.

What did you think I meant when I said that I loved you? You had, it seems to me, three main grounds for your belief. First, you had talked to Norton, and had found – it was rather horrid – that he seemed to think

---

1 In one of Brooke's 1907 notebooks is a poem titled 'The Spectator' which could be a response to this letter:

> Hate you? Ah, no! I've much to thank you for,
>   – New passion in my latest love-sonnets,
>   A fresh store of exotic epithets,
> A novel pose.....yes, Lilith-Eve, and more –
> You've stayed me with apples – from the Knowledge-Tree!
>   I dreamt; You taught me what the dream is worth.
>   I played my part (not clumsily!). Henceforth
> I'll sit in the stalls and watch the comedy.
>
> Ha! how that hero rants (as I erewhile!)!
>   I like the lad: his soul's one scarlet flame
> Lit by *her* lips (where lurks your subtle smile!).
> They win their heaven, – or lose – 'Tis all the same.
> In the end they fade and shrivel up and die . . . . . .
> We laugh at their brave antics, God and I.

'The Wayfarers', which Geoffrey Keynes has dated June 1907, follows in the notebook a few pages later, making it all the more probable (from the standpoint of chronology) that the poem was written in response to James's letter. If this is the case, Brooke probably intended a play on words in the title, as Strachey had been a spectator at the play and his cousin St Loe Strachey was editor of the *Spectator* (which James was soon to work for himself, and which already had printed several articles by Lytton). It is unclear which 'love sonnets' Brooke refers to in this poem, as the only published love poem from this period is 'The Beginning' (written in January 1907), which is indeed passionate, but not a sonnet – and which was probably written for Charles Lascelles.

the physical side of love less ugly than you did. Next, you had had an interview with Lytton.[1] Finally, a few days before, I myself had sent what now suddenly seemed to you an insulting letter. Obviously you could only think either the worst, or that I *did* have some, dark, infinitely degraded feelings, which deserved – what you gave. Am I right? Is this what you thought?

And if I *am* right, I am still lost, for I can never tell you what my feelings really are. I failed completely when I spoke; I can't even make an attempt in writing. Why should you believe me when I say that there is nothing of what you hate in them, that they are good feelings, that they are perhaps not altogether unworthy even of you. I have tried to be as simple as possible; but perhaps to you it will seem theatrical and affected and disingenuous. Please believe.

And if you do believe, you will be kind. You will let me know you as Mr. Dalton[2] knows you. Promise that it shall not be less, and I will promise that it shall not be more. I will never, never, never, mention this to you again.   Yours,

James Strachey.

RB, Sunday [7 April 1907], (Pension White, Piazza Cavallegieri [Cavallagieri], Florence.) (for a day or two) to JS, 69 Lancaster Gate [forwarded to Court Barton, North Molton, Devon]

My dear James

Your letter reached me on the eve of my starting for furrin parts, and since then I have been mostly in the trains. I admire your clarity and courage.

You are rather too logical for a sentimentalist like myself. All the reasons you advance for my conduct sound plausible; but I do not remember considering them at the time. For a little – a few days – I was rather selfishly irritated and felt a certain dislike for you. But, really, that was not great, and did not last.

Why did I not see you last term? You unbosomed yourself a little; let

1 Giles Lytton Strachey (1880–1932), James's elder brother, became famous in 1918 with the publication of his *Eminent Victorians*. Lytton attended Trinity College and was an active Apostle. His love affairs included Duncan Grant, Jack Sheppard, George Mallory, Henry Lamb and Bernard Swithinbank (1884–1958), a Balliol College undergraduate. Michael Holroyd's two-volume biography provides an excellent account of his life.
2 For a detailed account of Hugh Dalton's life, see Ben Pimlott's *Hugh Dalton* or Dalton's autobiography, *Call Back Yesterday*. In the autobiography, Dalton says of Brooke: 'No Cambridge friendship of mine meant more to me' (38).

me do so, too. Last December seems to me very long ago. A thousand ills have happened since then. I came back last term feeling hopeless about everything: I do still. Four days before I returned my brother, of whom I was fond, died; and my father became, suddenly, an old man. All the term bad news and sad letters were coming from home. My mother was quite ill once; my father twice, and is now. Also, things happened that hurt me more than all this.[1]

From all this I was depressed most of last term. I dwelt, if you like, in a rather useless and petty self-pity. Anyhow I felt, and was, generally unsociable. There are two Cambridge people who were my contemporaries at Rugby, in the same house, and my constant companions for years. These, (Geoffrey Keynes[2] and another[3]) I saw

1 Paul Delany believes this is a reference to a final break with Charlie Lascelles. However, there is confusion in Delany's book concerning Lascelles and Michael Sadleir. Brooke more likely refers here to the 'affaire' with Sadleir, which came to an end in July 1906. Michael Thomas Harvey Sadleir (1888–1957), the child of Sir Michael Ernest Sadler, was educated at Rugby and Balliol College, Oxford. Later, Sadleir joined Brooke in Eddie Marsh's social circle. He was present, for instance, at Marsh's breakfast party on 1 March 1913, during which Brooke read aloud his play *Lithuania*. Sadleir married in 1914. Following Brooke's death, Sadleir sent a letter of condolence to Mrs Brooke, including in it a copy of a remembrance of Brooke he had written for an unidentified magazine 'which circulates in India'. Sadleir later became the most noted collector of nineteenth-century fiction of his day, a distinguished bibliographer, and a writer of such novels as *Forlorn Sunset*.
2 Geoffrey Langdon Keynes (1887–1982), one of Rupert's two closest friends at Rugby. The two remained friends during their Cambridge years and afterwards, though they were never again close. Keynes was appointed a Brooke Trustee after Rupert's death and was given most of the responsibilities involved. Like Brooke, Geoffrey once proposed marriage to Katherine Cox and was refused. In 1917 he married Margaret Darwin, the younger sister of Gwen Raverat. They had four children. Aside from his role as Brooke Trustee, Keynes is also known in literary circles for his bibliographical work on Blake, Donne and Edward Gibbon. However, Geoffrey's primary life work was in the field of medical science. He served as a field surgeon during the war and later pioneered work in blood transfusion, thyroid surgery thymectomy, hernia surgery and the use of radium to treat breast cancer in place of radical mastectomy. His autobiography, *The Gates of Memory*, provides the details of both remarkable careers.
3 Hugh Russell-Smith (1887–1916). Photographs of Brooke's other close friend at Rugby show a solidly built young man with a friendly smile. Brooke cast Russell-Smith as 'Gluttony' in the Marlowe Society's production of *Faustus*, and he told him in a summer 1909 letter: 'Your head is like a fir-cone.' Brooke's existing letters to Russell-Smith show him at his silliest. On 29 June 1907, he wrote from Bournemouth: 'Both your suppositions are incorrect. (1) I did *not* write to your home in Thanet. (2) Your home in Thanet is, I feel certain, *not* being forwarded to you.' A letter from the summer of 1909 shows the affection with which Brooke regarded his friend: 'You were ever a dreamer (as you constantly say), an idealist, a thing of shreds and patches, not wholly of this world. [...] What shall we sing by the way, swan-like, my dreamer? Homer, Shelley, – ? [...] *You're not to wear a collar & a tie, Scrupkin.*' Russell-Smith studied history but appreciated literature as well. He defeated Brooke in the 1909 Winchester Reading competition, and two years later received a scholarship that enabled him to travel to America for research. A book resulted – *Harrington and his Oceana: A Study of a 17th Century*

often. I practically never saw anyone else, except by their invitation. I really did not 'drop' or 'cut' you uniquely. On Norton for instance I called once, – to explain why I had accepted his invitations to tea, and not turned up.[1] Sheppard,[2] though he lives so close & is elderly, I went to see twice (outside business) in the whole term. You speak of Dalton. I necessarily see him once a week at a foolish talking society. Beyond that he invited me once to tea, so I had him once to breakfast. That is all. He is merely a type. I hated other people's society so much, that I took refuge in my own; and found it quite as detestable.

All this explains my not coming to see you. No doubt it was very selfish. But as my friends will tell you, I am wholly selfish. I never think of others' feelings. I am entirely taken up with pitying myself.[3] Indeed, if you are still foolish enough to want it, you can know me 'as Mr Dalton knows' me, – or more closely, if ever you want to see any thing of me. When I come up (rather late) I will write and you shall come to tea, if you want to; – unless I suddenly vanish before next term; which is the sincere hope of   yours,
                                                                    Rupert Brooke

RB, Friday [19 April 1907], King's College, Cambridge to JS, Trinity College

If you got my last letter, and are in Cambridge, will you come to tea? On Saturday? at 4.30?   Rupert Brooke

---

Utopia and its Influence in America – published in 1914 and reissued in 1971. Found among Brooke's books after his death was a volume of Keats, a present from Russell-Smith. Following Brooke's death, Russell-Smith wrote a tribute for the *Meteor*, the Rugby paper. In it, he mentions that Brooke often quoted to him a verse of Hilaire Belloc: 'From quiet homes and first beginnings, / Out to the undiscovered ends, / There's nothing worth the wear of winning, / But laughter and the love of friends.' Russell-Smith married in 1913, shortly before going to war. A son, Roy, was born to Hugh and his wife in the summer of 1915. Roy reports that neither his mother nor his paternal grandparents said much about Brooke, Hugh or Denham while he was growing up. However, Mrs Russell-Smith did attend the unveiling of the Memorial to Brooke at Rugby in April 1918.

1 Strachey had written on 9 March to Grant that Norton despised Brooke.
2 John Tressider ('Jack') Sheppard (1881–1968), Apostle no.238, a classics don at King's College and member of the Carbonari. Sheppard later became a Brooke Trustee at the request of Mrs Brooke, but was content to let Geoffrey Keynes and Dudley Ward make decisions regarding the Trust. He served as Provost of King's from 1933 to 1954.
3 Geoffrey Keynes had recently criticized Brooke's attitude. Brooke wrote in response: 'I have thought over your idea of my at length giving up the pose of discontent and taking to optimism in my old age. I think not. The change might be refreshing, but I scrape along very well as I am; and the pessimistic insincerity pleases *me* at any rate, which is the main thing' (*LRB* 73).

RB, [Saturday, 20 April 1907]
to JS, Trinity College

3.55.

My dear James,

I suddenly remember that from 4.30 – I have a Review Committee meeting. I'll be back by 5.30 perhaps. In case I can't meet you.[1]   R.B.

I have it. – in the bottom right hand drawer of my desk: and the most phenomenal[2] & short paper in the world.

I think you misjudge them; – Mr D. a *ghost*?! no! no!   R

---

1 In a letter to Grant, Strachey provides a transcription of the dialogue he had with Brooke during this meeting. Apparently the second sentence out of Strachey's mouth was 'I suppose you know what's the matter with me. I'm in love with you.' Here, according to Strachey, is what followed:
   He: How distressing of you! Will you have a cigarette?
   [...]
   J: I suppose you don't believe I have any feelings.
   He: It doesn't interest me.
   [...]
   He: Besides, it annoys me.
   J: I don't see why it should.
   He: Because it irritates me: I *am* irritable. [...] I think I really ought to laugh at you. [...]
   J: I think I'd better go (Rising).
   He: I should advise you to go and make yourself a drink.
2 The words 'phenomenal' and 'phenomenon' were used to indicate everything the Apostles rejected. What they accepted was 'real'.

1908

Early in 1908, Brooke was elected to the Apostles. Lytton Strachey had written to James on 27 November 1907, asking if he felt Brooke might feel '*égaré*' (misled) if he was elected. But the next day James wrote back that Brooke had asked Norton to tea, which in James's opinion was 'really rather a violent step for him to take. [...] It proved that he was positively *asking* to be elected.' It fell upon James, as Brooke's sponsor, to issue the invitation. His letter to Lytton on 19 January expresses his misgivings after the fact:

> How dreadful it is to satisfy a violent desire. I daresay you'll get a coherent story out of Keynes – or me someday. [...] I really could scarcely speak at the beginning and I completely forgot, of course, to tell him it was secret – so he's probably retailing it all at this very moment to Geoffrey Keynes. [...] it was I alone who saw, in a ghastly moment as he went away, his incredible stupidity.

The Apostles had been known for romantic friendships since the days of Tennyson and Hallam, but, as Richard Deacon puts it, 'from the turn of the century the sublimated turned into the consummated and homosexuality became almost a creed' (55). There is no evidence to suggest that Brooke was either shocked or disappointed when he discovered the nature of the organization he had joined. He may have been discomfited when he realized the probable reason for his election, but if so he handled himself well. Far from being shocked by the romantic intrigues of his comrades, Brooke quickly adopted the lifestyle as the others watched carefully and anxiously to see if he would attach himself to anyone in particular. Harry Norton reported that he was falling in love with Brooke, and Maynard Keynes wrote to Duncan Grant on 2 February that James Strachey had 'stated the hypothesis that Rupert is falling in love with me!' Keynes wrote again three days later: 'James's ups and downs with Rupert seem to be almost more violent than usual. [...] There is an understanding between Rupert and Gerald [Shove] – they sit together every evening – to which he feels that he doesn't belong.'

Brooke also helped his brethren scout for new blood. The following autumn, James wrote to Lytton concerning 'the Central Figure of the day', Steuart Wilson, the senior scholar at King's:

> He is reported not only intelligent, but a Great Beauty – large & athletic, with masses of dark hair, and superb classical features. I quote Rupert, who pretends to be his dearest friend: & says he can easily snatch him from the thousand hawks who have made for him. R's story must of course be discounted, as he has evidently determined to fall in love with him. (13 October 1908)

Three days later, James reported that Gerald Shove, too, had fallen in love with Steuart and was 'violently jealous of Rupert'. The news of Wilson soon reached Maynard Keynes, who wrote to Duncan Grant (everyone's confidant, apparently):

> Tomorrow I lunch at Rupert's again and with the greatest excitement. There's a freshman called Wilson whom I've not yet seen. He's said to be by far the most beautiful person who has ever appeared. [...] James watches him from his tower through opera glasses and declares that, if he ever speaks to him, he will certainly fall in love. Rupert has had five or six meetings with him and has been so completely dazzled as to be quite unaware as to what happened at any of them. [...] Rupert now calls me Maynard, so I suppose the name may come into fashion in time. (29 October 1908)

The last sentence, though perhaps said with some sarcasm, illustrates Brooke's growing status among the Apostles. He was, in fact, elected the group's secretary – its primary office – the next year.

Brooke did not forget old friends, embarking on another walking tour with Hugh Russell-Smith during the spring vacation. Meanwhile, Strachey's pursuit of him continued. In April Strachey reported to Grant that he was seeing Brooke frequently but was afraid to 'propose' again. Strachey was thrilled when he and Brooke attended a socialist meeting in London together and Brooke exclaimed, 'Look here! don't you go and get lost!' and seized him by the arm. 'I felt decidedly at the time that he was deliberate,' Strachey wrote to Grant. 'That he'd been meaning to do it for some time, and jumped at a chance. I *can't* believe that he didn't know it was important. Why else was he so absurdly shy?'

At a meeting at the Green Dragon in Market Lavington 18–21 April, Lytton, too, had been struck by Brooke's beauty. He wrote to Virginia

Stephen – unaware that she had ever met Brooke – that among the others was

> a young undergraduate called Rupert Brooke – isn't it a romantic name? – with pink cheeks and bright yellow hair – it sounds horrible, but it wasn't. [...] whenever I begun to feel dull I could look at the yellow hair and pink cheeks of Rupert. James, too, is an interesting figure – very mysterious and reserved, and either incredibly young or inconceivably old.

But Lytton was taking a more cautious approach to Brooke than was James. Lytton wrote to Grant on 12 June: 'As for Rupert – I'm not in love with him, though it's occasionally occurred to me that I ought to be – but there really are too many drawbacks to him.' He wrote again on 31 July: 'James returned on Tuesday, and Rupert stayed here last night, which was rather a trial, I found. The atmosphere of deaf dumb and blind admiration gets on my nerves, like most other things, and I shriek and tear out of the room.' Earlier in the month, Maynard Keynes had written to Grant about Brooke's rehearsals for another play: 'One hears of nothing but Comus. James went to a rehearsal last night and declares that Rupert's beauty was so great that he couldn't sleep a wink last night for thinking of it' (10 July 1908).

At the end of the summer, Brooke and Strachey both attended the Fabian Summer School in Wales. Unfortunately, their hostess, Beatrice Webb, was not impressed with either them or their friends. She described Brooke, Strachey, Arthur Schloss, Gerald Shove and Dudley Ward as 'commonplace', and said that Brooke in particular 'put me off the track of his distinction by delivering a super-conceited lecture on the relation of the University man to the common herd of democracy' (*Partnership* 415). Even more damning, she said of the group as a whole, 'They don't want to learn; they don't think they have anything to learn' (456–7). Brooke enjoyed the camp, thought highly of Webb and was blissfully oblivious concerning her opinion of him. But his fellow camper Hugh Dalton, in *Call Back Yesterday*, admits, 'We were, I am afraid, cliquish, rude, ribald and irreverent' (49). Webb was no doubt especially sensitive on this issue because of H. G. Wells's address to a meeting of the Fabians two years earlier in which – noting their tendency toward private jokes – he complained that 'their supreme delight was to *giggle*, and they permeated English society with their ideas about as much as a mouse may be said to permeate a cat' (Cole 110).

It was at the camp that the friendship between Brooke and Strachey apparently came closest to developing into a romance. The possibility began in late August when they stopped over in Ludlow on their way to Wales. Strachey wrote to Grant: 'But how we stared last night before he went to bed.' A few days later, Strachey was writing to Grant from the Fabian encampment about his suspicion that Brooke was in love with a woman. 'Why did we think him a sodomite? No doubt he was once.' Strachey believed the woman to be Daphne Olivier, but only two days later he wrote to Grant that there had not been 'the smallest piece of evidence' to support his theory. In fact, he reports, Brooke had been 'pressed to join' a number of expeditions which included Olivier, but had instead remained with him 'nearly the whole time – and a great deal nose to nose'.

Three days later, on 4 September, Strachey wrote: 'My moment is coming. Good god – he's falling in love with me. No, no, no. I can't bear it. This is too vast. [...] Oh, I *know* it's true. [...] Didn't it possibly culminate yesterday evening? Doesn't he see today that perhaps he's wrong? [...] Why does he love me? Why *now* and not last Easter?' Then, on 8 September, Strachey reported that Brooke asked him for a walk – 'And in a few moments he was beginning to tell me; – but then panic fell – oh, on him perhaps too – and it all dissolved into air.' The next day he reported that Brooke had 'rushed off before dinner last night for a long walk – to recover, as he put it, his sanity'. Later on the evening of the 9th Strachey dashed off another letter to Grant: 'So everything's to end in utter misery, after all. We had a very odd conversation before dinner. But it seemed to sum things up. He had seen possibilities: but they had vanished.'

In his letters to Strachey, Brooke often seems to be teasing him with scintillating anecdotes involving homosexuality. But Brooke engaged in this type of flirtation with men and boys throughout his life – with Michael Sadleir, Charles Sayle, Lytton Strachey, Harry Norton, Hugh Dalton, Edward Marsh – even Henry James – and it was often far from a serious declaration of male affection.

For James Strachey, however, his being in love with Brooke was painfully serious. His feelings left him sick with desire, and ruined the possibility of his developing relationships with other young men – such as George Mallory and Gerald Shove – who were interested in him. To Strachey, they could never compare with Brooke.

In late November, when Strachey was in the sanatorium recovering from influenza, Maynard Keynes, Brooke and an unidentified third person took a cab to see him. The guard would allow only one person in, so Brooke went. After the meeting, Strachey hurried off a note to Lytton: 'He was here for half an hour; & was so superb & wonderful that it didn't seem the least macabre. I was even happy after he'd gone. He almost made me believe the most extraordinary things' (30 November).

Brooke once again spent Christmas with a group of friends in Switzerland.

JS, March 28th, 1908, 67, Belsize Park Gardens, Hampstead, N.W.

I'm in great despair about the reading party.[1] It'll be simply horrible. Everyone decent has refused; and we're reduced to a horrid set of politico-mathematicians. The only people who are certain are Maynard,[2] Hawtrey,[3] and Sanger.[4] [E. M.] Forster[5] may perhaps come for one night: I've asked Meredith,[6] but he hasn't answered yet, and will certainly refuse. Finally I'm sending a passionate appeal to MacCarthy.[7] If *he* can't come, I don't see how you'll be able to stand it. In fact I'm writing to recommend you to give it up – oh, well, anyhow to lay the case before you. I can only say that *I*'ld far rather not go – if *you* weren't to. But perhaps you aren't so cynical about them as I am. That's my one hope. After all I suppose it's only because I've seen them so many times that it seems to me so dreary. You are young.

Last week I walked about Peckham with a banner in support of the Cause.[8] Dicky Coit[9] was there too – really amazing, on a kitchen chair at the street corners. There was a great rapprochement in Cambridge, by the way, at the end of term; with tea parties and his cousin (whom you so greatly admire) from Ohio. Mr Towsey said: 'Dicky's charming, but his cousin's like an excited foxterrier.' But the party was rather marred by the unexpected entrance of Mr. Nigel Farnell (from Jesus) whom one really can't have about. I wonder if Dicky noticed that he makes up.

---

1 The philosopher G. E. Moore (1873–1958), Apostle no.229, whose *Principia Ethica* had defined the Apostles' attitudes on friendship had established in 1898 a tradition of inviting a select inner circle of Apostles to Easter reading parties. This one was not being organized by Moore himself, but by Maynard Keynes with help from James Strachey. Moore's philosophy influenced many Cambridge undergraduates, including Ivor Armstrong Richards – the literary critic, writer and mountaineer – who once remarked of Moore, 'Where there's a hole in him there's a bulge in me.' For further information, consult Paul Levy's *Moore: G. E. Moore and the Cambridge Apostles*.
2 John Maynard Keynes (1883–1946), the renowned economist, Fellow and Bursar of King's College, Apostle no.243 and elder brother of Geoffrey Keynes. See the biographies by Robert Skidelsky and Roy Harrod for further information.
3 Ralph George Hawtrey (1879–1975), Apostle no.235, a writer and economist at the Treasury.
4 Charles Percy Sanger (1871–1930), Apostle no.223, a barrister and close friend of Bertrand Russell.
5 Edward Morgan Forster (1879-1970), the novelist, was Apostle no.237, elected in 1901.
6 Hugh Owen Meredith (d. 1964), nicknamed HOM, Apostle no.236, elected 1900. He was a Fellow of King's and later a professor of political economy at Queen's University, Belfast. It was Meredith who introduced E. M. Forster to homosexual love. Their relationship was the model for the Clive Durham–Maurice Hall friendship in Forster's *Maurice*. Forster also dedicated *A Room with a View* to Meredith.
7 Charles Desmond MacCarthy (1877–1952), Apostle no.231 and literary and dramatic critic, was editor of the *New Quarterly* in 1908.
8 Under Brooke's influence, Strachey had taken an interest in Fabian socialism.
9 A student at King's and one of the first two Fabian undergraduates at Cambridge.

I forgot to say that Maynard has taken The Green Dragon at Market Lavington from April 19th to 21st. The place is said to be on the Great Plain of Salisbury.

Yours
James

It none of it seems to me very clear. One might think I wanted to make you refuse because I felt it my duty to go if you went, and was afraid of being bored. I suppose you understand what I really mean and want.

RB, [postcard, postmarked 8 p.m., 6 April 1908],
3 Beacon Terrace, Torquay.
To JS, 67 Belsize Park Gardens, Hampstead, London

I have been a long while out of the world.[1] Returning, I found your letter, and one from Maynard. I am going on Saturday the 18th (?) till the end. It would be arrogant in me not to; but I cannot, before; and, anyhow, I rather want to. I am not young; but having the pleasant tolerance of the old (or at least old-fashioned), I am not especially bored even with the wise . . .

Your account of a tea-party is strange & exciting. I did not understand it, but it filled me with extraordinary emotions. I should like to have been at Peckham.

your R.

JS, April 7th, 1908, 67 Belsize Park Gardens, Hampstead

Perhaps after all you're merely wise yourself. Anyhow things are looking up. There seems to be some hope of MacCarthy; and Bob Trevy[2] is certain – but he's to be early, and to leave, ha, ha, on the Saturday you mention. But they actually add that Moore himself is probably going. Your sad ignorance can't distinguish him I suppose from the others – bicycles, and so on. When you've heard him play the Appassionata – or sing Adélaïde – you'll anyhow think he's queer.

Of course Maynard has bought all the Maps and things, and worked it out completely. '. . And on Monday we might walk to Tidworth and come back through Westbury. That makes twenty seven miles and a

---

1 Brooke had taken part – along with H. G. Wells – in a Fabian debate at Oxford. He had then spent ten days in Torquay reading Greek for Walter Headlam and writing his sonnet called 'Seaside'.
2 Robert Calverly Trevelyan (1872–1951), Apostle no.226, poet and playwright. His 'Dirge' appeared in the first Georgian poetry anthology.

quarter: and there's an inn at Westbury marked with a star in Murray. We shall be able to get tea there, I expect. On Tuesday it'll rain, so . .'
'Bondage or Vagabondage?' one murmurs. Yours
James

I went yesterday and saw the Stage Society act that wretched play The Breaking Point.[1] Have you read it? The Rustic at the end was merely farcical; and the professionals in the audience tittered, so we intellectuals said Hush. 'Lord bless you, sir, she's passed away!' 'What – what do you mean by that expression?' JBS.

*RB, [20 June 1908], King's College, Cambridge
to JS, Trinity College*

Dear JamesAnn
People have suddenly accepted an old invitation & declared that they are coming to me tomorrow at *two* p.m. or so. May I, then, come at *one*, and in flannels? yrs.
The Devil

*RB, [11?[2] July 1908], King's College, Cambridge
to JS, Trinity College*

Breakfast at 9.15
(on Monday)
In *my* rooms
if you like RB

1 Apostle Harry Norton was stage manager for the Edward Garnett play, performed at the Haymarket.
2 The date is uncertain. Mrs Brooke had come to Cambridge to see *Comus* and had entertained Strachey and Frances Darwin at tea in her lodgings off Benet Street on 9 July. The next day, *Comus* was performed, and the day after, Brooke met Thomas Hardy. Then, on Monday the 13th he left with his mother for Rugby. Strachey apparently came to breakfast on the day of departure. On 18 July, the same day that Lytton Strachey's review of *Comus* appeared in the *Spectator*, Brooke wrote to Frances Darwin apologizing for not being around to clean up after the production. He said his mother 'packed me up and snatched me here to sleep & recover. I am now convalescent, & can sit up & take a little warm milk-and-Tennyson.' Hassall says Brooke had been in a state of nervous collapse due both to the strain of the production and to Walter Headlam's sudden death at the age of forty-two. Brooke said Headlam was 'about the best writer of Greek there has been since the Greeks' and said it was Headlam who had first inspired him 'to get *Comus* done' (*RBB* 162).

JS, July 18th, 1908, Trinity College, Cambridge

I find that I'm going down sooner than I thought – probably next Thursday – and shall be at Hampstead from then till about the first of August: viz. for rather more than a week. Will you come for a night *then*? (If it were for two, there'ld be the Pinafore.) The middle of September[1] seems so very far away.

Norton has arrived; very much excited of course about Mrs Piper and Mr Robert Sievier and the first letter he's had from Charlie for two years. You know about Charlie, with whom he has a Henry James love affair? Then there's Keeling[2] in a new red beard, like one of those dreadful creatures in the Natural History Museum – 'oorang-ootangs' I think they call them. Otherwise we're much as usual, though I admit that Mr Shove[3] begins to pall: he's really *too* much of a coarse-feeder – Mr Schloss[4] appears refinement itself in comparison.

Oh! and then somehow Mr Watts[5] came to tea (or was it a dream!) and

---

1 The beginning of Michelmas Term.
2 Frederic Hillersdon 'Ben' Keeling (1886–1916) of Trinity College, who founded the Cambridge branch of the Fabians and sponsored Brooke's membership. Keeling's socialism was greatly influenced by Edward Carpenter, a close friend of Hugh Dalton's father. Keeling was also president of the Fish and Chimney, a play-reading society Brooke had joined. It was in Keeling's rooms that Brooke met H. G. Wells and the Oliviers. During the war, Keeling, like Brooke, was offered a commission. He remained true to his socialist beliefs, however, and refused it. Soon thereafter, he was killed at the Somme.
3 Gerald Frank Shove (1887–1947). Brooke probably met Shove in the Fabians. It was Brooke who pushed through Shove's election to the Apostles in 1909 exactly one year after he himself had been elected (Shove was the first member elected after Brooke). In the beginning, Brooke and Shove were especially close as Apostles. Maynard Keynes wrote to Duncan Grant on 11 February 1909: 'Rupert and Gerald spend their time imagining copulations between every possible pair of people.' Shove was probably also imagining one between Rupert and himself, for he confided in a note to James Strachey written on 8 April 1911 that during his second year at Cambridge he had a 'lust for' Rupert. The same note seems to indicate an affair with Strachey during Shove's first year at Cambridge. However, his primary romantic interests at Cambridge were Francis Birrell and Ferenc Békássy. Shove, an economist, was strongly attached to the Bloomsbury group, and took part in the anti-conscription movement during the war. Among his friends he was probably most famous for toasting 'The King, God damn him' at a 1909 Carbonari dinner. He married Fredegond Maitland, the poet, in 1915. Brooke wrote to Geoffrey Keynes in May 1913, 'Give G. Shove a kiss from me, when next you see him.'
4 A. D. Schloss (Arthur Waley) (1889–1966), orientalist and poet. Like Brooke, Schloss went to Rugby and King's. However, problems with his eyes forced him to leave Cambridge in 1910. Schloss took his mother's maiden name in 1914.
5 If Strachey is inventing this episode, he could mean George Frederic Watts, the painter, who died in 1904. If the events in this paragraph are to be taken as fact, then obviously he is referring to some other Watts. Possibly this could be Walter Lamb, with whom Strachey had an affair (see footnote on page 128), and who he and Brooke called 'Watty' (though usually *not* 'Mr Watts').

we talked about Charles Sayle[1] and Leonardo da Vinci for many, many hours. He was very much épris,[2] and thought me extremely cultured, until unfortunately he found on leaving that the book I'd had in my hand when he came in was an edition de luxe of The Sorrows of Satan.

I'm going with Lytton at the beginning of August to an enchanted island in the Hebrides. We shall sit all day among the heather. He will write elegies in heroic couplets; I shall read our brother Pollock[3] on Torts. Good God I wish you could come too. Yes, and you may bring that mysterious figure Alfred[4] with you – as a support perhaps. Oh, I know it's out of the question: but as a matter of fact I was told to ask you. So there it is.

I go today to hear our brother Butler[5] welcome the extensionists in the Senate House.   Yours

                                                                          James

JS, July 23rd, 1908, Trinity College

I've ordered a pair of seats for Thursday night. Do I carry pessimism too far? Did you intend tactfully to announce that you'ld come – be delighted, of course – to the Empire; but that you couldn't stop the night; that you'd made other arrangements; that you were going to stay

---

1   Sayle was a Cambridge librarian who frequently entertained undergraduates in his home. For a period, Brooke was in his house every other day, often inviting himself to luncheons and dinners by sending postcards announcing his plans to stop by. Sayle gave Brooke frequent gifts and wrote in his diary passionate accounts of Brooke's physical presence. In 1909, however, he told Strachey that he had drifted apart from Brooke, a rift which he blamed on the Fabians (James to Lytton, 1 September 1909). Sayle was educated at Rugby and Oxford, but had left the latter due to a homosexual affair. He confided in a letter to John Addington Symonds that his first book, *Bertha: A Story of Love* (1885), was written about the affair. The 'Uranian' theme also shows up in his other books, including *Erotidia* (1889), *Musa Consolatrix* (1893) and *Private Music* (1911).
2   'infatuated'.
3   Frederick Pollock (1845–1937), Apostle no.160, jurist, legal writer, professor and editor.
4   Alfred Brooke (1891–1915), Rupert's younger brother. By all accounts, Alfred was an extrovert and skilful politician. He followed Rupert to Cambridge and joined the Carbonari. Both Mrs Brooke and Rupert tried to influence his politics, his mother hoping he would remain a Liberal and Rupert that he would join the Fabians. Maynard Keynes, meanwhile, complained in a letter to Duncan Grant that Alfred 'talks of nothing but Sodomy and the Budget' (quoted in Skidelsky 239) – a strange complaint, coming from Keynes. During the war, Alfred served as a lieutenant in the Post Office Rifles, and was killed in the trenches in front of Vermelles. After Alfred's death, Lieutenant. J. A. Webster wrote to Mrs Brooke: 'He had gone up to the trenches with a view to being instructed in the use of the machine gun, & was lying down under cover (it is supposed he was asleep) when a shell came over killing him instantaneously.'
5   Henry Montague Butler (1833–1918), Apostle no.130, Master of Trinity.

with – oh! no doubt God knows whom? Am I right? . . Perhaps I'm merely drivelling.

I don't seem able to leave this dreadful place – I can't hope to till Tuesday. There are hundreds of sordid details, you see, about leaving these rooms. My sofas are to go to London; I seem to see them driving down to the station in a hansom together. All these things revolt the Temperament of the Artist.

Then it's rather shocking about Mr. Shove. Dalton thinks he's developing along quite the right lines. *I* don't. At present the real question is whether he can be prevented from proposing to me before next Tuesday. Yes. Even Norton had to admit that poor dear Gerald at least *fancies* he's in love. A sad blow to you that he too should turn out to be hypertrophied. One had always thought him merely vague. In fact I still think so. If only he doesn't commit himself at all now, I'm sure he'll have fallen in love with Humanity again before next term. I must confess, however, that I feel rather filthily satisfied. I'd thought that at my great age I'd seen the last of such affairs. Oh! I can hear your snorts.

By the way, did you know that Ainsworth's[1] to be married to Moore's youngest sister? When Moore was told they were engaged, he said they didn't know what they *meant* by the word.

He and Sanger were here on Saturday; and on Sunday after lunch we all rushed off to your rooms where the only known piano existed. Mr Cane[2] was there. I wonder if he was surprised. – The horrid man's taken down your chinese lanterns, too.

I've just been reading an account of your appearance at Lord's as a performer. "Poor Rupert! I haven't seen the close of play but so far he has made no runs, taken no wickets and (according to my brother) fielded badly."[3] I'd fully intended to go myself and stay the night in London, and I made an appointment to go with Maynard by the 11.20. But I forgot to get an exeat[4] the night before; and Fletcher[5] was out all the morning. Even then I went as far as the station, and nearly decided to go for the day. Would it, I wonder, have been worth while?   Yours
James

It's rather gloomy here – in spite of everything. Another of your dilettante postcards would be a great relief.

1 Alfred Richard Ainsworth, Apostle no.234, elected 1899, died 1959. G. E. Moore had been infatuated with Ainsworth and was initially dismayed when Ainsworth announced his plans to marry Moore's youngest sister, Sarah. The character Ansell in Forster's *The Longest Journey* is based on Ainsworth.
2 Arthur Beresford Cane, Apostle no.213, elected 1886, died 1939.
3 Brooke, a decent cricketer while at Rugby, was taking part in the annual Rugby versus Marlborough match at Lord's. The report is from Maynard Keynes.
4 A pass for absence from a college.
5 Walter Morley Fletcher (1873–1933), tutor and administrator at Trinity College in 1908, later a renowned physiologist.

JS, July 28th, 1908, (just leaving) T[rinity].C[ollege].C[ambridge].

The second reason for taking a house in B[elsize].P[ark].G[ardens]. was that it adjoined Lord's. Via the Swiss Cottage – you understand. And if you don't, shall I really be able to explain it to you on Wednesday? Oh . . . tomorrow! I suppose I should find you if I shimmered round the Palace from half past two to three. Still, if you were generous and foned[1] instructions – but no, that, I feel, is what we nevah, nevah do.

Then there's no cause for dressing either for dinner or for the E[mpire]., unless you insist. (Dinner, I believe's at 7.30 – possibly 8). And then of course one goes there very late.

We had Mr Schloss on Relationships at the Fabs[2] last night. Daddy D.[3] (as we call him now) very gallantly made us all sit on the floor so that the ladies might have chairs.

Norton has suddenly become a habitué at Number 8 Trumpington Street.[4] That was the last connection I should have figured.   Yours
                                                                       James
Will you get this in time?

JS, September 12th, 1908, 67 Belsize Park Gardens, Hampstead

Dear Rupert,
Here are fifteen shillings for you. I'm sure there ought really to be at least three more.

They all got out at Oxford to view the quads and colleges: and I was left, as usual, in command of their traps and bicycles. So a French Jew came in at Reading while the sun was setting. And I told him that I'd got in by the shores of Cardigan Bay, and that where he'd put his bag – on the opposite seat – there, two hours before, had sat you. But he wouldn't believe me.[5]

I sit all day gibbering like this in an empty house. But tomorrow I shall rush out and spit at Cardinal Vannutelli and the Host as they pass down Victoria Street. Did you see that the United Protestants had asked Sanger for Counsel's Opinion about the procession? He fairly blasted the damned papists.   Yours
                                                                       James

1 'Hampstead 1090' is written above 'foned'.
2 The Fabian Society.
3 Hugh Dalton.
4 Charles Sayle's house.
5 Strachey and Brooke were returning from the Fabian Summer School in Wales.

I wanted to pray you to forgive me. I think I whined very much and seemed ungrateful. I'm *not* ungrateful. Did I really say 'cold-hearted'? You're kinder than everyone in the world.

RB, [postcard, postmarked 9.30 p.m., 17 September 1908, Rugby]
to JS, 67 Belsize Park Gardens, Hampstead

Thanks for the 15/-

I hope the poor afflicted Ward kept himself in till the end of the journey. I have reached solitude & books. It is probably the ideal. I cannot clearly recollect the Fabian Summer Delirium. It seems like the recollection of a review of one of Ibsen's farces.   Rupert

JS, September 22nd, 1908, 67 Belsize Park Gardens, Hampstead

Can you tolerate an occasional letter? There's no particular excuse: but it seems to give me pleasure. Of course you're not supposed to take any notice. I feel as though *I* hardly could – of Hugh [Dalton]. There was one from him this morning. Isn't he really too disjected? "In the flow of recent things," he suddenly exclaims, "we are borne along together among those who have achieved. Rising above the 'line of life' we survey the little undesirous people from on high with a smile." And he passes on to the Minimum Wage without the faintest jolt. Perhaps you're accustomed to it and can explain.

After all there seems to be nothing. There are no adventures. Mr Ainley[1] turns out to be *hideous*. So I rushed off to the White City in despair; and flirted with a charming French schoolboy in the Court of Honour. But even he had relations.

Oh! a dreadful meeting yesterday in Whitehall. I was in the vaguest possible condition – with a bad cold in the head, and the eye glasses for ever slipping from the nose – have you anything to correspond? Well, I was hovering dimly over some books outside a shop; when there, silently, by my side was Mr Colgate. All the usual horrors were redoubled. But he was certainly even worse. He couldn't speak: he couldn't decide whether to shake hands. Although partly blind, I managed finally to murmur: "Oh, have you been here ever since you came away from there?" He seemed to pick up a little after that; and we

1 Henry Ainley (1879–1945), the actor, was in the company of Herbert Tree at His Majesty's Theatre during this period.

talked quite a lot about 'Blanco' and Daphne.[1] Whether *they* were in love with one another or *he* was in love with both of them, I couldn't make out. But we parted most friendly, and he almost asked me to belong to the Fabian Nursery.

I read Tacitus in an infinitely Gibbonian translation.   Yours
                                                                          James

Did you notice that we succeeded in executing the guilty General?

RB, Monday [16 November 1908]

Your account of me, sometimes since, was so wrong, that I know you would like to see a true one; in here.

You, a social person, now envy me, I suppose, in the thick of this gay social Cambridge of ours. I envy *you*. Six weeks of solitude; in which to read books that shall subsequently be burnt! Oh Cambridge is more deadly than ever. I have had a freak evening. I have been sitting, trying to work, praying for peace. And in have come; in fantastic succession – , all the odd, Mr Dent,[2] Mr Firbank,[3] Mr Morrison[4] . . . But on Sunday I had tea with Sydney Cockerell,[5] who *is* Alive, & Neville Lytton[6] was there, whom I thought perhaps the Perfect Person. He plays Morris Dances on a Pipe. Tomorrow I go to see the Bacchae.[7] It will be very bad. I have been all round King's trying to borrow a blaque-bag, to go with & cannot.

1 George Rivers Blanco White – who in 1909 married Amber Reeves though she was pregnant by fellow Fabian H. G. Wells – and Daphne Olivier (1889–1950), the third eldest Olivier sister. Daphne, who attended Newnham College, suffered a nervous breakdown in 1915 following the news that Brooke had died. She eventually married Cecil Harwood.
2 Edward Joseph Dent (1876–1957), Professor of Music at King's during Brooke's years at Cambridge. Dent wrote Brooke's obituary for the *Cambridge Magazine*. Forster's Philip Herriton in *Where Angels Fear to Tread* is based on Dent. An 'angel', incidentally, was an Apostle who had resigned from active service. 'Angels' were allowed to attend all meetings for life.
3 Author Ronald Firbank (1886–1926) was known as a 'decadent dandy' at Cambridge. His *Odette d'Antrevennes* was published before he ever got to the university. Once there, he made his rooms the most elegant in Cambridge. Brooke was a frequent dinner guest, and Dent said Firbank was 'a great adorer of Rupert' (quoted in Chainey 174). Firbank's books were published at his own expense and ignored by most critics during his lifetime due to their homosexual subject matter.
4 Herbert Stanley Morrison (1888–1965), also known as Baron Morrison of Lambeth, the future English labour leader and politician.
5 Cockerell (1867–1962) was appointed director of the Fitzwilliam Museum in 1908.
6 Brooke probably knew Lytton from his having painted a portrait of Shaw in 1906 in imitation of Velázquez's portrait of Pope Innocent X, with Shaw in papal vestments.
7 The Gilbert Murray translation of Euripides, playing at the Court.

Saturday – or Friday? – the 13th, anyhow, you spent, of course, in mourning: Knowing it to be the anniversary of Bloody Sunday? Ha?

Here we had a most phenomenal paper. [Jack] Sheppard went out to dinner in Christ's & was drunk afterwards; very very maudlin, & sentimental.

I could not come that busy day you collapsed. Nor had I a thermometer. Not much. It will be Something to have a John Downing [?] – what a lot I have to do tonight –   yours
                                                                    Rupert

JS, Tuesday Evening, November 17th 1908, 8.15,
The sanatorium (or, less tactfully, The Borough of Cambridge
Infectious Diseases Hospital), Mill Road

This will be disinfected (by our Mr Moffat's kindness): and they promise me that it'll be safe. But you'd better burn it at once – perhaps even wash your hands? New idea: Put on a pair of gloves & read it out of doors.

I didn't mean to write – but this evening I suddenly feel that I want to talk a little: I suppose I'm rather sentimental too. Do you mind?

It was very superb getting your letter this morning. I hadn't expected one at all. And even when I saw the Granta[1] addressed by you, I didn't think there'ld be any more. Of course I'd been longing for news from you. I imagined you last Thursday at half past four standing on your hearthrug & teaching those phenomena Wisdom & Goodness; & then on Saturday night. But otherwise I knew nothing. Won't you, twice a week, instead of tearing off a *corner* of your Diary, tear off a whole leaf & send it here? It might make me too jealous. I already am of what you call the Odds – but who is Mr Firbank?

The Granta's article annoyed me very much: – nearly as much as Daddy D. did once – years ago, – in your second term – . He described how he'd first met you or seen you – at dinner with the Provost: he was sitting opposite "And I said to myself 'Who is this gurgeous creecha?'". Can't you hear him slowly mouthing it? Mon dieu!. I nearly strangled him.

I'm alone in this room. But there are eleven empty beds in it. In the next 'ward' there are several children. Every other Sunday their parents are allowed to come at two o'clock & stand outside the shut windows on a kind of platform. Then for two hours everyone shouts; & at four the parents go away, & the children cry for the rest of the evening.

---

1 Hugh Dalton had written a biographical sketch of Brooke for the *Granta*. When he showed it to Brooke prior to publication, Brooke suggested he put in something about his rustic, rural living and his past success in sports. Dalton did, and also threw in a line about Brooke bathing 'every evening at sunset'.

I've been talking now for nearly an hour & a half; but I haven't written down everything I've said. I shan't ever write to you again (perhaps I shan't even send this): oh! it's *much* too sentimental – & dreadfully egotistical.* There are at least 20 `I's' and only 17 `you's', & as for the 'he's' there seem only to be Mr Moffat, Mr. Firbank, & poor Daddy D. But then it makes one egotistical to lie without opening one's mouth all day – except perhaps to ask for a close stool.

Is Mr Shove going to be elected? Will you be his father?[1] I hope you'll manage it better than I did.

Give my love to the brethren, and especially to yourself,   Yours

James

I forgot to say before I was taken that the Bussy's[2] have been taken across (at the last moment). If you still think you can sell one to Dent, will you choose which you like best & hang it in your room? Perhaps they'ld ruin the colour schema of it?

* Besides I'm so afraid of giving you the disease.

RB, [28 November 1908, Cambridge]
to JS, The Sanatorium, Mill Road

They say that there is to be an excursion to you tomorrow: – Maynard says so. He is organizing it. We go on bicycles, have tea as we ride, & reach you between 3 & 4: Shout: & return. I to tea with Arthur Benson![3] I am moving always upward, in literary circles. Only last night I dined with Mr Morrison & Mr Anarchy B.: And today I have won two guineas in the Westminster.[4] It is all over Cambridge. Mr A.B. last night gave Mr M. & myself a list of all the really "brainy" and interesting people who had been at Cambridge lately. He began with Moore, and gave a complete list of the brothers & of noone else, up to date. I had to have many of the names explained.

1 In Apostolic jargon, a 'father' was a new member's sponsor.
2 Paintings by Simon Bussy who had married James's second eldest sister, Dorothy.
3 Benson (1862–1925) taught twenty years at Eton, then returned to Cambridge in 1904. Brooke met Benson through George Mallory, who had invited them both to his rooms. Benson at the time was suffering severe depression, and Mallory was determined to draw him out of it. Brooke did not like Benson's 'egoism' at first, but wrote years later, in a letter to Katherine Cox: 'My only friend is A. C. Benson. We had an infinitely affecting tête-à-tête dinner last night. He implored me to write to him. I nearly kissed him. Both were drunk' (September 1912).
4 Brooke won the *Westminster Gazette* prize for his poem 'The Jolly Company', which appeared in the 28 November *Saturday Westminster*. The competition was for 'the best new and original poem about stars'.

The Diary idea is really not so labour-saving as it sounds. My Diary only records the least amusing half of my engagements: & a lot of alternatives or speculations, which I don't attend. So its no good, uncommentated upon.

No real news. Eddie[1] [Marsh] is here again for the week-end. It is rather a scandal. And *I've* not even asked him to breakfast. Dennis Robertson[2] loves me & hates Norton. Mr Broad[3] has discovered all about the Society & told Mr Shove; who regards me with infinitely mingled & amusing emotions. I spoke a little ago at the Liberal Club & was agreed

---

1 Edward Marsh (1872–1953), an Apostle and London patron of the arts. There is no doubt that Marsh, who became Winston Churchill's private secretary, was later in love with Brooke. As Brooke set sail for the Aegean, Marsh wrote to him that he would 'live in a shadow' until he saw Brooke 'safe and well again', and added, 'I expect you know what you are to me' (26 March 1915). Brooke's mother knew, too. After Brooke's death, she wrote to Marsh, 'I know how he regarded you. Amongst his many friends he certainly placed you first, almost his Second Self [...] Before the war when he was going to London a good deal I suggested he had better take some rooms, he said, "No, Eddie wouldn't like it at all"' (April 1915). Marsh had, in fact, once written to Brooke: 'I think I'm prepared to love you under whatever transformation' (Hassall, *Marsh* 277). Although the *Dictionary of National Biography* attributes Marsh's bachelorhood to having had 'mumps and German measles in early adolescence', it was well known by all his acquaintances, including Brooke, that he liked young men. The painter Stanley Spencer sometimes accompanied Marsh and Brooke to London concerts and would spend the night at Gray's Inn (Marsh's London residence, which became Rupert's second home). Spencer was sure enough of Marsh's homosexuality to write him semi-erotic letters, such as the one in which he wrote, 'The boy we go bathing with is a Gladiator, only his muscles are not "bumpy" but evenly developed over his whole body. I love to watch the vapour rising from his body when he comes out of the water' (quoted in Hassall, *Marsh* 258). Marsh bought Spencer's painting *The Apple Gatherers* and hung it in the room where Brooke slept. What is clear from Brooke's last letters is that, at the end of his life, Marsh figured centrally in it. And, among all of Brooke's friends, it was Marsh who took his death the hardest. Marsh wrote the first memoir of Brooke – published at the front of *The Collected Poems of Rupert Brooke* (1918) – though he was frustrated at every turn by the poet's mother. She insisted, for instance, that Marsh ask Geoffrey Keynes to write something to be included, then, when Keynes declined Marsh's invitation to write, she withdrew her permission to publish. Marsh wrote to her expressing dismay that, after all the trouble he had taken, he should be made to suffer 'because someone else, over whom I have no control, refuses to write' (Hassall, *Marsh* 386). Later, Marsh sent an announcement to Sidgwick and Jackson of the *Memoir*'s postponement '"owing to wishes of the family" – I should like to insert the word "bloody" before "family", but I won't insist on this' (Hassall, *Marsh* 391). Marsh regarded his relationship with Mrs Brooke as the most distressing experience of his life; their dispute takes up almost seventy pages of Hassall's biography of Marsh. In later years Marsh continued supporting the arts in England, publishing additional anthologies of *Georgian Poetry* and aiding artists in financial difficulties. He was responsible for James Joyce's Treasury grant, though it was Ezra Pound – who had supplied him with Joyce's address – who sent Joyce the note of appreciation. Marsh's autobiographical *A Number of People* is a good source of information on his life and friends, as is Christopher Hassall's *Edward Marsh: Patron of the Arts*.
2 Dennis Robertson (1890–1963), economist, attended Trinity College and won the Chancellor's medal for English verse three times before switching to economics in 1910.
3 Charlie Dunbar Broad (1887–1971), philosopher, was a student of Apostle John McTaggart at Trinity College.

by everybody to be a complete failure: – except by Newnham, who felt protective & motherly.[1] Sheppard is aging. I am going to the (6.25) A.D.C.[2] tonight (!) with Mr Dent; with whom I dine. I shall go in a taxi cab. For I am rich. My income is £1825 per year – £7 a day: (£2 from Westminster, £5 from King's essay prize, just out).[3] Irene Dukes has gone off her head. I am going to Switzerland.

39 I's. 2 yous.

My love to the 17 children   Rupert

JS, December 31st, 1908, 67 Belsize Park Gardens, Hampstead

The International has its grand evening party at the New Gallery on the eighth. We've got some spare tickets; & it occurs to me that you might like to go. Hundreds of ghastly celebrities are always there – friends of yours, I expect. And possibly Monsieur Rodin to receive the guests.

But then I don't know where you are; I'm even rather frightened that you may be in Reggio di Calabria. Anyhow I shall be pleased with the cold refusal.There's of course a room here.   Yours

                                                                         James

We had Charles Archer here the other day at dinner – exactly like William,[4] but with hair mustaches – whiskas yellow instead of black.

---

1   Brooke wrote to his mother on 25 November 25 'Did I tell you I made my first public speech on Friday, to two hundred Liberals and Socialists, advocating "union among reformers"? It *was* bad: and I frightened.' 'Newnham' probably refers to Brooke's collective female friends at Newnham College, who included Katherine Cox and Margery Olivier. It might also refer to Gwen Darwin, who lived at Newnham Grange.
2   The Amateur Dramatic Club, whose theatre was on Jesus Lane in Cambridge.
3   Brooke jokes, of course. Though he had won £7 in one day, his actual income was £150 per year. Aside from the little money he made from his writing, this is what he lived on for the rest of his life. The figure of £1,825 is what his annual income would be if he made £7 a day, five days a week, for a year. In a letter to his mother the following day, Brooke multiplies the £7 by 365 days, coming up with an annual income of £2,555. The King's College essay prize was probably awarded for his paper titled 'Political Satire in English Verse', which he had read during the term.
4   Charles Archer (1861–1941) had recently translated Ibsen's *Rosmersholm* for the London stage (10–15 February 1908, at Terry's). His elder brother William Archer (1856–1924) had translated Gerhart Hauptmann's *Hanneles Himmelfahrt*, which opened as *Hannele* on 12 April 1908 at the Scala. William, the author of several books on the theatre, journalism, poetry and travel, spoke at the Fabian Summer School in Wales attended by Brooke and Strachey. In his speech he claimed that democratic social reform would mean an end of the arts, which he felt depended on a leisure class. Afterwards, Brooke referred to him as 'Whiskers, and no brains' in a letter to Geoffrey Fry (25 September 1909). In *Democracy and the Arts* – which he wrote to disprove Archer's position – Brooke called him 'a great living critic, a keen, able, solemn, whiskered, well-meaning man' (*Prose* 81). On another occasion, when asked his opinion of a new book by Archer, Brooke replied, 'Well, it weighs 2 lb. 13 oz.' (*Prose* 167).

1909

Brooke's involvement with the Fabians had increased throughout 1908. He had met H. G. Wells during Lent Term and then had made a point of reading Wells's books. *New Worlds for Old* made a significant impression on him, and after talking with Wells at some length he decided in April 1909 to sign the Fabian Basis and become a full member (his 8 April letter to Hugh Dalton announcing his decision is printed in Dalton's *Call Back Yesterday*, 47). Before long Brooke was calling himself 'a rabid Socialist', editing a newsletter with scathing criticisms of Conservative Party candidates, and canvassing the south of England on behalf of Poor Law reform. By 1910 his political views had become so firm that he declared after one of the two elections that year: 'I HATE the upper classes.'

In February, Brooke read his paper 'The Romantic History and Surprising Adventures of John Rump' to the Carbonari. The satiric attack on the English middle class is often farcical, as when God orders Rump – and his hat – out of heaven. Judging from this paper, the Carbonari membership was now discussing homosexual themes as openly as the Apostles. In the paper Brooke suggests that the duties of a housemaster consist in preparing the boys for Confirmation and turning 'a blind eye on sodomy', and he writes, 'I pass over John's amazing & sudden incursion into sodomy at the age of 15 under the guidance of the head of his house; also the many amorous adventures he himself arranged when he reached his last year or two at school.'

At the end of February, Strachey accompanied Brooke to Oxford, where he wrote to his brother Lytton on the 23rd: 'Oxford seems to overflow with Rupert's ex-lovers & ex-lovees. We meet them at every turn.' Duncan Grant joined them briefly and wrote to Maynard Keynes on the 25th: 'I dined with Rupert & James who seemed very happy.'

At the end of Lent Term, Strachey and Brooke went to the Lizard in Cornwall, where James joined Rupert for one of his characteristic nude swims then immediately wrote to Lytton (7 April): 'And this afternoon, for the first time in my life, I saw Rupert naked. [...] I was naked too. I

thought him – if you'd like to have a pendant – "absolutely beautiful".'
Brooke used the same trip to spend time with Hugh Russell-Smith at
Manaton in Devon and with Dudley Ward and the Olivier sisters in the
New Forest. He had met the elder Olivier sisters through the Fabians,
and in the summer of 1908 during work on a production of *Comus* he
met their younger sister Noel. She was only fifteen at the time, and there
was 'something distinctly boyish' in her 'unusual looks' (Lehmann,
Strange 32). Opportunities to see her were rare – especially once her
sister Margery began to suspect Brooke of too much interest – but
during this Easter vacation Brooke devised an elaborate scheme that
would enable him to spend a few hours with Noel in the New Forest. In
order to carry out the plan, he felt it necessary to deceive both his
mother (whom he was to join in Sidmouth) and Hugh Russell-Smith –
and to this end he enlisted the aid of both James Strachey and Dudley
Ward. Brooke seemed to take great pleasure in mapping out the details
of the plan, leading one, as Adrian Caesar says, to suspect that 'it was
precisely the difficulty of seeing her that Brooke enjoyed' (26).

Brooke was also becoming better acquainted with Katherine Cox and
Edward Marsh in 1909, and he stayed with Marsh in London before
returning to Cambridge for the next term.

During the lapse in correspondence from 12 April until 17 May of this
year, the following incident occurred. Strachey is relating the episode in
a letter to Duncan Grant. He had gone to Brooke's room and found him
in bed. He had then asked Brooke to give him his fingers, but this
request was refused.

> 'Oh, *yes*. It'll do no harm. Oh! You know you'll have forgotten
> everything tomorrow morning.' It was hysterical and it stiffened him.
> [...] 'I *shouldn't* forget. And it'ld only annoy me. Go to bed!' – There
> was a long dead silence. [...] You see; I found out something about
> him which *did* make me despair. He's a *real* womanizer. And there can
> be no doubt that he *hates* the physical part of my feelings *instinctively*.
> Just as I should hate to be touched by a woman. I think also that he
> has to some extent a dislike of *everything* physical – that he has a trace
> at least of virginity. [...] How I stared for something from him. How
> carefully he gave me nothing. (16 April 1909)

On 13 May Brooke read to the Apostles a humorous account of the
rumours surrounding his election, but couched in a fictitious future
inhabited by the present Apostles' sons. He called it, 'Why not try the
other leg?':

> By eight o'clock on Saturday evening, April 29th, 1948, the inner
> room of Brooke's rooms, on the ground floor of E staircase, Gibbs
> buildings, King's, was full of brothers, angelic and apterous. It was

thought to be rather an important occasion; possibly an amusing one. Young Brooke had been recently elected; solely, some of the angels thought – and especially those who had belonged to the brilliant and witty period of the early twenties, – solely for his name and his yellow hair. And it was his first paper.

The title of the paper comes from another section:

It is said that, a certain don of the college, when he had precipitately entered Hall for lunch, having been asked, what he had been doing all the morning, and having replied 'I have been trying to write Latin Prose, but have been unable to do so, owing to the painful rheumatism in my right leg,' it was quietly muttered by a propinquous scientist 'why not try the other leg?'

At the end of the Trinity Term, Strachey and Brooke both left Cambridge – Strachey abandoning his studies at Trinity College to become an assistant editor at the *Spectator* (the London newspaper edited by his cousin, St Loe Strachey), and Brooke deciding he could stand life in Cambridge no longer and would be happier in the nearby village of Grantchester, two miles west. James and Lytton began making plans to find rooms together in London, but these plans came to nothing, and James remained at his family home at 69 Lancaster Gate. Brooke moved to Grantchester primarily to escape some of his academic pressures at Cambridge and to obtain some solitude. Nevertheless, his two residences at Grantchester – the Orchard and later the Old Vicarage – both became gathering places for his circle of friends. Though he sometimes feigned exasperation at the frequent interruptions of his work, the friends generally showed up in response to his invitations. At this time in his life Brooke probably had more friends, and delighted in them more, than at any other. As Robert Pearsall, one of his biographers, put it, 'His friendships had become a cult' (68).

With the move to Grantchester, Brooke also moved further from his decadent stance, embracing instead the world of pastoral England. Those who think of him as the poet of laughter probably have the Brooke of this period in mind, for in his life, at least, he became a celebrant of youth, beauty and laughter. His poetry, although still frequently morose in subject, became less dismal in tone, and began to look more like Donne and less like Swinburne. As his enthusiasm for the Decadents waned, his interest in Shelley and Keats and the writers of the Renaissance grew. He was especially drawn to Donne, Shakespeare and Marlowe, writing papers on all three and helping to form the Marlowe Dramatic Society.

It was at Grantchester that Brooke and friends were dubbed 'neo-pagans' by Virginia Stephen, at least partially due to Brooke's habit of asking visitors to bathe nude with him near by in Byron's Pool. This is also the period in which he is said to have hated tobacco and red meat, preferring a diet that consisted mainly of fish. But Virginia later said of his semi-vegetarianism that he did not eat meat except when he stayed at her father's house, for he never liked to spend money.

Meanwhile, James Strachey was being pursued by George Mallory, a Cambridge contemporary who would later lose his life attempting to become the first man to ascend Mount Everest. On 8 February, Maynard Keynes had written to Duncan Grant that 'James and George Mallory fell into one another's arms!' Three days later he wrote to Grant that Mallory 'confided in Rupert that he did not know "whether he liked James or loved him" [...] James's feelings were, according to his own account, as mixed as they could be – George charming and impulsive and in beautiful good looks.' Then, on 28 February, Maynard wrote to Grant: 'James and George now stroke one another's faces in public.' In May, Maynard wrote again: 'How does James manage it? How could one help having *real* affection for him [Mallory], if he made love to one – or even if he didn't? Finally he has offered to copulate; and even that doesn't melt James's stoniness.' Strachey wrote to Lytton on 8 March: 'I've not even copulated with George. I don't much want to. In fact nowadays I see him so much that he bores me incredibly.' He eventually did have sex with Mallory, but never managed to fall in love with him. At the end of the year, Mallory wrote to James:

> There has never been anything to say since the day when I told you I loved you. Am I to repeat continually the wearisome news that I want to kiss you? [...] You had better forget that I was ever your lover. [...] How pleasant it was! for you I believe as well as for me, wasn't it? [...] You will see that I am unhappy which I believe will be unpleasant for you. But isn't there something also rather comforting about being loved? Or does it just make you feel you would like to kill yourself? (20 December 1909)

In August Brooke joined his family in Clevedon, Somerset, where he was visited by many friends. He then joined Strachey at the Fabian camp in Wales.

Strachey, as usual, spent part of the summer at his mother's ancestral home at Rothiemurchus in the Scottish Highlands. He invited Brooke to join him – and repeated the invitation for the next three years, but Brooke always found reasons to decline.

James joined Lytton in Sweden in September, after which he returned to his job at the *Spectator* in London.

Brooke lost his virginity this autumn by seducing Denham Russell-Smith at the Orchard. In December Brooke attended a ball at the Slade School of Art in London dressed as the West Wind, then – as had become his habit – he ended the year with a trip to Switzerland.

RB, [1 or 2 January] 1909, Rugby
to JS, 67 Belsize Park Gardens, Hampstead

Alas! The cold refusal is inevitable. With more than physical force they have tied me here till I go to Cambridge. If I show the least sign of knowledge of anything that lies beyond this house; or happened since A.D. 45., they lose their tempers, & I mine. A wearing life. Yet I am so sorry to miss M. Rodin, for whom I feel a lingering affection, & the Celebrities of London, who are my old, trusty, dear friends. Give them all my love. (In any case, there's the money difficulty.) (I only possess 11d. And I have spent the last ten days on a mountain trying to persuade the treasurer[1] that all is well concerning £2-9-8 which I received for Fabian Literature last term and which went to completing my collection of photographs of Donatello.) Which brings me to Switzerland: A most healthy & enjoyable time. Herbert Samuel[2] & I are great friends now. Many exciting things happened. At Zurich, on the way back, I saw (within three minutes) an English low-class tripper who looked exactly like our brother Dickinson,[3] & a Foreign Count who perfectly resembled Our Brother Browning.[4] At Klosters we wrote & played a melodrama. I

---

1 Margery Olivier (1886–1974), the eldest Olivier sister, was then treasurer of the local Fabians. Because Brooke felt that Margery tried to prevent him from seeing Noel, his comments about her were often mean-spirited. Like her sister Daphne, Margery suffered a nervous breakdown shortly after Brooke's death. She began psychiatric treatment in 1916 but became more and more violent. She was committed to a mental hospital in 1922, where she remained until her death. Margery outlived all of her sisters.

2 Herbert 'Bertie' Samuel (1870–1963), Liberal politician and philosopher, was in 1908 Under-Secretary of State at the Home Office working for legislation protecting children and workers. In a letter to Geoffrey Fry, written on 2 January 1909, Brooke described Samuel as 'a Socialist' and said, 'We Fabians were rather shocked at him.'

3 Goldsworthy Lowes Dickinson (1862–1932), Apostle no.209, the Cambridge don and political philosopher whose Dickinson's Society held discussion groups in his rooms. When Dickinson was awarded the Kahn Travelling Fellowship, which was intended to widen the mind of the Fellow who received it – Brooke remarked to Hugh Dalton, 'If they widen Goldie's mind any more, it'll break' (Dalton 56). His *Autobiography* describes his love affairs with Roger Fry, Ferdinand Schiller, Oscar Eckhard, Peter Savary and Dennis Proctor. There is an arrow drawn from his name in this letter to the margin, where appears 'or E.'.

4 Oscar Browning (1837–1923), Apostle no.142, had rooms across the hall from Brooke. Known as 'the O.B.', Browning had been dismissed as housemaster at Eton in 1875 over unspecified charges of 'intimacy' with the sixteen-year-old George Nathaniel Curzon (the future Viceroy of India) although the boys in his house – and their parents – rallied to his defence (A. C. Benson was among those Eton pupils who thought Browning wonderful). Browning returned to Cambridge, but he and Curzon remained close. When Brooke dined with Browning in 1907, Browning was excited at the prospect of a forthcoming Cambridge visit by his 'old friend' Curzon (*LRB* 85). Dickinson, in his *Autobiography*, says Browning had 'the homosexual temperament, and that explains his influence at Eton and at Cambridge' (64). Browning died in Rome.

was the hero, strangely enough. Quite bad, & most popular, I was. The *we* who wrote were Mr Clive Carey,[1] a great favourite with everybody, myself, quite a favourite with everybody, and our niece Miss Helen Verrall.[2] I have lately received a descriptive letter from Daddy, in Devon. "Daddy in Devon" – shall we write a novel? There is such shifting about the date of the London dinner – or meeting – or whatever – for Cambridge Fabians. They've altered the only possible date.   Rupert

JS, January 5th, 1909, 67 Belsize Park Gardens, Hampstead

Are you going to be at the F[abian].S[ociety]. dinner on Saturday? I thought it was possible that you might. Will you say on a post card if you are, so that I can telegraph to them that I can't after all face it – if you aren't?

I went to hear Mr Lloyd George at the Queen's Hall on Friday. I was utterly sickened, and decided that I couldn't possibly help those devils to get in again. The worst of it was of course the suffrage interruptions. I was only *just* too frightened to protest. The stewards are apparently ex-convicts; & the audience fairly howls with joy as sixty of them break poor Mr Mitchell's ribs. The Chancellor himself is just a very bad actor, & far from being scurrilous is incredibly sentimental & sanctimonious.

So I spend my time in carrying round a petition in favour of W[omen's].S[uffrage]. – I went into every house in Eton Avenue the other night – all Jews and R.A.'s[3] – and got 3 signatures. Not very useful, perhaps – except for the glimpse into the English Homes. Christmas makes them amazing – polished marble statues of naked Venuses holding bunches of mistletoe in their arms.

I hope Switzerland was nice. I went & looked at the slate at Charing Cross on the day you left. It said there was a hurricane – but perhaps you don't take that so seriously? And then there was the colonel who wrote to The Times & said the snow was so arranged this winter that everyone who skied would be killed. Perhaps you have been. Should I have heard?

It's so dull here. Not even St. Loe.[4]   Your
James

---

1 Carey, a baritone, also performed in *Doctor Faustus* with Brooke and later gave him singing lessons, at Brooke's request.
2 Helen Verrall (1887–1964) was the daughter of Arthur Woolgar Verrall, Apostle no.174 (and thus Brooke's and Strachey's 'niece'). Verrall and Brooke produced comic melodramas (*An Uproar in Three Acts* and *The Super-Ski*) on successive Christmas vacations in Switzerland and performed them at their hotel.
3 'Royal Academicians' – that is, members of the Royal Academy.
4 St Loe Strachey (1860–1927) whose books include *The Practical Wisdom of the Bible* (1908) and *Problems and Perils of Socialism* (1908?). During St Loe's term as *Spectator* editor, which lasted until 1925, at least ten Stracheys – including Lytton and James – contributed to the paper.

Have you heard that Adrian's[1] thrown up the Bar & is going onto the Stage? Perhaps it's a secret.

JS, *January 7th, 1909, 67 Belsize Park Gardens, Hampstead*

I'd thought it out so elaborately. You'ld be able quite easily to be here tomorrow, because you were going in for the University Scholarships & would have to be in Cambridge on Saturday. I suppose as a matter of fact you won't go up till next Friday – perhaps Thursday?

And then I thought that even if you wouldn't come here, you'ld come to the Fabian Dinner. So I unwisely accepted. Oh! they've insisted on Norton's going to it. Won't it be very awkward for him when they strike up our dear song about the Scarlet Banner?[2]

I've been reading Marshall.[3] Do you know what he says about the good fish? "As to the sea, opinions differ. Its volume is vast, & fish are very prolific; and some think that a practically unlimited supply can be drawn from the sea by man without appreciably affecting the numbers that remain there." Surely he must be a fraud?

I also read Henry James. But its fairly gloomy living here with a lot of people who don't in the least know what I'm thinking about, & who'ld hate me if they did. Then there's Lytton, whom I'm very fond of, & whom the Universe tortures quite incredibly. It'ld be some relief if I could talk to you about that, & other things that I really care about. Shall I ever? As it is, I have to make the best of Maynard, the iron copulating-machine, & Norton, the affable eunuch. Why are you so different? especially so far more intelligent? But somehow when I'm with you, there's always a damned awkwardness. *I*, at least, so often don't say what I mean. It was getting much better I think before I vanished. But I thought it was so very bad the last time I saw you. Can you explain it? Is it because facts aren't faced? But I think they are. Perhaps it's all my imagination, & I shall merely make it all worse. And anyhow the whole question must be infinitely less important to you than me, I know. And then I have the ghastly moments sometimes, when it all seems to be explained by your rather disliking me & wishing most of the time that I weren't there. But even if that's it, oughtn't I to face even that? Don't

---

1 Adrian Leslie Stephen (1883–1948), the brother of Virginia, eventually became a psychiatrist. He had studied law at Trinity College and then had gone to Lincoln's Inn. He and Duncan Grant became lovers in 1910. Later, he was rejected by Noel Olivier. He then married Karin Costelloe.
2 The socialist anthem, 'The Red Flag'. Norton was quite wealthy.
3 Alfred Marshall founded the Cambridge School of Economics. He published *Principles of Economics* in 1890. John Maynard Keynes was one of his favourite pupils, though Keynes later said Marshall was a 'very great man, but I suppose rather a silly one' (Skidelsky 427).

you agree that it's silly not to try to make it easier? – to talk, I mean. I'm sure it's all my fault; but I don't see how. Can't you help?

I'd no notion all this was coming when I said that I also read Henry James. Shall I burn it?

If it annoys you, it'll prove that you dislike me; because all this fuss is certainly me.   Yours
                                                                          James

Mrs Eden[1] thinks you're a new fangled young man.

*RB, Wed [13 January 1909, Rugby]
to JS, Trinity College, Cambridge*

My notable desertion of Classics (my sole topic of conversation last term) might have hinted . . . . . But it was rather a toss-up.[2] However I hope the feast succeeded. I rather wished to be there. Don't you admire & love them all?

Yes I appear on Friday very late. My love to Mrs Eden.

Really, of course, I think & live so utterly differently from you that I find it difficult to understand, often. I have to maintain (in reading your letter) a constant effort; lest I slip into my usual habit of mind, whence it all appears unmeaning. Like looking at a picture from the edge. For instance, your first sentence . . . "gloomy living here with a lot of people who don't in the least know what I'm thinking about" . . . . I continually fail to attach any meaning to it. The words seem all right: the syntax is admirable. But its like "so (he/she) went into the garden, to cut a cabbage," . . . .

And, then, resolutely, I remember how you think, & work out the sense . . . .

Also, you must remember, I (how pleasant it is to write about oneself always!) live much more transiently & without noticing, than is your standard. Or not? – I mean that I can't much remember now why I got out of the window when you came in, or didn't talk about Lytton. I can chiefly only deduce, imagine what I generally felt like. Various reasons I frequently don't like talking: & I frequently don't like Lytton. (I probably sympathise rather with the world.).

I have a theory of loving all things; but a practice of hating, or being violently irritated with, almost everything. More especially, of late, people & sounds. Partly, I have evolved a naife [sic] but passionate desire

1 Probably someone connected with the Strachey household.
2 Brooke was being encouraged to abandon classics and concentrate on English literature. He had not attempted the University Scholarships.

to be educated. And have been trying to get to work to remedy the barrenness of my education. That happened a lot. And always, in the quiet evening, people *came in!* . . . (Do you mind being one of a procession, for a moment. It's rather rude . .) Oh, I developed a feeling about the world! Once, (after you'd gone to the suburb) I made a scheme of sporting always. But I forgot, & it didn't work . . . .

You do not conceive how I love my own company: and thirst for knowledge.

Next term it will be worse. A play:[1] a performance of dancing:

. . . And I have planned a life for myself.   7. Rise.
                                        7.–7.45. Cold Bath
                                        7.45–8.15 Indian Clubs
                                        8.15. Butter and a nut –

and so on.

Really, if you could make me go a walk every now & then in the afternoon . . after my coffee with poor old C.C.C. I might scream at your window, & then we should trot off through Kings, & I should explain the Artistic beauty of the Backs . . . . . . Do you mind my being orderly? I'm so ungrumpy at 3.p.m.: & I want rather to go out in a day; and (at present) can't.

And then, I shouldn't imagine moments of awkwardness, if I were you. Like as not, I'm just bubbling on to myself about dear old [James Elroy] Flecker or something. Anyhow, I'll do my best to talk about anything in the world – even what people think – if you'll start the way at any particular moment. How the devil should *I* know what one talks about? (My rational silence in face of the Unusual is not a characteristic, personal to you, but general towards the world.)

I'll be less savage when I meet you. I've just been having a two hours row with my mother. And I'm tired & angry. R

JS, March 17th, 1909

Dear Rupert,
I'm sure it would relieve Moore's mind, if you sent him your dates.[2] His address is –
                6 Pembroke Villas
                    The Green
                        Richmond
                            Surrey

1 Brooke was to appear as the Prologue in *The Silent Woman*, produced by Reginald
   Pole of King's College.
2 G. E. Moore was planning his annual Easter reading party for the Apostles – to be
   held this year at the Lizard in Cornwall.

Ben [Keeling] has written to ask me to go to Walthamstow on Friday. He says that you're going to be there. Can it be true? I wish I had enough strength of character to refuse.

I gathered from Daddy that you hated me even more than before – because I said last night that: Mr Alston made a speech to him in defence of Sodomy. The end of the story was rather amusing.

Poor Sheppard's very much upset about Mr Hamilton:[1] the latest turn, you know, which I suppose Daddy described to you.

Maynard has just been – but all this is forbidden.   Yours
                                                                                       James

RB, Thursday [18 March 1909], School Field, Rugby
to JS at Trinity College, Cambridge
[forwarded to 67 Belsize Park Gardens, Hampstead]

The worst part of sentimentalists who are *quite* ignorant of human beings – (people whose existence on many other grounds I have always defended) – people like you & Daddy, – is that when they get together they are *so* mad, & that, in such ways, they elaborate idiocies, the explanation and the destruction of which occupy much of the valuable time of the clear-headed men of the world.

My brother Alfred is not an idiot. It does not pain me that any ignorance of his should vanish. His prejudices do not interest me. None of his feelings affects me in the slightest.[2]

A lot of other comments could be made; but these will do for the time.

Thanks for Moore's address. I shall write to him. Most of my plans are upset by my mothers illness; & the fact that I may have to be plagued by

---

1 Probably Granville Hamilton, a close friend of Maynard Keynes at Eton who attended King's College with Sheppard. In his biography of Keynes, Roy Harrod calls Hamilton 'good looking and charming' and reports that he later served for thirty years as Clerk to the House of Lords (33).

2 Strachey wrote to his brother Lytton on 16 March: 'Alfred Brooke is here [...] Rupert says he's extremely debauched and lascivious. [...] Oh, one has rather odd feelings towards Rupert's younger brother. At least, *I* have.' In August, Strachey went to visit Brooke and wrote to Maynard Keynes from Rugby: 'Alfred is very pink and white – perhaps almost buggerable.' When Alfred joined Rupert at Cambridge soon thereafter, he was the subject of much speculation concerning whether he would be willing to engage in sex. Hugh Dalton, one of those interested in both Alfred and Rupert, wrote to Strachey on 16 September: 'O dear no, he is not completely "higher".' The term *higher*, short for 'higher sodomy', was used to refer to those who subscribed to the idea that love of man for man was superior to love of man for woman. 'Higher sodomy' did not involve physical sex; 'lower sodomy' did. Although Brooke professes not to be concerned with Alfred's sexuality in this letter, he had apparently recently involved himself in defending someone else's sexual inclinations. Maynard Keynes had written to Duncan Grant on 8 February that Brooke had taken it upon himself to argue for leniency in the case of a Rugby schoolmaster accused of 'buggery' of a student.

the family most of the creation. I think however, that, though reluctantly, I shall go for the weekend to the Party.

I believe I am going to see Ben on Friday evening at his flat & stay there. But I'm dining with St. John:[1] so I shall arrive late.

I don't suppose I know what the `latest turn' about Mr Hamilton is.

I thought Alfred would upset you.   Rupert

JS, March 21st, 1909, 67 Belsize Park Gardens, Hampstead

It was very nice to find an unexpected letter from you sitting here when I got home yesterday morning.

I quite agree with your general reflexions on the Sentimentalist. But I don't think I took the Alfred story very seriously – though as a matter of fact I *did* imagine that I'd made you angry in some other way. You know how it must always happen. There were other small things, but it was chiefly that you wouldn't have seen me before you went, if I hadn't broken all the rules & gone in on Tuesday night. And then when I *was* there, you were wishing perhaps that I wasn't: and anyhow chiefly when I dragged myself out you didn't give me a word or even a look which should belong to me. I saw that after all I was much much less than poor old Sheppard, – the shadow of a shade, – nothing.

I suppose all my tears have been unreasonable. But *now* I'm unreasonably happy. You can do that too. You can do *everything*. And wasn't it everything to be with you for those last three minutes yesterday?

There doesn't seem to be much excuse for writing. I suppose you don't ever feel that you want to tell people things? I don't mean gossip; – things about your own feelings. *I* do violently. But who can I tell unless you? You aren't interested: but you may understand a little. The others – oh! even poor Daddy D. – would be quite hopelessly stupid.

Damn.

Will you anyhow tell me the name of your place, so that I can look it up in the Times Atlas?

1 St John Lucas-Lucas, the poet of aestheticism and future editor of the *Oxford Book of French Verse*. Lucas, from Rugby, was an early mentor for Brooke. They met when Lucas was twenty-five and Brooke sixteen. Mrs Brooke apparently never approved of their friendship. Lucas was so distressed when he learned of her dislike of him and of her insistence that none of his letters from Brooke be placed in Marsh's *Memoir* that he wrote to Marsh, 'I never had the faintest idea that Mrs. Brooke had any objection to my letters being used by you. Why in the world should she? I *did* know that she objected to my name appearing in your memoir; [...] I am sending you the letters & Rupert's letters too. Please keep them & tell her that I never want to see them again.'

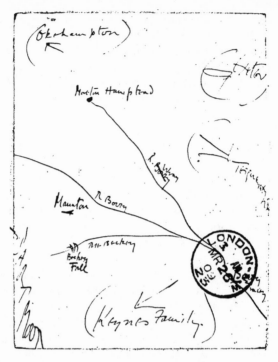

Brooke's post card of 25 March 1909 providing Strachey with a
rough map of the Manaton area where Brooke was staying.

In my study of the Modern Drama, I've at last reached Mr Jones.[1]
Mon Dieu! quel homme! Surely infinitely below the terrible Mr Pinero.[2]

Yours
James

JS, April 3rd, 1909, Penmenner House, The Lizard, Cornwall

Moore says you're coming on Tuesday; but he seems to think you're
so incompetent that you won't find the way here unless I explain it.

There's mainly a most alarming motor bus for ten miles from Helston
to here. And probably you can 'book' to the Lizard from wherever you
may now be. If you sent a postcard with your train, I'ld meet you at the

---

1 Henry Arthur Jones (1851–1929).
2 Arthur Wing Pinero (1855–1934), the dramatist and director whose *Mid-Channel*
   was then in the middle of a fifty-eight-performance run at the St James's Theatre.

Hotel de Ville here – where the bus stops.

We arrived last night: the others are Norton, Gerald [Shove], & Moore. It's very painful – Purgatory, in fact – with torrents of wind & rain into which the others have just (2.30) plunged. I'm crouching by the fire between the Poor Law Report[1] and Middlemarch. (By the way, have you heard the latest rumour? – Beatrice Webb is enceinte; & has been hurried off to Spain, where she will give birth to – what? a copy of the Minority Report? Heaven knows the name of its father.)

[Desmond] MacCarthy is expected on Monday, and [Charles] Sanger & Crompton Davies[2] on Thursday.

That's believed to be all.

I went to 'Strife'[3] again & sat next Daddy & Mr Foss.[4] They seemed to be more or less married. Daddy is really a little too quick even for me: –

For the Academic Year	1906–7	R. C. B.
" " " "	1907–8	Gerald.
" " " "	1908–9	Mr. Foss.
" " " "	1909–10	Alfred perhaps?

Notice that they are always freshmen, and always elected in the following January.

You can imagine how excited we all were when they announced a play by Arthur[5] called 'A Boy's Proposal'; to be acted, too, by dear Philip Tongue.[6] Lytton & Norton rushed off to it: but I gather that it was a disappointment.

Yours
James

Do send the train. And then perhaps it wouldn't be *too* absurd if I

1 The Poor Law Commission majority and minority reports had been published in February 1909. Fabian leader Beatrice Webb was co-author of the minority report.
2 Apostle no.218, elected November 1889.
3 The John Galsworthy play, which was ending a brief run at the Adelphi after successful runs at the Duke of York's and the Haymarket theatres.
4 Although Brooke refers to a 'Michael' Foss in his next letter, Strachey must mean William 'Billy' Foss of Emmanuel College, a Cambridge Fabian and Marlowe Society member. For several years, beginning in 1910, he and Dalton lived together in London at 4 Brick Court, The Temple. Dalton describes Foss as 'good-looking, small', and 'a perfect companion', and says 'it was his acting which first caught Rupert's eye and mine' (68). Due to financial problems, Foss left Cambridge after one year. Dalton was the best man at his wedding, soon after which Foss was killed in the war.
5 Arthur Eckersley, playwright and contributor to *Punch*. St John Lucas-Lucas had once brought Eckersley along when he called on Rupert at Rugby. Like Lucas-Lucas, Eckersley was an ardent follower of 'decadence'. *A Boy's Proposal* played at the Adelphi from 29 March to 3 April (the same dates as *Strife*).
6 Philip Tonge (1892–1959), a veteran of the London stage at age seventeen, played the part of Tom, the boy.

went to Helston & came back with you in the bus? It can only get up a hill once in five times: so the conductor stands on the step with a wedge in his hand, ready to put it behind the wheel instantly, to prevent the whole thing from rolling down backwards.

RB, Monday [5 April 1909, Manaton], Devon to JS, Penmenner House, The Lizard, Cornwall

I knew, indeed, *all* about the way. And I had long decided to take the 5.25 MotorBus from Helston. If you reason at all practically (and not as in a house of four filosofers) you will see I am hardly likely to be able to get to Helston in time to catch the 7.45 or the 11.15 a.m. motor bus. Turn now to page 103 of your little green book. I leave Newton, you will see, at 1.16, and, perhaps, reach Helston at 5.15. Really, there is a connection. But, in case, it will be very nice if you meet me, for then, if we missed the bus, we could walk 11 miles, carrying my portmanteaux.

I received a lot of press-cuttings from Arthur [Eckersley]. He is all over himself, as we say. Every weekend Philip T[onge]. goes down to Bournemouth & stays with him there, in his little lodgings on the West Cliff. I told Maynard, & he was very much shocked. Maynard, with his family & La Kox,[1] we met half-way over Dartmoor on Friday; the day on which we, quite cavalierly, walked 27 miles in 6½ hours. So proud we are (We: Mr Smith[2] & I: *not* the Keenses.).

I do not think this will get to you in time. Your letter appeared this morning: & I catch the next post. But I think it is no good. I am spending a happy morning voting. I am getting it done now because I am afraid you & Gerald [Shove] will try to canvas me. I hope you are voting for Mr[s?] Standring[?].

I do not believe about Beatrice. Unless Daddy . . whose *spermatazoa*

---

1 Accompanying Maynard Keynes were his brother Geoffrey and Katherine Laird 'Ka' Cox (1887–1938). Known for her motherly nature, Cox was loved by most of the women of Brooke's circle and pursued by many of the men. The daughter of a Fabian stockbroker, she lost both parents before going to Cambridge, where she enrolled at Newnham College. She refused proposals from Jacques Raverat, Brooke and Geoffrey Keynes, then in 1918 married Will Arnold-Forster, a tall, slender naval officer and painter. With her husband and son (Mark Arnold-Forster), she moved in 1928 to Cornwall, where she died ten years later of a heart attack. The relationship between Brooke and Cox is chronicled extensively in Paul Delany's biography of Brooke.

2 Hugh Russell-Smith. Brooke wrote to Dudley Ward that Russell-Smith 'accompanies me, uncomplainingly. I call him many pet-names: "Guts" "Little Grub" and (sometimes) "The Liberal Party". He addresses me only as "Uncle Rupert". So we progress.' In the same letter, Brooke encourages Ward to visit Eckersley in Bournemouth: 'The poor thing's very lonely there. I may be going to B'm'th myself after Our Walk.'

must be *very* powerful.

I invented Mr Michael Foss. So I am content to watch.

What is Middlemarch?   Rupert

> *RB, [9 April 1909], Osborne Hotel, Exeter*
> *to JS, Penmenner House, The Lizard, Cornwall*

My dear James,

Could you so far aid in my deception[1] as to post the letter I enclose? And, being most hurried, I forgot to give that tall young person, who

---

1 In order to meet secretly with Noel Olivier (1892–1969), Brooke and Dudley Ward arrived in Bank, where the Olivier sisters were staying, on 10 April and remained for four days. The youngest of the Olivier daughters, Noel was born on Christmas Day 1892. Her father was Sydney Olivier, a founding member of the Fabian Socialists and an atheist who became Governor-General of Jamaica in 1907. Noel was pursued by both Brooke and Strachey. Much of her personality can be gathered from her letters to Brooke, recently published along with Brooke's to her in *Song of Love*. The woman who emerges from those pages matches fairly well the woman Christopher Hassall described in a series of letters to Margaret and Geoffrey Keynes written in 1962. At the time, Hassall was writing his biography of Brooke and had contacted Olivier through James Strachey, asking her to look at his manuscript. She agreed and soon took possession of it. When she failed to get back in touch, he contacted her again through Strachey and was informed by her that she had not yet looked at it but would get in touch with him later when she was free. Hassall then asked permission to call her, but Olivier forbade him to phone, claiming she was incapable of thinking quickly. Instead, she gave him a date on which to write a letter of inquiry. Hassall reluctantly agreed to her terms and eventually did meet her a second time. He wrote to Geoffrey Keynes afterwards: 'She arrived punctually, and let me tell you we talked and argued for nine hours. [...] Joan [Hassall's wife] offered Noel a bed for an afternoon rest, but she declined. She was tireless. *I*'ve *rarely* been so exhausted. [...] My God, we did "go at it"!' (8 December 1962). Hassall quotes Olivier on Katherine Cox: 'I knew she could take nothing from me, for my relationship with R[upert]. was of quite a different order.' Hassall then notes Olivier's history of being contrary to the wishes of others, and proceeds to blame her 'understanding' for some of Brooke's problems, arguing that Brooke's subsequent nervous breakdown was brought on by Olivier not reacting 'normally' and forcing him to make a choice between herself and Cox. Hassall says 'she gets *real* satisfaction out of *not* "acknowledging" her position with Rupert now, just as she did, years ago, *to his face*'. Two days later, Hassall wrote to Margaret Keynes: 'Yes, Noel was not in love with R.B., as you say, though she doesn't admit it. But I think she lacks the nerve to fall in love at *all*.' Even at the time of the Rupert–Noel flirtation, many of their friends doubted their sincerity. Jacques Raverat addressed the question of whether the two were in love in a May 1911 letter to Brooke: 'I *think you* aren't and I *know she* isn't' (quoted in *SOL* 89). Olivier wrote to Brooke herself the same month: 'this thing that you will insist on calling our love [...] I don't believe we are [in love ...] You seem to *want* us to be in love so much; why do you?' (*SOL* 91). Brooke replied that she was 'a codfish' and 'a *Bloody* woman' (92). Part of the answer to Olivier's question about why Brooke so desperately wanted them to be in love may be ascertained from his letter to her on 23 December 1911:

> We could be such you & I that thousands of people, afterwards and now, would make us names for the heights they knew the best. 'Rupert & Noel', – I'm solemn and serious. Don't you guess, even now, what people like Geoffrey

makes our meals & beds, a sovereign.[1] And I love her. If (it is a minor matter) – if (and only if) – if you find yourself, at the end, approaching her, in that spirit, please add, to your own, mine, (saying some formula, such as "The young man with the hair, who went early, forgot to give you this – 1/7½ {or whatever it may be}") and pressing in her delightful hand that sum, which, together with the 9d for the bag, I will, next term, repay. But all that is a mere aside. The letter is the thing. And were my addresses legible?[2] *Lyndhurst* is one of the important words. I walked each mile in 14! and met a thousand motor cars.   Rupert

JS, Monday Night, April 12th, 1909, Penmenner House, Cornwall

Dear Rupert,

I'm afraid you must almost certainly have been exposed by now. There came first (on Saturday morning) a letter from Rugby, which I sent on to Lyndhurst. Did you find it? That one ought, of course, to have been answered by the one that you sent me to post; which moreover only arrived this morning. Won't it be very irrelevant? and won't the date be wrong? – However, I posted it at once, & hope for the best. And the bag?

Desmond [MacCarthy] & I leave for London tomorrow by the night train. You can imagine how he's been working out the maddest details: how we're to leap out at midnight, and plunge for two hours through the streets of Plymouth; and how, when finally we reach Paddington at six, we're to drive straight off to a Turkish Bath and Breakfast in Jermyn Street.

Poor dear Gerald came out the other day with 'I'm very miserable.' I

think about us? – Oh, I'm not meaning that people's *opinion* or praise is the thing to go for. (*SOL* 148)

Still, after Brooke's death, Olivier wrote to James Strachey that there now remained no hope that she would ever marry for love. She did marry Arthur Richards in 1919. She also became a Member of the Royal College of Physicians in 1922, and in 1932 renewed her old affair with Strachey, though both were married. They were lovers for ten years. Olivier died after suffering a stroke in 1969.

1 Brooke was either having some financial problems or was in a state of forgetfulness: Hassall reports that he also forgot to tip the maid when he departed from Hugh Russell-Smith.

2 Brooke had left with Strachey the following written instructions:

Bag to Cloak Room
          Exeter (St. David's)
Letters that come at or before first post Monday morning to Poste Restante
    (or English Equiv.)
    Lyndhurst
after, to Gloucester House
          Esplanade
          Sidmouth
(not to be sent till Tuesday morning)

asked him why. 'Oh!' – he wouldn't let me have it – 'for various reasons.' Does he feel 'out of it'? *I* can't help him much to feel in it: but I've asked Norton to be kind.   Yours
                                                                                              James

I thought I made out a good deal of you in the Westminster.[1]

JS, June 18th, 1909, 67 Belsize Park Gardens, Hampstead

You seem to have left (at least)
> 1 Shaving-brush
> 1 Tooth-ditto
> 2 Sponges (Lord! made of india rubber)
> 1 Bag.

I suppose there's no hurry, so I'll bring them tomorrow afternoon.

George[2] stays here tonight. I'm most nervous, as Lytton spends all his time in trying to persuade him to rape me. I feel that I ought to enjoy it.

---

1 Brooke's 'A Love Poem', which appeared in the 10 April issue of the *Saturday Westminster* and won the prize for a poem written 'to a voice'. The poem was published as 'The Voice' in Brooke's *Poems*, 1911.
2 George Herbert Leigh Mallory (1886–1924), the mountain climber, who was becoming frustrated in his efforts to win Strachey's affection. A note from Mallory to Strachey scribbled on the back of a King's College 'Arrangements for Hall' memorandum dated 7 July reads: 'Will you, dam [sic] you, come to lunch tomorrow?' Mallory, the eldest son of a rector, attended Magdalene College, Cambridge, where he was an oarsman, a Fabian, an actor and a representative of the Woman's Suffrage Association. His closest friends in his early years at Cambridge were Jacques Raverat and Geoffrey Keynes. Unlike James, Lytton Strachey was much smitten with Mallory. Lytton wrote to Leonard Woolf: 'His [Mallory's] body – vast, pink, unbelievable – is a thing to melt into and die' (Woolf, *Letters* 149n). Lytton courted Mallory for two or three years, finally giving him an ultimatum in 1910, which Mallory refused. Edward Marsh was also much taken with Mallory when he met him, and complained in a letter to Brooke that he should have been introduced sooner. Brooke replied on 25 February 1912: 'I've known him [Mallory] so many years, discontinuously. I'm rather fond of him: but I never have a warm enough affection – no, it's a sharp enough interest I lack – to see him a great deal – I've meant to go & find him at Charterhouse, but never done it. I always, or generally, have a vague feeling in his presence – as if I'm, momentarily, dull, not he, especially. But what's one to do? But I like him.'
   Mallory published a study of James Boswell in 1909 and took a job teaching at Charterhouse in 1911. He married Ruth Turner in 1914, joined the army in 1915, fought at Ypres in 1916, and was best man at Robert Graves's wedding in 1917. Mallory loved mountain climbing and set a record during his second attempt on Mount Everest by reaching 26,985 feet. He died two years later, in June 1924, making his third attempt. He had told Geoffrey Keynes before leaving that he did not expect to come back. Mallory was last seen 800 feet below the summit; thus he may well have been the first modern man to ascend Everest, for it is possible that he made it to the top and died on his way back down. The narrator of a BBC documentary on Everest aired on 30 May 1993 made a point of mentioning that on Mallory's final assault he took with him the young, good looking climber

Shall I?

Oh, didn't you hate Norton last night? I did. Was he really drunk, or only pretending?   J.

JS, July 1st, 1909, 67 Belsize Park Gardens

Then you'll come.

I'm fairly plunged into the theatrical monde. (Last night I went to `Orfeo'[1] & met – among [Charles] Sanger & Syd [Cockerell] & Sir Richmond Ritchie[2] – dear Mike; I could at last talk to him on equal terms about Coshum & Leon Quartermain.)[3] They're a surprising lot.

I expect I shall stay here till it's over. And then I might go up for a little – though there'll be no excuse.

Will you come and read your books for the last fortnight or even ten days of July in a cottage by Lock an Eilan? If you like solitude, there's the pine forest and the heather and most of all the mountains. And as for me, couldn't you treat me as some cat or other? I wouldn't speak. All your expenses should be paid of course. Won't you even think about it? It's been a dream for years that I should make you love Rothiemurchus. My God! The smell! The Colour! One can *live* there.

For a week?   Yours
                                                                                    James

I was sorry to see that poor Kitty[4] was arrested.

Andrew 'Sandy' Irvin of Merton College, Oxford, rather than a more experienced partner in his team. The narrator, himself a mountain climber, said the decision could only be described as 'odd', though Mallory's letters written during the expedition and sent back down the mountain indicate that he believed Irvin was best suited for the final assault. Geoffrey Keynes wrote to Mallory's widow: 'I knew long ago that this was going to happen, but that doesn't make the fact any easier to bear. [...] You are the only person who could possibly know how much I loved George, and so I feel that I know something of what you have got to bear' (quoted in Robertson 253).

David Robertson's biography, *George Mallory*, provides a good account of Mallory's professional life but leaves out much of his personal life and contains more photographs of mountains than of Mallory. Duncan Grant's painting of Mallory now hangs in London's National Portrait Gallery.

1 Gluck's *Orfeo ed Euridice* played for one performance at Drury Lane.
2 Ritchie (1854–1912), a civil servant, was a Trinity man. He married a second cousin seventeen years older than he – Anne Thackeray, daughter of William Makepeace Thackeray and the sister of Leslie Stephen's first wife.
3 Leon Quartermain (1876–1967), the actor, and Ernest Cosham, the dramatist and actor who died in 1910 aged forty-four. Quartermain and Cosham both had roles in *Press Cuttings*.
4 Kitty Holloway, a suffragette.

RB, [postcard], Saturday [3 July 1909], The Orchard, Grantchester,
near Cambridge to JS, 67 Belsize Park Gardens, Hampstead

Rose gardens & a cat & my meals outdoors, & I don't know where
your last letter is. But I suppose I shall appear on Tuesday some where.
I'm going *not* to have *either* lunch *or* tea with you, I don't know which,
yet,[1] – oh! a codicil, & so on . . . (*not . . . either* – *or* = that I'm going to
have *one* of the two with you, if you like: it reads unclearly.).
There's a bloody devil in my rooms in King's: the Worst Limit in
England, who's read *every*thing (in brown paper). I'm afraid Scotland's
out of the question you know.   R

I *may* only be able to inform you when I can meet you, by telegraph
on Tuesday.
Forster's tale (English Review)[2] is perhaps the best to be written.

JS, [telegram, 9 a.m., 5 July 1909, West Strand]
to RB, The Orchard, Grantchester, Trumpington

The fact of its precisely being one that the day is Friday intamate [sic]
that after all my old friend may be perhaps not quite all there James

RB, Monday noon [5 July 1909], The Orchard
to JS, 67 Belsize Park Gardens, Hampstead

I enclose 4 documents: which may explain where I stand; – in
bewilderment.
I am writing directly your telegram has come, to make you more
certain (*certiorem facere*)[3] what I shall do. Though I expect a following
letter.
I shall not come tomorrow; that is right, I think. (a [Charles]
Saylism.). I shall come on Friday, mn?
My remarks about meals hold. – Oh, dear. I must write to Charlie
[Lascelles] & rearrange either lunch or tea on Friday. You may see
Charlie if you're good, for a second. But not talk to him.
Poor Mr Buxton[4] (is it?) doesn't understand your style. Does 'one'

---

1 Brooke was arranging to have one of the meals with Charlie Lascelles, the boy
   with whom he had been enamoured at Rugby.
2 E. M. Forster's 'Other Kingdom'. In a letter to his cousin Erica Cotterill, Brooke
   omitted the 'perhaps', calling it 'the best story ever written'.
3 'to inform'.
4 Sydney Charles, Earl Buxton (1853–1934), was Postmaster General from 1905 to
   1910.

mean 'a fact' or what? And did you want to say intimates?

Oh, I hope Friday is right.   Rupert

(2)

Extract from my communication of the 29th ult.

Yes I will (or shall) come on the 8th

(3)

Opening words of your letter dated July 1

"Then you'll come."

RB, [postcard], Wednesday [7 July 1909], Arcadee [Grantchester] to JS, 67 Belsize Park Gardens, Hampstead

I am afraid I must return on Friday evening. I'm not (luckily) wanted for the Saturday *Conference*. Even, I've refused to stay the weekend with the Oliviers & Mr [H. G.] Wells: La! I have to lunch with Charlie, meeting him at 1. Are you going to be about in the morning (I shan't arrive early) or will you send me a pass port? The Treasurer is *clamouring* for information about the play.[1]   R

JS, Wednesday Night, 12. [7 July 1909], 67 Belsize Park Gardens

Dear Rupert,

I've just got back from my place & found your post card. I'd so hoped you'ld stay. May I see you a little after the performance? I expect you'll want to catch the train.

Do you want me to ask who Charlie is? or am I supposed to think it's Sayle? Oh! I can see who it is. But you needn't think I'm jealous of a ghost. And is Charlie more? But by all means serve him up for me at the door of the Court at half past two.

I'll put your ticket in & a postal order tomorrow morning before I post this.

I'm so sleepy & unhappy. I wish I could dance on my toes always like you.   Goodnight.

                                                                         James

1 Brooke had agreed to help Strachey distribute announcements for Shaw's *Press Cuttings*, which was written in support of Women's Suffrage and forbidden by the censor. The performances were at the Court Theatre on 9 and 12 July.

Conference?

I sent Syd – *Sir* Syd[1] – a stall & *pit* stalls to the Treasurer & Bryn[2] this afternoon.

JS, July 11th, 1909, 67 Belsize Park Gardens

I think I shall manage to escape tomorrow evening. Am I really to go and see you at once? How? In a taxi-cab?

Oh dear! Such an awful party just now (after Sunday dinner). Uncle Bartle[3] playing the Hammer-Klavier Sonata on the Pianola, and Beatrice Chamberlain (Joe's eldest daughter, you know) shrieking through it about Papa & the House of Lords. "Papa says if *he* were the House of Lords – Papa of course with his idea that the Will of the People *must* prevail – it should be thrown out."

Poor Beatrice (she's a leading Anti[-suffragette]) & Ellen Terry[4] are to be in her Ladyship's[5] box tomorrow.

I'm outraged to discover that Mr Sharpe[6] *does* cook the words of his Folk Songs. "It has been necessary entirely to rewrite the words of 'Johnny my Jingabe' with the exception of the refrain. The original words were too coarse for publication." And so on with most of them – including 'O No! John' & a great many of the best ones. What infamy! And this, of course, is Dear Old Science. Mayn't we even suspect some of being sodomitical?

Sheppard's getting a room for me, until I can communicate with Hom [Hugh Owen Meredith]. So I don't know where I shall be. Your

James

If you write a play, I'll undertake to have it performed by the Civic & Dramatic Guild.

JS, July 16th, 1909, Cambridge

I want to go with you to the Library tomorrow morning – if you wouldn't mind.

1 Sydney Olivier, Noel's father.
2 Brynhild Olivier (1887–1935), Noel's elder sister and the second of the four daughters. After a half-hearted flirtation with Brooke (described by Pippa Harris in *Song of Love*), Olivier married Hugh Popham (1889–1970), a diving champion from King's. She later divorced Popham and married Raymond Sherrard. She died from Hodgkin's Disease in 1935.
3 Bartle Grant, brother of Strachey's mother and father of Duncan Grant.
4 Ellen Terry (1847–1928), the actress, had recently created the character Aunt Imogen in Walford Graham Robertson's *Pinkie and the Fairies*, which opened at His Majesty's Theatre on 18 December 1908.
5 Strachey refers to his mother, Jane Maria, Lady Strachey.
6 Cecil Sharpe, collector of English and Scottish folk songs.

I don't know when you're going; so will you call in for me on your way? If I'm not there, I shall be in Sheppard's rooms having break-fast.

Yours
James

Lunch with Flecker today was simply Hellish – old cold bloaters, sardine paste, & the relics of your gooseberries – oh! and dirty! hairs in the butter! soot in the cream! Why does he creep so?[1]

Poor George [Mallory], too, didn't distinguish himself. It came out that he thought Ibsen was a celebrated English dramatist. "Translations? Then what language *did* he write in?"

JS, August 4th, 1909, The Little House, Burford, Oxon.

Dear Rupert, May I come on Saturday instead? I shan't at all be wanted here after that: as ther'll be just the two married (?) couples, & I should be de trop at almost every moment. Besides, I rather want to finish off my life as soon as possible – and retire into the North.

If you'd even infinitesimally rather I shouldn't, will you send a p.c. & I'll go instead for a walk to Bristol? I'd probably quite enjoy that.

Sheppard seemed very anxious to be here with "Mr Taylor",[2] but was terrified that you'd never forgive him if he stayed. I tried to convince him that you might be a human being & understand.

This menage is at present very comfortable; but after Duncan's arrival tomorrow it will really be rather hot.[3] Sheppard's quite mad – & describes all day his liaisons with German waitors [sic].

The Burford Revels took place on Monday – a performance of Mr Kipling's poem 'A Song of the English' with Canon Beeching as Neptune. There was an enormous & entirely cynical audience, who roared with laughter when the Band struck up Chopin's funeral march, & Mrs Cyriac Wilkinson drove upon the scene on a dray with a coffin as the Spirit of the Dead. The proceedings closed with the Recessional sung by the audience; followed by an undressing race (for boys only).   Oh the post!

Yours
James

1 James Elroy Flecker (1884–1915), the poet and dramatist. Hassall quotes this entire paragraph but attributes it to Brooke (*RBB* 188).
2 Cecil Francis Taylor (1886–1955) was elected Apostle no.249 in November 1910. His election was pushed through by Jack Sheppard, who was in love with him, and with whom he remained a life-long friend. Taylor became a schoolmaster at Clifton College.
3 Strachey's return address indicates he was staying with Maynard Keynes, who was currently romantically involved with Duncan Grant.

*RB, [postcard], Aug. 5 [1909], The Vicarage,[1] Clevedon
to JS, The Little House, Burford, Oxon.*

I'm writing to poor Sheppard, forgiving him. Lord, what fools these
mortals are! Oh, you can come on Saturday, or when you like; I rather
thought of you managing Desmond [MacCarthy], if he came; I'm not
good at Celts. But as one'll never know when he comes, it's no good
trying to think it out. There's a lot of books here that you'll like. The
Dictionary of Religious Anecdote is good. You may meet Mr Saunt[2] in a
train.   Love[3]   R.

Bring Maynard & the rest if Burford's near.

*JS, [picture postcard of HM King Edward VII, 6? August 1909, Burford]
to RB, The Vicarage, Clevedon, Somerset*

Saturday, then, at 3.12. Are there cabs?
Sheppard devient de plus en plus[4] – well, I really hardly think, on a post
card, that one *can*. He let it out (for instance) at dinner last night that
poor Cecil [Taylor] has 3. Was there ever such a brick? J.

*JS, [picture postcard of HM Queen Alexandra,
no date, no stamp or address on card]*

3 what?
Positively, my dear,
    B A L L S !

(an envelope for Her
    Majesty, I think.)

*JS, Monday midnight, August 16th, 1909, Milton Cottage,
Rothiemurchus, Aviemore, N[orth].B[ritain].*

[In top margin: *'Tuesday morning*. I've just read this, & find that it's in

1 Brooke's parents were renting the Victorian house.
2 W. Henry G. 'Boxer' Saunt, of School Field, Rugby, a close friend of Hugh Russell-
   Smith, with whom he had gone to France in 1908.
3 Here it looks as if Brooke has written 'Love', then crossed it out.
4 'is becoming more and more'.

rather bad taste. Please don't read it till you can laugh at it without being angry. J.']

Mustn't *you* have a Collins[1] as well? Do you, I wonder, realize how much it humiliates me that I can never give you the smallest pleasure in return for what *you* give *me*? I struggle with a Max[2] here & there; but how many million Maxes ought I to pay you for a smile? Yet when I give you *one*, you're furious at having to accept a present from such a person as me.

I think you were relieved when I came away – naturally, I suppose. But God knows I tried hard to behave properly. Isn't it rather wonderful that we should ever be able to speak to one another? And nowadays we manage to a great deal. No doubt it's mainly your dreadful control of everything.

I was rather depressed towards the end. I'm very sorry. But it was because of my thinking that I shouldn't really ever see you again, & that I should very soon stop even knowing you. I know you consider that I'm very mean and contemptible because I'm unhappy. But thank heaven I don't *entirely* depend on you. You can't by being angry prevent yourself from having existed: and sometimes I remember that it's You and my love that make the universe magical – and not the fact of your coming with me to buy some trunk-tallies. And isn't it splendid to be the only person in the world who loves you? You don't pretend that the others do? They may *say*, but I *know* that the curve of your nostril is beautiful, and that you're cleverer than I am, and that you're the greatest poet in the world.

But there *is* another kind of happiness, which I should have most, I suppose, if you were fond of me, but which I have a great deal when I sit on the grass beside your chair and sometimes hear your voice. And I suppose I must have hardly any more of that. May I struggle for it a little longer? There are so many things I want. I think the most important is letters. Without them I shall vanish – become a Tatham,[3] even a Hobbes[4] – almost at once. Couldn't it amuse you to write them, although it bored you to read? I want them, of course about essentially you. Surely you're interested (it would be the inside wouldn't it?); and you have a great many adventures. Are your letters perhaps generally dull for you because you're dishonest in them? You might in any case

---

1 A 'Collins' is a letter of appreciation for hospitality received. The name comes from the character in Jane Austen's *Pride and Prejudice*.
2 Strachey had occasionally presented Brooke with drawings by Max Beerbohm (1872–1956), the critic and caricaturist.
3 Herbert Francis Tatham, Apostle no.211, was elected in 1885 but was never an active member of the Society. He died in 1909 without ever having bothered to resign.
4 Probably Arthur Hobhouse (1886–1965), Apostle no.244, who was elected in 1905. Robert Skidelsky, in his biography of Maynard Keynes, says Hobhouse was

feel sure that you wrote for immortal publication (in Paris and a hundred years).

This one must stop. I write too wildly, I fear. It must be because you've never broken my heart in writing. But I've hundreds of times expected it – a post card in your coldest and thinnest writing, with simply 'I didn't like your letter.' Perhaps it'll come now.

My family has much less Soul than yours. And it's Soul that I long for. Also there's no bed; & I'm writing this at 3 in the morning on the sofa which I shall be asleep on in five minutes. I expect I may rush off somewhere tomorrow – & to Wales after all on the 27th.

Goodnight Rupert. I wish I might see you for a minute.   Yours
                                                                          James

RB, God's day [Sunday, 5 September 1909], Vickridge [The Vicarage, Clevedon, Somerset] to JS, 67 Belsize Park Gardens, Hampstead [forwarded to Rothiemurchus, Aviemore, and then to Badanstalten, Saltsjöbaden, invid Stockholm, Sweden]

Oh, yes, my nostril still curves exquisitely, while a slight bump (quite transient) on my left ankle, produced by a rock, *added,* even, to the incomparable beauty of that limb for a week. There is no other really important news about the things which most interest you. But there are one or two remarks I wish to make (I almost apologize) about other topics. Where, for instance, is your French list?[1] We should like to have it in our hands.————That reminds me that I heard from Charlie [Sayle] today, about such matters. He referred to you as Strachey. Oh I *did* think it had got to James, – to James Strachey at the nearest. Why is the coldness? Where [sic] you ruder to him that evening than you ever told

---

'stunningly handsome' (127) and the 'first great love' of Keynes's life (128). It was Keynes who pushed through the election of Hobhouse (after winning a battle for his affections with Lytton Strachey) – an action that began a trend of selecting new Apostles more for their looks than their brains. In *Moments of Being*, Virginia Woolf quotes Vanessa Bell as saying that Brooke 'has been twice to bed with Hobhouse' (174). Hobhouse did have an affair with Duncan Grant in 1906. Grant said it came to an end suddenly: 'He was desperate to keep his mother ignorant of our affair, but my passionate remonstrations and expressions of despair must have reached the butler's ears. Anyway, Hobhouse told me not to visit him again' (Roche 89). Hobhouse is referred to as 'Edgar Duckworth' in Holroyd's biography of Lytton Strachey – and given the unflattering nickname of 'Dicker'. Like Tatham, Hobhouse faded from the scene soon after his election.

1 Brooke had asked for Strachey's help in compiling a list of French literature for the library of the Union Society. The interest was due in part to Brooke's having read Lytton Strachey's essays and reviews in the *Spectator*. In 1910 Lytton was commissioned by the Home University Library to write his *Landmarks in French Literature*.

me? Or did you try to rape him, and a little half-heartedly? Poor Charlie is, in any case, and in all cases, quite bitter & broken. His letter to me was a monument of reticence & genteel efficiency. All business, till the last – "I note you are coming up in the last days of September.

> Yours ever
>
> C. Sayle."

'I note' you must appreciate. I had, oh! very *cheerily*, written to *him* "I'll be seeing you again in three weeks, old cock," or something such. His heart burns towards the date (you heard of him & Daddy & "my swans"?) but he must only *just* let me know. And yet how can I fail to see? The business-like brevity of the rest of his letter, – Fires are concealed by the dingy frock-coat. Observe the tight-lipped pathos & pass on to the post-script (he writes from Ross in Herefordshire.). "The Wilsons[1] are at Worcester. They have very kindly asked me to go & stay there, which I shall do." The 'they' was *almost* underlined. Did I ever tell you that my people once, meeting him, said "Oh, you must come & stay with us, Mr Sayle." He said "When!" but nothing was arranged. And since then they have been told by my uncle the Dean[2] that Charlie has a bad influence on young men; so all is over. We can't have anything to do with a Rake.

Sheppard appeared for a week-end. He's rather nice. I suppose your surmise is (you will be conceited) correct. At any rate, I sat in the Summer House writing, & they, Sheppard & Gerald [Shove], walked round the garden, saying, at the top of their voices, the most *dreadful* things; which I redly heard whenever they passed my retreat. I don't mean obscene. Their purity was as notable as all their other noble qualities. They (I gathered) simply, in ecstatic generosity, flung Mr Taylor at each other. They held him down for each other. I was, I swear, greatly impressed: till that devil of Scepticism (in these matters) whispered to me. Dreadful in this way: – (I report quite accurately.). The first time they passed they were both talking confusedly at once,

---

1 Hugh and Steuart Wilson, brothers from Winchester and both students at King's College. Steuart (1889–1966), the senior scholar at King's, was the young man whom Strachey had reported Brooke to have been falling in love with the previous year. Steuart was wounded in the war but became a professional tenor. Among his famous interpretations was Vaughan Williams's setting of *A Shropshire Lad*. Brooke seems to have known Hugh better. Hugh had written to George Mallory from Brooke's rooms in 1907: 'I hope you two will see a lot of each other next year: he [Rupert] is a quite unique creature, one of the few men for whom I have a profound *intellectual* respect, up here' (quoted in Robertson 36). Hugh served briefly as a master at Rugby but was killed in the war in 1915 soon after Brooke. Before his death he wrote to Mrs Brooke, 'Rupert's last book of poems is in my valise & I often read him & look at his picture before I go to sleep.'
2 Brooke's uncle, the Rev. Alan England Brooke, was Dean of King's College. He was known among the students – much to Rupert's annoyance – as 'Brookie'.

expostulating "Yes, but don't you see . . ." "I cannot allow . . ." "I don't think you quite understand . . ." They were always arm-in-arm, Gerald's left in Sheppard's right, and, very painfully, looking *outwards*, Gerald to his right, Sheppard to his left, and occasionally each on the ground, – but always each at his *own* toes, never at the other's. I think they never saw each other *at all*, much less met each other's eyes, that morning. Both faces were red (especially Gerald's) with nobility, and just perceptibly nervous. They seemed to be saying "We are behaving in the highest & most sensible way. We will not be sentimental about anything except nobility & each other's feelings. We will quite impersonally and academically discuss any little feelings we have ourselves . . ." The second time Sheppard was saying "My dear Gerald, your generosity is simply splendid!" And Gerald, more puffed than ever, was murmuring "Oo, no!" The third time, I heard Gerald say "Oo, I shall go right away for ever." and Sheppard in a high voice was beginning "Don't you see that your very absence may put a factitious value on you? . . ." Then they honourably passed out of my life for a time. It's all very fine. I hope you don't laugh at them. I do. And since you left, there have been recurring millions of people.[1] All hated by my Family. "I have met so *many* brilliant, conceited, young men," said my mother, bitterly, last night, *àpropos* of Maynard. But she'd said, a week ago, "I don't call poor James *clever*." Sheppard heads you, however, in popularity. There was nobody else they could *stand*.

Did you ever hear of Portishead? It is seven miles up Channel from here. Campbell[2] & I (I'm glad it was no narrower companion I had then. Had it been Dudley.[3] . . .) went a walk thither, and in a wood, two miles this side, passed three *pairs* of women, two pairs lying asleep, tightly embraced, *in pleno gaudio*,[4] the other awake, but in a tree, & no less inextricably impleached. Two more pairs we met walking thither. It must be the Headquarters in the United Kingdom. Amazing! But I suppose you know all about it.

Master Birrell[5] came, & was disgustingly obscene in his private habits:

1 Among Brooke's other visitors to the Clevedon vicarage: Edward Marsh, Hugh Dalton, Dudley Ward, Gwen Darwin, W. G. Saunt, Eva Spielman and William Foss.
2 A. Y. 'Archie' Campbell of St John's College (1835–1958), the poet and future Greek scholar. He read the part of Elder Brother in *Comus*.
3 Dudley Ward (1885–1957), who later became an economist and Fellow of St John's College. His job as Berlin correspondent for the *Economist* led to his often hosting Brooke during Rupert's frequent visits to Germany. When war broke out, he returned to England and worked for the Treasury alongside Maynard Keynes. Mrs Brooke named Ward a Brooke Trustee and left the Old Vicarage at Grantchester to Ward in her will.
4 'in full pleasure'.
5 Francis Frederick Locker Birrell (1889–1935), son of Liberal Cabinet member Augustine Birrell and grandson of Tennyson, was considered as a possible Apostle

kept scratching and titillating himself in public. Mr Bill Hubback has been here, & told me what it was like to be an embryo.[1] His love of the Society is very touching. The treasurer & her sister Brynhilde have been about; which, of course, pleased my vulgar tastes enormously. I discern a Meredithian Earth–Our Mother tint in the blood of Sir Syd. that takes me. I pine to watch dusky women snaring parrakeets, – you'll find it all in our brother Tennyson; I forget the exact emotion.

– O, I saw Hallam's[2] grave. It was almost blâsphemous in the inscription. It said that in leaving the Society for J[esus].C[hrist]. Hallam was to be congratulated: though it was rough on Alfred [Tennyson]. They were coarse in those days.

I go to Rugby tomorrow. The date at the beginning of the letter was true then, but is not now.[3] Does your philosophy allow that? Are you watching King Lear? Why is poor Mr Milward Edmund?[4] He won't do. It is a part I always wanted to play.

Another bit in Queen Victoria[5] – did you see it? – is near the beginning. I found it last night. "Princess 'Vikky' was a great favourite, and on one occasion, when out for a walk near Osborne, shewed both courage and sense. She sat down on a wasp's nest and was badly stung."

End of paragraph. It goes on about something else.—My dear James, what *does* it mean. You know these things. Who *are* our rulers, any-way?

Rupert

but not elected. David Garnett reports that Birrell's first words upon seeing him were, 'Who is that handsome fat man over there?' (*Echo* 259). Birrell had affairs with Maynard Keynes, Gerald Shove and Garnett. His relationship with Garnett sent D. H. Lawrence into such a rage that Garnett decided to end his friendship with Lawrence. Birrell and Garnett served together in a Quaker relief camp in France during the war (one of Birrell's final actions before going to the front was to go to bed one last time with Maynard Keynes), and they ran a London bookshop together from 1919 until 1924. Birrell also edited a series of books on 'Representative Women' and an anthology of 'last words' called *The Art of Dying*. Birrell was operated on for a tumour of the brain in 1932. Raymond Mortimer, his closest friend during the last part of his life, looked after him until Birrell died on 2 January 1935. His photograph can be found in Robert Skidelsky's *John Maynard Keynes*, volume one.

1 Francis William Hubback, a handsome Trinity man, was, like Birrell, considered for election but ultimately passed over. A Fabian and an economist, he was one of Brooke's first new acquaintances at Cambridge. He was an avid climber and was part of the 1909 Christmas ski trip at Klosters, Switzerland. He married Eva Spielman, another of Brooke's Cambridge acquaintances. Hubback was killed in France in 1917.

2 Arthur Henry Hallam, friend of Tennyson, was Apostle no.68. Hallam was elected in May 1829 and resigned in May 1831, but such a short tenure was not uncommon for the Apostles of his era. Tennyson, in fact, was elected in October 1829 and resigned in February 1830. While a member, Hallam delivered a paper on 'Platonic Love'.

3 The letter was posted on the 6th.

4 The actor Dawson Milward (1862/70–1926) was playing Edmund in a new production of *Lear* at the Haymarket.

5 Sidney Lee's *Queen Victoria* (1903). Lytton Strachey later gave his own biography of Victoria the same simple title.

JS, *Monday, September 13th, 1909, Badanstalten, Saltsjöbaden, invid Stockholm, Sweden*

Your letter followed me round the world, & only arrived here this morning. I'd thought that perhaps you'd decided there should never *be* one. But you *weren't* insulted. I pass on with a pirouette or two of thanks.

You should *never* come to Sweden. There are very low hills covered with mangy conifers (as Bob Trevy [Robert Trevelyan] calls them) and telegraph poles and art-nouveau villas. 'Isn't it *pritty*?' say all the visitors. I've been here a week, looking after Lytton, whose escort suddenly left him.[1] The other guests include Miss Quick, from New Zealand, and the Housekeeper of the Royal Palace at Stockholm – a wonderful vast woman with a heavy cavalry moustache. But life's rather dull.

While I was in Scotland I had a letter from Daddy describing a walk he'd had with Alfred [Brooke]. 'I was delighted with the boy', he begins. They plunged at once, according to the rather worm eaten convention, into Sodomy, its uses & abuses. Alfred was of course 'very sound' – was very sentimental, I imagine this means, and oh! infinitely Higher. There are also hints of other things. Won't you have to square Alfred to prevent his dragging apart, when he's launched at Cambridge, just *too* many pairs of curtains? But perhaps, if I'm not there, no one will take the trouble to look at what's behind; excepting of course, in his wallowing plagiarism of a fine old tradition, Daddy – who may be trusted to *see* what's not. But I dodder.

Your account of Sheppard and Gerald is unconvincing & even careless. It all comes of trying to combine Mr Belloc & Mr Henry James.[2] Wasn't what you were witnessing in reality a proposal? Fishes, I think you once admitted, can be very attractive.

Oh! The French list. It's practically done. But I haven't got it here. I believe it's in London – so you can't possibly be sent it till I return. And

1 Lytton had intended to leave Sweden at the end of August, but his health was improving so much that he decided to stay longer. His companions, however, left; thus, James went to keep him company. No sooner had James arrived than Lytton once again fell ill, delaying his and James's departure.
2 Brooke met Hilaire Belloc (1870–1953), the writer and Liberal MP, in 1907 when Belloc spoke at Pembroke College. Brooke provided an escort home, reporting to friends afterwards, 'He was wonderfully drunk and talked all the way' (quoted in Chainey 182). Brooke became an admirer and hosted a dinner party for Belloc in February 1909, with James Strachey and Maynard Keynes in attendance. Brooke met Henry James – who was immediately taken with him – on 12 June 1909, when James came to Cambridge at the invitation of Geoffrey Keynes and Charles Sayle. Brooke punted James down the Cam, and later told Frances Cornford that he had done his 'fresh, boyish stunt' to great success (quoted in Lehmann, *Strange* 51). The novelist's Cambridge visit has been well chronicled by Keynes in both *The Gates of Memory* and *Henry James in Cambridge*. Henry James wrote of it himself in

even then I shan't send it to you but to *Him*[1] – so that I can have the opportunity of a letter. Mayn't I begin `dear Charles'? What's all that about swans?

Poor George [Mallory] has returned, he tells me, from the Alps. By the way, I never had the courage to tell you that he insisted, before we parted, on copulating. No, I didn't in the *least* lead him on. In fact I was very chilling. But as he seemed so very anxious, & I couldn't pretend to have all that virgin horror, I submitted. So we went through with it – in poor old Dickinson's bed. Are you dreadfully shocked? *I* didn't enjoy it much – I was rather bored. Nor, oddly, did he. He, I think, *was* shocked. At anyrate he shewed no desire to repeat the business. Really, you know, it's only in the most *special* circumstances that copulation's tolerable.

We leave here on the 23rd, & reach London about three days later. Would you possibly pass through on your way up? For King Lear? Anyhow do please write again.   Yours
                                                                               James

JS, September 22nd, 1909, Saltsjöbadens Badanstalt invid Stockholm [on letterhead from the spa – thus, the different spelling]

If you *do* happen to write, will you to Hampstead? We leave tomorrow for London via Gothenburg. (Have you ever heard Sanger on the Gothenburg system of public houses?) The voyage lasts for two days and nights in a shockingly small ship. I'm utterly shattered by the prospect. When I came there was a hurricane; & my terror & pain were so great that I could only think that if they told me that all my wildest dreams of happiness had come true I shouldn't be even faintly interested. Isn't it *awful* to think of the vast sum of evil at the present moment caused merely by seasickness? It really doesn't seem to me a subject for jokes.[2] Perhaps if you get this in time you'll offer up a prayer for me

his preface to Brooke's *Letters from America*. Having seen Brooke's physical beauty and having been told that Brooke was also a poet, James remembers the 'surprise (on one's own part) at his having to "be" anything' (19). James grew fond of both Brooke and his work, and, after reading Brooke's war poems, wrote to Marsh: 'Tell Rupert of my pleasure and my pride. If he should be at all touched by this it would infinitely touch *me* . . . . I think of him quite inordinately' (quoted in *RBB* 503).

1 That is, Charles Sayle, Cambridge under-librarian.
2 Brooke, on the other hand, did think it a subject for poetry: he wrote 'A Channel Passage' three months later while on holiday in Switzerland. As Henry James put it, the poem 'performed the extraordinary feat of directing the contents of the poet's stomach straight at the object of his displeasure' ('Preface' 29). The 'object of his displeasure' was apparently Noel Olivier.

– sing, even, that dear hymn for those in peril on the sea?[1]

I saw a marvellous picture of Rembrandt in the Stockholm gallery today. It's well worth the journey from Cambridge – enormous, unfinished, & in the latest style – misty brown figures taking an oath with their swords over a torchlit dinner table – (Sarmatians perhaps) – & over them towering an amazing barbaric king in a triple crown and a divided beard.

There was a remarkable literary letter from Desmond [MacCarthy] to Lytton the other day. If his novels are like that! He said he'd been very much flattered by your invitation – but he calls you Brooke.

I read War & Peace, & oh! the Times. We're *frightfully* excited about the Constitutional Crisis.[2] Is one in England?   Your
                                                                            James

I gather that Lytton's corresponding with you about a house in Grantchester. Would you hate anyone being near you? – though I suppose you both dislike one another too much to meet often. I wonder if you think it's an intrigue of mine – a desperate attempt at a connection? I think perhaps it *is* rather; though he, poor dear, 's completely unaware of it. Lord! I am a baby. If you say you object (and won't you, if you figure the cog-wheels & chains?), I expect I can douse it all – what with the damp & one thing & another.

My mania for running things, you see, again.

RB, [postcard], 7.0. p.m. Monday [27 September 1909], The Orchard to Lytton Strachey, 67 Belsize Park Gardens, Hampstead[3]

Mrs Neave,[4] it subsequently appears, has a Colonel & some young ladies with her, & is under the impression she can let you have sufficient rooms apart from them! But I think the Colonel *must* be going very soon.

If you are rich, you get here in a cab. If not, there is a carrier, for bags etc.   RB.

1 'Eternal Father, Strong to Save' by William Whiting, found in both the *English Hymnal* and *Hymns Ancient and Modern*.
2 The crisis occurred when Unionists in the House of Lords rejected the budget and refused supply, making new elections inevitable. The highest percentage turnout in electoral history gave victory to the Liberal and Labour candidates in the general election of January 1910, allowing the Liberals to continue in office. The Unionists, however, did gain ground over their showing in the previous election.
3 See Brooke's longer letter to Lytton, dated 19 September 1909, in *The Letters of Rupert Brooke* (185). The letter is not among Brooke's letters to the Stracheys in the Berg Collection and is the only letter to a Strachey to be included in the *LRB*. The letter also appears in *RBB* (203).
4 Florence Neeve and her husband Henry owned the Old Vicarage. They were taking in lodgers to help pay for the education of their thirteen-year-old son, Cyril Anthony, who wanted to become a Congregational minister.

JS, October 10th, 1909, 67 Belsize Park Gardens

Are you going to be in Cambridge this week or will you be away? Lytton seems to be going as an experiment on Wednesday;[1] and I think they'ld let it be an excuse (as he's rather ill) for me to go & help him to arrange himself. But if you wouldn't be there (you said you were going to Bushey)[2] Ild put it off. I don't begin my affair regularly till November 2nd, so if I dared I might be in Cambridge till then. But of course I don't.

Political life turns out to be just what poor Mr Belloc describes – so the man hasn't even any imagination. On my first morning St Loe had just been told by Margot what a state Henry was in because the Suffragettes had threatened to throw vitriol at the children;[3] and so on about everything – oh! yes! Royalty, even, Itself. "Of course, we say everything before you, (oh! I know you're very discreet) – secrets of the prison house! what?" So the readers of the Spectator must never know that – but nor, Rupert, must you. And if the Editor's brother is Treasurer of the Household,[4] can we be surprised that Mr Graves is Sir Edward Grey's[5] brother-in-law?

I spent this afternoon at the Marble Arch listening to the speeches. They were mainly as one expected – Tariff Reform & the Dooks were merely scoffed at. Even the King (fat-head Edward) seemed unpopular. Finally there was a rather sequestered Suffrage meeting at which the chairman suddenly said: `I will now call upon Mr Laurence Housman'. Don't you think literary men should be prevented from stumping the platform? He was a brilliant speaker & most violent. The things he said! things that couldn't, he admitted, be printed. How the plain clothes policemen by Government Orders pinched the ladies' breasts. And so on & at last the old Trina [?] story about the Liberal Stewards who committed indecent assaults on the women as they ejected them. But finally as the climax 'And now, of course, women are not admitted to the meetings, but men supporters interrupt; and now the indecent assaults are committed on *them*!' Qu'est-ce qu'il veut dire? Does he really splendidly accuse all Liberal stewards of unnatural crime? Oh! oh! At

---

1 Lytton Strachey went to stay with Brooke at the Orchard in order to look over the Old Vicarage.
2 Bushey Park near Hampton Court Palace in south-west London.
3 Herbert Henry Asquith (1852–1928), Prime Minister 1908–16, and his second wife Margot Tennant (1864–1945), whom Brooke later counted among his friends. As for the vitriol, Rupert wrote to Edward Marsh on 10 December: 'I hope you've evaded the Suffragettes so far. What do you do when they fling vitriol at you? Is an umbrella any use?'
4 St Loe's brother, Edward Lord Strachie (1858–1936), lived at and managed the Stracheys' family home (Sutton Court) in Somerset.
5 Charles L. Graves was chief assistant editor to St Loe at the *Spectator* and also a contributor to *Punch*. Edward Grey (1862–1934) was Foreign Secretary from 1905 to 1916.

Limehouse he said he'd known an Army captain & a naval officer, both of whom were indecently assaulted. But what, after all, *is* an indecent assault?

Towards the close I became aware of Mr Reitlinger. We had some pleasant words together. He writes, a little, on the Evening Standard.

Your loving
James

Will you send a post card on your movements?

Did you win your examination?[1]

Oh! The Grafton Gallery! I was there to see the crowd on Saturday afternoon – everyone in Europe from our brother Carlisle[2] through Mr Barker,[3] Mr Epstein[4] & Sanger down to poor Cosmo.[5] The pictures were invisible. Mr Barker was lecturing Mr Shannon on the beauties of Father Benson's[6] Ghirlandaio; but I couldn't catch the words.

RB, [postcard], Tuesday [12 October 1909], National Liberal Club,
Whitehall Place, London
to JS, 67 Belsize Park Gardens, Hampstead

If Mr Housman had played Rugby football he would understand it is inevitable under the circumstances.

I go to Cambridge on *Thursday*: leaving King's Cross at 11.10, perhaps. But that can scarcely be certain. I shall then be there for ever. Mrs Neaves [sic] almost had despaired. She will be delighted. But it *is* a little murky.   RB

1 Strachey may refer to Brooke's classical tripos. Brooke had sat for the exam in May, taking a disappointing second. This result cemented his decision to switch his concentration to English literature.
2 George James Howard (1843–1911), ninth Earl of Carlisle and Apostle no.158, an artist.
3 Harley Granville-Barker (1877–1946), the theatrical producer, whom Brooke met at the 1908 Fabian Summer School. Granville-Barker also appeared at Cambridge as a Fabian lecturer. Lytton Strachey published an article about him in the 28 March 1908 edition of the *Spectator*.
4 Jacob Epstein (1880–1959), the sculptor, who in 1912 carved a tomb featuring a naked male for Oscar Wilde's grave at the Père Lachaise cemetery in Paris. It was covered with a tarpaulin due to the disapproval of the French authorities, who ignored a petition organized by Lytton Strachey asking them to reconsider. The tarpaulin was removed in 1914 without comment.
5 Cosmo Alexander Gordon (c.1885–1967), a friend of Geoffrey Keynes. Keynes, who met Gordon at Charles Sayle's house, wrote in *The Gates of Memory* that in retrospect it seemed 'I derived over the greater part of my life a more continuous delight in his company and influence than from any other' (55).
6 Monsignor Robert Hugh Benson (1871–1914), the younger brother of A. C. and E. F. Benson. He converted to Catholicism and wrote several books defending the faith. Benson is the model for Father Robert Rolle in Shane Leslie's *The Cantab* and for Reverend Bobugo Bonsen in Frederick Rolfe's *The Desire and Pursuit of the Whole*.

JS, Tuesday Night, October 19, 1909, The Union Society, Cambridge

Here is sixpence that I owe you.

I wish I could say something about your poems. I've been trying all day. But how can I separate them from your reading them? It was all infinitely more wonderful than I'd imagined. I think what I'd left out was the feeling. Was it very absurd of me to have forgotten that? You always hide it, don't you? But I believe I always knew it in my heart – that's what I've really meant when I've thought you supreme. But it all seemed plain for the first time last night. And then the absolutely perfect expression. Why can your voice express more than [the] greatest symphony of Beethoven? And there's the pure beauty of it too. Most, though, I suppose, the beauty of your face as it moves – its wonderful subtleties and softnesses – your eyes and your lips – oh Rupert I'm simply mad.

If I could write poems like yours, I shouldn't do silly things like sending this. But I feel my head so stuffy that I *must* do something. No one in the world can sympathise or even understand. And no one could believe any of this except you. What would Norton say if I tried to describe to him what you were like last night? You know that all I pray for is to be allowed to do something to please you. But I spend all my time in doing what annoys you. Why?

Everything's so complex. 'Candidly' as Mr Barker put it (*really* he's rather an ass) 'I can make nothing of it.'   Your

James

Was Mrs Peters'(s) letter like this?

RB, [postcard, postmarked 12.15 p.m., 20? November 1909], The
Union Society, Cambridge
to Lytton Strachey, Pythagoras' House,[1] Cambridge

Thursday lunch will be admirably suitable. I shall be there all Thursday, so if the weather's awkward at lunch time, you'ld find me at any other meal time, probably.   R.B.

To drink, I have, now, only common country things. If you require anything special, anything alcoholic, you must warn me . .

---

1 Strachey had decided against lodging at the Old Vicarage after Brooke warned him of the damp. He instead rented George Mallory's former rooms in Pythagoras' House on the outskirts of Cambridge.

RB, Monday [22 November 1909], The Orchard
to G. L. Strachey, Pythagoras' House, Cambridge

Dear Lytton,

I am going to Oxford.

Next Saturday there'll be a great many wings[1] flapping about Cambridge. A paper from the Ark[2] would, I feel, be a pity, a last resort. And that devil Norton says he's going away. Will you, as wingless, be able to interrupt your Tragedy[3] so far as to write a paper?

If not do you know of any angel, who'll be on the scene, who *would*?

I return on Wednesday.   Rupert

JS, November 25th, 1909, the Spectator, *1. Wellington Street,*
Strand. London, W.C. [newspaper letterhead]

I find that I've got after all to see the *Wasps*[4] – officially – on Friday night.

There are two tickets. I suppose that either you're going already, or that you won't want to that evening at all. In case you *do* care for it, will you arrange dinner in Gerald's rooms? And anyhow leave a message for me there, as (unless you get this tonight) there'll be no time for an answer. I shall be at G's by tea time.

I suppose one would have to dress.

Sir P. FitzPaatrick[5] is BLOODY. And I'm a pro-Boer at last.   Yours
                                                                        James

I'ld rather (but I suppose you won't pay any attention), that no one knew *why* I'm in Cambridge.

I look forward to the Great Tea Party, & Full-Bottomed-Wig Meeting on Saturday.

No paper?

1 Apostles who resigned were said to 'take wings' and were afterwards known as 'angels'. Resignation had its benefits: angels were welcome to attend meetings but were not expected to contribute papers.
2 The records and papers of the Apostles were kept in a trunk, known as the 'Ark', which had been donated by Oscar Browning.
3 Strachey was working on *Essex: A Tragedy* – a blank-verse play he submitted to the Stratford on Avon Prize Play Competition, but which failed to impress the judges. Brooke, newly elected to the Apostles' highest office of secretary, was responsible for seeing that a paper was read during meetings. When no one could be found to write something new, the Apostles reverted to reading old papers kept in the Ark.
4 A Cambridge performance of the Muriel Carmel Goldsmid play.
5 James Percy Fitzpatrick (1862–1931) was a member of the Transvaal delegation to the 1908–9 National Convention of the South African Colonies. Strachey has spelled his name as if he were a Boer, knowing Fitzpatrick would consider it an insult.

JS, December 1st, 1909, 67 Belsize Park Gardens

I shan't be in Cambridge on Saturday,[1] so will you write and say what you're going to do? The Ursula play is on Monday afternoon at the same time as the Stage Society.[2] (I'm going to it as D[rama].C[ritic]. on Friday.) So I'm afraid that's no good.

It would be very nice if you spent a night here, and stopped it for a little from being so grey. But I expect you've arranged to go to Rugby or perhaps to Ben [Keeling]'s. I don't think anyhow that it matters about Marjorie;[3] but if there's something else –

There don't seem to be any plays, except La Princesse Bariatinsky in Hedda G.[4] on Tuesday afternoon. The Blue Bird[5] begins I think on Wednesday.

I see there's no reason for you to stay.

Mr Wells has sent what seems to me an utterly disingenuous answer. Why can't the man *say* that he's in favour of people who are in love copulating? that it's a good thing? I believe he really thinks that. Hasn't he the nerve to say it? Or is it simply his circulation he's afraid of losing?

My attempt at even a flirtation with Alfred ended in the usual dust and ashes. I could only come back to my old mumblings that there wasn't a trace of the Magic. He seems to me to have died five thousand centuries before you were born.

Please don't look at the thing about the play.[6] Isn't it dreadful to produce such bilge – and with such enormous difficulty and care?

Yours

James

I suppose you won't come on Sunday and go to a strange evening concert at the Opera? May we anyhow look at some pictures together on Monday morning? But the play's really enough to make me happy till January.

---

1 For the Founder's Feast at King's College. Maynard Keynes wrote to Duncan Grant that Alfred Brooke, Frankie Birrell, Gerald Shove, Freddy Hardiman, Jack Sheppard and himself were all kissing in public at the event (quoted in Skidelsky 235).
2 *St Ursula's Pilgrimage*, in which Eileen Wellesley was an extra (at the Court), and the Stage Society's production of *The Workhouse Ward* (at the Aldwych).
3 Marjorie Strachey (1882–1964), James's sister. She was the ninth child, falling between Lytton, who was two years older, and James, who was five years younger.
4 A single performance of Ibsen's *Hedda Gabler*, in Russian, was held at His Majesty's.
5 Maurice Maeterlinck's fairy tale was being staged at the Haymarket. Strachey reviewed it for the *Spectator*.
6 Probably Strachey's review of *The Wasps* in the *Spectator*.

Duncan [Grant] reports what Albert Rothenstein[1] says of Sheppard: 'Such wonderful spirits! he's the kind of man one would expect to see at the Empire with three whores on his arm.'

His repper[2] seems after all safe enough. What?

JS, December 4th, 1909, 67 Belsize Park Gardens

Dear Rupert,

I've got a ticket for the Burlington F[ine].A[rts].C[lub]. If you like pictures of the Umbrian school, you could go there on Monday. And in that case I suppose you'ld go to the New English[3] afterwards, as it's nearer St. G[eorge].'s.[4] Will you send another post card if you want to make the new arrangements? Otherwise I expect I shall see you at the N[ew].E[nglish]. If you wrote by your 8 o'clock Sunday post, it would be all right. The play's at half past two, at the Aldwych Theatre. Praps I'd better send a ticket, in case we don't meet.

St Loe & I sat in the front row of the stalls at the Court yesterday. They really did look remarkably beautiful, – at least the ladies. The gents were unluckily mere professional actors. So *you*'ld have enjoyed it much more than I did. Perhaps the prospect of a two hours' erection will make you after all stay till Tuesday afternoon, when it happens again. Personally I liked the audience best. It was mainly, I admit, the aristocracy; but among the odd jobs were Lord Roberts[5] and Sir Oliver Lodge,[6] The Prime Minister [Asquith] and Mr Henry James, besides, of course, our brothers [Bernard Henry] Holland, [Edward] Marsh, [Henry John] Cust, and [Charles George] Lyttelton. Poor Eddy! It was dreadful for him to have to recognize me in such a place.

Margery Olivier asked me (with, I imagine, your permission) to go to Switzerland. The Lord, whom one can always depend on, has made it impossible. Six months ago I should perhaps have gone in spite of everything. But I'm too weak now to struggle out of the clutches of the

1 The painter and art critic (and younger brother of painter Will Rothenstein) who designed the sets for the Marlowe Society's production of *Comus*.
2 'Reputation'. Sheppard apparently did not want it known publicly that he was homosexual. This is perhaps the reason that he alone, of Brooke's homosexual acquaintances, enjoyed the favour of Mrs Brooke, who appointed him a Brooke Trustee after Rupert's death.
3 The New English Art Club exhibition contained two works by Duncan Grant, one being a portrait of James Strachey stretching out in a chair (the painting is now in the Tate Gallery).
4 Brooke wanted himself and Strachey to have lunch with the Oliviers at the St George.
5 Frederick Sleigh Róberts (1832–1914), first Earl Roberts of Kandahar, Pretoria, and Waterford, a Unionist field marshal.
6 Oliver Joseph Lodge (1851–1940), a physicist.

Phenomenal. I sit and cry and feel rather like Gerald. (Have you noticed how one's tears always run down one's cheeks into the corners of one's mouth? or is it only so with people like Gerald? They taste most extraordinary, and quite out of tone.) Should I have liked going to Switzerland? You all seem to me very brutal when you're together. It's got something to do with your bodies, no doubt.   Yours

James

JS, December 6th, 1909, 67 Belsize Park Gardens

Dear Rupert,

Will you come with me to Florence next Easter? I think I could behave myself very well, and I would promise.

I want it, to be able to look forward to. Otherwise it makes me too unhappy to see you every week or fortnight for two or three hours, and to know that I shall only see you like that for year after year, less and less, perhaps. Did you understand what was happening in me this evening? Nothing, I suppose. I didn't either really. It seemed so much worse than usual, and for no reason. But some of it seemed to me to be thinking of all the people who didn't care – Daddy, & Mr Pudsey Dawson,[1] & the waiters at the Union – who could see you as much as they liked, while I could hardly ever. Oh there's infinitely more than that. I doubt now whether that even matters. I want something: but I can't at all tell what. But I think that today makes me want it too much. If I were brave I suppose I should never see you. Or would it be cowardice? Do I seem just ungrateful? I'm not. You're always so kind now that I think sometimes you must be very old. I can explain nothing; but perhaps you'll understand. Would it make me happier if I went with you to Florence? If not, I haven't asked you; and even if it would, I wasn't serious, unless you choose to think I was.

What am I like as a companion? Boring? irritating? which? I can't tell. So I can't be sure *how* monstrous it would be. But I must say that personally I should prefer myself to Alfred. But then I'm not Narcissus – which makes all the difference.   James

JS, December 7th, 1909

Oh! Oh! I've just dug "Rupert and other Dreams" out of a dust-bin, and find to my horror that – well, look: –

---

1   A bull-terrier living at the Orchard. Brooke's visitors report that Pudsey would often join Brooke for swims in Byron's Pool and would sometimes sit in the garden while Brooke – standing under a tree with an open shirt – read *Faustus* to him.

The poem's in Omar Quatrains; & after a short introduction beginning,

> "Whether in dream or in the flesh I knew
> His face 'tis hard to say."

we are presented with our Hero.

> In his own countenance I could not find
> One look that was not wholly to my mind:
> His face, so full of shy romantic grace,
> Was beautiful and humourous and kind.
>
> True poet he, with eyes like music mute,
> And voice recalling 'cello rich and flute,
> His brow (by thought, and sorrow, footstep lined)[1]
> Answered to lips gracious and resolute.
>
> In stature he was tall, of soldier make,
> With nerves of steel, wide work to undertake,
> And few would guess how tenderly his heart
> Could beat and suffer for another's sake.
>
> Rupert his name. . . . etc.
>   . . . .
> . . Small children's tears his gentleness would move
> As intimately as a mother's soul.
>   . . . .
> The bigger children hailed him chief of all –
> A sportsman every inch, they said, whose ball
> Was never off the wicket – thus he won
> His popularity with great and small.
>   . . . .

He was, I regret to say, unfortunate in his love affairs; but I don't know the details.

> No more I guessed, nor did I seek to know,
> For man's good confidence all soon is chilled
>
> By tactless questions – and he was too proud
> A friend's impertinence to have allowed.

---

1 '(Oh! we've always admired that)' is written above the second half of this line.

Not that I blamed him for his want of trust,[1]
Because the reticence brought us no cloud.

His poems live . . . .
Nature in all her moods was part of him . . .
His wit and satire had a friendly sting . . .

A few remarks about the Children of the Sun lead to the observation
that

Like them, he could adapt himself with ease –
As readily he'd sleep beneath the trees
As be in comfort – since his wants were few
And he'd no self indulgence to appease.
. . . .
Youth's Atheism lured him for a while
But he was far too humble to revile
The Crucified, and to the Cross returned
A proven one in whom was found no guile.

(I don't quite understand that.)

No doubt his faults were Adam's . . . . .

But I suppose after all that you've read it a hundred times. The author, I
realize at last, must be Geoffrey Keynes. It must go back now to its dust-
heap.   James.

RB, Sunday [12 December 1909], Rugby
to JS, 67 Belsize Park Gardens, Hampstead

My Dear James,
    Your questions are not wholly easy for the unreflective nature of the
hour to answer. `What are you like as a companion?' Well, chiefly, I
suppose you're intelligent, interesting, and witty, compared to other
people. Most other people, you know, aren't in the Society: and its
barely blasphemous, though it's offensive, no doubt, to say it makes a
difference. On the other hand, like the sea in Mr Chesterton's[2] poem,
you sometimes leave nothing but a mood of vague ironic gloom. Not

1 '(oh dear me no)' is written alongside.
2 Gilbert Keith Chesterton (1874–1936), journalist, author and poet. He was
   included in the first Georgian anthology.

indeed my imagination, but my experience, enables me to be respectful, if unintelligent. My "kindness" is, yes, due to old age; but partly to feeling it, gently, a pity you don't seem to enjoy things for the moment. Why, by the way, don't you write a book or two?

I rather doubt if I can go with you to Italy. But I am very certain I can't decide in the slightest, yet. There are two vague probabilities that oppose you.

(1) I shall quite probably not go. . . . Money . . . . . Etc . .

(2) I have partly promised several other people I'd go with them.

It sounds nearer likelihood that I should drift from party to party in Italy. If I go out with anybody, I guess I shall desert them after a week, to return, perhaps, after another. Do you, by the way, quite realise that you are proposing to accompany me into very ODD places in Florence, Venice, and Naples; and to Sail in a boat with me in the bay of Spezia?

Moreover, I want (if Moore wants me) to be on the Reading-Party a week or more this year. That would date and limit an Italian sojourn.

Your quotations from "Lilian"'s[1] poem allure me and inflame. I have come to the conclusion that you did not invent them, as I thought at first. If you're passing your dust-heap, could you pull it out again? Otherwise I shall have to buy one.

On Thursday I am going to the Café Tour Eiffel, Percy St, Tottenham Court Road, to be Born.[2] I shall be p.a.p.,[3] I think, about 9.45 (It's *like* a London Society, isn't it, to meet at such hours!). Tell me where to be at or about 9.50. As I shall certainly lose count of time, you'd better make it, if you can, some covered, or easy, spot. But I suppose you can't. If the time don't suit, any other will. I suppose there's no Music Hall we could Drop Into?

And can I sleep at your house that night? I can easily get another place. But let me know. R.

JS, December 13th, 1909, The Union Society, Cambridge

I shall enjoy, because of you, even tonight at Commem. and "Jackson's".

On Thursday at 9.50 I'll wait in what they call the Booking Hall of the Tottenham Court Road station of the Hampstead Tube. It's

1 'Lilian' was Brooke's nickname for Geoffrey Keynes.
2 T. E. Hulme, the poet, philosopher and translator of Bergson, had begun a discussion group that became heavily influenced by the French Symboliste poets. The group had no formal name, but is sometimes called the 'Hulme group', or the 'Thursday night group'. Hulme died in the war.
3 Probably an abbreviation for *prêt à partir* ('ready to go').

underground, I suppose you know, at the place where T.C.R. and Oxford Street cross. I couldn't think of anywhere else, & I hope it's near Percy Street. If you're too much attracted by Pound's nose,[1] you can be as late as you like. I can easily go into a trance.

Young King's[2] (don't you think?) is going just a little bit too far. But perhaps you've not heard – I'm told they're trying to keep it dark. Cross-examine poor Albert[3] in any case, as I gather that he pretends to be quite innocent. What a story!

There'll be a room for you.

They thought Duncan was ridiculously sentimental when he said Maynard was `Absolutely Good'. Besides it wasn't true. But it's very difficult *not* to think things like that. At least one's muddled. I believe I used to think you were rather a Beast, and yet that too.   Your loving
                                                                                            James

---

1 This meeting of Brooke and Ezra Pound took place shortly after Brooke had unfavourably reviewed Pound's *Personae* in the 2 December *Cambridge Review*. As the review was signed 'R.B.' it is unclear whether Pound knew Brooke was the author when the two poets met. In 1909, Pound had become disenchanted with the Poet's Club and was attending meetings of the 'Hulme group'. Later, when Marsh published his first Georgian poetry anthology in 1912, Brooke encouraged him to ask Pound to contribute.
2 A group of recently elected King's Fellows led by Maynard Keynes. They were agitating for radical changes within the college.
3 One of Alfred Brooke's nicknames, along with 'Podge'.

1910

Parker Brooke became suddenly ill in January 1910. Rupert and Alfred were summoned from Cambridge and arrived on the 24th to find their father unconscious. As he took turns sitting by the bedside that evening, Brooke wrote to Dudley Ward: 'His face is twisted half out of recognition: and he lies gurgling and choking and fighting for life. He is much weaker now. Probably he will not last the night. I hope not. It is all terrible for mother.' Mr Brooke died before midnight and was buried a week later, the same day the fifty-four boys in his house returned from the Easter holiday. Rupert reluctantly agreed to postpone his studies at Cambridge in order to take over his father's duties as housemaster for the remainder of the Lent Term. This allowed his mother to remain in School Field while she looked for other accommodation. Rugby historian John Hope Simpson says of Rupert as housemaster: 'The young Brooke professed to have enjoyed the experience, but he was an unusual schoolmaster and his Sixth found it rather difficult to support him' (160).

Brooke's primary romantic interest during the year was Noel Olivier. Some biographers have written that Brooke and Olivier became secretly 'engaged' at Buckler's Hard in 1910, though Christopher Hassall wrote to Margaret Keynes that Olivier told him that nothing of the sort occurred: 'The "pact" (at Buckler's Hard) *was* cleared up; there was no such thing' (10 December 1962). In any case, by the end of 1910 Brooke had abandoned Olivier in order to pursue Katherine Cox. Still later, when Cox became interested in Brooke, he briefly returned to Olivier, only to abandon her again. Adrian Caesar believes that Brooke's love for Olivier was dependent on 'non-consummation or non-reciprocation' and says that 'as soon as the affair with Noel threatens to become physical Brooke sheers off, frightened and repelled' (34).

It is Cox who has received the most attention from Brooke's biographers – and for good reason. Certainly, of all Brooke's amorous encounters with women, his affair with her was the most intense, the most complicated and in the end the most tortured. Even more than Brooke's relations with Noel Olivier, his entanglement with Cox ran hot and cold by turns. Whenever she was reluctant to get involved, he was obsessed with having her; whenever she was willing, he was cold and remote.

In the best of times, Brooke treated Cox almost as a mother-figure. She always looked older than her years and, unlike Brooke's own mother, was matronly and infinitely sympathetic. Frances Cornford speculates that it was, perhaps, 'the very lacks in his mother's temperament that did make him turn a young woman [Cox] into a mother' (quoted in Hastings 160). In the worst of times, Brooke denigrated her with verbal abuse. Caesar says the two were 'caught in a circle of mental sado-masochism' (37), which seems true at least for Brooke.

Strachey's life in 1910 centred around his continued adoration of Brooke and his increasingly demanding position at the *Spectator*. Among his contributions to the *Spectator* this year were numerous reviews of plays and articles on such diverse topics as the Elizabethan stage, 'A French View of English Politics', Swift, Swinburne's morality, 'The Progress of Psychical Research', Tolstoy, and the Incas.

When Strachey could get away from his duties at the paper, he often visited Brooke in Cambridge. He was also able to join Brooke and Lytton Strachey in Lulworth for a few days in April, and at the end of the summer he and Brooke once again attended the Fabian camp in Llanbedr, Wales (Strachey's future wife, Alix Sargant-Florence, also attended with her brother Philip).

RB, Tuesday [18 January 1910], School Field, Rugby to JS, 67 Belsize Park Gardens, Hampstead

My dear James,

Alfred says you think me ill. I am not. I did not answer your letter about the Fabian Dinner,[1] because I got here too late. I ate poison in Switzerland and that laid me a-bed for a week. I still am not allowed to eat apple-dumplings. I walk solitarily through the gray country: indoors I compose Hardyesque poems. Certain events have conspired to fill me with gloom. The last is this. I pray you keep it a secret.

My father has been ill & unable to see for a week. Today, secretly, he has gone with my mother to a "specialist" in London. At this hour (12) precisely, the interview begins. It is supposed the specialist will say he has a clot on the brain. Then he will go mad by degrees and die. Meanwhile we shall all live together in a hut on no money a year, which is all there is. Alfred is sombre, because he thinks he won't be allowed to continue a brilliant political career at Cambridge. It is pitiful to see father groping about, or sitting for four hours in gloom. And it is more pitiful to see

---

1   The letter is missing.

mother, who is in agony. But I am not fond of them. But I rather nervously await the afternoon, with their return. Will it be neuralgia, after all? Or really a clot? or blindness? What will one do with an old, blind man, who is not interested in anything at all, on £600 a year? Shall I make a good preparatory-school master? Will it throw me back to the old, orthodox ways of paederasty?

Daddy & Maynard have been here, electioneering, on different weekends. Alfred is a great success in the villages. His speeches are all stirring up hatred against Mr Blatchford[1] for being an Atheist.

What does one do in a household of fools and a Tragedy? And why is Pain so terrible, more terrible than ever when you only see it in others?

But breathe no word. If it's kept dark, the school goes on paying us.

Rupert

JS, January 18th, 1910, 67 Belsize Park Gardens

Perhaps, if you liked people, it would be a little relief to know that what hurts you hurts them. But you don't; so I suppose you must be alone. Dear, dear Rupert; I wish I could stop you from being unhappy.

I can say nothing. I can only sit here and wish avidly that Fate had given this to me and not to you. What has your yellow hair to do with Pain? If we were Christians – –

Perhaps thinking about poems helps you to escape? But I've known how impossible it really is in a house. Do you go sometimes for walks and forget?

I asked Alfred about you, because Duncan had heard something vague from Maynard – and threw out, in his artistic way, something about typhoid.

Interests here are very political.

I must catch a post.

Goodbye. I am praying that everything after all has turned out well. Tell me.   Your loving
James

---

1   Robert Glanville Blatchford (1851–1943) published the *Clarion*, a socialist weekly that had recently embarked on a campaign against religious orthodoxy. Alfred Brooke, like his mother, favoured the Liberal Party, but the idea of attacking Blatchford on religious grounds may not have been his own. In a letter to Katherine Cox written this same month, Brooke writes, 'Dr. Clifford was in Rugby last night and made a vastly popular speech for the Liberal cause. His chief point was that Robert Blatchford was an ATHEIST. Oh, my country!' He goes on to say that 'Alfred makes highly successful speeches everywhere.' Brooke wrote to Geoffrey Keynes on 14 January: 'Were I but well, I would be helping some jolly Labour man.'

RB, Tuesday eve [18 January 1910], School Field, Rugby
to JS, 67 Belsize Park Gardens, Hampstead

Eh! well I've had a bad time with Mother; and she's wild, praying for his death and so on. The London doctors are vague & ignorant, but not cheering. That we may have another term's profits from the House, we're going to beg the new Headmaster to let us stay on. We'll be thrown out at Easter, all right. *Now*, we're to get a youth to take a form, and Mother and I will run the House. So I don't go to Cambridge this term. I shall, as a matter of fact, go across for various week-ends (cheap ticket, 6/6 return) to get books, etc. So the Society will rub along. But what will it do in the weeks neither you or I are there? Norton Gerald & Maynard! Will they discuss Liberalism?

I go, as a matter of fact, next week-end. Will you be there? I want to know what I do about the Secretary.[1] Just leave the book to Norton, I suppose? I'm writing to prepare him, & find out Saturday.

The Fabians, the M[arlowe].D[ramatic].S[ociety], the . . – What a man of affairs I am! I suppose, in this place, I shall write several masterpieces by April.

One of my Rugby week-ends, you may come here (if things go well, and visitors are allowed). We will eat a whale[2] quietly in my bed-sitting room.

We call it Neuralgia: we shall shortly call it Nervous Breakdown, for the term: I think. So say you heard of bad Newes, when you all talk about it in your London club. I really write to know if Lytton, or anybody, wants my rooms. Books, private letters, and all. Let me know if you know of anybody. Between Now and April. And don't let your emotions run away with you, & make you urge them on the unwilling Lytton. He probably wants them less distant, and more light: and he might repent of kindness. Meat is there. 30/- includes it.   Rupert

JS, January 19th, 1910, 67 Belsize Park Gardens

Yes. I shall be in Cambridge from Friday to Monday. May we have a meal together? I suppose you'll be at Grantchester. Lytton says he won't have your rooms; in fact he's not going up at all this term. (There'll not be much left of the Society.) I can't think of anyone else to take them – & there's P. Dawson, hanging over them. I expect Flora Keynes[3] would find you a person.

---

1 Brooke means that he is not sure what to do about his post as secretary of the Apostles since he will not be in Cambridge.
2 Sardine on toast.
3 Florence Ada Keynes (1862–1958), mother of Maynard and Geoffrey.

Even when I try to be calm, your Future seems to me quite intolerable. Won't life at Rugby be *Hell*? And apart even from your horrors you'll be very desolate, won't you? But I suppose you mind that much less than most people. And afterwards? – I feel myself relapsing into sentiment.

At least you shall never be a schoolmaster. We've *proved* that it's perfectly easy to make 250 a year from journalism – very dilettante too. And none of the horrors of a fixed life. No dam paederasty either.

There's nothing to do, I suppose, except to try & make jokes. And *I* can't do that.

Yours
James

RB, Thursday [20 January 1910], School Field, Rugby
to JS, 67 Belsize Park Gardens, Hampstead

[with ink blot on paper and line drawn from it to top margin where is written 'not a TEAR']

My way of disregarding people's emotions seems to me superior to going all squashy about them, as you did in your first letter. Really, of course, I don't disregard them. Being immensely egotistic, I am as delighted to see other people suffer, when I am suffering, as any of your common selfish sentimentalists. I can't really agree that it's a high emotion. But I am most proud if it really gives me a claim to have "a heart."

I shall be up Saturday morn till Monday eve, or Tuesday. Yes, in Grantchester. At any rate let us all dine in the Union that evening. And if you've got rooms you can give me some meal & tell me about Journalism. Anyhow's there's Sunday breakfast. I look forward to an emotional meeting with Mr P[ugsy].D[awson]. Perhaps he'll have forgotten me, though. He may bite me: or worse. I shall be very briskly *about* all Saturday. I have to straighten many messes. The certainty slowly gathers that I'll also find myself here May to August. That will be an even worse Hell. But I get April, anyhow.

250 sounds well. But none of my cousins edit prosperous yellow journals. They are all in the Church. And the assistant-clergy only get £120. Still, you might enthral the Editor of the Nation,[1] and push me in.

But even that won't avail for these months.

Rupert

[1] H.W. Massingham. The *Nation* – known as the *Speaker* until November 1906 when Massingham became editor – was the leading radical weekly during this period. The *Speaker* came into being to counter the editorial policies of the *Spectator* following the split in the Liberal Party over the question of Home Rule in Ireland, and had been pro-Boer during the Boer War. Despite family ties to the *Spectator* Lytton Strachey had been a frequent contributor of book reviews in the early days of the paper. However, Desmond MacCarthy, who had solicited the reviews, was let go by Massingham when he took over. Nevertheless, both Lytton and James knew that their political views were closer to those of the *Nation* than to those of the *Spectator*.

JS, January 21st, 1910, The Spectator, *1. Wellington St.,*
Strand, London

How wonderfully you can penetrate the mysteries of the human heart! You really are most feahfully good at psychology. Does your amazing flair enable you to foresee the exact moment when I shall "go" melodramatic and cut your throat? or when my lust will be so frenzied as to force me with the help of a pennyworth of chloroform (ah! I've worked out the details) to rape you? Surely it's impossible that my penis should have escaped your notice? You can't doubt whether I have any balls? At least I assure you that I have, and also (en passant) that if you would like them, they're entirely (as poor Mr Scott-Coward said) at your disposal.

Well, well, the address at the top is turning a little pale. And I must begin reading through the "pages".

I have a room under Maynard's auspices in King's. Perhaps you'll have Sunday supper with me. I should borrow Norton's room.

The counties are going badly, aren't they?[1]

Has it reached the provinces that Mr Carnegie gave a million to the Liberal party funds a fortnight ago?[2] And that Lord Percy was killed in a duel by Winston?[3]

Isn't it sad about poor old Crooks?[4]

But I'm pleased that Hilaire [Belloc] got in.

I hope I put you thoroughly at your ease?

Yours,
in Wellington Street,
James

JS, January 28th, 1910, 67 Belsize Park Gardens

Is anything happening to you?[5] I suppose not. As for me, I've been having influenza – caught because of you, I imagine, from Gerald. I'm just out of bed & do feel rather an egoist. I mean that if you were in the chair there, instead of wanting very much, in the usual way, for *me* to give *you*

1 A reference to the general election of January 1910.
2 Scots-born Andrew Carnegie (1837–1919) supported the Liberal Party and later presented Liberal politician and future Prime Minister David Lloyd George (1863–1945) a stipend of £2,000 annually for life.
3 Winston Churchill (1874–1965), who entered the House of Commons as a Conservative in 1900 but switched to the Liberal Party four years later.
4 Member of Parliament William Crooks (1852-1921) took Woolwich from the Conservatives in 1903, lost his seat in the general election of January 1910, then regained it in December of the same year. Known for his good nature, Crooks was popular even among the Opposition. He lectured at Cambridge as a guest of the Fabians and on at least one occasion visited Brooke at the Orchard.
5 Brooke's brief silence – a mere ten days – was due to the death of his father. While Strachey's letter of 21 January went unanswered until the 31st, Brooke did not reply to a 16 January letter from Noel Olivier until 20 March.

the sugar, I should want very much for *you* to give it to *me*. Something about the eternal male & female, + and –, Martha & Mary – or was it Christ?

When I was at 103[1] I worked out a story that you'd had a fresh crisis. The details I find misty. But the two chief bits of evidence were that poor Albert should have figured at the debate on Tuesday: & what else could have stopped him but a telegram from Rugby? the next was that you didn't stay your extra night.[2] For Charles Sayle saw you driving in a taxi to the station on Monday "like a young god going into battle". Perhaps if I'd seen Wednesday's *Times* it would all be explained. But I didn't; because on Wednesday I was – well, at 103.

And that reminds me of what I've also worked out. I really had already on Sunday – and should have mentioned it, but that I'm always utterly terrified of you physically, morally, & mentally owing to the *purely* irrelevant fact of my being in love with you – I've given up even *attempting* to deal with you face to face. Fortunately, your commas are less paralyzing than your eyelashes,[3] & one can always (in moments of controversy) put them in one's pocket. – Well. What I want to say is that I think it's hard that you should have erected the preposterous convention by which no one may ever be serious unless he's satirical, for fear of being considered 'squashy' or 'sentimental'. Of course I care rather about my letter;[4] but I take it really but as an instance. You knew it didn't for a moment pretend not to be full of literary badness. It couldn't hope to express my feeling perfectly. (But who could express even a *squashy* feeling perfectly?) All that was supposed was that people who knew me well, & especially you, might be able to guess the feeling from it. Can you seriously tell me that after all your unpleasant adventures with me you still think me capable of writing down a sentence about 'Pain & your yellow hair' without smiling? Do you think *I* don't see as well as *you* that the words 'Dear, dear Rupert' sound very ugly, & might possibly remind you of 'dear-dear, Rupert'? Was it that from things like these you invented a feeling which I really hadn't felt (& which I sh[oul]d probably have agreed in calling sentimental)? Or was it that you *did* make out from the general 'tone' what my feeling was, & called *that* sentimental? The latter, I thought. So I replied briefly that I couldn't agree. And I still think it's the latter. But I now merely write, because it occurs to me that the 'sentimental' feelings include all the ones

---

1 Strachey is referring to his temperature.
2 Rupert had been at the Orchard on 23 January to retrieve mail and a few belongings, and intending to stay for the Marlowe Dramatic Society's performance of *Richard II*, when a telegram came saying that his father had suffered a stroke. He and Alfred left for Rugby the next morning.
3 Strachey has written in the left margin, with an arrow drawn to this place in the text: 'Do I add a note here to say "Not intended to be squashy"?'
4 Strachey refers to his letter of 18 January and Brooke's reply of the 20th.

connected with friendship. Love in some odd way you seem to pass. One may be irritating when one's in love, one may be offered a cigarette; but one isn't, I gather, called 'squashy'. It's when one for a moment stops, it's when one becomes so to speak merely 'Dudders',[1] that one must be so particularly careful to wind up one's letters with a 'yours sincerely'. Dudders, in fact, & his class, is what I plead for. May he never, in the dreadfullest moment of your life, & though he be lain with six hundred women, take your arm in his, unless he says 'How fearfully slippery the pavement is today!'? He hasn't, you see, the Resources that I have – the murder, I mean, and the rape, – But this is leading to other and even less pleasant subjects.

It *is* superb that you're the nicest person in the world. And, oh, I was awfly jealous when I saw on Sunday that there was *nothing* you weren't better at than me. I wish you'd been here really all this time, instead of only thought about. Send me a letter to make me supreme on Monday or Tuesday. I must creep back now into bed.   Yours
                                                                                 James

My last conscious recollection of 'The Office' was a letter *very-very* private from Margot A[squith]., saying that they all thought the collapse due to Lloyd George & his *stupid, disgraceful,* vulgar speeches. Rather mean.

RB, Jan. 31 [1910], School Field, Rugby
to JS, 67 Belsize Park Gardens, Hampstead

Your letter found me, too, with influenza: and a High Temperature. (I can only claim, with honesty, 102: but then they wouldn't always tell me). It has gone down to the other end now – hovers between 96 & 97. So they're trying to feed me up.

So I shouldn't have handed you the sugar.

I am up for an afternoon for the first time. Your delirious deductions were correct. We *were* sent for on Monday morning. All the details are too horrible – smell, and so forth – and I've not seen people dying before. So, even more than previously, I've got to rule the House (who returned in the middle of the confusion). Mother is rather bad.

I cannot argue so well as you, when influenza has me. As far as I can remember, it was a good deal the unpleasant literary tone of your letter that deserved the epithet 'squashy'. The general psychological atmosphere I only slightly thought of. But a good deal the particular phrase – the letter, in this turmoil, like everything else, isn't here – "why should God put such Burdens on your yellow head? . ." or something. It reminded me only of

1 Dudley Ward.

two things (1) The Oxford style – which doesn't go well on you (2) The letters of Messrs [Ronald] Firbank, Goldschmidt,[1] and the rest – which you always stood up for, but I never much liked. The humour you detect in the phrase did not occur to me; because when I am absorbed in domestic (or any emotional) situations I lose whatever sense of humour I ever have. After all, if you write these things to me, as a mere literary man, who doesn't understand the emotions of love, I may at least criticise its *phenomena*.[2] It's my profession: and if your letters are to be published, you may like to know what cultivated literary opinion will think.

About friendship & Dudders I don't begin to understand at all. Perhaps you think too much in categories –

I go to Cambridge this week-end. To get the books I didn't get –

Rupert

JS, February 1st, 1910, 67 Belsize Park Gardens

I suppose you'll scarcely believe that I'd no conception – till Duncan, back from Cambridge, mentioned it vaguely only last night. Otherwise I doubt if your letter would have explained.

I'm afraid it's been scarcely pleasant. One doesn't die prettily, does one? But I only hope its being got over is really a relief.

---

1 Ernst Goldschmidt, a Fabian from Trinity College, whom Brooke stayed with in Vienna a year later, and who became a bibliographer and author of *England's Service* (by 'Sarpedon'). Michael Holroyd says he had a 'sinister reputation' which prompted Maynard Keynes and Lytton Strachey to introduce him to Oscar Browning (*Unknown* 253n).
2 This exchange is possibly what prompted Brooke to write 'Sonnet (1910)' this same month:

I said I splendidly loved you; it's not true.
    Such long swift tides stir not a land-locked sea.
On gods or fools the high risk falls – on you –
    The clean clear bitter-sweet that's not for me.
Love soars from earth to ecstasies unwist.
    Love is flung Lucifer-like from Heaven to Hell.
But – there are wanderers in the middle mist,
    Who cry for shadows, clutch, and cannot tell
Whether they love at all, or, loving, whom:
    An old song's lady, a fool in fancy dress,
Or phantoms, or their own face on the gloom;
    For love of Love, or from heart's loneliness.
Pleasure's not theirs, nor pain. They doubt, and sigh
And do not love at all. Of these am I.

'The fool in fancy dress' may refer to a fancy-dress ball at the Slade School of Art that Brooke and Strachey attended less than a month before this poem was written (Brooke was dressed as the West Wind).

The rest of your letter I hardly understand at all. The wall in between seems to be blacker & higher. I had that to expect, I suppose. I imagine that you're rather bitterly angry. I thought at first it was with me – but now I hope it may only be with the universe. But I've floundered enough in all this fog. My side of the correspondence is like Sheppard's speech at the Dinner – an apology for apologizing for apologizing for an apology. So I shall relapse into a rather triste silence.

It's obvious that I won't be in Cambridge this week.   Yours

                                                                                James

I wish, though, that you weren't so often ill

JS, February 3rd, 1910, 12 Devonshire Place, Eastbourne

Sorry to appear again so soon.

A rumour has arrived by the *most* irregular channels – viz. Duncan – that those devils at Cambridge are taking advantage of our absences to hurry through the election of Frankie [Birrell]! Had you heard? Is it conceivable? But the story is circumstantial. Pozzo[1] has *always* had diarrhoea – & his new friend Gerald [Shove] is anxious to avoid a dinner at all costs. One can see how in their mean way they thought it out. Last Saturday Sanger was up. They discussed it, & Norton, feeble as ever, half agreed. They'd arranged to have F. to Sunday breakfast. And then proceeded to the usual farce of asking Sanger's opinion. Was there ever such cynicism? Dear Charlie [Sanger] remarkably "saw no objection to him".

There it remains. Could they possibly have intended to do it without any consultation? They might ignore Lytton & me on the grounds of our age. But you? Duncan really seemed to think he'ld be proposed on Saturday. Well, *you'll* be there.

Don't you think it ought to be prevented? Of course if you're in favour, it's quite final. But I can't think that you are. And I merely prepare you; and, in case you might feel swayed by them, strengthen (as they say) your hand.

After all, is there any great pressure? In a year from now, everyone will still be up. Won't possibly even you? And Mr Birrell won't solve any problems. Think how he'll go squash. Oh much worse than Gerald.

I leave it at that. But you know how weak they all are – how any display of determination shatters them. I expect they'ld at once try and pretend it was all only a joke.

I'm here with some queer relations in a kind of 'sanatorium'

---

1 John Maynard Keynes.

recovering.[1] The other boarders are Lytton, a morphio-maniac, Mrs Eden (incredibly cynical), & Mrs Eden's Step-Mother. The last is thought to be a *religio*-maniac. She sits on the corner of a high chair, very old, muttering "Oh! God! . . oh! God!" and writing out prayers on half sheets of note-paper.

Yours
James

RB, Friday [4 February 1910], Rugby to JS, 12 Devonshire Place, Eastbourne

You alarm me. The more that I am not going to be there tomorrow. The doctor has made me put it off a week. They couldn't, with nobody there. Imagine 12.50, and they face to face with it, and Tomlinson[2] on the hearth-rug, listening . . . Surely they will wait? Of course, in weaker moments, I had contemplated the possibility of Franky: – as a stop-gap. But only in my weaker moments. Really, has he a mind at all? I, as a matter of fact, shan't be up next year, I feel. And I had wanted to elect before I vanished. Otherwise, afterwards, they'd choose – whom? Marchand?[3] Alfred? Mr Churchill?

But *Franky* . . .

Well, I hope they'll put it off till next week.[4]

Mrs Eden? *Our* Mrs Eden? And what about her "step-mother"? Isn't it Tommy, in the last stage before death?[5]

---

1   Duncan Grant's maternal aunt, Daisy McNeil, ran a private nursing home for the well-to-do at 12 Devonshire Place in Eastbourne. Lytton had been sent there earlier in the month to recover from gastric influenza. James apparently joined him to recover from his own influenza.
2   Bishop Tomlinson was the founder of the Apostles.
3   Probably Geoffrey Marchand of St John's College, a Fabian.
4   Brooke complained in a letter to Jack Sheppard that 'the worst of it is that now I'm away & James edits the *Spectator* there's nobody practical, or even social, left' in the Society.
5   Although Strachey probably means the Mrs Eden who seems to have been a member of the Strachey household, Brooke is asking if the Edens he refers to are Mr and Mrs 'Tommy' Eden of Hillbrow prep school. Tommy Eden was the headmaster of Hillbrow while Brooke, Strachey and Duncan Grant were pupils there. Paul Roche reports that Grant told him Mr Eden 'liked visiting the little boys while they were having their baths. And he did . . . he did do . . . improper . . . gestures towards those little boys he was fond of while they were having their baths. And one of them split on him one day. This little boy's father was a master in the big school at Rugby' (46). In Roche's account, Grant goes on to relate how there was a 'frightful scandal', how Mr Eden was 'told he must leave within twenty-four hours', and how he disappeared. According to Grant, this is where Brooke, at age fifteen or sixteen, comes in: 'Rupert discovered – I don't know from whom – that he was hiding in Liverpool. So Rupert went off to Liverpool and tracked him down; told him he must *not* be in this state of mind; he must go back to the school, pack up quietly and leave in decent order. Rupert saved him' (47).

I devoured Spring's Awakening.[1]   Rupert

P.S. Up, towards Beachy Head, at High Coombe, The Meads, lives my Uncle Cotterill,[2] a very beautiful old man with white hair and a Roman nose. Erica is not there.

RB, [postcard], Thursday [10 February 1910], School Field, Rugby to JS, 67 Belsize Park Gardens, Hampstead

It was more impossible than one can think: though alluring.[3] I can barely get away for one week-end to collect essential books, in Cambridge. Many thanks, though.

You know I've got the responsibility of the souls brains & bodies of fifty boys of riotous character. One has yellow hair. I take prayers every night: Hymns only on Sundays.   R.

JS, February 10th, 1910, 67 Belsize Park Gardens

Will you have dinner with me somewhere on Sunday?

It doesn't seem as though we should after all manage to get our eight seats – there's such a rush. By the way it suddenly came out to-day that Miss [Elizabeth] Baker (you know her? St Loe's typist, who takes down all the leaders in short-hand) – that she's *the* Miss Baker, the dramatist, the author of "Chains". She'd kept it dark for fear of St Loe being shocked & angry. Of course he's delighted – so much that he's to give me a stall for the series. But we don't mention that.

Did you hear of the Abyssinian prince & suite, who reviewed the fleet

---

1 Frank Wedekind's *Frühlings Erwachen* (*The Awakening of Spring*), a play that tackles in rapid succession all the horrors of adolescence. The suicides in the play were not, unfortunately, mere melodramatics: between 1883 and 1889, 110 Prussian schoolboys killed themselves as a result of the conditions described in the play. The drama was not allowed on the German stage until 1906, fifteen years after publication, when it was performed (with mandatory cuts) at Max Reinhardt's Kammerspiele at the Deutsches Theater in Berlin. Brooke saw one of the hundreds of performances in Berlin before the play was again banned at the outset of the First World War.

2 Brooke's uncle, Clement Cotterill, was a retired schoolmaster, a follower of William Morris and the author of *Human Justice for those at the Bottom from those at the Top*, which Brooke anonymously reviewed in the *Cambridge Review* (28 May 1908). Before Brooke became a full member of the Fabians, he had written to his uncle saying that he had lately come across 'a good many Socialists' and that he wished he could get them, 'especially among the Fabians, to accept your definition of Socialism'.

3 Strachey had invited Brooke to the Repertory Theatre.

at Weymouth? They were chiefly Virginia & Duncan.[1] If the Tories find out, the Government will resign.

Is Richard II really all that?[2]

Give my love and a kiss to the one with yellow hair. But we're sufficiently educated here for Marjorie [Strachey] to have thought your postcard "a bit thick".

I go now to Fitzroy.[3] Ottoline and Philip[4] will be there.   Yours
                                                                      James
Are you recovered?

RB, 17th [February 1910], School Field, Rugby to JS, 67 Belsize Park Gardens, Hampstead

O yes, next week – by which I mean the one after – that is to say come on Saturday the 26th. My mother says she will be perfectly impassive.

On looking up early M.S.S. I find I wrote H[enry]. J[ames]. some years before I had read, or even handled, a volume of that impalpable, that so slightly contagious, contemporary of mine.

God! Aunt Gertrude will be here! But you must be firm with her. Do you mind?   Rupert

JS, February 18th, 1910, 67 Belsize Park Gardens

I can face even Aunt Gertrude. But is she, as Young Mr Wick once asked, or is she not a Brooke? "Is she your father's or your mother's sister or sister-in-law?"

We had a visit here yesterday from Gerald, in a fawn-coloured jacket and bowling hat.

1 Strachey refers to the *'Dreadnought* Hoax'. On 10 February 1910, HMS *Dreadnought* (the world's first battleship equipped entirely with big guns), anchored just south of Weymouth at Portland, received a visit from a party that claimed to include the Emperor of Abyssinia, three of his countrymen, an interpreter and a representative of the Foreign Office. They were in fact Adrian and Virginia Stephen, Duncan Grant and three friends, but their scheme was successful and they were given a tour of the ship. Later, after the hoax was revealed, indignant sailors 'kidnapped' Grant in reprisal but were totally won over by his good nature and, fearing he might catch cold in his bedclothes and slippers, released him without incident.
2 Brooke had written an article on *Richard II* for the 10 February *Cambridge Review* to publicize the work before the Marlowe Dramatic Society performance.
3 To attend one of Vanessa Bell's Thursday Evenings group Bloomsbury gatherings. Virginia and Adrian Stephen lived at 29 Fitzroy Square; Maynard Keynes and Duncan Grant shared a studio at no. 21.
4 Lady Ottoline Violet Cavendish-Bentinck Morrell (1873–1938, known primarily for her role as social hostess in London artistic circles, and her husband Philip Edward Morrell (1870–1943), a Liberal Member of Parliament (he had lost his seat in the January 1910 election but regained it in December).

Otherwise nothing has arrived but our eight seats for Monday night.

The question used always to be whether you *had* read H. J. Did you ever see this?[1] It was written, yes, nearly five years ago, just before you came to stay at Kettering. You'd written me six letters (there they are), & they were handed to Lytton, for him to give his opinion on whether you were Apostolic. So he gave it in writing. Awfully crude and rather cruel, isn't it? As he himself was later to admit. Do you still respect yourself as you were five years ago? Perhaps this'll hurt your feelings. (Bobby Longman is of course a combination of St John [Lucas-Lucas] and Arthur [Eckersley].) But I suppose chiefly the whole thing's just out of date. And how my own detestable figure shines through it!

After I left you on Sunday I had a long promenade sentimentale with Daddy. He was wonderful as ever, and came out with: "It is better to pass from a short period to an infinite period by a gradual period than by a sudden period." Masterman[2] or Sir Thomas Browne? I gather he admires both writers. Comforting in any case.

Yours
James

You'll give me back The Dossier?

RB, Friday [25 February 1910], School Field, Rugby to JS, 67 Belsize Park Gardens, Hampstead

I once met Mr Frank Lascelles. It was in Oxford; and we became great chums for a short while . . Did you fall in love with him?[3] His character is attacked by everyone I know. Is Mr Dennis Eadie a success?[4] And so on.

1 Strachey refers to 'the dossier' Lytton wrote in 1906, which is quoted in *RBB* 70–1. Among other things, it says that Brooke's egoism can be excused 'when we remember the adoration of the young [Geoffrey] Keynes, and, I presume, the whole of Rugby'. It ends with: 'Let us add, please, to Sarawak's [that is, Brooke's] good qualities a general innocence, and an interest (though perhaps not deep) in interesting things. These encourage me to believe that with the wiping out of Bobbie [Longman] something might be done. But I admit one other consideration, which seems to shatter my main hope – The Rajah, very likely, had not read Henry James. But Mr. Longman?'
2 Charles Masterman (1873–1927) had published *The Condition of England* in 1909. The book, a great success, addressed class divisions in English society.
3 Alan Frederick Lascelles (1887–1981), the future royal secretary, whose speech at the Savoy had been covered by Strachey for the *Spectator*. At the time Brooke knew him, 'Frank' was a tall, attractive student at Trinity College, Oxford.
4 Actor Dennis Eadie was playing the part of William Falder in John Galsworthy's *Justice*, which Strachey had just seen (his favourable review appeared in the *Spectator*, 26 February). *Justice* played at the Duke of York's, 21 February–14 March, 1910. Beatrice Webb said the play incorporated 'the philosophy of the Minority Report' on Poor Law Reform (*Partnership* 449). It is also credited with leading to prison reform in England.

For Life trickles to me through the Labour Leader & letters. I still believe the plays to be bad. But why are they reviewed like that?

Aunt Gertrude really *is* – I hadn't met her for years.

Come when you like: only bring a book, for I have to work at intervals. You will have to choose between lunching in the Dining room, with mother and Aunt G. – neither you nor they would be very happy – and lunching in hall with me and the House. You'll like that, I suppose. And as you mayn't come to prayers it's your only opportunity of seeing them. My embryo's[1] away, but may be back by tomorrow. You must not laugh when I say grace: you must eat meat; you may say anything about politics (they are very keen, Liberal & Tory,) most things, wrapped up, about Religion, & scarcely anything about Sodomy, unless its very Higher. We sit among the Sixth – the intellects, & there are vistas of babies. When you enter 108 – no, 106, for Turner is away this term – curious & hostile eyes will be turned on you. Can you bear it? Our surroundings will be very shy & silent, so you will have to talk. They all love me.[2] They are very ugly: though God knows if you will think them beautiful or not. When "drawn out" they become animated. They are quite up-to-date, and highly intelligent. I eat eggs, but you must eat flesh. You must not behave like the gentleman in Morgan's tale:[3] though I am incredibly like the Schoolmaster there.   Rupert

All this about lunch refers only to Saturday: I have Sunday off.

JS, [telegram, 26 February 1910, Steeles Road]
to RB, School Field, Rugby

You alarm me and Lytton says its bad form [to] go before luncheon so I arrive three forty James

JS, February 28th, 1910, 67 Belsize Park Gardens

Dear Rupert,

Here's the 2/-.

I hope you weren't all the time bored. I was very happy.

Does your Mother expect a Collins? I couldn't manage saying good bye to her at all. Perhaps she thought me rude.

Rapid Transit plays the Devil with Time and Space.   Yours
                                                                                               James

1 Brooke refers to the boy with yellow hair.
2 Brooke wrote to Edward Marsh on 3 March that the boys 'remember I used to play for the School at various violent games, & respect me accordingly'.
3 Probably Forster's *The Longest Journey* (1907).

JS, March 4th, 1910, The Spectator, *1. Wellington Street*

Here is a letter from Moore.[1] You'd better read it before going on with this . . .

Very well. Are you prepared to risk it? If so, I shall issue invitations, and order the rooms. I propose to ask:

(1) Norton
(2) Gerald
(3) Bob Trevey
(4) Sanger

The last two are of course very unlikely to come. What do you think, too, of

(5) Morgan [Forster]
(6) Sheppard
(7) Crompton [Davies]
(8) Hom [Hugh Owen Meredith] (*No!*)

or any one else you like?

Be explicit, if you please.

I caught such an awful cold and congestion in your drafts, that I couldn't go to see poor George Meredith.[2] But I hear that Will's clothes were lovely. He's promised to get Duncan to do the scenery for one of the later plays. Old Masefield gave a dreadful account of how the stage caught alight in the middle of the trial on the first night of Justice. Mr Galsworthy had to run for the engines.

I'm sorry to say that I hear sad tales against Granville[-Barker]. His whole reputation, one gathers, is fraudulent . . . . However . . . one can't believe a word.

I shall send you the stage book; but it's quite unreadable.   Yours
                                                                     James

I figured you as not being able to leave Rugby early enough on Thursday April 7th to catch the ten o'clock train from Pad[dington Station]. You'd stay Thursday night in London, perhaps, & go to a play & the [Café] Tour Eiffel or Fitzroy;[3] & go on on Friday morning.

I've a tendency, you'll observe, like poor Pozzo, to be a little statistical.

---

1 Asking Strachey to arrange the Apostles' annual Easter reading party – but to plan it for some time after Easter, which fell early (27 March) in 1910.
2 Meredith's *The Sentimentalists* opened at the Duke of York's on 1 March, with Dennis Eadie in the lead role, and with costumes designed by William Rothenstein (1872–1945).
3 For Vanessa Bell's Thursday Evenings group.

*RB, Monday [7 March 1910], School Field, Rugby
to JS, 67 Belsize Park Gardens, Hampstead*

Thanks for the large book with pictures. I've not yet tried to read it.

We breakup on *Wednesday the 6th*. So I can *easily* manage Thursday morning – Wednesday, even, perhaps. I might find a way by Birmingham. I should think it ought to begin as early as possible. I may stay only nine days. I should want to be roaming off about the 17th or 16th. I tell you I like *all* the brothers. So its no use asking me who. I can see that Eddie [Marsh] would be too unpleasantly sentimental in public: & I can understand the little man from New Zealand[1] being left out. But I don't find myself anything but fond of the idea of the rest of the Society coming. So write swiftly to successive batches. Your tabulated list looks very jolly to begin on. I hope Sanger & Bob Trevy will come & that Moore's sister[2] will be punctual. Pozzo, I gather, will be on a sentimental journey.[3] Sheppard would keep us cheery nicely. Lytton is a devil. There's no reason why, if it helps these old men, you shouldn't do it from (say) April 2nd for 15 days: or earlier. Then I'd come in in the middle. It might suit better. If one must go to the end of the world, Cornwall sounds best. If both your places fail I know of one on the edge of Dartmoor.[4] It has the advantage of being a house *not* an inn, & having a piano. But there are only four bedrooms certain. But more could probably be arranged.

Moore's funny about the baby. But what a superb prose style!   Rupert

JS, March 9, 1910, 67 Belsize Park Gardens

I've issued the invitations as you directed.

This morning, crossing mine, came a typically ineffective letter from Gerald, trying to get up a party of his own. Have *you* had one too? I shall disregard it, of course.

I've been sitting for an hour with this letter. I suppose you think it's an awful waste of time. I was trying amongst other things to make you out – and me too. Do you seriously tell me that my intellectual, moral, and aesthetic judgments are all obscured? Oh ho!

---

1 Leonard Hugh Graham Greenwood (1880–1965), elected Apostle no.242 in November 1903 (falling between Leonard Woolf and Maynard Keynes). A King's man, Greenwood later became a director of classics at Emmanuel College. His *Aspects of Euripidean Tragedy* was published in 1953.
2 Moore's youngest sister, Sarah, who had married the Apostle Alfred (Fred) Ainsworth in 1908. Their first son was named after Moore, who had overcome his initial dismay at the marriage (see page 41) and was enjoying having Ainsworth as a brother-in-law.
3 Maynard Keynes was planning a romantic trip abroad with Duncan Grant.
4 Becky House at Becky Falls, near Manaton. It is now a fifty-acre private nature park, with the main attraction being the seventy-foot waterfall.

Damn. I must go and dress for dinner and the Madras House.[1] They say it's very bad. Why should that ugly-looking man from Cambridge be there? I dislike almost everyone. Why do you like them? Perhaps because you've never copulated with them? What kind of state would a person be in who'd never forthed? Perhaps McTaggart[2] never has.

Nothing to amuse you – except that Eddie has gone off at last with Henry Lamb[3] – and this poem about Sodoma.   Yours affectionately

James

JS, March 11th, 1910, 67 Belsize Park Gardens
to RB, School Field, Rugby

Things are looking black.

Norton can't come.

Bob can't come.

Sanger can't come.

Sheppard & Morgan haven't answered.

So we're probably reduced to Gerald & a possible Moore. If Moore didn't come, there'ld be a very painful group – which I don't think I could bear – even if *you* could. If Moore *does* come, it's even worse – for no one could say a word.

I might have added:

Hawtrey can't come.

Crompton can't come.

There's also the complication that all these people *can* go at Easter & want to & had half arranged with Gerald to go with *him* then.

Consider, then, whether (if Sheppard refuses – for Morgan would make things worse – it's a talker one must have with Moore) I shall send Gerald off with the riff-raff at Easter and give the whole thing up.

It's for you to decide. If the horrors seem to you chimerical, I'll of course face them. But when you're thinking of the case of 'Gerald only', try to remember, academically, what I'm like. (Not because it matters what happens inside me – but because I don't always behave properly if I'm in a state. But I daresay it'ld be all right.)

---

1 A play written and produced by Harley Granville-Barker, playing at the Duke of York's.
2 John (Jack) McTaggart (1866–1925), Apostle no. 212, a Hegelian philosopher and political conservative. McTaggart's paper titled 'Violets or Orange Blossom', a defence of homosexual love, was one of the most popular in the Apostles' archive.
3 Henry Taylor Lamb (1883–1960), the painter. It was Lamb whom Katherine Cox later fell in love with, provoking Brooke's jealous rage and effectively ending his relationship with Bloomsbury. Lamb was the son of a professor of mathematics in Manchester. 'Eddie' is probably Edward Marsh.

Could you write and say if you'll go anyhow or on what conditions? If I heard by tomorrow night, I'ld write at once for your rooms – it's getting late.   Yours

James

[Back of envelope reads: 'p.p. Morgan can't come.']

RB, Saturday [12 March 1910], School Field, Rugby
to JS, 67 Belsize Park Gardens, Hampstead

(How I gauge the woman's[1] taste! I *am* clever)

Black as night (or blacker: for night – but we won't go into this. Do you ever go out after dark? Do you sleep with your blinds up?).

I should think it had better all collapse. There seems now no possibility left that would stand an evening's strain. I bet Sheppard won't come. So its only a case of *shov*elling Gerald off & persuading Moore to be a midwife in any case.

How splendidly Gerald steps out of it all. Where's he going to take a house? In Lowestoft? You'll go down for the Easter week-end and keep them going? On April 6th I expect I shall just shoulder a *ruck-sack* and vanish. I may drop in & see Daddy on Dartmoor. I don't know. It's frightfully exciting to have the whole world open to one. Shall I go to Manchester as a super to Miss Horniman?[2] Shall I put on a beard and go through the workhouses of Warwickshire? Perhaps I shall go to Paris or Amsterdam? I shall see you in London at the end of the time, may be.

I enclose a cutting which you may give me again one day. It is for my pseudo Ark. Do you find it so funny as I do? I keep the Bazzi a day or two. Is it yours to have back? Why is it in Lytton's writing then? And why did he write it in Mr Schlösser's[3] rooms?   Rupert

Is it our A. J. Butler[4] who died? It is, no doubt. Have you a spare Times of him? yrs The Secretary

1 Brooke refers to Naomi Royde Smith, co-ordinator of the literary competition in the *Westminster Gazette*. On this day the *Saturday Westminster* published an untitled poem by Brooke beginning 'When the lips and hands are done with', and signed 'Mnemon'. Brooke had used the same alias several times in 1909 and had won several prizes.
2 Annie E. F. Horniman (1860–1937), director of the Manchester Repertory Theatre Company.
3 Henry Schlösser, who was prominent in the National Committee for the Prevention of Destitution, a Fabian group formed by Beatrice Webb in 1909.
4 Arthur John Butler (1844-1910), Apostle no.164.

RB, Monday [14 March 1910], School Field, Rugby

Dear Lytton

Yes, it would be agreeable. But I am half-pledged to a man in Utrecht,[1] to which I can get for nine pence in a coal-boat. The man however may not be able to come. But I shan't know till some days hence. If he can't, I shall come to Cornwall. But that may be off by then. I have explained the whole situation carefully to James, but there really isn't one. In a week one may know. The only thing is, can you control Moore? Can you talk to him about aesthetics? Have you ever seen Gerald doing it? And will you climb the Great Auk with me? (That may not be its' [sic] name.)

If Josephine Preston Peabody is not, after all, your *nom de plume*, what are your feelings about it/her/him?   Yours ever
                                                                  Rupert Brooke

JS, March 16th, 1910, 67 Belsize Park Gardens

It's perhaps hardly worth while to go on worrying the poor thing. However – .

Gerald has only two pound nine; and says he can't possibly come on to us. He seemed immovable.

At the very best then, there'ld be only four of us – You & I, Moore & Lytton. Wouldn't even the very best be too bad for you? And at the last moment, perhaps, there wouldn't be a Moore.[2]

Then, as to me, I could find out at any moment – nearly asked today – but I've got a mania for not facing facts. It's so nice to hope. – If I couldn't go, even though *you* could bear them, *Lytton* couldn't bear *you*.

And there's always Dudders.

But if you wonderfully *didn't* go to Prague, would you say whether you thought the prospect of the partie carrée[3] as horrible as you must? And then, if you didn't, I'ld ask St Loe.

But these are miracles; and that kind of thing doesn't happen.   Yours
                                                                       James

You heard about Goldie?[4] He summoned up his courage one night, and

---

1 On hearing from Strachey that the Easter reading party was not working out, Brooke had written to Dudley Ward in Germany proposing that they meet in Holland for a holiday together.
2 The Easter reading party did, in the end, fall through – for only the second time since 1898. The other year when there was no party was 1906.
3 The usual meaning is 'a pleasure party of two men and two women'.
4 G. Lowes Dickinson.

proposed to Mr Eckhard.[1] Exactly *what* he proposed is uncertain. But Mr E. rose and walked to the other end of the room and then gave a lecture on the Limits of Friendship. What a devil! Has he your sympathy? Goldie, at least, has mine.

And oh! it came out through Mr Eckhard, who told Daddy. Rather mean of him?

I think of sending you a very beautiful photograph of our brother Jackson.[2] I'm having it framed. But when you're tired of it, you could tear it out & put it in the Ark. But I may like it too much to give away.

> ### RB, 18th [March 1910], School Field, Rugby
> ### to JS, 67 Belsize Park Gardens, Hampstead

Dudders has not answered. So I am still without the disgrace of Knowing Where. The non-appearance of that bright boy Gerald seems to alter the prospects of our domestic forbearance, in your eyes. It is odd. What sort of a scene can it be that you think Gerald's tact might have averted? I should think if we could all four go it would be all right for eight or nine days. If anything tottered, I could slip onto the road a day or two earlier. If you can't come I suppose nothing will happen at all. If Moore, – I don't know. I should think I might (Moore fading at the last minute) come for a week in that case, or less. And you & Lytton would be happy together for the rest.

What Goldie proposed must have been (I use the active standards) very slight. But I should think people who propose to Mr Eckhard deserve what they get, even if that isn't Mr Eckhard.   Rupert

I'll send you a card when I hear from Bavaria, directly.   R

1 Oscar Eckhard, a contemporary of Brooke's at Rugby, was the third of Dickinson's four loves. Dickinson, at forty-six, was much older. The proposal is described in his *Autobiography* (13–17, 123–6), part of which reads: 'If I can make out of this relation, too, something permanent and beautiful, it will be one of the chief gains of my life. I do not know whether it will be possible. But upon the possibility, or the reverse, must turn a great part of my happiness in the future' (14). On 16 June 1911 Eckhard told Dickinson everything – that he had showed Dickinson's letter of March 1910 to his mother, who urged him to be considerate. Eckhard finally 'came to bed' with Dickinson in November 1915, when he was home on leave from the trenches of France. Dickinson says of their years together thereafter: 'We usually also went to bed together' (125). The photograph of Eckhard in Dickinson's book shows an attractive young man, but Brooke, in a letter to Mrs Brooke, called Eckhard 'the ugly friend of the Simpsons''.
2 Henry Jackson, Apostle no.157, elected in 1863, whom G. E. Moore once described as having 'a very disgusting appearance' (Levy 47).

RB, Monday noon [21 March 1910], School Field, Rugby
to JS, 67 Belsize Park Gardens, Hampstead

I have just heard from Dudders. He wrastled with himself but his gleaming conscience conquered. So I am free for Cornwall. Find out if it is going to happen. And let me know. Did I make the position as I saw it clear? I expect you so sympathetically saw my vision? It is a broad and easy one. Understand, if you can isolate this thought for a moment in the Universe – that I am not cast astray and quite lost if at any last moment I am told that nothing happens. If I only hear that it's "off" when the train gets to Bude, I can, after all, get off there, have tea with Mrs Steel; & walk to Leeds to see Ben [Keeling].

I'd rather like to learn your opinion of time-limits, though, in the various combinations (or permutations?). And I privately beseech you, if you're selecting between hotels, to get the cheapest, compatible with Lytton's comfort – – not to mention the least Oxford.

Confirmation tomorrow.

And is the Repertory Theatre to shut up in a fortnight?   R.

$\overline{\text{over:}}$

The question of time-limits, I find, works thus. Let the combinations be A. B. C etc. The possible time there α, β, γ etc., and – – No; it won't do. I have forgotten that way. Imagine any combination at the Lizard for two years. "Impossible!" you say. Very well. On the other hand 10 minutes of even the pleasantest party wouldn't be worth going to Cornwall for. We must consider, then, if there are any combinations for which the longest possible period of harmony is less than the shortest time which would make it worth while going to the Lizard. Such would be out of Court. – Save that the ratio of the distance comes in. Two ends that just didn't meet at the Lizard, might meet in Dorset, overlap in Sussex, splendidly bloom in Tunbridge Wells? But who wants to go to Tunbridge Wells?

This is all very clear: & you must keep making your mind up. As for Cornwall – I have just discovered, while "turning out", two old photographs, 1893 perhaps, of me, Dick, Adrian Virginia Vanessa Toby Leslie[1] .... all very sporting and odd. Virginia & Vanessa are incredibly old in it: a little gawky: Virginia very fat faced.   R

---

1   Richard Brooke, Leslie Stephen and Leslie's children Adrian, Virginia [Woolf], Vanessa [Bell] and Thoby. The place was the Cornwall seaside town of St Ives, where Rupert and Virginia played together on the beach.

JS, March 21st, 1910, 67 Belsize Park Gardens

Dear Rupert,

I daren't say anything – for I've hardly a doubt that God's only doing the Cat trick.[1] Tomorrow morning I must ask St Loe – and there's not much hope. Lytton's furious with me. He seems to think one can control Destiny; and even threatens to drive up to the Office in his furs and motorcar. – I'll write as soon as I know the result . . . But (as I've just heard a fat person singing) "O Freunde, nicht diese Töne! Sondern lasst uns angenehmere anstimmen, und freudenvollere!"[2] The allusion escapes you?

The Stage Society, too, this afternoon – with Ashley[3] and other friends. Yes, and last Wednesday I went so low as Will Rothenstein's salon, with H.G. [Wells] and Max [Beerbohm] and all the rest. It's really rather painful about H.G. I can't help pitying the Little Man.[4]

I became today finally aware (I'd for some time suspected it) that I'm what Lytton calls an effréné[5] womanizer. My shame is intense. Lust – mere rabid lust – for a schoolgirl oh my God of seventeen. (Is she a little like a boy perhaps?) The whole story is horribly like one of Mr Picciotto's. And the whole thing's been rammed down my throat by a vindictive Creator. I might have been spared this! But at least I've never spoken to Her. I sat next her, in the beginning, at Mr Ll[oyd] George's speech at the Queen's Hall in January. I lost her in going out. But fate began at once; and a quarter of an hour later she was incredibly in the tube carriage when I got in. The whole thing then fairly faded till a fortnight ago when she was on[c]e more in the tube. Then came today in Oxford street, when I completely collapsed, and confessed to Lytton. That was hard enough. But oh! half an hour ago, again, returning from the concert, underground, She.

You can sympathize, can't you?

Yours
James

1 Possibly Strachey means to suggest the Magnificat: the canticle of Mary found in Luke 1:46–55.
2 'O friends, not these sounds! Rather, let us strike up more pleasant and more joyful ones!' From the 'Ode to Joy' in Beethoven's Ninth Symphony.
3 Ashley Dukes (1885–1959), drama critic and translator.
4 In 1909 Wells had published *Ann Veronica*, a novel which drew on his relationships with Catherine 'Jane' Robbins and Amber Reeves. The book was met with a wave of criticism, denounced as 'immoral' and banned from many libraries. The scandal made it difficult for Wells to find a publisher willing to take on *The New Machiavelli*, but it was published (with its caricatures of Fabian leaders Sidney and Beatrice Webb) in 1910.
5 'unbridled'.

RB, Thursday [31 March 1910], School Field, Rugby 'still'
to JS, 67 Belsize Park Gardens, Hampstead

I have delayed to write, and to return this, because I always thought I might be certainer next day & never was. I have a sore throat ("run down" . . .) and so I may just stop here, in the house in the Bilton Road,[1] a week. But if I recover I shall almost certainly go to Holland. Nobody will come with me, from Dudders down to St John. So I go heroically solo. Maybe it is best. If that happens, I shall appear in London on Wednesday, & go to Holland on Thursday. So could there be the refusal of a bed on Wednesday? The worst of it is I can't make you certain yet. If I come, I shall go to Justice[2] on Wednesday evening, or Earth fails. Can you stand it again? Anyhow it will be the Pit. I'll not stay over Thursday even for the Eiffel Tower and your Saloon.[3] I fear them. I know your family just *will* be at home on the 6th: but what's to be done?

Arride, my dear chap, is an English word, and means "affect with a slight glow of not transient but not violent kind eyed content."[4]

We are "moving out". It is too disgusting – but you have experienced it. My mother grows bleaker moment by moment. The drawing room was raped today. The dear old kitchen cat ("Tibby") is going to be "put an end to". She is sixteen, and one ear has been going for some months, and, it is agreed, the Bradbys[5] would never keep her, and she'd not settle anywhere else . . . . Poison, in milk. I cannot sleep for thinking of her quite stiff on her right side, all four legs straight . . Will *her* face turn grey and impossible, in a moment?

Lytton's note interrupted this: & made much of it a little dusty. My letter to him explains everything. I can only add that I caned a boy on Tuesday. It is an extraordinary sensation. He had broken his furniture to small pieces with a coal-hammer. But I had no consciously sexual emotions.[6] I cried a little after he had gone.   Rupert

---

1   With the end of term forcing the Brookes out of their School Field residence, Mrs Brooke had rented a three-storeyed house on Bilton Road.
2   The John Galsworthy play mentioned in earlier letters.
3   Brooke means the Thursday night meetings of the 'Hulme group' at the Café Tour Eiffel and the Bloomsbury group at Fitzroy Square.
4   Brooke had written in a short note to Strachey: 'This matter of your woman, though, arrides me. Is it that that makes you sorry for Wells (the man?)' (23 March).
5   H. C. Bradby, already a housemaster at Rugby, was assuming the duties at School Field.
6   Sexual emotions regarding his schoolboys were, nevertheless, much on Brooke's mind. He had written a poem, included in a letter to Dudley Ward, on 27 March containing such lines as 'Nor buggering Bishop went to taste his boy,' and ending with a view of the fifty-three boys under his charge:
    They are upper-class. They do not know the Light.
    They stink. They are no good. And yet . . . in spite

RB, March 31st, 1910, School Field, Rugby

Dear Lytton,

Your letter has come[1] and I have arranged possibilities for an hour and a half. The situation is particularly clear. I have sent off a letter to Mrs Hern[2] of Dartmoor, asking if her rooms will be free. She will telegraph to me, so that I shall know on Friday evening or Saturday morning. Then *I* shall telegraph to *her* (if the rooms *are* free,) to say if we are coming.

I was going alone to Holland. Would you like to come there? (Or Belgium.) That you are in frail health makes me think you may prefer the English country-side. If you daren't risk Holland, *and* Mrs Hern refuses; we shall have to reconsider the situation. As I am alone and content, I need not get a ticket for Rotterdam till I start; so my plans will be secure. If Mrs Hern accepts, you must face the choice between her and Holland. Holland means seeing Rembrandts and travelling from town to town twice a week on barges. There are also further alternatives, such as a hut in a village in the New Forest – which I could find, but I don't know its address, – and any suitably wild place you could discover or know of. I really don't care where I go. All I want is Intellectual Conversation and to avoid Rugby. If it were Holland or the Forest James might join us for the weekend – or even Devon. *Cornwall,* I think, is a bit far, for any purpose? Do I gather that Moore's sister is going to have a hard bearing after all?

The only difficulty is that I am at present slightly ill; and may be unfit for movement on Wednesday; probably not.

On Dartmoor one goes out runs in football clothes. So remember to bring your football clothes.

I forget what you mean about Henry. Everything is so disturbing here. James? or Lamb? or the Fifth (Shakespeare)?[3]   Yours ever

                                                Rupert Brooke

> Of the thousand devils that freeze their narrowing
> views
> (Christ, and gentility, and self-abuse)
> They are young, direct, and animal.
> [...]
>   So I love
> (Partly because to live it, once, I found
> All glory, and . . . there are . . . spots of holy ground
> – Oh, mildly holy! – about the place!) each line
> Of the fine limbs and faces; love, in fine,
> (O unisexualist!) with half a heart,
> Some fifty boys, together, and apart,
> Half-serious and half-sentimentally . . .

1   Strachey had written to Brooke earlier this same day: 'Is there any chance of your being able to go with me, only, for a week or so? . . . I fear its hardly possible that you're still free. If you were I could go as soon as you liked, with songs of Thanksgiving.'
2   The proprietor of Becky House.
3   Strachey had mentioned Henry Lamb, with whom he had become infatuated.

The Brooke family's first home in Rugby, at 5 Hillmorton Road.

School Field, Rugby.

RB, April 1st, 1910, School Field, Rugby
to Lytton Strachey

Yes, your telegram turned me through Bradshaw. Your medical man is a fool. Exmouth is dreadful. No brigs or sailorboys or sea: mud, dagos, and trawlers. It is a vast flat of huts and clay. I once had croup there. No! no! Dartmoor is, as a matter of fact, just as healthy as the Sea (and far healthier than a large town or the mud, like Exmouth.) and Mrs Hern is an angel with fires & food & ministering. It is not particularly warm, indeed. In North Devon we might try Lynton, etc. But I fancy the South Coast would be warmer, at this time of year. Kynance Cove . . . . but it *is* far. We have thought of Lulworth in Dorset: a fishing village, which had a beautiful left-handed boy in it two years ago. I only know the *address* of rather poor rooms, so I should have to go down and find the better ones which I know by sight. There is also Bonchurch in the Isle of Wight, which is very small, & has the Landlip & Swinburne's shade.[1] There are places in Devon & Cornwall. It might be best if I (or we) went to an Hotel in a Large Town & then prospected in the villages for forty miles around. Do you own a motor car? I'll leave here on Wednesday. Either I'll stay that night in Hampstead & go off next morning: or go straight hence to (say) South Devon: and rush wildly round till I find a farm on the Sea. At certain moments – when, for instance, I think about Cornwall (where one bathes) – I am bothered because I don't know James' week-end radius. Is it at all defined? Would Moore be difficult for a week-end, if we're accessible? if James were there? I long to go to some wild spot & *look* for a House. But that takes time & means hurry. Do write something by return, if only about Henry – Lander? Lee-Warner?[2] ['Boxer'] Saunt? RB.

JS, April 4th, 1910, 67 Belsize Park Gardens

Dear Rupert,

When you telephoned, did you say definitely that you were coming? Lytton was very vague.

There's one of the coils that family life is always offering. Till yesterday there were four empty rooms. Today there are two. But Cousin Minnie (Mrs Elton, you know) is arriving; and so is a working-woman or

---

1 Landlip is a tourist resort. Swinburne was buried at the Bonchurch graveyard in 1909. Brooke had written to Hugh Dalton at the time: 'Did you see that, against his desire, the bloody parson mouthed Anglicanisms of blasphemous and untrue meaning and filthy sentimentality over him? God burn him! Do you know Bonchurch? I twice dwelt there for months. Once, we will go to the grave, and put flowers there, and spit at the Rector, bathe, and weep' (16 April 1909).
2 Henry Lee-Warner, Apostle no.154, elected in 1862.

sempstress. So that there'll be no *room* on Wednesday night. There will, however, be a *bed* – if you'ld care for one in the same room as me. I daresay you'ld be safe enough: but if you have any hygienic or moral scruples I could sleep on plenty of sofas. Lytton said you *must* come here, because he wanted to discuss his plans. He fairly snapped at me when I said there was a difficulty. So I think you'd better come anyhow.

What about Justice?

I've got to interview Mr [Harley Granville-]Barker tonight. I'm to go to the Duke of York's where he'll be watching in a box, & send in my card in the interval. Will he have me in to see the rest of the play?[1]

Will you go to the International on Wednesday? and Carfax [Gallery]? Could we meet? I shan't have anything in the afternoon, I expect. But perhaps you will.   Yours
                                                                          James

Lytton went to the Zoo yesterday with Bertie, Alys, and Jane.[2] Jane & Alys were allowed past the outer rail, so as to feed the bears with marmalade. They were occupied with two of them, when one in the next cage but [sic] its claws through the bars and seized Alys by the sleeve. There was an awful scene – but fortunately someone rapped it over the knuckles before it had done more than tear out the whole of the arm of her coat and combies.[3]

RB, [telegram, 7 April 1910, West Lulworth] to Lytton Strachey, 67 Belsize Park Gardens, Hampstead

Cove Hotel Friday then admirable cottage very Expensive Thousand Rooms Bring anyone George[4] for instance will meet you Warm Rupert

1 It was the final night of *The Madras House*.
2 Bertrand Russell (1872–1970), his wife Alys, and Jane Harrison (1850–1928), a classical anthropologist. Russell, Apostle no. 224, was lecturer at Trinity College, 1910–15.
3 'combinations' – that is, underwear for the upper and lower body.
4 Ironically, Strachey received simultaneously an invitation from George Mallory urging him to come to Paris. He would have preferred the Paris holiday, but stuck with his original plan to join Brooke at Lulworth Cove in Dorset. Holroyd writes: 'Far from sounding off songs of Thanksgiving, therefore, he felt particularly embittered, cursing himself for having written off to Brooke in the first place simply because no one else seemed free. The expectation of West Lulworth now singularly failed to thrill him, but on his arrival there all this bitterness and disappointment quickly melted away. Rupert was a charming and decorative companion, and the hotel was warm and cosy. "Rupert read me some of his latest poems on a shelf by the sea," he wrote to James, "but I found them very difficult to make out, owing to his manner of reading. . . . I found him, of course, an extraordinarily cheerful companion. I only hope though, that he won't think me (as he does George Trevy) 'an old dear'. I thought I saw some signs of it"' (*Unknown* 455–6).

JS, April 12th, 1910, 67 Belsize Park Gardens

It felt very dingy to be opening the letters as usual this morning.[1] Do you think it Oxford of me to prefer being with you on a hill? I feel I'ld like to explain everything to you in detail. But of course I mustn't. I suppose you wouldn't blame me for being 'jolly' for three days – but only for *not* being all the rest of the time. But you'll agree that it's rather going to bed with the worms to find oneself talking to Mr Harold Cox[2] again.

Dear St Loe was very nice about you. He cross-examined me very severely as to who I'd been with – insisted first on your name – any relation of the Rajah? He then asked if you were a sollicitor [sic], and I replied that you were a poet. "Oh! then we must notice his book when it comes out – has he published one yet?" Only a few things in papers. "Oh! tell him to give you some to bring me! Oh! I should like to see them! Oh! yes! we must have some of those! Unsuitable? *Oh* no!"

I must now begin a Subleader on Memory and Individuality.[3] It was rather a triumph to have done my 1500 words in the train in spite of everything – though I *did* leave my bag on a seat at Wool.   Your

James

The India Office is the only one of Arthur's[4] appointments that I should hardly have expected even from him. But how'll he manage about Supply?

RB, [postcard], Monday [25 April 1910], King's College, Cambridge
['At length!' is written below 'King's College']
to JS, 67 Belsize Park Gardens, Hampstead

I came up by the 5.30 this morning. I left Jacques[5] with your

1 This was James's first day back at work after joining Rupert and Lytton at Lulworth.
2 Harold Cox (1859–1936), the economist and journalist, was a leader-writer with the *Spectator*. He had previously served as a Liberal MP and started a co-operative farm at Tilford, Surrey, on which G. Lowes Dickinson once worked. In his later years he fought for political individualism.
3 'Memory and the Individual', *Spectator*, 16 April 1910, p. 618.
4 Arthur Balfour, the former Prime Minister, who in November 1909 had used the Unionist majority in the House of Lords to defeat the Finance Bill, refusing supply to the government.
5 Jacques Pierre Raverat (1885–1925), the French painter. Raverat studied mathematics at Emmanuel College. After twice proposing to Katherine Cox and being refused, on 27 May 1911 he married Gwen Darwin (1885–1957), the painter and engraver of woodcuts (and granddaughter of Charles Darwin, and sister-in-law of Geoffrey Keynes). Brooke said of the couple in a June 1911 letter to Cox, 'Gwen's the only woman in England, & Jacques almost the only man, I've never lusted for.' Gwen appeared with Brooke in *Comus*, and both she and her husband became close associates of Brooke and Virginia Woolf, although their strong anti-German sentiments alienated them from the Woolfs (and the Stracheys) during the war. After reconciliation with

bag:[1] & he swore to give it you. He was very notionless, though: & could only think of inviting you to dinner & making you take it away. You are warned.   R.

RB, Thursday [28 April 1910], King's College, Cambridge to JS, 67 Belsize Park Gardens, Hampstead

Poor Jacques has the Artistic Temperament[2] and doesn't think much about these things. I must say I *thought*, to begin with, he was going to pay for your dinner. But then he showed a disposition to expect you to pay for it . . . I paid for mine. On the other hand, I expect he has forgotten by now, completely.

Two days' quiet reflection convinced me I oughtn't to take the ticket. The break in my not too quiet life, the extraordinary difficulty of conveying dress-clothes to the station . . . . many thanks, however.

Mr Dawson's[3] Christian name turns out to be Archie. Not even Archibald.

I suppose you've heard what Oscar Wilde used to call Charles Sayle?
                                                                                    Rupert

RB, [postcard, postmarked 2.30 p.m., 12 May 1910], Cambridge to JS, 67 Belsize Park Gardens, Hampstead

The probability of women makes it seem rather – to you – uninviting *this* weekend.[4] Shall we call it *next*?   R

Virginia Woolf, Jacques – in 1923 – said, 'Rupert had more to do with' his anti-Bloomsbury feelings during the war than anyone (quoted in Delany, *Neo-pagans* 217). Jacques suffered from multiple sclerosis, which eventually caused his early death.
1 The bag that Strachey had left 'on a seat at Wool', which Brooke had managed to retrieve for him.
2 Later in the year, when Frances Cornford experienced problems coming up with women willing to play one of the Seven Deadly Sins in a Marlowe Dramatic Society production of *Doctor Faustus*, she wrote in exasperation to Brooke: 'If you know a likely Sin I should be very glad to hear of her on a p[ost]. c[ard].' She also mentioned difficulties with their friend Reginald Pole, who was playing Mephistophilis. Brooke wrote back (8 July) claiming to have found an edition of the play with an extra part suitable for Pole: 'an Eighth Deadly Sin, called "The Artistic Temperament"'. Brooke had made frequent references to 'the artistic temperament' since reading Wilde's *De Profundis*, in which Wilde suggested that Lord Alfred Douglas had the 'germ' of an artistic temperament.
3 A former lodger at the Orchard who Brooke presumed had been the owner of 'Pudsey'.
4 Dudley Ward was scheduled to visit, and was bringing his future wife Annemarie von der Planitz and her sister, the dancer Clothilde von Derp. Brooke wrote to Ward: 'I've had dreadful scenes with the Stevensons [his landlords at the Orchard]. The village "talked" because of bare feet. So they [Annemarie and Clothilde] MUST keep their boots on! Otherwise they mayn't stay! This is true' (May 1910).

RB, Wednesday [18 May 1910], The Orchard
to JS, 67 Belsize Park Gardens, Hampstead

This week-end's clear of the ladies: so will you come? Lytton came to tea yesterday; and Mr Dawson *killed* a cat.   R.

P.S. Miss Macaulay's[1] coming to tea.

JS, May 18th, 1910, 67 Belsize Park Gardens

Oh! la! la! Will you then be prepared for me on Friday? I gather there'll be *Sunday* trains: so I'll arrive about 5.30, I suppose. – London's incredible. It may be *caused* by hypnotism, but there it is. Black and thick and hot: (Good Friday)[2].[2] Did you hear of the Queen Mother? The deputation from the House of Commons arrived at the Palace – 3 Unionists & 3 Liberals. She led them into the Death Chamber, lifted the handkerchief, and, turning to the Liberals, exclaimed: "Gentlemen! It is you who have killed him!"[3]

. . . .

I'm wrestling with Miss Baker's Chains.[4] Really not so bad.

. . . .

I haven't nearly recovered from Monday. There was a phosforescent cow who mooed; and finally only a Mr Walker's (a clergyman's) bed to share.   Yours

James

. . . .

1   Rose Macaulay (1881–1958), who frequently cycled over for tea from her home at Great Shelford. Her feelings for Brooke are revealed in her novels *The Secret River* and *Views and Vagabonds*. Rose's father was George Campbell Macaulay, a former master at Rugby who was currently Brooke's English tutor at Cambridge. Her uncle, W. H. Macaulay (an Apostle elected in 1876), was also a tutor at King's.
2   London was in mourning for King Edward VII, who died 6 May at age sixty-eight. The first '2' in superscript after (Good Friday) is James's, and is apparently meant to liken the King's death to the crucifixion squared. George V became the new King.
3   Prime Minister Herbert Asquith, a Liberal, had introduced the Parliament Bill on 14 April. It would have removed from the House of Lords all authority (except that they could delay legislation for two years) over matters of finance: this became the Parliament Act in August 1911. In introducing the Bill, Asquith made it known that if the Lords rejected the proposal he would appeal to the country, with King Edward's consent, to create enough new peers to form a favourable Liberal majority. If, however, the King refused, the Asquith government would resign, leaving Lord Balfour to govern the country from a minority position. This had placed the future of the government squarely on the shoulders of the King, who had reluctantly agreed to co-operate with Asquith.
4   Elizabeth Baker's *Chains*, with Dennis Eadie, was playing at the Duke of York's. Strachey's review of it appeared on 21 May.

JS, May 24th, 1910, 67 Belsize Park Gardens

I'm afraid I may seem to take things as a matter of course. Your kindness is so dazzling that I can say nothing.

Do I seem very querulous sometimes? It's not what I feel. I shouldn't, even if you said you'ld never speak to me again. Most often it's a desperate anxiety to please you, when you're bored and irritated. On Monday morning for a few minutes, for instance. Sometimes too just before you vanish, things seem rather black. But after you've gone I'm soon happy – you can't imagine how much. After all, isn't the real difference between me and Frankie [Birrell] that I've got *you*? and in the most important way of all?

– – – – Maynard is waiting somewhere for me to go to a play – The Naked Truth.[1]

How did Mr Crooks[2] go off?   Your
                                                                James

You can tell Lytton if you see him that George [Mallory] is coming here for Wednesday night – so I suppose he's going to Cambridge on Thursday.

JS, June 3rd, 1910, 67 Belsize Park Gardens

If you judge it wise, will you offer the Society these subjects tomorrow night? Then, if you told me which was chosen, I might rub something up for Saturday week. – If you think it'ld be unpopular, pray sink the whole affair.[3]

Last night I met a plenipotentiary, a proconsul, and an ex-president. The entertainment was deplorably middle-class. It was obvious that the

---

1 By Emily Morse Symonds and W. B. Maxwell, playing at Wyndham's.
2 William Crooks had addressed the Cambridge Fabian Society. Brooke wrote an unsigned report on the meeting for the 26 May *Cambridge Review*.
3 At the conclusion of Apostles' meetings, it was customary for the person whose turn had come to conduct the next meeting to offer up four topics for a paper – three serious and one playful. The members then chose one of the four. Strachey was to be the next moderator and is asking Brooke to present the choices on his behalf. However, in the end Strachey could not attend the meeting. Brooke composed and delivered a paper in mid-1910, possibly for this meeting, titled 'Are the playing at cards and the attendance of the theatre amusements inconsistent with the character of a clergyman?' It ended with: 'The lawn faded, and the intimate appeal of the blue of the buttons of the peacock's trousers grew dim and vulgar. I was almost left alone with the super curate, awaiting some most exquisite refinement of lustful address. He came slowly up to me; protruded his tongue, and began licking the insides of my nostrils, round and round.'

Colonel was SOFT. He talked a lot – about big-game hunting and the inapplicability of the jury-system to non-Aryan nationalities. You could hear the fizzz as my words dropped lightly among his turndown collar and rimless 'glasses'. As a man of action and weight Lord Cromer[1] smashes him. His lordship, by the way, was rather testy over the Guildhall speech. Arthur Balfour was pleased by it, and Grey[2] delighted. The only person who was really shocked by it was Beauchamp[3] – and, as the Colonel remarked 'Who's Beauchamp anyway?' We did what we could to explain ... ha! ha! ha!

The Queen Mother is being rather a nuisance – insists on flying the Royal Standard;[4] & of course poor George is too good natured to object. She also always pretends not to hear when they begin to suggest that she might Clear Out of Buckingham Palace. So the drains will have to get out of order.

You heard, I suppose, how dreadfully upset poor Pichon was because his coachman was dressed in black. He asked the Colonel to join him in a protest. Even the Duc d'Aumale's was in red. Oh! perhaps *that*'s who Beauchamp is – Pichon, I mean.

Well, that's the end of the London Budget, I fancy. I met Maitland Radford[5] in the tube yesterday, and Morgan [Forster] at the Japanese Ex. this afternoon. Funny how, when one's with him, the world takes a turn. A lady as we passed exclaimed: "And he put Polly down so *roughly* that he hurt her wing."

You've missed the first lot of pictures already – amazing they were.

Yours
James

On Sunday night I go to dear Ashley D[ukes].'s play.[6] There's of course a seat for you, if you ask for it.

Poor H.G.'s portrait of McTaggart's not exactly *profound*, is it?

---

1 Evelyn Baring, Lord Cromer (1841–1917) had served with James's father, Sir Richard Strachey, on the India Council. He was godfather to (Evelyn) St Loe Strachey, who listed him as one of the 'Five Great Men' in his autobiography, *The Adventure of Living*. When Cromer died in 1917, St Loe wrote in his obituary: 'The British people may be stupid, but they know a man when they see him. That is why for the last thirty years they have honoured Lord Cromer.' St Loe was deeply hurt by Lytton Strachey's hostile portrayal of Cromer in *Eminent Victorians* and several times criticized Lytton and his book in the *Spectator*. Oscar Wilde also respected Cromer: in 1893 he suggested to Lord Alfred Douglas' mother that Douglas be sent 'to the Cromers in Egypt' where he would have 'proper friends' (Wilde 346).
2 Sir Edward Grey, Foreign Secretary.
3 Earl Beauchamp, one of the few wealthy landowner ministers in Asquith's Cabinet.
4 The flag designating the presence of a sovereign.
5 Hugh Popham's cousin, who, like Popham, fell in love with Bryn Olivier.
6 *Civil War*, written by Dukes, was playing at the Aldwych.

RB, [5 or 6] July [1910], 24 Bilton Road, Rugby
to JS, 67 Belsize Park Gardens, Hampstead

Dear Comrade,

I have written to signor Marinetti,[1] asking them to join the Society *en bloc.* How superb they are! I am reading Mr Meredith's novels,[2] & preparing my Poor Law Orations.[3] Sometimes I bathe with the boys, & tell Arthur[4] about it afterwards. His emotions are ungovernable. I have been planning to write to you, ever since Friday. I was rather afraid, because . . ck! what *is* to be done with him? Is it because of his quarrel with Lytton? or because he never was elected?

Did Duncan tell you, I went with St John [Lucas-Lucas] to *Cosi Fan Tutti?*[5] In the intervals, between my flirtations with O[scar]. B[rowning].,[6] (who *was* "too poor to come to the dinner, dear boy!"), St John, Adrian [Stephen], Mr Bell, & I chatted. Mr Bell began to tell us all about his secret society for buying the National Gallery.[7] ". . . Secret Society . ." he suddenly shrilled ". . *Brooke* knows all about Secret Societies . . . he! he! . . . don't you, eh? . . . . in Cambridge . . . . he! he! . . . . eh? . . . he! he! . . ." We all said nothing, and I was a little red. He went on at it for an amazing time. I felt sharply and suddenly what you perhaps meant when you said he was no gentleman. Everyone was a little troubled. He went *on* so, appealing to me, if I didn't know what he was talking about, turning to Adrian "I thought you didn't see what I meant at first. You do now?", sweeping St John of Oxford in the circle of knowingness, rather

1 Filippo Tommaso Marinetti (1876–1944), the Italian intellectual and 'prophet of Futurism' in the world of art. His first Futurist Manifesto had been published in *Le Figaro* on 20 February 1909. It called not only for a rejection of the past, but also for a renewed patriotism and glorification of war.
2 Probably *The Ordeal of Richard Feverel* (1859) and *The Egoist* (1879) by George Meredith (1828–1909). However, Strachey thought Brooke meant Owen Meredith, the pseudonym of Edward Robert Bulwer-Lytton (1831-91). Brooke had reviewed George Meredith's *Last Poems* in the *Cambridge Review* (18 November 1909).
3 Brooke and Dudley Ward were preparing to embark – in a horse-drawn caravan owned by Hugh and Steuart Wilson – on a speaking tour of the West Country to drum up support for Poor Law Reform.
4 (Arthur) Clive Bell (1881–1964), art critic, had been up for election to the Apostles, but ultimately was rejected. The offspring of sporting landed gentry, Bell, in his days at Cambridge, was often seen in full hunting gear, including horn and whip. He married Vanessa Stephen. Their first son, Julian (1908–37), was an Apostle and a fervent communist. Leonard Woolf, through Hugh Dalton, obtained a position for Julian in the Labour Party, but he rejected it and went to Spain, where he was killed fighting in the Spanish Civil War. The Bell's second son, Quentin (b. 1910), became a writer and art historian. A daughter, Angelica (b. 1918), was actually the child of Vanessa and Duncan Grant.
5 Mozart's *Così Fan Tutte* had been performed at His Majesty's on 27 June.
6 Brooke wrote to Dudley Ward on 3 July that Browning 'tried to kiss me'.
7 Bell helped Roger Fry arrange the first Post-Impressionist exhibition, 'Manet and the Post-Impressionists', held at the Grafton Galleries, 8 November 1910 to 15 January 1911.

vaguely . . . . adding details "my Society will be . . . . just about as secret as *That One*!" Early I murmured something about The Fabian Society. It was weak; but I couldn't go on *long* looking as if I didn't know he was talking at all. Adrian was magnificently unperturbed. He never stirred, but gazed above us, looking as if he never understood anything, wagging his head dimly when addressed. He seemed tired of Clive, the whole evening, before & after. St John blinked and said "All King's to me has always been a Secret Society!" in his Little Joke tone. It might have been Oxford Banality: but I suppose it was TACT. The whole thing lasted several hours.

I felt, – I always do on such occasions – red & silly-looking & shocked. I never look quite so silly as I feel at those moments, I find. So I *may* have appeared fairly glacial. I wonder. I was at least rather silent, not without loftiness.

But, really, what does it mean? Is it frequent? Is it what Mr Bell & Lytton's boisterous generation called "chaff"? Or is it accumulated spite? What a weasel! Rupert

I hear Lytton's less ill. Is that so? I hope so. Give him a slap on the back from me.

> *RB, Sunday [24 July 1910], Black Bear Hotel, Wareham*
> *[posted 10 p.m., 28 July, from Lyndhurst]*
> *to JS, 67 Belsize Park Gardens, Hampstead*

I've been being wild. But it came on to rain so, today especially, and then Pat[1] was killed by a motorcar, so we, for a night, gave up & came in here, to a lobster-tea and beds. And tomorrow I go to speak for Mr Cavendish-Bentinck[2] at Corfe.

As for the summer school,[3] no woman I at present love will be there, alas! So I shalln't (unless new cases occur) be at all turbulent. I suppose I shall bask a bit. So do what you like. I don't know how long I'm going for – not less than five days & not more than ten I guess. And I don't know *when*. But I'm partly tied by a date – which you know better than I, at this distance. I suppose I'll go *about* August 27th. But things may alter this either way. I should think you might enjoy it. I can at least promise you I

---

1 'Pat' was a cat that had accompanied Brooke and Ward on their walking tour for Poor Law Reform.
2 Lord Henry Cavendish Bentinck, Ottoline Morrell's brother, was described by Leonard Woolf as 'one of those curious Tory aristocrats who are always more liberal than the Liberals and continually vote against their own party' (*Beginning* 193). Duncan Grant once named a sheepdog puppy in his honour after Lord Henry bought one of Duncan's paintings.
3 The Fabian Summer School in Wales.

shan't climb.[1] But if you come you must be good as a means some hours a day.

I had, last night (it is why I write) such a dream – lying out under a full moon. It was of two people – Charles Sayle & Kenny Cott (the latter in his eighteenth year, perhaps – or even younger) and . . . Charles got at it by pretending he'd lost a Penwiper, and making out Kenny ("naughty boy!") had taken it, and searching his pockets! – his trousers pockets – for it. Kenny accepted it, giggling. Excitement rose; & finally they left the room together. There were other details. I expect it all happened, really, sometime. There's a curious obviousness, finality, certainty about it, somehow, when one hears of it, isn't there? Kenny and Charlie.

I see that the illiterate part of the Society is well-represented in the British Academy of Letters. Otherwise one knows little of what passes, down here. Though yesterday I met a man who'd acted with Wilson Barrett[2] in *The Silver King*.

Lytton will be in Wales any how, I suppose?   R

JS, Thursday evening [18 August 1910],
Beech Shade, Bank, near Lyndhurst

My dear Rupert,

Frightfully thrilling this life of adventure to us sedentary men. Only a week ago tonight I arrived at the summit of Beachy Head and found the American cripple with his attendant Italian gnome. Since then –

Of course it was a disappointment that Vera was away; and it rained a good deal. Brighton was remarkable. Were you ever in a boarding house? Mr Bennett[3] is at least partly wrong – for the Corporation have got an exhibition of Modern French Pictures quite unparalleled. It shuts unfortunately at the end of August. But if you've any moral sense you'll go to look at it. The pointellistes are of course out of date. But there's a whole roomful of symbolists – Gauguin, Mattisse, Derain, – My God! the colours! I nearly bought you one of the Embankment as a birthday present with the sky blue road and the bloodred trees that we know so well.

1 Beatrice Webb was in the habit of leading those attending the Fabian Summer School on strenuous walks up hillsides. In addition, the influence of George Mallory had made mountain climbing a popular pursuit among many of Brooke's acquaintances, including Geoffrey Keynes and Bill Hubback. Brooke did not share their enthusiasm and, along with Gerald Shove, formed an 'anti-athletic league' in protest.
2 The actor and playwright (1846–1904) known for religious messages in his work. Shaw's *Androcles and the Lion* was a response to Barrett's Christian melodrama *The Sign of the Cross*.
3 Arnold Bennett, who in 1928 attacked Virginia Woolf's *Orlando* in a review for the *Evening Standard* only to run into her the following evening at a party. Woolf, who had attacked Bennett as a materialist in 'Modern Novels' (1919), said to him, 'You can't hate my books more than I hate yours, Mr. Bennett,' and then settled down with him for a talk (Woolf, *Moments of Being* 190).

On Tuesday morning your letter arrived at a very fashionable Hotel in Brockenhurst filled with diamond merchants and Indian civilians. My unpopularity reached its climax there. So the same morning I started off, and the finger of [Bishop] Tomlinson led me blindfolded to Mrs Primmer. She was very indiscreet, I may add – had a lot to say of the gentlemen and ladies from Trinity College Cambridge. In the afternoon, I had another divine impulse and started on my meteoric flight. Perhaps you heard a rumour of it?

I've just arrived back – and God knows why I'm being so garrulous. The point is to say that I'm very excited to think of next Friday. It's very kind to ask me to stay the night. I believe there's a wonderful train that goes straight from here to Rugby. If so, I shall take it; but I'll tell you more precisely later on. I've asked for a bed as you recommended.

Everything round here seems to be on the fuck – hens, ponies, horrid little black dog-pigs in flocks – and even Mrs Primmer has a Lancashire visitor from next door. I alone am inordinately chaste.　　　　Your
　　　　　　　　　　　　　　　　　　　　　　　　　　　　　　　James

RB, Thursday [18 August 1910], Old Vicarage
[apparently hand-delivered by Norton – see Strachey's next]

Tomorrow Friday

Breakfast at 9
　　or
Lunch at 1.30

Come to whichever you
like. There are few
people here & they long
for you

　　　　　　　　　　　　　　　　　　　　　　　　　　　　　　　Rupert

JS, Friday night [19? August 1910], Beech Shade
[Bank, New Forest]

Dear Rupert

Your invitation's just come on from Norton. I'm very sad, of course, not to have been there. I hope you didn't despise me very much for going away: but you probably didn't notice. Anyhow, if an excuse is needed, I needn't rake up my actual chimaeras; my dear old traditional terror of your friends will serve.

I'm feeling a little worried by one or two things. Wattie is coming here tomorrow.[1] He practically invited himself – or perhaps merely forced my mildness to ask him. And he'll read me the first four acts of his tragedy in couplets. Also, I've heard from the Manager of the F[abian].S[ummer]. S[chool]. to say that there isn't a bed at Caermeddyg but that "a bed or a tent is available at Pen-yr-Allt." What he of course *doesn't* say is where you're to be. But I fear the worst.

Mrs Primmer tells me that you spent Bloody Sunday under these very trees. You remember Bloody Week; when Gaye[2] shot himself, and Duncan divorced poor Maynard at the Triason,[3] and Swinburne died, and Lytton had the staggers in Piccadilly Circus? Mr Belloc, too, as we learn from his latest book, was in the Forest at the time.

Any how, you're damned mistaken if you think I didn't get two pounds' worth of pleasure out of Wednesday evening.

This week seems longer than all the other eight put together. Please send me a short letter, even an angry one, to make it go quicker.

Oh! that creature that person, Mr Lamb, had the effrontery to say that he didn't think much of Mr Rupert Brooke's performance![4] You may depend on it I gave him a pretty severe rap. A miserable bald castrato from Manchester! and coming here tomorrow afternoon!   Your

                                                                                          James

They said you were leaving Cambridge on Saturday – but whether for Rugby I don't know.

1 Walter R. M. Lamb (1882–1961), the elder brother of Henry. Nicknamed 'the Corporal' by Lytton (meant to reflect what Lytton perceived as his mediocrity), and referred to either by that name or 'Watty' (or, in this case, 'Wattie') by James and Rupert, Lamb lectured in classics at Trinity College. He later became secretary of the Royal Academy, wrote a book about it (*The Royal Academy*, 1935) and was knighted. Duncan wrote to Maynard on 26 August: '[James] & Corporal Lamb apparently have been living together very scandalously in the New Forest & now James is going to Wales for a week to stay with Rupert.' Lamb and Strachey did have a brief affair. Strachey apparently told Brooke about it, for Brooke wrote to Katherine Cox in March/April 1912: 'Did I tell you what Watty said to James when James accepted him? Did I tell you what Watty said to James when James (months later) Declared it was all *zu Ende*? I shall, in confidence, when we meet (But don't tell James.).'
2 R. K. Gaye had a temporary classical fellowship at Trinity and was inseparable from his friend G. H. Hardy (1877-1947), the mathematician. Hardy was an Apostle; Gaye was not. Shortly after Hardy cut himself off from the Apostles, Gaye committed suicide. Lytton Strachey believed it was over his failure to receive a permanent Trinity fellowship, and over an estrangement with Hardy. After Gaye's death, Hardy left Cambridge for Oxford.
3 During a visit to Versailles, Grant told Keynes that he was no longer in love with him. However, the two got back together shortly after.
4 The Marlowe Society had repeated its performance of *Doctor Faustus* for the benefit of fifty visiting German students. Brooke played the Chorus. He wrote to his mother on the day of the play: 'After the performance we are all going in a great brake to have supper at the Cornfords, in our dresses: which will be rather fun.'

RB, Aug. 22 [1910], 24 Bilton Road, Rugby
to JS, c/o Mrs Primmer, Beech Shade, Bank, near Lyndhurst

I came home this afternoon to find that my mother had just been jostled by a horse & hurled down. Her nose is dislocated & enormous, her face cut, & her mouth in ribbons. She is cheerful. But what is called the shock may affect her in a day or two. So it's just possible I can't go to Wales. Unlikely though; and I want to. Still, be warned. Of course, if I *don't*, you can come for a week-end here, unless she's at her last gasp. Providing for the journey, will you look out trains, or shall I? I, I think. I wonder if I can go quite cheaply. Yes, they've promised me a bed at Caer-Meddyg. I am writing to insist on the stable, & to put forward your claims. But I rather fear for you. However, once there, one can shuffle meals & beds, if one has sufficient cheek, like you, or sufficient prettiness, like me.

The Old Vicarage was expecting you, a good deal. Bryn was especially eager. And I'd very carefully brought Noel up to the point at which she could & must meet an Apostle. So there's a year or so lost for *her* education. And even you might have Widened a little. Jacques was all over himself at your note. Was it true? I was prompting, & could see nothing. You needn't, by the way, consider yourself bound to praise, or to monopolise criticism, on all occasions. Watty may be right. For I was preoccupied, & didn't remember it very well. And we all agree I can't act. So that even as a Chorus . . But he scores off you in the end. I've met a great many people who have heard his Tragedy lately.

I'm, for me, just on the limits of queerness, at present. Oh, oh! Perhaps it is being with Dudley for so long; & having read only one book in six weeks. Come & calm me. Play for the wise & good. I saw Roger[1] for a moment, & even that was wonderfully real. But Norton says he is going to organize a joint meeting of the Carbonari & "the other old thing" at the beginning of next term. To wind up both.   Rupert

I wonder how the Devil you discovered Mrs P[rimmer]. If she remembers me, give her my love. But I wonder what she thought of Bill & Eva – [2]

Mr Belloc's latest . . .? Can you bring it? Or *some*thing Modern –

---

1 Roger Fry (1866–1934), who organized the two Grafton Gallery Post-Impressionist exhibitions, which critics described as pornographic. Fry was the first lover of G. Lowes Dickinson and remained his friend for life. In his *Autobiography*, Dickinson says that in Fry's last year at Cambridge, 'every night I used to see him to bed and then kiss him passionately' (90). Although Dickinson goes on to say that he had 'a kind of married feeling' towards Fry, Fry in fact married Helen Coombe in 1897. Virginia Woolf wrote his biography.
2 Eva Spielman (1886–1949) of Newnham College and Bill Hubback. They married in 1911.

JS, Tuesday the 23rd [August 1910], Primmer House, [Bank]

Tuesday afternoon, and I've escaped it so far! I've been told the plot once though, and had the characters described to me twice. He's just come in, too, with a suspicious looking red manuscript book, so I suppose I'm doomed.

As for criticism, I trained myself some years ago to tolerate it (intellectually, at least) from people who might reasonably be considered good judges. But I shall never encourage Frankie to call you stupid, nor shall I salaam to Gerald's verdict on your poems. And since you raise the question, one may point out that I've quite as much the instinct for monopolizing praise. Has Fanny [Frances] Cornford not given you an account of my reply when, at our first meeting, she informed me that you were a true friend, upon whom she felt she could rely in an emergency? Oh! my icy analysis of your character was most effective – though I fear most of the vitriol ran off Mrs. C.'s back. Not very admirable habits, these of mine, are they? But ever so natural. There seems to be some horrid private property idea at the back of it all.

Well, now you shall hear what it was that Watty actually said – which I've ventured up till now to conceal. He said that you couldn't pronounce English properly. So I replied that of course they did all that kind of thing much better in Manchester. – A sordid little adventure, my dear Rupert; but one gets accustomed to such when one deals with that melancholy gib-cat.

Your mother's condition sounds alarming. Wouldn't it be better, if I still *am* to go to Rugby on Friday, for me to stay at the George? I leave for London on Thursday afternoon – so if you want to write and stop me after then, you'd better write to B[elsize].P[ark].G[ardens].   Yours
James

Jacques had some story of an International Congress of Conversazione Societies. Are you to be one of the delegates of the English Club?

RB, Wednesday [24 August 1910], 24 Bilton Road, Rugby
to JS, 67 Belsize Park Gardens
['To await arrival.' written after address]

"We do think that the emotional contemplations of a natural scene, supposing its qualities equally beautiful, is in some way a better state of things than that of a painted landscape: we think that the world would be improved if we could substitute for the best works of representative art *real* objects equally beautiful."

Isn't there something Queer about this?

Oh, no, you'd better come here. My mother is really quite well; only battered. I don't suppose you will see her. And Alfred will not be here. I wrote to the School, describing our train. I said *we* should walk from the station, unless it rained. But that our bags wouldn't. Is that at all right? And have you got enough labels, the right colours & shapes?

I've not heard about my letter to the Secretary about Accommodation. A note from . . Lytton!   R.

> *JS, Thursday night [25? August 1910],*
> *143 Fellows Road, South Hampstead, N.W. [London]*

Yes; it always seemed rather fishy.

I shall arrive then – is it too immoderately early? – by a train that gets to Rugby at twenty to four.

Shapes? Colours?? Labels??? Is one then not admitted without 'em? Christ! – but does one obtain such things at Clement's Inn?

Praps you could forge some.   James

> *RB, September 11th 1910, 24 Bilton Road, Rugby*

Dear Lytton,

It must be your heartless satirical playfulness, or indeed a depth of respectability in your surroundings, that makes you angle for "a little scandal" from *me*. It is so well-known that scandal, as that word is understood, never reaches my ears till everyone else has grown tired of it, and rarely then. In my little cottage, and even more in the roamings of late months through the Country, and the Camp, I am so far away from such things. Anyhow my scandal is not your scandal, nor your – I don't know how it goes on. It wouldn't stiffen you even at all to hear of what it was the rosiest chatteringest delirium for me to do, – bathing naked by moonlight with the ladies. For I, of course, am with Jane[1] in these matters. And you despise us. On the other hand, all other sorts of scandal I have only through Daddy, and that muddies them dreadfully. How Daddy borrowed Goldie's poems from Mr Eckhard and found inside the rough draft of Mr Eckhard's famous letter to Goldie, written this Spring; and how, on reentering his room one night he found James busy making a hasty copy of the letter, delighted at finding "a human document", you've probably heard. Daddy was stilted enough not to let James go on: which is a pity. Daddy himself, by the way, was in the oddest state at the dear old Summer School, a week ago. We all shared the Billiard-Room –

---

1 Jane Harrison and Lytton's sister Pernel were with Lytton in Saltsjöbaden, Sweden, where he had once again been sent for health reasons.

Daddy & James & Mr Foss and myself. – and, of course, Mr Julius West.[1] Daddy was a schoolboy in dormitory; & conceived a light lust for James, – who, I thought, was quite dignified about it. He would steal up suddenly behind him and tickle him gently under the armpits, making strange sibilant cluckings with his mouth meanwhile. And when James was in bed Daddy stood over him, waving an *immense* steaming penis in his face and chuckling softly. Poor James was nearly sick. It was really very terrible. And Mr West, of course, thought he was seeing Life: and tried to keep *his* end up with Tales of the Fabian Office, and of Mr Wells' flat *amours*.

We all loved Beatrice [Webb], who related amusing anecdotes about Mr Herbert Spencer[2] over and over again. She was very inquisitive, too, about the Society as represented by James & me & Daddy. She'd a long story about handing *Principia Ethica* to Mr Arthur Balfour; who skimmed it swiftly & gave it back, saying "Clever, but rather thin. The work of a very *young* man." Beatrice believes everything Mr Balfour says: so it was difficult to say anything.

Oh, I've just been reading it – *P.E.* I'd never read it before. Of course I knew all it was about. It seems very amusing. Though I don't know . . . is the last chapter completely accepted nowadays?[3] And, oddly, I've just had a little private note from Gerald, in Norfolk: trying to borrow it from me. "I have long felt," he ends, "it is a book one should read." So, you see there's *something* up.

It's a pity you didn't *quite* join Beatrice's show. James has; & sent £5. Didn't you like the bit where the imbecile boiled the baby?

1   Julius West, a Fabian. Lytton wrote to James on 15 September: 'I had a letter from Rupert yesterday, from Rugby, giving the most frantic account of the Summer School. Who on earth is Mr. West?'

2   The philosopher (1820–1903). Though Brooke seems fond enough of Beatrice Webb (1858–1943), she continued to be unimpressed with him, numbering him among those young men who were more interested in who was attending the Fabian Summer School than in what was being discussed. However, Brooke's notebooks reveal that he took many notes during his stay in Llanbedr, and it is difficult to doubt his seriousness regarding socialism. Hugh Dalton wrote in an unpublished memoir of Brooke (1915) which is now in the Brooke Archives at King's College, Cambridge: 'He remained a Fabian longer than most of us; in fact I do not know that he ever formally ceased to be a member of the London Society.' Brooke's papers recovered from the Old Vicarage include a considerable number of articles on the subject, and he was arguing the side of the Labour Party as late as 1914, just a few months before his death (Nesbitt 92).

3   Strachey, too, had expressed misgivings about the last chapter. In a letter to Moore, he wrote: 'Your grand conclusion made me gasp – it was so violently definite. Lord! I can't yet altogether agree. I think with some horror of a Universe deprived for ever of real slaughters and tortures and lusts. Isn't it possible that the real Ideal may be an organic unity so large and of such a nature that it is, precisely, the Universe itself?' (quoted in Holroyd, *Unknown* 234).

I hope you're going to continue to study Cambridge next term, now you've got rid of all obesity & rheumatism & whatnot in Sweden. There'll be lots to do: all the coming generation to review, and the new brothers to elect (putting off for once your *frigiditas*),[1] and Watty's tragedy to have read to you, & Frances'[Cornford] Friday evenings, – oh, my god, what a whirl! You can't intend to miss it. And, really, the prospect of a Saturday night with Gerald & Bertie [Bertrand Russell] & Maynard & Norton – Oh, I want a little literary flavour to help me out. (Otherwise, even, they'll elect Broady, {the logician}).[2]

Oh, yes! & there's our brother Raleigh's[3] literary lectures . . . I've just finished, by the way, one of the later volumes of *The Yellow Book*[4] – all I read nowadays. What a wicked scented lot they were! Raleigh & Mr John Buchan[5] are the chief contributors. I wish I'd been born a year or two earlier. "To be alive in those days . . ."

Shall I see you on the 10th prox. at the London & Cambridge dining club? I had dinner with the President or whatever he is, the other day, Mr Hilton Young;[6] who lives with a young married couple in a house once inhabited by Talleyrand. He seemed rather disillusioned & tired. He said he was a relic of Moore's generation. There's no other news of London, I think: and none at all of Rugby, except that the cinematograph in the Town Hall is a *great* success, and little Julian's scarlet fever was a false alarm.

I suppose, now I think it over, this won't reach you in Sweden; but'll come back & find you with James next week. (I wonder where that'll be. Not within reach of Rugby, I suppose? – there aren't any places within reach). I think it's rather funny. I suppose it'll even seem a little homely to you, Scandanavianism, now? Anyhow, it makes it doubtful if it's worth while even risking sending Jane my love, as I so much want to do. Would you have delivered it delicately?

Oh, Laddie's[7] climbed the window and eaten a fly. Oh!   Rupert

---

1 'frigidity'.
2 Charlie Broad, mentioned previously in Brooke's 28 January 1908 letter to James.
3 Walter Alexander Raleigh (1861–1922) – the critic and essayist – was a graduate of King's College and Apostle no. 204. Raleigh published his *Six Essays on Johnson* in 1910.
4 A London periodical extant 1894–97 that published much of the work of Aubrey Beardsley. Brooke once advised his cousin Erica Cotterill to educate herself on 'one third of Swinburne, all Oscar Wilde, and the drawings of Beardsley' (*RBB* 81).
5 John Buchan (1875–1940), author, whose early books were noted for their youthful freshness.
6 Hilton Young (1879–1960), a writer and the future Minister of Health. Young was a Trinity College graduate and a friend of Forster's. He was also a climbing companion of Maynard Keynes, and once proposed to Virginia Stephen. One week before writing this letter, Brooke had written to Dudley Ward: 'Poor Hilton! He is in love with Alfred . . . But I shock you.' The letter is included in the *LRB* with this section deleted.
7 A puppy.

RB, [postcard], 24 B[ilton].R[oad]. S.22.10. 3.30. N.W.N. ∞.
[22 September 1910]
to JS, 67 Belsize Park Gardens, Hampstead

Oh, I wonder if you met Mrs. Candish Betik[1] . . .
Kimmeridge, know it, – by George yes!
I go to Grantchester on Tuesday, London a week later.
What I really want is Morgan Forster's address.[2]   Rupert

It is *next* Sunday I lecture to the New Bilton Adult School on "William Shakespe[a]re, The Man and His Age."[3]

JS, Friday morning [23 September 1910] [The page is folded in the middle with 'F.W. Lewis 130 Murray Rd' written on the back]

I make out Morgan's address to be – Harnham, Monument Green, Weybridge. Daddy walked over to visit me one day at Mrs Stickland's. His father was apparently dying of some appalling internal disease. You can imagine his brutality about it all. He had to watch one night at the bedside – the Canon[4] groaning & tossing continuously. From time to time Daddy

1   Rupert refers either to Ottoline (Cavendish-Bentinck) Morrell or one of her relatives (Strachey had been staying at Corfe Castle near the home of Ottoline's brother, Lord Henry). Brooke came to know Ottoline well enough to write about her in an April 1913 letter to Katherine Cox: 'My dear child, don't worry about me & Ottoline Morrell. She stank: filthily. If ever she dared to mention you to me, I'd stop her bloody mouth by telling her what I thought her. I only pray I shouldn't hit her. [...] She's primarily & centrally filthy, nauseous, degraded. It made me feel dirty for days, having seen her. [...] I'll even promise not to "discuss" you with that slut.'
2   'Do tell it me.' is written in the right margin.
3   Brooke wrote about Shakespeare in one of his Grantchester notebooks, possibly in preparation for this talk: 'This glutton, drunkard, poacher, agnostic, adulterer and sodomite was England's greatest poet. Mind you hush it up. [...] I like telling the story of Shakespeare's love affairs. It shocks the Puritans, who want it hushed up. And it shocks the pro-Sodomites who want to continue in a hazy pinkish belief that all great men were Sodomites. The truth is that some great men are sodomites *and* womanizers, Shakespeare, Angelo, etc. [...] Pure sodomy is a pretty affectation in the young, but if it is anything more, leads to secondrateness, sentimentality, fluff, gentle dilettante slush. John Addington Symonds, and x___ and y___ and z___. That's the general rule, if you want one.' In the same piece, after observing that Shakespeare sometimes exhibited a revulsion towards sex, Brooke writes, 'The fact of sex is fundamentally filthy.' This document sums up much of Brooke's sexual attitude: his underlying Puritanism regarding sex even as he tries to distance himself from the Puritans, and his feeling that homosexuality and heterosexuality could both exist in one person. Brooke seems to have held the view that homosexuality should be limited to one's adolescence – even though he himself waited until the age of twenty-two to engage in sex with another male.
4   Hugh Dalton's father, who tutored the royal princes, Edward and George. The post had been offered to Edward Carpenter, who refused. The Canon, like Carpenter, was homosexual (Pimlott 66, 77–9). He did not die at this time.

would remark in his most sententious fortissimo – "Are you suffering a considerable amount of *pain*?"

Tomorrow I go to – Hove, to spend Sunday and the dear 26th with my brother Ralph and a lot more of my family. And on Tuesday the Office reopens.

Ainsi soit-il.[1]

James

What the devil is N.W.N.?

Life in America

———

Bennie (the control): Father papa papa Pa Pa father talk to me as you did before I left so suddenly.

Mr. Nathaniel B. Junst: Well, dearie, I want you to study and work hard and get along in that life you're in now, and then daddy'll come too, Bennie, and we will get along together just as we did in this life.

Bennie: Do you ride any now.

N.B.J.: Yes, sweetheart, – yes, sweetheart, and think of you every day when I ride.

RECTOR: We shall have to let him go again for a moment, friend, not because he is tired, to use thy expression, but because he becomes a little confused.

———

JS, October 19th, 1910, The Spectator, *1. Wellington Street, Strand*

My dear Rupert,

(1) There's no news yet from the Stage Society. But I've made a provisional intrigue for the tickets.

(2) I handed over the Books to our brother Norton yesterday afternoon.

(3) With the greatest diffidence I venture to remind you of the N[ational]. L[iberal]. C[lub]. They say: "Letters should state that the Candidate is a Liberal, and personally known to the Writer." Daddy writes: "I have known Mr James Strachey for many years . . . etc." By the way, praps you've sent a letter to the Sec[retar]y *direct*? This would be a grave mistake.

———

Shall I go to Cambridge on Saturday? You seemed simply not to regard it as a thing that could *possibly* happen. So I suppose it won't. But Sunday at Hampstead? And then, there are only about seven weeks before you

1 'So be it.'

finally vanish.[1] On the other hand, I find it so hard not to be oofish. Did you think me awful on Saturday? or didn't you notice? and on Sunday did you think me better, as I tried to be?

Lytton seems to have had a hot time of it with George [Mallory] . . . I gather that on Sunday he only didn't go right through with it out of terror that someone would come in – as there way [sic] no key to the door.[2] But on Monday evening they had a conversation which left Lytton as he put it quite déchiré.[3] George said in fact that such things couldn't ever be repeated. They bored him so. No, he felt no actual repulsion. He was just 'indifferent'. Lytton hastened to agree that there was no point in anything short of actual copulation. But surely, as he was merely indifferent, he'ld be obliging enough to allow that. No. Just once? No, never.

Another of these virgins.

However, he was awfully upset in the end because Lytton said he never wanted to see him again on those conditions – as it would be simply boring. It appears that the poor fellow had imagined all along that Lytton was deeply in love with him.

But what a bad habit our brothers have of losing their self respect like this.   Yours
                                                                    James

RB, [postmarked 21 October 1910], Cambridge to JS, 67 Belsize Park Gardens, Hampstead

Next week's too soon, I fear. Perhaps the Electra'll come again at Pompey Time.[4]

Isn't this[5] *too* farcical?

I'm sorry I forgot.

And you may be in Cambridge at this moment.

Edward[6] is staying with me *this* week-end.

I may see you – *apud Tertium*;[7] on Saturday.

1 Brooke planned to spend several months in Germany.
2 Mallory had taken a temporary position as schoolmaster at Charterhouse, and it was there that Lytton went to see him.
3 'sorry' or 'torn'.
4 The Hugo von Hofmannsthal/Richard Strauss opera was being staged at Covent Garden on 24 October. It was, in fact, performed again on 26 November, not long before John Masefield's *Pompey the Great* opened at the Aldwych on 4 December.
5 His letter of recommendation for Strachey's National Liberal Club application.
6 Edward Thomas (1878-1917), the poet, whom Brooke and Dudley Ward stayed with on their way to campaign for Poor Law reform. Thomas lived at Petersfield, conveniently close to Bedales, where Noel Olivier attended school. He thought Brooke's 'clear, rosy skin helped to give him the look of a great girl' (quoted in *RBB* 240).
7 'around the third [hour]'.

Henry Schlösser yesterday.

Austin[1] has finally disgraced himself.

And I've had a second litter of pigs in three weeks.

Do you know what happens when a Sow has fourteen piglets and only twelve Teats?

My dear fellow – two of them DIE.   Rupert

JS, October 21, 1910, The Spectator, *1. Wellington Street*

Dear Sir,

I am directed by the Editor of the Spectator to ask you whether you would care to undertake to review for him a book in two volumes by Mr John Tucker Murray upon "English Dramatic Companies, 1558–1642", which has today been published*. He understands that you have made a special study of the period in question; but what he would like is not so much a technical discussion of the book as a general essay upon the subject with which it deals. If you should feel inclined to accept his suggestion, he will have the books forwarded to you at once. He asks me to add that he wishes the notice to be a short one – of not more than 750 or 800 words.   I am,

Yours faithfully,

James Strachey

*(Price 31/6 net)

JS, Friday night [21 October 1910], 67 Belsize Park Gardens

I've returned haggard from dinner at the Sangers',[2] and found your letter. Thank you so for the word to Mr Dawson Hicks[3] (or whatever [h]is name is). I'm afraid it was a worry.

I went last night for the first time to Tristan.[4] Do you know it? It seems to me something that really makes up for a good deal. Certainly it "expresses" – I don't know what that means – LOVE in a way quite unparalleled so far as I know . . . Some bits of A. and C.[5] perhaps . . . – But

1 Alfred Austin (1835–1913), the Poet Laureate and former editor of the *National Review*. Brooke met him in 1908 at a dance following the performance of *Comus*.
2 Charles Sanger and his wife Dora.
3 Again, Strachey is referring to the letter of recommendation Brooke wrote for him. The recipient is probably George Dawes Hicks (1862–1941), a Cambridge philosopher who was greatly influenced by G. E. Moore.
4 Wagner's *Tristan und Isolde*, at Covent Garden.
5 Probably *Antony and Cleopatra*.

on the other hand the depths that that person reaches of platitude and general ineptitude! And the fearful entourage of Kings and Knights in wigs & false beards! – the brown cardboard castles with dog tooth carving on their arches! In fact the whole ghastly gothic revival! – However, it's worth while to drop in for Act II at least.

Otherwise I read books on Syndikalismus[1] – an obscure subject, a *very* obscure subject. Oh! we're not *near* the bottom of it, believe me!

And you? Obscure too, ever. Give my love to Edward and Austin . . Chamberlain? Johnson? Birrell? . . . And your piglets! *I* have a couple of teats to spare: so send 'em along – and doubtless as to milk the Lord will provide.   Yours
                                                                                                              James

I imagine that Lytton will be in Cambridge tomorrow. The indications are at present that *I shan't*.

JS, Monday evening [7 November 1910],
The Union Society, Cambridge

Dear Rupert,

Would you very much mind explaining a few things I don't under-stand? If it bothers, you mustn't answer.

Why were you suddenly angry tonight when I asked about the footlights? Was it my imagination? I'm sure it wasn't. Was it just that you were at the moment annoyed by my damned insistence – my coming back? Or was it that you wanted to show that I'd somehow reached some limit or other? Are you utterly sick of seeing me? – – I really understand nothing of your view. Only, you seemed nice for a great deal – and then suddenly you were cold and angry. I was rather frightened &, if that's the word, 'upset'.

Have I seen you a great deal? I suppose I have. I'ld much rather not come again to Cambridge soon. But Norton began to make a great fuss about next Saturday – so perhaps I must then. After that I shan't this term. You see, I'ld rather *anything* than bore you. Partly, perhaps, because when you show that I do, its simply hell.

You don't mind this, do you? It doesn't make it worse? You see, I want to know things, because I'm sure it's no use pretending about this kind of thing.   James

1 Syndicalism, a system of economics in which workers own and manage their factories. Gerald Shove espoused syndicalism while studying economics at King's.

RB, Tuesday, Nov. 8 1910, Ye Olde George Hotel, Chatteris to JS, 67 Belsize Park Gardens, Hampstead

My dear James,

I don't remember that I was angry. I felt annoyed at remembering there was another thing I wanted to do & had better not. Constipation is wearing. Ask Lytton. You've probably never tried to write poetry for three weeks and failed. Even if one succeeds it's wearing. I returned and went to bed at 9.30. & got up at 11 this morning. Twelve of those hours I slept. That showed me I was very ill. So I came here. I am well again. Perhaps I shall never return again. There are a great many people in this room. They are like people in plays. But when they get by twos they say the most awful things to one another. I have made the extraordinary discoveries about commercial life. About Bedrooms.   but my chop comes

Rupert

You are in the same state of confusion I used to be. You think of everything except yourself as stabile [sic]. It makes life simple: but it is not true. Other people vary as much from moment to moment, and are as disorganized, as yourself.

JS, Lord Mayor's Day [11 November], 1910, 67 Belsize Park Gardens

My dear Rupert,

You make me feel beastly and stupid. All the same, I think you've only escaped from the difficulty by a Glissade. And is that after all more reputable than my method of Simplification?

I'm very sorry you were involved in Monday's explosion – though the tails of Norton's poor peacocks got the worst of the wetting. I really didn't know I was still liable to that kind of thing. – But I do rather want to know, even now, how you feel about it all. I seem so incredibly in the dark about you; and isn't obscurity awfully bad as a means? But you seem so to hate talking about such things – and I'm too frightened to carry it through. Couldn't one have an absolutely cold & unemotional conversation? It might really be quite interesting and funny. But of course the whole affair would depend on your masterly handling of it. Rather like the central scene in Miss Hamilton's latest play?[1]

---

1   Cicely Hamilton (1872–1952), the dramatist and actress. Her latest play was *Just to Get Married*, at the Little Theatre.

Lytton and I watched the Show this afternoon from the N.L.C. Yesterday we saw the pictures,[1] which are simply superb. Even that cynical Jacques of yours was converted. We had tea with Desmond [MacCarthy] & his telephone in a vault below the gallery. He says he'll be in Cambridge on Saturday – and I've written to Moore.

I dare say I'm almost the only person in the world who feels sorry about your constipation – Daddy too perhaps. Were you really ill? And has that funny looking place set you up again?

James

You should have seen The Mairciful Soul last night! The hero, an elderly ghost, dressed in cinque cento tights, was a german jew.[2]

Fé-or-dé-leeeeee-sa! You have *betrayed* me! Blank verse or Prose?

RB, [postmarked 10 p.m., 11 November 1910], The Orchard
to JS, 67 Belsize Park Gardens, Hampstead

I don't know what a Glissade means; but no doubt it's something very degrading. If you really think its time for another of the unemotional and clarifying conversations, I dare say you're right. I gather we meet with Dickinson on Saturday. He's going to be away. But he told me that we *had* to meet where the Ark was, because we all laid our hands on it & swore, at one point. Eddie's turning up – I didn't invite him. Norton is at his dying mother's bedside: and that makes complications.

I am better. I wrote fourteen lines yesterday. I envy you your quiet life. I don't understand about peacocks.   R

RB, [postcard, postmarked 3.30 p.m.,
22 November 1910, Cambridge]
to JS, 67 Belsize Park Gardens, Hampstead

Rev. Headlam,[3] the Fabian, is now put off for the Monday. So it doesn't matter. Monday perhaps even almost best. But as it happens.   Rupert

---

1 'Manet and the Post-Impressionists' at the Grafton Galleries.
2 The leading role ('Geoffrey') in *The Merciful Soul* at the Little Theatre was played by Everard Vanderlip.
3 The Rev. Stewart Duckworth Headlam (1847-1924), who had lost his position in the Church due in part to his political beliefs, and who had stood bail for Oscar Wilde in 1885.

JS, November 30th, 1910, 67 Belsize Park Gardens

Dear Rupert,

You see that Salome's[1] not till Thursday? And the Chineses[2] are, I fear, dubious. Have you any other choices? Well, well, there'll always be a music hall with election results. I have the darkest views as to them. How many seats will Government loose [sic], d'ye think? *I* put it today at nearly a hundred. Lancashire has gone, of course. Oh dear dear.[3]

I've been seeing Ben [Keeling] a good deal lately. He seemed a little perverse if not hysterical about Lord Shove – though I can well imagine that That Great Man was irritating enough.

Norton I met for the first time since his trouble[4] yesterday. He showed his usual flair for purely chimerical rats. By the way he's come round typically with immense gusto to the very old world view of you as by far the most delightful person in Cambridge, charming, imaginative, etc etc etc. Funny how he catches things on the turn always.

And how *is* the old place? Very fit, I hope. Wasn't there some man elected to something or other?

Oh! Pompey's[5] at 2.30. No tickets have come yet – but I expect it's all right.

If you catch your train may I meet you opposite the dear Gangangrenous pussy cats?[6]   Yours

James

JS, Saturday night [10 December 1910], 67 Belsize Park Gardens

These old things seemed to me so bright, I thought they might cheer your defeat.[7] You heard of the Typewritten Ballads, done by different people line by line? Here are three selected ones in very various styles. Please return them.

1   The Strauss opera based on Oscar Wilde's play premièred in England (in a censored version) on 8 December at Covent Garden.
2   *The Dragons of Wrath*, directed by Gertrude Kingston (1866/8–1937) and playing at the Little Theatre.
3   A constitutional conference between government and Opposition party leaders had been held in the summer to reform the role and membership of the House of Lords and to debate the question of Irish Home Rule – an issue that ultimately led to the dissolution of the conference and, consequently, to a call for new elections.
4   Norton's mother had died.
5   Masefield's *Pompey the Great*, which Rupert felt 'just failed, really. Though the acting didn't give it much chance' (letter to David Garnett, January 1911).
6   Probably Landseer's four bronze lions at the base of Nelson's statue in Trafalgar Square.
7   Strachey refers to the election. Though fifty-six seats changed hands, the election of December 1910 was a virtual stand-off with the Liberals maintaining control of the House of Commons. Brooke wrote to Katherine Cox: 'So tired I got, working at our election all day and half the night. I did "conveyances". And we had twenty motor-cars promised; and *twelve* came! . . . Man after man we had to give up. Couldn't get

I had a very distinguished tea party after I'd written to you: Messieurs Squire,[1] Jukes, Clifford Sharp[2] and [A. R.] Orage;[3] StanHope[4] of Chester; and finally the President of the L.G.B.[5] I was quite converted to John, who seemed to me to have the Artistic Temperament. He advised me to marry before I was thirty, so I said 'never'. He then asked me whether I was at Oxford or Cambridge, and when I answered 'Cambridge', murmured 'Ah! that explains it.'

The others I thought a bit what you'ld call Grubby. And Mr Sharp defended the Incest Act & Bestiality Laws against the charges of Chester & me.   Your

J.

RB, Thursday [22 December 1910], 24 Bilton Rd, Rugby to JS, 67 Belsize Park Gardens, Hampstead

Many thanks. I like – it is a sign of what I'm coming to – Professor Mostigu the best. I shall send you two reviews in two days.[6]

I hope you enjoyed Ben. I had a Crisis[7] and went to London & back. Saw the pictures. They don't seem to me odd. Why do they say so? I thought

them to the poll. . . . The next day came pathetic letters, reproachful. "We was waiting in the rain for three hours for that motor." They can't afford railway fares. . . . It is not true that anger against injustice and wickedness and tyrannies is a good state of mind, "noble". Oh, perhaps it is with some, if they're fine. But I guess with most, as with me, it's a dirty mean choky emotion. I HATE the upper classes' (December 1910).

1 John Collings Squire (1884–1958), poet, essayist, Fabian and literary editor of the *New Statesman*. His work was included in the *Georgian Poetry* anthologies.
2 Sharp was the *New Statesman*'s first editor.
3 Alfred Richard Orage (1873–1934), the proponent of guild socialism (and later Social Credit economics) and editor of the *New Age*, a paper whose subtitle – 'An Independent Socialist Review of Politics, Literature and Art' – accurately reflected its mission. Among the paper's contributors were Shaw, Belloc, G. K. Chesterton, H. G. Wells, Havelock Ellis, Arnold Bennett, Katherine Mansfield, John Middleton Murry, Wyndham Lewis and Ezra Pound. Orage could attract such a relatively wide sample of writers because as editor he 'was very careful not to give his editorial support to one brand of socialism in preference to any other' (Flory 46).
4 Philip Stanhope, a Radical MP.
5 John Elliot Burns (1858–1943), president of the Local Government Board. Although he was one of the radical ministers in the Lloyd George Cabinet, Burns bitterly opposed Sidney and Beatrice Webb's proposals in the Poor Law Reform Bill. Burns had been imprisoned in 1887 for his part in the Trafalgar Square riots. Note that Strachey thinks Burns has 'the Artistic Temperament': Burns and Oscar Wilde had worked together for prison reform. Wilde even thought of asking him to write a preface on prison reform for a sixpenny edition of *The Ballad of Reading Gaol* (Wilde 733).
6 Brooke's unsigned review of *William Hunnis and the Revels of the Chapel Royal* by C. C. Stopes appeared under the title 'William Hunnis and his times' in the 28 January edition of the *Spectator*. The review of 'Professor Mostigu' is untraced.
7 He had hurt Katherine Cox's feelings while they were in a bookshop and was subsequently disgusted with himself.

they were just what painters would make if they were less dull than painters generally are.

Now, I'm awful. [squiggly line spiralling downward], you know. I hope no one I respect will ever speak to me again. Will you write an article denouncing me in the Public Press?

I don't think you'd better go to Munich, you know. If it was in April (& I there) it might be different. But I want to *begin* by learning German.

Alfred is playing Patience. He & I just put the Westminster on the fire; it burned; & then the fire played drum and fife. Also, at 1.30 a.m. a week ago, in the dark, someone called me in my ear twice. And on Friday just before tea they called from the road – no one there – and, just after, I was sick in my handkerchief. That's why I went to London.   Ever,

but my God! how desperately
Rupert

JS, Christmas Eve 1910, 67 Belsize Park Gardens

I don't understand your letter. Are you ill? or have you been? or is it something else? Could you tell me?

I'm rather bad, one way and another, so I'd better not go on. Do *you* ever hope that Self abuse may solve everything?

Shall you be about again? Jacques said you were going to Lulworth. And when's your final departure?

You weren't *asked* for two reviews. And I hope you've kept them short.

Ben is incredibly simplified, and lives in a fools' paradise. I found it hard to communicate with him there.

Do write and say what it's all about.   James

[There follows in Strachey's album a pen-and-ink drawing (see page 144) on a postcard (addressed to Brooke at The Orchard, but the name and address have been scratched out) titled 'L'indécise' ('The Indecisive One'), which was probably enclosed in the above letter.]

RB, 24 Dec. [1910], 24 B[ilton].R[oad]., Rugby
to JS, 67 Belsize Park Gardens, Hampstead

Dr Sir,

I have tried to write in the proper style for your magazine. I am afraid the result is not very good. I hope it is not too long. If your Editor thinks so, explain to him that these books are both very important contributions to the History of Literature. And cut as much out as you like. Also please will you look through and see if the French words are right? I do not know about your habits – what you want in the post[s]cript which gives the

name etc. of the books, and when you use italics, for names quotations etc. These Old English quotations look very *quaint* in Italics. I have tried to be at once quaint & well-informed throughout; I have succeeded, I think. But oh! dull
    dull
      dull

          dull DULL   ever R.

Strachey's pen and ink drawing on post card to Brooke

JS, December 31st 1910, 67 Belsize Park Gardens

I daresay you'll get a proof one day. The tone wasn't bad on the whole – though there was one dreadful passage in Mr Hunnis, which I struck out. . . . and one or two words here and there.

I take this opportunity of complaining about *"naïve"*. Is it intended to be

French? There's a French adjective *'naïf'*, whose feminine is *'naïve'* – but why is the feminine used? On the other hand I've heard it said that there's an English word 'naive' (knave) – but in that case why the diaeresis and why the italics? But I suppose you're familiar with all this & put it in for our sake: and indeed, as the word's so very Spectatorial, I let it stand.

Carrabee! carraboo!

––––––––––

My pale soul feeds on Salome and water.   Yours
                                                                                                    James

1911

The new year found Brooke at Lulworth Cove with a party of friends that included Katherine Cox and Jacques Raverat. Not long after the outing broke up, Brooke left for Munich. After living three months in Germany, he visited Vienna and Florence before returning to England in May. Back in Grantchester, he took rooms at the Old Vicarage, which became his permanent residence. Although he often spent time elsewhere – in Rugby, London, Germany and America – he kept most of his private papers and manuscripts at the Old Vicarage from May 1911 until his death.

The focal point of London's summer of 1911 was Covent Garden. Brooke and Strachey were frequently in the audience; together and with an array of other friends, they took in a series of performances by the Grand Opera Syndicate and by Serge Diaghilev's Ballets Russes, featuring Nijinsky.

Strachey's contributions to the *Spectator* this year included articles on Slovak art, Winston Churchill, 'Doctors and Advertising', the Greek Anthology, 'The Foundations of Mathematics', English palaces, the Franco-German Agreement and at least three articles on China.

Strachey and Brooke ended the year where Brooke began it: at Lulworth Cove.

RB, [postcard, 2 January] 1911, Lul'[wor]th
to JS, 67 Belsize Park Gardens, Hampstead

I suppose you got my reviews later. Burn them or exenterate them or as you like. I'm quit of them. And I'm going to Germany. Only an imbecile would want *one* review on two books about wholly unconnected subjects. – –

Jacques sends greetings.

Oh, I only had a Spasm. A Spasm you know. A Spasm.   R.

JS, January 3rd, 1911, 67 Belsize Park Gardens

I say, Jane, would it be possible to send me a p.c. (you've one always on your person?) to say if you think it's likely I'll see you before you leave? Perhaps you sail from the Cove: and at any rate you'll not I expect be long in London. I'm merely inquisitive because I rather want to fix up my arrangements for *my* departure . . . for Sardinia or Sevil[l]e . . . But if there's a chance of a few moments of you, I'd rather stay in London till you've gone – even if its only a dim one. But of course if there's none, I shall hur[r]y to some place rather soon. And the people I'm going with, if I'm going with anyone, are a little restive.

You heard that Duncan danced the Gillie Cullam[1] so badly that he cut his toe off with one of the swords?

Give my love to Jacques   Yours
                                                                       James

RB, 5th Jan [1911], 24 B[ilton] R[oad]
to JS, 67 Belsize Park Gardens, Hampstead

I hear you have been in constant communication with my mother. Mr B. just got me as I drove off on Wednesday morning. Many thanks. I've not read him yet. But a glance or two seemed to show that the glamour even struggles through print. My eyes swam a little. But it didn't quite conceal a phrase or two & two thoughts or three that weren't, Miss [Katherine] Cox & I thought, θυιτε Cambridge – or rather, just not Wise and Good. But I shall investigate further as I pack. A man sent me proofs. They had already been corrected by an ape with no knowledge of Modern English. But I occasionally humoured him. "Nâîvê" they presented as native, with an imperial. I never murmured.

They will fill παγεσ of your paper. Why did not you cut them down? I was shocked when I saw them. I suspect you of undue favouritism. Also, they're much too true & good for an unliterary paper. But hadn't Mrs Brigham ever a chance? I was sick she went.

I pass through London on Monday (probably) and Wednesday or Thursday. I'll try to see you. I'll telegraph. But at present I don't know times. – But, good god! are you away on your holidays?

Jacques thought Carrabee! Carraboo! the wittiest thing he'd ever heard.

                                                                       Rupert

---

1   A traditional Scottish Highland dance.

JS, January 6th, 1911, 67 Belsize Park Gardens

Dear Rupert,

Daddy D. (in seaweed and felt) was shown up to the sanctum yesterday morning. Why, I wonder, did he make out that you'd gone – to "Galatia" as he put it – that morning at ten? It made me pretty severe on ηµ, while we lunched at some Cock or other – especially as he would tell me the history of all your love affairs, which he'd had from Mr Gaunt in the strictest confidence, and which Mr Gaunt had had (in the strictest confidence) from "Denham".[1] God knows the creature didn't manage to

1 Denham Russell-Smith (1888-1912), Hugh's younger brother, whose seduction by Brooke is described in a forthcoming letter to Strachey. It was not until 1980, when the publication of John Lehmann's *Rupert Brooke: His Life and his Legend* brought the incident to light, that Russell-Smith's name became irrevocably associated with his seducer for all time. In the many years between, virtually all trace of him was lost.

Denham was born on 16 December 1888 and was only a year younger than Brooke. Like his elder brother Hugh, he went to Rugby and was enrolled at School Field. He lived in Parker Brooke's house from September 1902 until July 1906.

Brooke's enchantment with Denham began in 1906 when he went with Hugh for a summer holiday at the Russell-Smith home at Brockenhurst. Rupert and Denham exchanged letters, though none has survived. In September 1906, Brooke wrote to Hugh, 'soon I shall exude an epistle to your brother. But this, you understand, is to you. [...] On the whole I think you are the happiest people I have found in my search; all the more so that you do not know it.' A January 1907 letter from Brooke to his mother mentions 'a letter from D. Russell-Smith', and in a 9 September 1907 letter to Dudley Ward, Brooke complains of 'Denham who answers long letters by return of post'. Brooke invited Hugh to a play by Shaw in September 1906, and added, 'Bring Denham too if you like.' The next summer, Brooke again stayed with the Russell-Smiths and noted, 'Denham & Alan [Russell-Smith, Hugh and Denham's younger brother] seem well; Denham older.' Brooke wrote to Geoffrey Keynes in April 1907: 'I know it was arranged Denham should be there. But [...] he didn't want to be in the same town as my mother [...] Remember me to Denham. I expect I shall miss him.' Brooke wrote to his mother from Lulworth, 30 July 1907: 'I hope Denham & Alan have taken my racquet, as agreed. Hugh & I were rather sorry for ourselves as well as for Denham when we heard of his accident: – at least if it is his right hand. It will spoil all the tennis at Brockenhurst.'

Denham's name appears in several more of Brook's letters from this period, as when Brooke warns Geoffrey Keynes regarding Alfred Brooke's planned visit: 'Denham was the last person you thrust on your people. If they're looking forward to another Denham, they'll be disappointed in Alfred' (12 August 1907). He goes on to say: 'I loathe you with a deadly jealousy because you have B'hurst to look forward to. I shall probably kill you on Saturday morning. I have just returned from the dear Smiths. I was asked for a week & stayed two and had to be thrust out. Half the time I was impossibly rude. Don't corrupt them with your modern decadence! Denham is more fascinating & bewildering than ever. I am afraid he found me, generally, too old. Be very young to them. To watch Denham's behaviour towards the rest of the family turns to sweetness (for a moment) even the dour pessimism of Yours Rupert.' Brooke affected much the same type of ending in another letter to Keynes on 29 September 1907: 'There are about two who pretend to remember me. On such I inflict myself & my sorrows occasionally. They are polite. But they yawn: heavens, how they yawn! Such is Denham (who is younger). I sat in his study tonight & was violently morbid all over the sofa. He smiled a charming smile outwardly: but loathed it and Yours Rupert.' Denham's name also appears in letters from the following year. On a 21 July 1908 postcard to Geoffrey Keynes, Brooke wrote, 'Well then, you may come, next Saturday. You will find Denham here! Bring a tennis-racket, give

get through more than two or three sentences – but can you *imagine* the insolence of that excremental shadow mouthing and giggling – *oh*!

As a matter of fact I sent another letter to L[ulworth]. (which was really why I asked for the address). I presume you never got it & that Mrs Leavenworth[1] has read it – but there was nothing in it but some enquiries & you've answered those.

My holiday began this afternoon, but I shall be in London. Will you stay a night here? It would be so nice. If you hate this house, couldn't we go to the Strand Palace Hotel & have a private sitting room? It's only in H.G. [Wells]'s novels that that involves copulation – and though I should like that, what I want's only to sit in a room with you. Have you made all your arrangements? and is it hopelessly impossible for you to wait one more day? I want you to so much. Please do, please, please, please, please.

I'm sorry you're so beastly about our Mr Bedford, the reader. He's a member of the I[ndependent]. L[abour]. P[arty]. and I'm sure knows a lot more M[odern]. E[nglish]. than you do. Ape, indeed!

I've been trying to draw a picture called "Dogs must not occupy seats", but I haven't succeeded yet.

Oh Jesus! I must go & dine with Mrs Sheppard at the N.L.C.   Your
                                                                 James

You and your new triangular writing! Good God!

[Charles] Sayle my love, & pray without ceasing.' On 6 October, he was suggesting to Keynes that they 'meet Denham at tea, perhaps', but on 29 November 1908 Brooke wrote: 'Denham R-S has typhoid, Hugh says.' On 3 January 1909, James Strachey wrote to Duncan Grant, 'Today Maynard came; & said that he'd heard that the small Mr Russell Smith was dying of typhoid fever. Hope had been abandoned. R. mentions nothing [...] I think he really was fond of him.' However, four days later, James wrote to Lytton that Maynard 'said that Mr Russell Smith had recovered. But you didn't know that on Sunday he said that Mr Russell Smith was dying. And you've never heard of Mr Russell Smith.' Denham did recover, and was healthy enough by autumn for Brooke to seduce him at Grantchester. At the time of the seduction, Brooke was twenty-two and Denham twenty. Shortly before Denham's visit, Brooke had written to Hugh, 'Love to Denham' (*LRB* 174).

After a series of further illnesses, Denham died at 1 a.m. Wednesday morning, 10 July 1912, at the age of twenty-three. His nephew Roy Russell-Smith, born after Denham's death, was told the cause of death was septicaemia from an abscessed tooth. Geoffrey Keynes was among those upset by Denham's death. In a July 1912 letter to Katherine Cox, Brooke reported, 'Geoffrey writes, snapping at the Universe, – & a *little* puzzled – (you know his eyes & hair when he has the *migraine*) – over Denham's death. Rather lovable, then.'

After Hugh Russell-Smith's death in 1916, Mrs. Brooke wrote to Geoffrey Keynes on 16 July, 'Denham died 3 or 4 years ago after several bad illnesses, both Rupert & Alfred liked him very much.'

1 The proprietor of the Cove Hotel in West Lulworth.

Brooke's post card of 7 January 1911

*RB, [postcard, postmarked 6.15 p.m., 7 January 1911], Bilton Road
to JS, 67 Belsize Park Gardens, Hampstead*

I shall get to Euston 11.10 on Monday. If you're there you can take over
control. Thence I drive to Charing Cross. Then I'll go to the N.L.C. We'll
have lunch somewhere. At 2 or so I depart. I'm afraid I can't stay an extra
night. Frightful rows already.

I daresay Daddy didn't[1] get it very right, you know.

Percy's triangles[2] – ha! how I worship him.   R

1 Brooke refers to the reports on his love life.
2 Henry Algernon Percy (1871-1909) was a politician, world traveller and author
  who, after visits to Turkey and Egypt, began studying hieroglyphics.

Strachey imitates Brooke's 'new triangular writing'.

JS, January 20th, 1911, 67 B.P.G.

I'm afraid you had the most dreadful gale. I prayed to God for several hours one night that he might chain the winds. But perhaps it was the wrong one.

I've been till yesterday at Corfe Castle and the New Forest. Gerald & Norton were there some of the time. Gerald, did you hear?, had been in Exeter dealing with a family quarrel. It appears that Mrs Herbert Shove (Herbert, you know, is the one in the sub-Marines) has a mother who cohabits with her husband in a ménage that's run by her 'lover'. Southsea will therefore have nothing to do with her. But Herbert condones her conduct and has therefore been cut off by Gerald and the rest of the family. They all gathered in two hotels in Exeter and the whole question was discussed in three immense conversations with speeches à la Mr Shaw. Gerald took a moderate and Centre line.

Norton read Love on Optics. He talked very little, and all of a sudden a dreamy look would come over him, and we knew he'd discovered a formula.[1] He was also ashamed to say that he wanted to copulate with the horrid red-hatted Dorothy who waited. We only had two conversations. One was on the nature of Beauty. Norton thought it was immoral to think of a picture as being anything more than an arrangement of lines and colours. The other was about my love affairs. I said I'd written to the Duc de Conde to ask if I might stay with him, and fall in love once more with his dear sister Vera. 'To my great Surprise' Norton was deeply pained, and assured me that it would be best for me to avoid a woman as I would the devil himself. Really I never saw anyone go more utterly off the rails, and mix his tones more hopelessly. And when he went away he made a fuss because they charged 6 and 6 a day instead of 6. Gerald all the time seemed sunk in grubbery. I only had him alone once, and cross-examined him about Daddy D and your letters. As I suspected, it was worse than he'd told you. He'd gone through quite a series, and gave Gerald an account, as typical, of one I'd sent when I left Clevedon. I have only a dim memory . . . . but why don't you burn 'em?

I didn't like my companions much, but when they'd gone it seemed worse. Jacques said I'd better go to Cambridge, and it *was* rather a good idea. So I'm halfway there. If I stay 10 days, mayn't I elect someone? I shall have no other distractions.

This afternoon I dropped in for a couple of acts of Peter Pan. I'd no conception it was so devastating. My memory was of something rather bright. I fairly turned pale with the horror of it. And the way it's done. The strained miawing voices! Good God . . . All the same, I wanted most awfully to bugger Pauline.[2] . . . It's to be hoped that Charlie's Aunt[3] where I go tonight with Jacques'll be more hopeful.

I don't know if you care to hear all this dull gibber – by the banks of the Weezer.[4] Perhaps things in Cambridge 'll be more amusing. But it can't help being a kind of diary. It's simply a method, intolerable, perhaps, of conveying gossip. Say if you'd rather not have it.

I've just read your review of the C.H. of E.L.[5] I think it's superb. But aren't you too bold? Can even a person as immaculate as you defend incest so openly? (Mr Strachey regrets to add that the proofreading appears to have been most careless. He counted as many as five 'literals'.)

I must start for the Avenue.   with Love,
                                                                      James

1 Norton was studying the numerical theories of the nineteenth-century mathematician Georg Cantor.
2 The actress Pauline Chase (1885-1962), who was playing the part of Peter Pan.
3 Brandon Thomas's *Charley's Aunt*, being staged at the Savoy.
4 Strachey probably refers to the Weser River, though it is actually in northern
   Germany and runs through Bremen. The Isar runs through Munich.
5 Brooke's review of *The Cambridge History of English Literature*, volume VI, which
   appeared in the 19 January *Cambridge Review* (he had also reviewed volume V in the
   8 December 1910 issue, remarking that 'It is amazing that experts and professors of
   English literature, familiar with so many live and glowing styles, should write such
   uniform lustreless English, with all the faults of journalese').

We were a quiet little party at Norton's last night. There was a knock at half past eleven, and I thought that perhaps after all . . . but when I opened the door there was dear old Maynard in his shiny dresser, just back from the fourth best dinner he'd ever eaten in his life. We had a conversation about Companionship, and whether one could prevent people from finding out what one's soul was like. Norton preferred to call it a fundament; and Gerald confused it with one's character, till I explained the difference. Sheppard stared at Cessil,[1] and Cessil simmered, and Pozzo [Maynard Keynes] cleared his throat several times and said that anyone who copulated in a hammock when he might in a bed was a foolish fellow.

There was a most unpleasant story (in confidence of course) about Duncan's latest debauch. The duc de Condé was in London, & asked him to the rooms of a friend of his – a Mr Workman (late of Trinity apparently, and ex-friend of Dent's). It was after the theatre and the room was very richly furnished in the Turkesque style. The three of them sat and drank champagne for hour after hour, and Duncan has only a misty recollection of the rest. But he remembers that at the Duc's instructions, he and Mr Workman took off all their clothes and copulated on the floor, while the Duc sat watching them and "tossing himself off" – and explaining all the time that this was the latest vice – Mixoscopy . . . But doubtless, beside the Weezer, you're familiar with it already.

Materially, Cambridge seems much as usual – except that Mr Strood or Strowd is gone, but that there's a new fireplace in the Union dining room, and that Sheppard's in the O[scar]. B[rowning].'s rooms. They present the gloomiest appearance. Every one of the old beauties is there; but spread over an immensely vaster space, their general effect is even more desolating than before. Oh yes, they've all gone across – the ex-pianola, the Hamlet chair, the portrait de ma mère – even those thin wooden basket-shaped horrors (God knows what) with primitive designs on them, from the mantle-piece.

It's after dinner at the Union, and I must shortly proceed to the Salon, where I hope to meet poet Williams.[2] Maynard thinks it quite probable that I shall fall in love with him. How wonderful that'ld be!

I tried to find the Pinsent & Wardley[3] last night, but they were out. The stagnation is incredible. Norton positively wouldn't have either of them to breakfast this morning.

I've accepted an invitation to the Lamb dinner!   Your
                                                                                                      James

1 Cecil Taylor.
2 Iolo Williams, a King's College poet.
3 David Pinsent and his friend Wardley were possible embryos.

Oh, do you get any papers sent you? Would you like any? Perhaps you take no interest in such things? Or would you like the Nation or Newage [sic] or some such? even the Times?

————

There was such a fuss about the Book last night. However, it was found today at Pozzo's.

RB, [postmarked 28 January 1911], Pension Bellevue,
30 Theresienstrasse, München
to JS, 67 Belsize Park Gardens, Hampstead

It was, of course, careless of me. But – this accursed language! It is so like this coarse nation to insist on having a definite, unmistakable, sign, in those things, flapping, suddenly, a great gaudy banner in your face! Where are the delicate intimacies, the faint and intricate progress, in which one has learnt to find, perhaps, the deliciousest part of life? Can you slide with averted face, humming, into a . . . 'relation', if, somewhere, you have to stop, pull out a bit of chalk, scratch a Line, stand on it on one foot, and blow a fanfare on a Bugle? We Northerners, with our Extra inch of handkerchief showing, our graded stress on pronouns, and atmospheric adverbs, feel a little helpless in such surroundings. . . . . Of course, it's all right now. With half Germany and all Austria between us, I sleep on my back o'nights without a second's uneasiness. But if I go to Bucharest . . .! or when he comes to Cambridge in July . . ! If, indeed, Mr Lang (the Australian sheep-farmer)[1] hadn't been, with the door ajar, at the time, waiting outside my bedroom . . . . ! For, indeed, my dear, if my proposal *had* been intended, would it have done? Could I have 'made anything' of my life, joined to (so kind, and even, so delightful, as he was) the Assistant Professor of Physics at the University of Bucharest? Dr phil. C. Statescn (Calea Mosilov.zog. Bucarest – I have his card) is, after all, only half my height, getting on for forty, and darkly Oriental. Of course, everything, in that remarkable eight days, *had* rather led up to it – our common isolation (in this German-middle-class-hell of a pension), our swift friendship, our conversations, – where so *much* lay unsaid, – in mixed German, Italian, and Attic Greek, our agreement about Ibsen, our common condemnation (did *this* first fire him?) of that nasty little too-much-womanizing Franco-German dancing-master with the movable scalp, opposite, and then, our meeting at the *Café*, our eating (was it? – oh, it *was*! – but I was *mad* that

————

1 In a letter to Noel Olivier, Brooke described the other guests at his pension as consisting of two English ladies, 'a Romanian economist, his brother, Professor of Physics in Bucharest, an Italian count who is a cavalry-colonel, an Australian sheep-farmer, my age, a Franco-German dancing master, and about eight Germans, male & female'. He also says that he is going to Bucharest to stay with the professor (*SOL* 78-9).

night – *too* naughty of me!) with two teaspoons out of one pot of *Yogurt*. So I wasn't really surprised when, dashing in that afternoon (his last) to snatch, with Mr Lang (the Australian sheep-farmer), a quarter-of-an-hour's supper, between an afternoon concert and an early theatre, I found the Professor (God knows how long the poor little creature had squatted there) on my door-mat. I brought him in here. His train left for Vienna at 9. – in two hours. I think perhaps he noticed that Mr Lang (the Australian sheep-farmer – perhaps he had a sheepy standard, or – but Australians are so *odd*) stayed outside in the passage, humming the *Leib-lied*. Anyhow, with that and my vast, ghoulish, quivering, Ibsenite white Stove, towering into the upper dimness of this room, as a background, we said good-bye, grasping hands in the warm, Continental fashion. And, just as we were making final arrangements about Bucharest and Cambridge, and giving the last shake, my German slipped, and – wholly, oh! *wholly*, without wanting to – I whipped out a *Du* ("Kommst Du . . ."),[1] just on the final squeeze. There was, just for a fraction of a second, a dead pause. The Professor, the Stove, and I, were motionless. Even Mr Lang (a nephew of Andrew's) stopped humming. Then I was confusedly conscious of a wrinkled dark nose – down there – a round Slavonic mouth; and an on-the-point-of-grabbing-left-hand, and, concurrently, of myself, hat-on-head, half-way-through the door, screaming "Leben Sie wohl, Herr Professor! Leben Sie wohl! Leben Sie wohl![2] . . . . ," & leaping downstairs, into the street, with an harassed Mr Lang (a second cousin of Francis ("Billy") MacCann's) firmly held by the elbow. The Professor was left alone with the Stove. But whether he raped that, or merely abused himself in my bed, I don't know. I didn't return till 11. And, as far as I can gather, he said nothing at all to his little brother, the Economist, whom he left here, and who sits taciturnly by me at meals, and who abuses himself every lunch-time with a fork, under the table.

I am quiet now. Even Mr Lang (from Victoria) leaves tonight, for Berlin. It is true I am momently expecting Herr Dellephant. But I have a feeling he will be restful. I am hoping you have elected Dennis [Robertson], or Philip,[3] or Fred,[4] or Albert: and begotten M. Pinsent, if not Wardley. And I am sure you have succumbed to Iolo. Mixoscopy is, surely, as old as Heliogabalus, who enlivened so the Drama? München is very pure, the

1 'Are you coming?'
2 'Goodbye, Professor! Live well! Live well!'
3 Probably Philip Baker (later Philip Noel-Baker), a King's undergraduate and member of the Carbonari. Gerald Shove was completely smitten with him and would often show up to watch Baker, a runner, practise for the half-mile. 'Philip' might also be Philip Sargant-Florence, the brother of Strachey's future wife, Alix. He had attended the 1910 Fabian Summer Camp with his sister Alix, then gone to Cambridge.
4 Frederick McMahan Hardiman (1891-1914), of King's, a friend of Maynard Keynes. Hardiman was killed in the war.

Münchener child-like. I see Ibsen every day. They aren't bad at it; though Ella Reutheim, who looked exactly like Miss Stewart (Minnie, *not* Alice.) screamed too much. It seemed so absurd to find Miss Stewart (Minnie, *not* Alice!) running about, and shrieking! She wouldn't, you know. Ramer was made up as Jesus, which seemed a good touch. Rebecca as Lady Strachey (*aet.* 35) – less illuminating.

I see *The Times* every evening in the *Café Bauer*, over my hot milk.

Thanks.

Rupert

RB, [postcard], Sunday [29 January 1911], Café Bauer: with Keats. [Munich] to JS, 67 Belsize Park Gardens, Hampstead

If you've got it *about* – the old copy of The Times that – a week ago – had two columns on *The Rosencavalier*[1] – could you send the columns here, before *Friday*? It doesn't matter much.

I've just been to the Flying Dutchman, an old simple tuneful affair – and full of Mr E.W.[2] of course. Oh Germany! Oh the – but I *can't* tell you.

I suppose you're all much pleased with Hugh's[3] success. Oh – send Lytton's Spanish address. My[?] hot milk – Prosit![4]

Rupert

JS, January 30th, 1911, 67 B.P.G.

You seem to keep things on the move out there. It's all very well to blame the language; – but even in Cambridge, you know, it'ld be thought a little marked for two people to eat the same boiled egg. The poor Professor. I think I'll drop him a line to the Calea Mosilov and exchange condolences.

I returned just now from my ten days in that place, feeling at Liverpool Street rather, perhaps, like your Stove. (Mightn't I, by the way, even *become* it?) Austere, stuffy, disillusioned. The letter made me a lot brighter.

---

1 Strauss's *Der Rosenkavalier* made its debut on 26 January 1911, at the Hofoper Theater in Dresden. The production was directed by Max Reinhardt. It was to open in Munich on 1 February.
2 Brooke may refer to Wagner, the composer of *The Flying Dutchman* (*Der Fliegende Holländer*), though the first initial is wrong.
3 Hugh Russell-Smith had received a research prize in history from Trinity College that enabled him to study in America for a year. The result was his published thesis, *Harrington and his Oceana: A Study of a 17th Century Utopia and its Influence in America* (1914; reprinted 1971).
4 'Cheers!'

The whole thing moved through its inevitable fluctuations, from the moment when I found Norton picking holes in the kinetics of the Ether, to the moment when I left him in his chair gazing at Vanessa upon the sofa opposite, and being tolerant to Clive [Bell], who rather proudly was muttering about exsupplicate and blown surmises. – – My flirtations I fear lacked vigour; but half way through I had an unexpected and entirely unpleasant wet dream, with Jim Butler[1] as its hero. I melted towards Alfred for two days. But he turned out to be more beastly than you could imagine. Mr Perrin was attractive as ever, but very remote, except for a moment when he told me I had a hat just like his. Most awfly touching, wasn't it? With Iolo the case was different. I laid myself out with such care, and produced so many apt quotations from Lionel Johnson[2] and Padraic Colum[3] that there is actually some alarm that he may develop into another George [Mallory] – a George, alas, wearing heavy black spectacles and a shocking bad complexion. He's a great admirer of Charles Sayle – and "Rupert Brooke"'s poems.

Davie Pinsent really didn't seem to me altogether without hope. Character feeble, but "quite nice", and mind perhaps adequate. Even Norton was forced to admit that "none of the obvious objections applied". He came to breakfast with me (& the rest) in [G. H.] Hardy's[4] rooms where I was for the last week. Oh! have you been in them? There's an appalling life size head of the Dear Departed over the mantle piece with an eye that one's for ever catching. The whole suite has the air of a mortuary chapel and I felt sure that the drawers contained endless love letters and relics. I only ventured to open one – and found a pair of poor [R. K.] Gaye's fives-gloves, and an old cricket ball. – – On Saturday Norton read an old paper of his on whether we want to copulate when we're in love, and why we do, and whether it's any help to us. The only amusing thing was Gerald's quite irrelevant recount of how Daddy proposed to him. He came into the room with a great sheaf of papers, apparently, and announced that, as he found his command of language on such occasions ineffectual, he had written out an analysis of his state of mind – which he now proposed to read. So they settled down on each side of the fire, and Daddy went through a regular Carbonari paper, including the quotation from Swinburne and the peroration by Mr [Charles] Masterman. What, I wonder, was his Lordship's reply?

As Sheppard is thought to have the measles, we all went last night to

---

1 James Ramsey Butler (1889–1975), the son of the Master of Trinity. Butler became a historian.
2 A poet of the Rhymer's Club, which also included Yeats and Dowson.
3 Padraic McCormac Colum (1881–1972), dramatist, whose play *Thomas Muskerry* had been presented in June at the Court by the Irish National Theatre Society. The play had impressed Brooke.
4 See Strachey's letter of 19 August 1910, and note (page 129).

Greener's salon for a change. The room was crowded with greyish black persons; and as we entered it poor [Cecil] Taylor (who was of our party) fell into line and vanished with a click, leaving Norton and [Jack] McTaggart and me like incredibly conspicuous rocks of grotesque outlines rising out of the Norfolk Broads. It seems that I was next a Mr Stokoe from Caius and Guernsey, who knew Miss Wilson & the Hampstead set, and had lived previously in the Euston Road, and felt worried about predestination. – – The only other public events were a debate upon Home Rule at the Union, which Mr Stephen Gwynn carried by 40 votes; and the Fifth Symphony conducted by Mr [Thomas] Beecham. (Mr Gwynn turned out to be that quiet man we once found with [Henry] Jackson when we called, d' you remember?)

Gloomiest of all, perhaps, was my immense conversation with Goldie [Dickinson]. The chief fault he had to find with us was our lack of Reticence: "... and apart from its being a joke, Lytton's end[l]ess description of it all as Buggery is a misrepresentation of the facts ..." Oh dear! Shall we ever be like Goldie?

I must go to bed. Breakfast tomorrow at half past eight. Wellington Street at ten ... However, it means January's over, thank God!

I send you my organ, in case you care to see your début before the clergy.   Your

                                                                          James

Oh, did you hear of Mr Towsey and Lady Abdy? He advertised as private secretary, & she gave him an appointment at Eaton Square. She received him in bed, and most elaborately painted; and they talked for several hours, in the course of which she explained how she'd had to divorce Sir William because he would insist upon putting oysters up her cunt and then sucking them out. She asked how much Mr Towsey wanted, and he suggested 340 a year. She was horrified, however, and said: 'My poor boy! you can't possibly live on less than six hundred!' The story goes on rather like that for a long time.

Have you seen the Rosenkavalier? It sounds awfully bright.

JS, February 8th, 1911, Hampstadt

The cameleopard, I understand, hired a boat and a boy, and went for a sail, last Long [Term], on the Broads with Mr Applegate.[1] Herbert, though

1 Strachey appears to be relating a story involving Maynard Keynes ('Leigh, the cameleopard'), Duncan Grant ('Mr. Applegate'), and Francis St George Nelson ('Herbert'), a Cockney youth who was seventeen in 1909 when he began modelling for Grant and first had sex with Keynes. 'St George', as Keynes called him (also, at times, 'Bubbles'), was a pantomime in a travelling theatrical company. In the following years he frequently called upon Keynes for financial assistance.

a member of the lower classes, was just seventeen, at the amiable age when one's on the turn – hoping, a little shyly, for a pair of breasts to put one's hand between, but oh! ready in one's randiness for narrower hips and shorter hair. Well, as it rained so, Leigh said one morning: "Let's go up to London for the night, Herbert, and I'll give you a woman." So that evening they all three found themselves sitting in the brilliantly lighted saloons of the Hôtel de l'Europe. It very soon became clear that Herbert was much attracted by the lady who sat next him sipping her whisky and soda. (Leigh, who understands these things, at once pronounced her nineteen, and a lady, not a prostitute.) After they'd chatted a bit, she leant across to the cassowary and said that she'ld very much like to go to bed with his little friend; "and as for *you*, dear, it's easy enough to see which way *your* tastes lie, you and your other friend" – and she nodded to Mr Applegate. They went on talking of Cambridge, which she knew all about, of course, from her brother at Caius; and, as she couldn't manage that night, they settled to meet again a few nights later . . . . . Next day the three of them returned to their boat.

When the Saturday came round, Leigh and Herbert alone met her in the Soho restaurant for dinner. They drank a good deal, and after it was over Leigh got up and, "theetering" rather meaningly, said he'ld leave them together. But oh no, she insisted, they must all three go to a little hotel she knew of at the back of the Palace Theatre: There was nothing, she explained, that she'ld enjoy more than seeing "you two boys having a bit of fun together". But Leigh was by this time getting nervous, and refused. So, after an argument, she suggested that she and Herbert should go off at once, while Leigh went out and found a boy and came on later . . . He walked along quite vaguely "looking for a boy", and just outside The Corner House saw an attractive enough youth, took him by the arm, and as they walked down Rupert Street explained in his voluble way that they'ld find the other two in a little hotel behind the Palace Theatre, and that he was sorry to say one of the other two was a woman. Poor Leigh's so impetuous! but he *did* look round at last and see that his companion seemed worried. "We're going to lie together, you know." His companion gasped . . . "but . . . but . . I don't understand . . . I didn't know . . . I've never . . . even with a girl . . ." However, Leigh was bound to see it through now: and at length – out of adventurousness? – the stranger consented to go. . .

The waiter received them with comprehension: "Madame is waiting for you in number 23." They went upstairs, knocked, and opened the door. On the bed lay Herbert, quite naked, – except, of course, for Madame's boa and muff. Madame herself, in the middle of the room, wore a pair of stays. "And now," cried she, "off with your clothes!" But once more Leigh was seized with shyness and refused; and the poor little initiate, with his back to the door and fumbling with his bowler, stared with his alarmed eyes, and took of course the cue from Leigh – his only protector in this strange new world . . . She was full of resource: "Well then; go upstairs together first (I've taken number 48 as well) and come down again presently." . . . They reached the other room on the floor above and shut the door. But by this time the stranger was growing excited, so that, when Leigh stood there and threw back his arms, he flung himself into them and covered his face with kisses. After long embraces, they undressed and lay on the bed and embraced again for a long, long time, and copulated, and remained at last in a quiet naked ecstasy . . . Then the door opened in full view of the bed: and there was Herbert in a blanket and the waiter behind him, peering through. "We've been expecting you" said Herbert, while the waiter sympathetically vanished. So they all went down (it was one o'clock by then) quite naked, and she was waiting for them quite naked in Number 23. "Enfin," she exclaimed, '"now, into bed, all of you!" And in they all got, Herbert on the left, with her next to him, then Leigh, and on the right the little unknown. Herbert was upon her again in a moment, and had 'come off' (as St Loe would say) before Leigh had given his young friend more than a preliminary caress. Instantly, she abandoned Herbert and turned to Leigh: "'No, no" she said "stop that! No!" and she raised her voice "you must have *me* now. I mean to cure you" she fairly sang, "of your ridiculous habits. Before the night's out, you shall have learnt to love a cunt." – Poor Leigh was horrified; all his elevation of spirits left him, he was repelled and sickened. "Oh, leave 'im alone" said Herbert, and grasped her shoulder. But she shook herself free, and threw herself upon her reluctant Adonis.

> Even as an empty eagle, sharp by fast,
> Tares with her beak on feathers, flesh and bone,
> Shaking her wings, devouring all in haste,
> Till either gorge be stuff'd or prey be gone;
>   Even so she kiss'd his brow, his cheek, his chin,
>   And where she ends she doth anew begin[1] . .

Oh but she kissed more than that – his buttocks, his balls, my God, his penis, she kissed them, she licked them, she bit them . . . But he lay icy cold, and in the greatest discomfort. Most of all, perhaps, he was annoyed to notice that his mysterious little companion, whom he'd felt sure of for the true cause, was becoming visibly more and more excited, and even at last stretched out a trembling finger and stroked for a moment the flesh above her navel. She paid not the slightest attention to it, but offered herself with even more frenzied caresses to the wretched Leigh. Then, suddenly, she pulled herself up. "Eh bien!" she declared, "I have another card to play;" then to the others: "at him, you two!" and immediately he

---

1 From Shakespeare's *Venus and Adonis* (lines 55-60).

found himself seized by the now unwilling arms of his friends. But she slung them on . . . and he was happy again, and grew warmer, and stirred his legs, and panted a little, and was passionate at last. The six arms wreathed together, the six legs were interlaced, the kisses rained – then, like lightning, he felt them whirled away from him, and her body was close to his instead. Loathing seized him – it took less than a second for his immense and swolled [sic] penis to bend and sink and shrivvle [sic] up into a dry shadow . . . But she was not discouraged. Again and again she flung her legions upon him and brought him to the wildest heights, and then, at the last ecstatic moment, leapt into their place, and was hated . . . Well, there isn't much more. At about four o'clock she managed to whisper in his ear: "I give in . . . but before them . . . my disgrace . . ." and to save her honour he went through a mockery of the necessary movements. Then, after a pause, the unknown youth said he must be getting home to his parents at Ealing; and, after letting him out, Leigh returned to sleep in his upper room. Next day He and Herbert joined Mr Applegate once more upon the Broads.

Did I tell you, by the way, that she was a Mrs Anderson, whose husband (the doctor) has a considerable practise at Brighton?

———————

I'm very sorry about this being so long & dull, after all. But at least it's absolutely true. But so was the story of Mr Towsey who took tea with his friend in a bed-sitter in a Bayswater lodging house. His friend asked him to undress, which Mr Towsey obliging, did. His friend thereupon produced a razor and said that his particular vice was shaving people's bushes.

You can imagine who I've been meeting.

Tomorrow I dine with Jacques & Mr Gill[1] the sculptor. On Friday I go to Cambridge for the Lamb dinner . . . I've got a book by Erica "An account" partly novel, partly play. Strikes me as being a little dotty. Why did you never block that woman and save her?

Good night Rupert. Your
James

RB, Wednesday [15 February 1911], [Hotel] Bellevue, [Munich] to JS, 67 Belsize Park Gardens, Hampstead

What with househunting & poetry &, you know, the odd Mr de Ravelli, – to say nothing of Mr Xenba[2] . . . . But I'll write someday. Munich, you

———————

1 Eric Gill. Brooke thought Matisse's paintings and Gill's sculptures the best things in the Post-Impressionist exhibition, and he purchased some of Gill's work to give as presents to Katherine Cox and Cathleen Nesbitt.
2 Di Ravelli was the Italian count staying in his pension. Mr Xenba may be the 'Franco-German dancing master.'

know, isn't up to your London level: though I suspect the Cameoleopard improved it. He – Leigh – was, I gather, in this house, even this room, up to six weeks ago. So you may imagine what excitement your letter caused in the *pension*. Did I tell you that I wasn't allowed to correct my proofs for the Cambridge Review? Did I tell you that I didn't like the Spectator? – I read the number you sent me very carefully though. The essay on a man we ought to have elected, at Trinity, was funny. Who was he? St Loe has sent me a cheque. Shall I acknowledge it: or merely sign & pay it in? And isn't it typical that the bugger calls me "R. Brooks"?

I'm really writing about the photograph. I tried to compose a letter to M. Bedlam: but I don't even know his address. Nor do I know which of the three you want [here Brooke draws sketches of the three choices]. I expect if you want one, you'd better see all. Daddy's choice *mightn't* be yours.

I have them all . . . . . if you can wait till July? . . If not, give me more information.

I go to continue to seek my studio.[1] Fifth Symphony tonight. Tomorrow [Wagner's] Lohengrin. Friday Debussy. Saturday Schnitzler.[2] Sunday Valkyries. Yesterday The Wild Duck. On Sunday I saw Ghosts for 6d: played as a farce. Mr Wedekind[3] turns out to be a music hall singer: & has coffee at the next table after lunch. No other news.   Rupert

I say, would you go round to 7 Denning Road & stick Charlotte? She keeps writing to me . . . .

JS, Sexagesima Sunday [19 February], 1911

Dear Rupert,

Everyone here, of course, is talking about that tin man, who's just having some more taken out.

I was here last week as well – for the Lamb Dinner, which wasn't very exciting. After Raleigh's speech, which sounded as though it must be full of deep & beautiful thoughts, Gerald & Cecil & I got up & filed out. It was

---

1 Brooke was searching for new lodgings – preferably a studio apartment – near Friedrichstrasse in München-Schwabing so he could be near his new friends, Frau Doktor Ewald (1859–1931) and her son, Paul. Frau Ewald was an artist and proprietor of a Munich pension. Paul, who was Brooke's age, had attended Cambridge's Caius College for a year. Frau Ewald's portrait of Brooke in a broad hat is now well known thanks to postcard reproductions in the National Portrait Gallery. E. J. Dent, who had stayed at the Ewald pension previously, provided Brooke with a letter of introduction.
2 Arthur Schnitzler (1862–1931), the Austrian physician, dramatist and novelist.
3 Frank Wedekind, author of the Brooke favourite, *Frühlings Erwachen* (*The Awakening of Spring*). Brooke wanted to translate Wedekind's work into English and had ended an address on contemporary theatre to the Cambridge Heretics Society with a tribute to Wedekind.

only when we'd reached the door that we noticed that Watty[1] was with us. "Ah!" everyone murmured, "there go the Apostles!"

The state of the Society is simply deplorable. Norton, for instance, ought to have read on the first Saturday – but, as I told you, only produced an old paper. The week after, when I didn't come, he was away from Cambridge, and they had an old thing of Sheppard's. Last week, again he hadn't written, but read us an ancient affair that he'd done years ago for the Sunday Essay & had never read to it. That had to count as his paper! – – But far graver is Gerald's behaviour. He's apparently decided to leave Cambridge the day after tomorrow & not return till his Tripos[2] starts. The excuse is that he can't do any work owing to distractions here, and that it's essential he should get a first so that he may be given a fellowship later on. Meanwhile the Society will be reduced to an ex-ghost and a posthumous abortion.[3] You can imagine that I made a fearful scene last night. Sheppard was even more uncontrolled than me. Even Norton was magisterial & pursed his lips. Pozzo declared that the balance of probabilities wouldn't in his opinion justify Gerald in his departure. The Taylor – I forget. The upshot was that he seems quite unshaken; and I gave notice that next week I should move a vote of censure . . . But I do think it's pretty scandalous, don't you?

The Vice President [Cecil Taylor] read his first paper last night. It was supposed to be stiff (a kind of echo of that conversation we had with Moore – "is pleasure a quality of consciousness?" kind of thing.) But it had come rather unstarched. Altogether the V-P seems likely to rank soon as "one of our failures". His self confidence grows & grows, and he's really *not* the Perfect Man. One of his worst features is that he always has an air of understanding one au fond – with the brisk hollow sympathy of a hospital nurse. Norton jumped fairly severely on his argument – but he's utterly obtuse to doubt himself for a moment.

Other Cambridge news is scanty. I'm here this week end to hang an Exhibition of Simon [Bussy]'s pictures in the "Nate Room" of the Guildhall. They open today for a week & are creating quite a stir. Gwen & Jacques superintended all the arrangements.

I flirt half heartedly with Michael [Sadleir] and Alfred.

The Friday Club dance[4] was quite amusing. We went as pictures by

1 Austin 'Watty' Smyth (d. 1949), Apostle no. 232, librarian in the House of Commons.
2 Gerald Shove did receive a 1st in the Economics Tripos, Part II in 1911.
3 An 'abortion' was the Apostles' term for a rejected prospect ('embryo').
4 The Friday Club was founded by Vanessa Stephen (Bell) in 1905 to discuss fine arts. The club held periodic exhibitions and had a larger membership than Vanessa's famous Thursday Evenings group, which was limited to her closest friends. This particular dance was a benefit for Women's Suffrage hosted by James and Marjorie Strachey in Crosby Hall, Chelsea. James appeared in a costume based on Bakst's design for Nijinsky's slave dance in *Schéhérazade*. David Garnett described Strachey's costume as 'chiefly grease-paint from the hips upward', with Turkish trousers 'cut low enough at the waist to reveal his navel' (*Echo* 207).

Gauguin – viz. Clive & Nessa, Virginia, Adrian & Duncan, Roger Fry, and I. We were incredibly beautiful & very naked with a few brilliant clothes. Mine had a lovely P.I.[1] Rocking horse painted on them by Roger & Duncan. Roger was amazing with his face like that awful creature in the Esprit du Mal. We were very unpopular, because everyone thought we were so damn cleeky.[2] Also, we danced properly & beautifully, – instead of their absurd waltzes and things. I was rather in love with one or two of the young women – and I've discovered that the essential quality of a woman one loves is that she must have two pigtails. – Perhaps that may be because it shows the shape of the head . . . . But the most romantic thing . . Suddenly a young quasi-Jew in invisible eyeglasses and a kilt came up and said "D'you remember me, Strachey?" Of course I didn't. "I'm O'Malley"[3] – and the whole pathetic affair flashed back to me. He was fairly bursting to know whether Rupert Brooke was there . . . but he seemed to have his consolations among the ladies. We had three minutes of brilliant Oxford talk – & agreed (as he's in London coaching for the F[oreign].O[ffice].) to meet.

I shall go to Sheppard's now. Do write & tell me about your admirers or admirees . . .

By the way, wouldn't *you* feel excited if you got a letter from someone asking you to tea and enclosing a pattern or silhouette of his penis cut out of tissue-paper? . . .   Your
                                                                          James

JS, [early March 1911], 67 B.P.G.

Dear Rupert, these marriages are dreadfully unsettling, don't you think?[4] I hope you're not going off secretly with a Grossherzogin?[5]

News is very scrappy at present. I wasn't in Cambridge last Saturday, but I was the week before. Gerald had gone, and there was no paper. The final news is that Norton's going too. He seemed to have a better excuse. His health has collapsed, and he never sleeps for figuring out his p's and

---

1 Presumably, 'Post Impressionist'.
2 Strachey may mean *cheeky* or he may be coining his own combination of *cheeky* and *cliquey*.
3 Sir Owen O'Malley was a contemporary of Brooke's and Strachey's at Hillbrow preparatory school. He enjoyed a career as a British ambassador (to Hungary and several other countries). He is the recipient of the earliest surviving letter written by Brooke.
4 Jacques Raverat and Gwen Darwin had announced their plans to marry in July. Gwen had written to Geoffrey Keynes in February that after the engagement was announced, Katherine Cox had become despondent and thrown herself at Brooke – who told her that he was in love with Noel Olivier.
5 'grand duchess'.

q's. So at the end of this term he's going for at least three months or six for a voyage to the South Seas.[1] The Vice President will therefore meet himself every week in April. – However, I daresay Gerald may be forced back. And I imagine there's a chance of you eventually.

I called on a Trinity fresher called Mr Burnaby (or Budge), who's rather queer in a Trinity way. He admires Turner and MacWhirter,[2] Browning and Beethoven. He's ignorant, ugly, and possibly interested. Not at all the kind of Ganymede one expects to meet a little further along the street.

My brother Oliver returned from India last Friday. He's the divorced one, you recollect, (Eton & Balliol – age 35) of whose second child you are the putative father.[3] He was in England for two years, six years ago; and was very modern then. He went away in my first term, and the last person he heard of (and the first he enquired after) was a brilliant young Austrian Jew, who had declared himself to have been the principal catamite in Vienna. 'Was he in the end elected?'[4] he asked – for Mr H. James was much admired in those days. It all gives one a wonderful sense of mummydom. He stayed in Munich a few days on his way – and I so regret not having sent him to you. You'ld get on awfully well, I expect. He's the very antithesis of Haschisch. Bright and breezy! – Free and easy! And moreover follows your particular predilections with acharnement.[5] But perhaps you sympathetically met a strange eye during you[r] Fanking[6] or whatever you call the dam thing?

On Sunday I took a walk and lunch at the Public Schools Club with Mr O'Malley. (By the way, what's his Xtian name? This is *important* & should be answered by return.) He came out ever so strangely. Indeed, it began better than it ended. You remember we met at the F[riday].C[lub]. Ball? and – tho' praps I wasn't explicit – about a gurl with 2 pigtails? Well, almost the first thing on Sunday he asked if I'd seen the gurl at the Ball who looked exactly like Rupert Brooke. As it happens, I *had* said to myself that she wasn't in the least like 'Rupert Brooke' – so of course I knew at once who it was he meant. But it was really rather funny, for apparently the faithful creature had gone up to her (she was a complete stranger) and said in his cynical Oxford way – for he knew you had no 'female relatives' – Miss Brooke, I believe? She answered that her name was Lynton. "Well, I'll call you Miss Brooke for short." I thought at first that he must be delightfully vague about the Sex Question. But I fear that his feelings

---

1 Norton suffered from manic depression, which led to a complete nervous collapse in 1920. To get away from Cambridge this year, he accompanied Roger Fry and Vanessa and Clive Bell on a trip to Turkey.
2 John MacWhirter (1839–1911), the landscape painter, died on 28 January.
3 Oliver's second child was named Rupert.
4 This may refer to E. P. Goldschmidt, a Fabian from Trinity College who was Jewish and from Vienna. Goldschmidt, though not an Apostle, is mentioned in Brooke's forthcoming letter (7 April 1911).
5 'eagerness'.
6 *Fasching*, Germany's Carnival.

towards *you* are all too pure . . . However, he told me a lot about you. "He's just come through the stage when one sits all alone in a darkened room with a picture by Botticelli; and he's just reached the stage when one hears the World throbbing like a violin-string." He also explained that you were in love with a connection of his called Brynhild Olivier. – How one does pick things up in these days!

Subsequently he turned out to be a particularly filthy kind of Oxford Christian – although even then he was rather funny when he gave an account of the "Darker Cambridge" view of life.

We've been having rather a painful Galsworthy scene this afternoon – a deputation from the London Society of Compositors to ask St Loe to give his printing contract to a Society House. Poor old St Loe quoted Bastiat, and Mr Naylor quoted Webb – all on the friendliest terms, of course.

"Business", a play by Mr John Goldie, comes out on Sunday week.

———————

I went & dined with Jacques last night. I like him very much. But there are somehow difficulties . . I don't know. Last night seemed especially uneasy. Perhaps he was bored at my being gloomy. But I couldn't help feeling jealous.

Do you think, Rupert, I might go and see you for a week-end? At the beginning of April? I've worked it out, and it *is* possible. I'ld get St Loe to let me off a Friday. Then, by starting on Thursday night, I should reach Munich at half past ten on Friday. I should have all Saturday & Sunday there; and start back on Monday morning & get to the Office on Tuesday by ten. Why shouldn't I? It wouldn't cost much more than ten pounds. But I expect you'ld hate it. – It'ld be much better if you came back for Easter. Won't you accept a first return? Then you could see everyone you wanted, and go if you liked to their reading party[1] for a little, and stay for only one night here, perhaps, or not that. – Oh! it's so grey all the time. And I don't recover as they said I would. I suppose it's incurable.

Didn't you think the Doctor's Dilemma wonderfully bright? If only our Bernard [Shaw] could think a little more clearly.

And the Professor of English Literature! What a triumph! but what a scandal!   Yours

                                                                                                  James

Do you know this poem?

As Lord Rosebery[2] said to Lord Crewe[3] the other day: "If poor Peggy's delivery's as slow as yours, she'll have the deuce of a time."

———————

1 The annual Apostles' Easter reading party.
2 Archibald Philip Primrose (1847–1929), fifth Earl of Rosebery, had been Liberal Prime Minister, 1894–5.
3 A minister in Asquith's Cabinet. 'Peggy' is his wife.

RB, [postcard, postmarked 13 March 1911, Munich] to JS, 67 Belsize Park Gardens, Hampstead

I live, see you, at Obenstrasse 3, Gartenhaus I[,] and Bellevue sends letters on fitfully & to the wrong address.

We rhyme *anything* on the chance of 10/6. But *saw* & *for* are gone, to rhyme in future. So are *dawn* and *morn*. You Kelts are going to be shut down. Your *poem* plagues me because I know it well & like it. [Thomas] Traherne? or only Strode? 17th century, anyhow!

April 7th I go to Vienna, till 13th. 14th–17th at Bucharest 18th–20th Constantinople 21st Athens 22nd–30th Dalmatia. 31st–8th Venice. 8th–12th Munich. I reach Cambridge 10 pm May 13th, spend the next week at Rugby. Thenceforward the Vicarage for ever. I shall be here all weekends till April 7th. I'd like to see you. The German objection had better be given up. Frankly, I don't speak a word, all day. But two days is absurd. Why not be ill & take a fortnight – at least a week? The April weekend will give you the first half of [Wagner's] *The Ring*. You'd like Munich. But my life would tire you. I *very* nearly came to England ten days ago. But I shan't now, of course. Mlle. Van Rysselberghe[1] has appeared since then. God! God! I've been so busy writing to these people.[2] It was necessary you know. They were going a bit . . . . But it's all right now. Jacques even, I gather, has blossomed. But I confess I was nervous. In 1917 I will tell you all. I am tired.

Owen St Clair,[3] of course. You didn't think it was C.A.G.?!! I shall certainly have tea with him when I return.

Yours are the only letters that convey any idea of what's happening in England. (I wish, though, I hadn't forgotten who Peggy is.) That is because you have a plain mind. Why don't you write a novel? Mr J. M. Dent is a devil. I detest Gerald. And I am broken about Norton.

Mr Lamb – well I hardly know *how* to explain how he takes Mlle [Elizabeth] Van R[ysselbergh]. You can figure him! I have chucked Bisman Di Ravelli. Leo Dallinger[4] has chucked me. The Ewalds have gone.

---

1 Elizabeth van Rysselbergh (1889/90–1980), the Belgian sculptress. She pursued Brooke for several years, writing him many letters, which Brooke, before dying, instructed Dudley Ward to destroy. After Brooke's death, she claimed to have been his mistress and expressed regret that she had not conceived his child. Years later, in 1923, van Rysselbergh had a daughter by André Gide.
2 Brooke had been writing long letters to Katherine Cox, Jacques Raverat and Geoffrey Keynes.
3 Brooke is responding to Strachey's request for O'Malley's Christian name.
4 Identity unknown, though probably a member of Karl Wolfskehl's social circle, which Brooke adopted while in Munich. Brooke had been introduced to Wolfskehl by the Ewalds. On the first Thursday of each month, Wolfskehl hosted gatherings of young writers, artists and musicians in his Schwabing home. Wolfskehl was part of the inner circle of the George Kreis, the group of devotees to the poet Stefan George

Fraulein Runge[1] goes on Wednesday. And I have finished my Yogurt.

[Written across right side of card: 'Please send Henry Lamb's address.']

RB, [28 March 1911], 3 Oben strasse [sic]
to JS, 67 Belsize Park Gardens, Hampstead

Your Parisian card has arrived. I expect my yesterday's card will have explained all. But perhaps it got rubbed out on the way. It seemed rather poorly when it left me.

I *shall* meet you. If I don't, you get a porter, called Träger (I believe) & give him your documents. He vanishes & you meet him and all your luggage again in the Soul-revision.[2] There you say "Nients!" determinedly. They let you go. You say to the porter "Owtô!"' and he puts you in a machine. You ask the porter, who has a fixed tariff, "Vefeel?" & give him what he tells you. The *owto* is told "Dry Oben schtrâsse."

The Gartenhaus, you see, is behind & separate. Press the bell for Gartenhaus, 1st storey, right. Nothing will happen, & you will sit on the step till I come.

My flat is kept by Fraulein Grübel. I daresay Jacques lied. There's nothing in the stories except Human Interest. The later ones are much better: & even less happens. Ammoniated Quinine is working wonders. But my life is in tatters. (I hope you will bring *plenty* of handkerchiefs; I've run short.).

My editions of the Bible & other works by Sir Arthur Q.[3] are good. "Let him [caress][4] me with the [caresses] of his [hand]: for thy [affection] is better than [lemonade.] or Shakespeare would come out well –

"Nay but to live

in the [perspiration] of an enseamed [room] [Hot] [with] [emotion], honeying and [flirting] over the [unpleasant place] . .

Dull! Dull! dull!

Thine – , too-sunken Rupert

known (as is George's poetry) for its adulation of blond, attractive young men. Brooke recited Swinburne to the group on one occasion. For an account of the Wolfskehl gatherings, see *RBB* 252–3.

1 Iris Runge, a friend of the Ewalds who played the lute and sang French and German folksongs.

2 *Zollrevision* – that is, 'custom's examination'. Brooke continues giving phonetic spellings of German words in this paragraph. 'Nients' (that is, *Nichts*) means 'nothing' (as in 'nothing to declare'), 'Owtô' is *Auto*, 'Vefeel' (*Wieviel*) means 'How much?' and 'Dry Oben schtrâsse' (i.e., *drei Obenstrasse*) is the address: 3 Obenstrasse.

3 Arthur Quiller-Couch (1863–1944), the English author and editor of the *Oxford Book of English Verse*.

4 These brackets – and those that follow in this letter – are, of course, Brooke's.

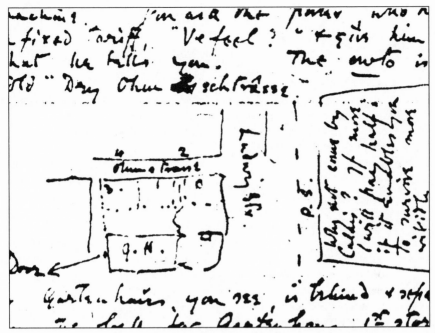

Brooke's post card of 28 March 1911 with map providing directions
to his rooms in Munich.

P.S.

Why not come by Calais? If more I will pay half if it enables you to
survive more vividly. R.

I suppose the April *English Review* won't be out?

RB, Friday [7 April 1911], The Old Place [Munich]
to JS, 67 Belsize Park Gardens, Hampstead

James dear,

The world moves very rapidly and I'd like to prosecute my academic
enquiries. It's so difficult, here. You tell me the syringe (sirynge?) is best.
What I want to know is the exact name of the *stuff*. One's at such a
disadvantage in dealing with a foreign chemist. And I don't want to poison
anybody; least of all myself. In fact I want further information than one
can get even from German textbooks – when one doesn't know the
language. Perhaps Daddy's Block helps? "Any chemist", I'm told, does. But
if one could breathe the German – or Italian – name, it might save a scene
that'd be very painful to a Gentleman . . .

In fact, if you could just forward any information you can heap
together, – or even a neat little package . . . – you might save a ball or two
for the nation, at the risk of preventing a future Brother –

I go tomorrow for a week to E.Ph. (!) Goldschmidt[1]
IV Heugasse 12
Wien –

from there I'll send future addresses which'll be vague . . There's no great
hurry – a fortnight about. But earlier would oblige. Don't write to Wien
after I leave. Ernest will open my letters.

– Oh, of course I shall consult him about it all – but he's not very
trustworthy . . . 40.80 to hand, with thanks. Is it right?

in a hurry & with oh!
a stomach ache
Rupert

*JS, Monday April 10th 1911, Hampstead
to RB, bei Herrn E. Ph. Goldschmidt,
IV Heugasse, 12, Wien, Austria*

Dear Rupert. Very well, I now know every detail of the whole sordid
business. Here is the gist of it.

Preventives are of three kinds: (1) letters, (2) pessaries, (3) syringes.

(1) Letters are condemned on all accounts; for (a) you get hardly any
pleasure out of them and (b) they are most likely to get torn in the
excitement of the moment and are consequently dangerous. (I may perhaps say here that all this information comes from my brother Oliver,
who is an adept, and who thinks that I'm on the brink of fucking Dieu
sait qui).

(2) Pessaries are unpleasant things. A picture of one is to be found on
the enclosed sheet – with the title of Rendle's Wife's Friend, obtainable at
all chemists in cardboard boxes as shown. It's made of quinine and oil –
and you shove it up the lady's cunt before you start. One result of this is
that after a little it makes a filthy soapy mess that comes out over
everything. In general it's efficient.

(3) Two pictures are to be found enclosed of two sorts of syringe. The
article is known as an 'enema', and has two alternative attachments
according as it's used to make you forth (anal enema) or to clean out the
lady's inside (vaginal enema). If you buy one at a chemists', it's generally
provided with both – or you can ask specially. The syringe itself can be
(as I said) of two kinds. The ordinary one is just a tube with a kind of
swelling in the middle. You put the attachment at one end and dip the

1   Ernst P. Goldschmidt had invited Brooke to stay with him at his residence in Vienna.
    In a letter to Mrs Brooke, Rupert referred to Goldschmidt as 'a very rich and clever
    Jew'.

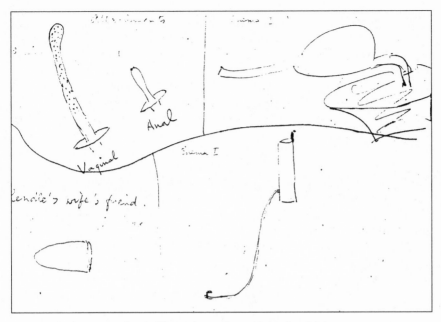

Strachey's illustrations of contraceptive devices.

other into whatever liquid you want to inject, and then squeeze the swelling in the middle of the tube. The more recommended kind is a glass (or metal) cylinder with a hole in its bottom out which the tube leads, and ends in a kind of tap (before reaching the attachment). You hang the cylinder – with the liquid – on a nail in the wall, and all you have to do is to turn the tap at the bottom of the tube, and the liquid rushes out. The enema is far the most popular instrument – and is generally effective. But it is essential to use it immediately after you've emitted. You can't just lie in bed for half an hour or so before using it. With regard to the liquid used, any doctor will give you a prescription. (Oliver unfortunately hasn't one with him at present.) The principal ingredient is quinine, which is fatal to spermatozoa. It's also *most* important that *cold* water should be used. It's unpleasant, but *far* more effective.

General Notes. The chief thing is that *no* method is certain. If you're careful, you *probably* succeed – but you must always be prepared for a failure.

Whatever else you use, you always have to clean things out with a syringe – unless you particularly want a child – if only for the sake of cleanliness. And one can merely repeat – do the washing thoroughly, thoroughly! Quinine will kill anything it touches – so make sure it touches everything!

It's important to choose the right date – as nearly as possible half way between the "monthlies". If you do it just before a "monthly" you're most likely to have a baby. To do it *during* a "monthly" is too *incredibly* disgusting.

. . . "My dear boy", he wound up, "I recommend you to content yourself, if you're dealing with a girl, with "playing about" with her – you can get plenty of pleasure that way. But if you *must* block someone, my final advice to you is – let it be a married woman."

———————

Surely, Rupert, you can't want any more about this? Would you like me to send you an enema? or a box of Mrs Rendle's friends? – Oh, but isn't it all too incredibly filthy? Won't it perhaps make you sick of it? – Come quietly to bed with me instead . . . .

I wonder if you'll see the Bell group in Constantinople. They *ought* to have been in that train. But Vanessa fainted at the last moment, so they went three days later.[1]

Do write & give me an address in any case. I like to know vaguely where you are.

Lytton & Oliver have taken rooms in Cambridge for the May term – over the late Mr Stroud, next door to Queen Bays – Mr Morrison's rooms in fact.   Yours
                                                              James

I forget to remind you of Henry [Lamb]'s method – withdrawal before emission. But *that* requires an iron nerve – and if it fails –

RB, [postcard, postmarked 21April 1911], München (the last night) to JS, 67 Belsize Park Gardens, Hampstead

Many thanks. I don't admire your attitude. Cheer up, though: Elizabeth [van Rysselbergh] rather agreed with you, & has funked it. (She's sorry now.) . . All my plans shattered by – did I tell you? – poor old Bob Whitelaw,[2] after whom – in Florence – I have to look. So everything's *too* flat. Ernst (or Ernest) was charming as ever. He has given a bit, in mind, however. Plays picquet in a Jew's café all day . . Told me an awfly jolly tale about [illegible] Brown. I saw Mr Schnitzler's

1 Vanessa Bell was pregnant. She had a miscarriage in Turkey.
2 Rupert's godfather, Robert Whitelaw, a housemaster at Rugby, had recently lost his wife of forty-two years. Alfred Brooke had accompanied him to Italy and left him there in good health, but Whitelaw soon became ill; thus, Rupert was summoned to Florence to accompany Whitelaw back to England.

latest,[1] in 18 acts. And Richard III. Good God! I was very ill though. Now, only remains dinner with Gordon Craig[2] in that cellar; and Bob. Well, well!

One day I shall telegraph a list of theatres & dates. That will mean please secure seats (not dress) – or, if you're engaged, *one* seat for me. This is in view of Pavlov etc, or the Russian ballet. But don't let on to anybody when I'm coming.

I am a wreck. I can only echo Norton's advice to you, my dear fellow, & subscribe myself.   ever R.

I go to Hotel Berchielli, Lung' Arno

JS, Monday [24 April 1911], Belsize

As far as *that* goes, my sympathies are entirely with *you* & not the least with Elizabeth or myself. I never *could* understand the damn sentimental view of copulation . . . .

This is to make you acquainted with our Creator's last little joke. Lytton has got the mumps. He came out with them (or it) on Bloody Friday in that beastly little Greyhound [Inn] at Corfe – to which he & Gerald and I had gone for our post apostolic reading party. The situation was dreadful . . . but I won't linger on it. The beauty of the disease is that it takes between a fortnight and a month to 'incubate', after which infection lasts for six weeks. On the other hand one's not infectious till it actually comes out. It seems fairly certain, then, that (as I was with him the whole time) I shall be seized. It may come on any day from next Friday (April 28th) to the following Monday fortnight (May 15th). Funny, isn't it?

The only thing I'm interested in is whether you'll be back in time. I expect the dear Lord has booked me for the day before. Only think of the battle going on inside, too. And again, his Lordship [Gerald Shove] with the glanders! What a sight *that*'ll be!

One of the brighter features of the disease is that it attacks the balls as well, and often does for them finally.

Dudley & Jacques do nothing but laugh at it, damn them.

---

1 *Der junge Medardus, dramatische Historie in einem Vorspiel und fünf Aufzügen,* which Brooke called a 'Hebrew journalist's version of *The Dynasts;* but rather good' (letter to Edward Marsh, 25 April 1911).
2 Edward Henry Gordon Craig (1872–1966) – the artist, writer and stage designer – lived 1907–14 in Florence, where he began his theatre magazine, the *Mask.* Craig was the son of the actress Ellen Terry and architect E. W. Godwin. His book *The Art of the Theatre* had been translated into German in 1905 and was influential in the move towards Expressionism. Brooke reviewed another of his books, *Towards a New Theatre,* in the *Nation* (20 September 1913, p. 920).

Why couldn't I have had mumps and everything else between January 9th and March 31st?

I've been in Cambridge for the week-end. Mere stagnation – except for our brother Taylor's accounts of the Sistine Chapel and Maynard's dissertations upon Sicily and its Urnings[1] (or earnings, as Hawtrey would say). Oliver has proposed to Ray,[2] and converted Gerald to Hetero-sexualismus. We have decided to elect the Ladies.[3]

Have you received the manifesto of National Liberal Club Forward Movement?

I went to the first performance of Fanny's First Play.[4] Ashley [Dukes] thought it deplorable. Bill Foss wondered what had become of Shaw's Intellect. Iolo [Williams] was delighted. With whom would you agree?

I see the Spectator's brought out your review at last. That'll be three pounds.

I hope your parting with Elizabeth wasn't too painful.

And that you'll appear soon.

Your
James

1 Homosexuals.
2 Rachel Costelloe, who became Oliver Strachey's second wife. It was Costelloe who introduced Katherine Cox to Virginia Stephen.
3 Gordon Hannington Luce (1889–1979) and Ferenc Békássy were elected Apostles in January 1912 at the request of Maynard Keynes, who had an affair with Luce the following summer. Luce later taught in Burma at the University of Rangoon. His *Poems* was published in 1923 by the Woolfs, with Duncan Grant providing artwork.

The son of a Hungarian aristocrat, Ferenc Istvean Denes Gyula Békássy (1893–1915) was educated at Bedales – where he fell in love with Noel Olivier – and King's College, Cambridge. Delany says that following his arrival 'at King's in October 1911 he soon got into the swim of homosexual Cambridge' and that 'he at once caught Maynard's eye. Even with such a patron, he must have had unusual charm to be elected an Apostle only three months after his arrival' (142). He was only eighteen when elected.

Békássy and Brooke did not always get along. When Békássy showed a renewed interest in Noel Olivier at a time when Brooke himself was courting her, Brooke returned without comment some poems Békássy had given him to read. Delany says, 'Rupert's real problem with Békássy, one would guess, was that the younger man's game was too close to his own. Békássy was a disconcertingly fluent bisexual [...] and himself loved a kind of *doppelgänger* for Rupert named Frank Bliss' (142). Bliss was elected an Apostle the following November. Though Bliss and Békássy were best friends and probably lovers, they were killed fighting for opposing sides during the war. Maynard Keynes raised the money for Békássy to return to his native Hungary to fight for England's enemy. He was killed in the Bukovina on 25 June 1915, at the age of twenty-two. His name appears in King's College Chapel on the pillar of the war dead, but it is on the opposite side of the English soldiers, alone. The Hogarth Press published a book of Békássy's poems, *Adriatica*, posthumously.
4 The Shaw play was being staged at the Little Theatre. Shaw's name, however, did not appear on the programme.

RB, *[picture postcard of Andrea del Sarto's S. Giovanni Battista*
from the Pitti Gallery in Florence,
postmarked 27 April 1911, Firenze]
to JS, 67 Belsize Park Gardens, Hampstead

Just a Levelezö-Lap[1] to let you know we're enjoying ourselves. The first of May, of course, is the Day I shall reach (don't breathe a word of it!) England.

Who should we meet but Jeremy Hardwich, and, later, Geoffrey Scott![2]
Excuseia Dopisnice.[3]   R

RB, *Thursday again [27April 1911], Pension Erica [Florence]*
to JS, 67 Belsize Park Gardens, Hampstead

I went to the [Hotel] Berchielli and found your letter. Thought I must just write and tell you about *Mumps*. I had them when I was 16. Of course it's infinitely worse at 23. As for Lytton . . . . . It's not so much the pain, – though that's incredible, – as the Disgrace, – and the madness. After a few days, when your month's set, – They begin. At first they just swell and swell and swell, till they're tight and shiny and cracking, two monstrous red balloons. Then, all of a sudden, they go hard, – hard as a rock. You lie and stare at the mountain under the bed-clothes, and pretend it's your knees. The doctor strips you and eyes them till you have an erection, and then thinks you're a bad lot. You cannot pumpship[4] and your semen turns green. And night and day the thought and torment of these vast twin scarlet bleeding pineapples is with you. It lasts for months. I suppose the fatal cases are when they grow too far and explode.

I suppose you'll be able to convalesce at Grantchester.

———

With Iolo.
But is it certainly Mr Shaw's?
Oliver sounds a fine fellow.
The parting with Elizabeth was most painful. I felt an awful snake.

1 'Postcard' in Hungarian. The word *postcard* is written in seven languages on the back of the card.
2 Scott (1883–1929) was an Oxford undergraduate who had accompanied Maynard Keynes to Tuscany in 1906. Keynes had written to Lytton Strachey: 'Scott is dreadfully Oxford [...] Even in his sodomy, which he takes more solidly than anything else, he seems to want to worship an idealised vision in which he has clothed some good-looking absurdity rather than come to close quarters' (2 April 1906). Scott is the author of *The Architecture of Humanism* and *Zélide*.
3 The meaning appears to be 'excuse the postcard' (referring to the semi-nudity in the Del Sarto painting). *Dopisnice* means 'postcard' in Slovenian.
4 Brooke and Strachey use the term 'pumpship' to mean both masturbation and the semen ejaculated during masturbation.

Especially when she said she would kill herself, and I felt frightened of the police. She's quite come round, and apologized for her telegram; and, it appears, we're to have a week at Marseilles in August. I am very bitter with myself, and frightened of England. Of the scene when the maid-servant suddenly brought two students to see the room, and found her with her hair down, weeping, at full length, on that *plateau* of a sofa, and me in great pain on one leg in the middle of the room, saying "Yes . . . . yes . . . . yes . . . .", very wildly, in a tone that distractedly wished to be Wedd's[1] but was, I fear, only Daddy's – of that I will tell you later. But, anyhow, do assure me that one *ought* to tell the truth: and that it's not honest to want to be raped.[2]

On Monday. Leave a note at the N.L.C. with the address of your sanatorium. *If* you're still whole, I'll see you, Monday or Tuesday – – –

desperately

Rupert

JB, Wednesday night, [17] May 1911

Oliver and Ray suddenly arrived here from Oxford just now; and their engagement is announced – how publicly I don't know. I can't help feeling a little withered about it. Oh who is Oliver that he should be on such terms with St Peter? And does it seem to you credible that two people should fall in love with one another? Dear me! I asked *him* that just five minutes ago, and he most sleekly replied that it seemed to him the natural thing to expect. And now here I am sitting alone while they're together upstairs – in Lytton's bedroom, I fancy.

I want to know if I'm to go to Cambridge on Saturday.[3] I've looked up the trains, & find it's just possible – if I travel in my topper – to arrive by ten. I'm rather black at present, and can't quite see why I should go, but I

---

1 Nathaniel Wedd, Apostle no. 215 (elected 1888), a classics teacher at King's and co-founder of the *Independent Review*. Known as a radical atheist, Wedd was instrumental in encouraging Forster to write.

2 Van Rysselbergh later visited London in the hope of seeing Brooke again. While telling Elizabeth he wanted to see her, Brooke, pleading fatigue and confusion, appeared to do everything he could to keep it from happening. She eventually left England without seeing him. They met again several years later (for lunch, according to Brooke's biographers), after Brooke returned from his trip to America and the Pacific. Van Rysselbergh was then living in England while studying at the Royal Horticultural College.

3 For a meeting of the Apostles. Lytton Strachey read a paper that reflected his changing political views. Brooke, by converting James to Fabian socialism, had influenced Lytton. According to Holroyd, 'Under the influence of his brother James he [Lytton] had, since leaving Cambridge, grown more interested in politics, and was in the gradual process of rejecting his vague, high-bred Conservatism in favour of a more combative, left-wing position, mildly socialistic and violently anti upper-class' (*Achievement* 17).

1. The Brooke family on the steps of School Field, c. 1901. Rupert is in the front row, second from left, between his brothers Richard and Alfred. Their mother is in the second row, far left and their father is in the back row, second from left.

2. The Strachey children, c. 1893, from left: Marjorie, Dorothea, Lytton, Joan Pernel, Oliver, Richard, Ralph, Philippa, Elinor and James.

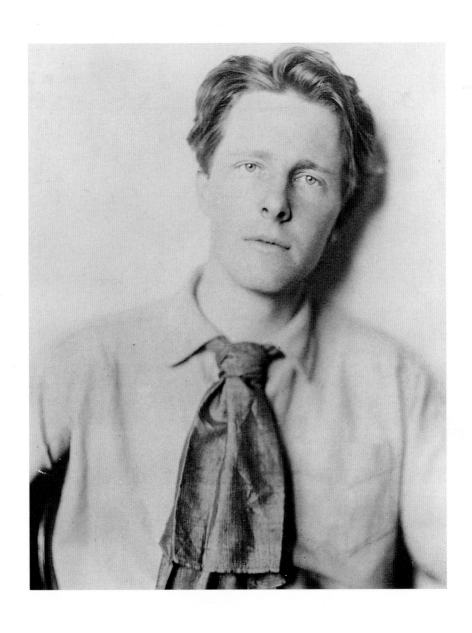

4. Duncan Grant's 1910 painting of Strachey.

facing page
3. Brooke in one of Sherril Schell's 1913 studio photographs.

5. Hillbrow School, c. 1901. Alfred Brooke is in the second row, far right; Strachey is in the third row, sixth from right; Rupert is in the fourth row, second from right.

6. Brooke in 1903, aged seventeen.

7. Denham Russell-Smith from 1906 Rugby School photograph.

8. Brooke with the Russell-Smith family at Brockenhurst Station, c. 1904. Denham Russell-Smith and Brooke are on the far left. Also present are, from left: Denham's cousin Christine Goodman, his sister Elsie and brothers Alan and Hugh, his mother, Ellen, and uncle, Frank.

9. Parker Brooke's house at Rugby, 1906. Charles Lascelles is (most probably) in the second row, second from left. To the right of him are, left to right, Denis Browne, Brooke and his father, Geoffrey Keynes and Hugh Russell-Smith. Denham Russell-Smith is in the back row, second from right.

10. Rugby School summer camp, 1906.

11. Brooke reading *Doctor Faustus* to Dudley Ward and Jacques Raverat at Grantchester.

12. A picnic during May week, 1908 with, left to right, Frances Darwin, Francis Cornford, Eva Speilman, Margery Olivier and Brooke.

13. Margery Olivier (far left), Justin Brooke, Geoffrey Keynes and Dudley Ward (last three on far right) watch Donald Robertson wrestle with Brooke (in foreground) at a picnic between Baitsbite and Clayhithe, 23 May 1909.

14. Brooke on a skiing holiday at Lenzerheide, Switzerland, December 1909.

15. Brooke, Bryn Olivier, A. Y. Campbell, Jacques Raverat and Geoffrey Keynes at a breakfast party.

16. Brooke, Evelyn Radford, Margery Olivier, Dudley Ward and Noel Olivier outside Mrs Primmer's cottage, Bank, Lyndhurst, April 1909.

17. Buckler's Hard, Beaulieu, August 1910 with, left to right, Dudley Ward, Katherine Cox, Ethel Pye, unidentified man and Brooke.

18. Estrid Linder's photograph of Brooke working on their translations of Swedish playwright Gustave Collijn in the Old Vicarage garden, Grantchester, 1911.

Three views of Brooke with friends at Clifford Bridge, Devon:

(*above*) 19. In 1908 with, from left, Noel Olivier, Maitland Radford and Virginia Woolf.
(*right*) 20. With Noel Olivier, August 1911.
(*below*) 21. With Gerald Shove, August 1911.

22. George Mallory.

23. Geoffrey Keynes.

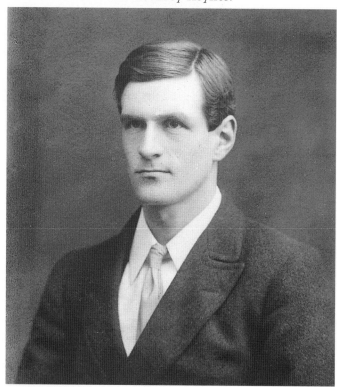

24. Katherine Cox.

25. Cathleen Nesbitt.

26. Alix and Lytton Strachey.

27. St Loe Strachey.

28. Taata Mata (far left) and Brooke (second from right) in Tahiti, 1914.

29. Brooke, unwell, on a cot at Port Said, Egypt, 2 April 1915.

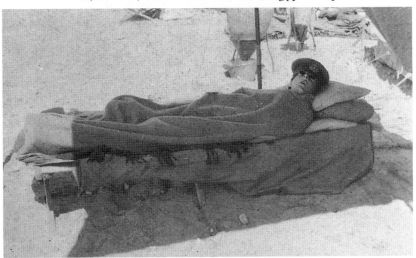

30. The original marker for Brooke's grave at Mesadhi on Skyros.

31. Detail of the Brooke memorial statue in Rugby.

think I want to. Will you send me a post-card to say what *you* think? I suppose it's monstrous to ask that.

You can't imagine how sordid the Office seemed on Tuesday morning after nearly three week's being away.

Will you kindly speak to Mr A[rnold]. Bennett about the stuff he writes in the New Age on the Copyright bill? "The consequences of pillage cannot be ultimately beneficial to anybody." – It might be Lord Cromer on the Budget.

I dined with Dudley tonight & we went on to see Ka afterwards – but only found her dull sister.[1]

What must it be like to walk down the Strand, knowing that your beloved's photo is being sold for a halfpenny by every newspaper man?[2]

It would be awfully nice if you wrote.

James

> "From twelve to two
> I've plenty to do
> Helping Lord Roberts the troops to review."

RB, [18 May 1911], King's College, Cambridge to JS, 67 Belsize Park Gardens, Hampstead

I'll tell you on Wednesday what it's like to "walk down the Strand, knowing that your beloved's photo . . . . . newspaper man." After all, eleventh out of seventeen, gives one some *data, nicht wahr?*[3]

I don't know what to do about Oliver. I think I shall write to Elizabeth.

As for Saturday: I think it's a good thing to be at meetings, if one's an active brother. Me, I'm busyish over the week-end: settling (in three 5 hour interviews) the souls of (a) Justin[4] (Sunday 12-5) (b) Mr Allen[5]

---

1 Hester Cox, Katherine's elder sister.
2 Strachey refers to Dudley Ward's romance with the dancer Clothilde von der Planitz, who was to appear at the Comedy Theatre. Dudley eventually married not her, but her sister Annemarie.
3 'Is it not true?'
4 Justin Brooke (1885–1963) went to Bedales and Emmanuel College, Cambridge. His circle of friends at Cambridge included Brooke and many of Brooke's friends, though he was known among them for his remarks that he had never been sorry to bid anyone goodbye, and that he had no idea what friendship was. He gradually lost touch with most of them after marrying in 1917.
5 Clifford Allen (1889–1939) was a student politician in the Fabians while Brooke presided over the Cambridge branch. He had attended the Fabian Summer School with Brooke. In 1911 Allen was appointed general manager of the *Daily Citizen*, the first official Labour daily newspaper. He was also chairman of the University Socialist Federation, 1912–15, during which period he led the resistance to conscription and was imprisoned several times. Allen suffered a complete breakdown in 1938, dying a year later.

(Sunday 5.15–10.15) (c) Ka Saturday 3–8. And on Monday, for a bit, my own. But I shall be in to some of the breakfast on Sunday: & perhaps about o' Monday.

Just finished Clay hanger:[1] Did you notice the adverbs?

Oh!

Rupert

RB, [24 May 1911 – the date appears on the letter written in pencil, probably by Lytton], The Old Vicarage to Lytton Strachey

Did you hear what he – Mr Luce – said about the expression on the faces of men pumpshipping?

I promised to go to Gwen's[2] to supper on Sunday: to meet M. Raverat and Virginia [Stephen]. You're going to be asked. Couldn't you come there and have Mr Luce another day? It'd fit so much better. I want to meet him in your presence. I found Cecil [Taylor] didn't draw him out. If he could be changed to any time except Monday & Tuesday nights . . . . .

But tomorrow (or Friday) no doubt I'll learn. Tomorrow, I gather, you'ld find a friend or two extra here, Bertie [Bertrand Russell] (on Jacques' invitation) and, I'm sorry to say, Olwen. Friday nobody that I know of, except me, & Jacques, & the Colonel [Walter Lamb]. But I hope you've made it up with Olwen –

Oliver [Strachey] & Karin [Costelloe] to tea today.   yours R

JS, Wednesday night [24 May 1911], 67 Belsize Park Gardens

"Beenham", writes Mr Jukes, "will amuse you . . ." I wonder . . But whether "Beenham"'s the place, or merely poor old Charlie Charring-ton's[3] knicker, I'm unaware.

I had such a dreadful party last night – dinner at St Loe's & the Follies.[4] I wish the circles I moved in were slightly less bourgeois. And it was something of a nightmare going through that whole performance again – sitting between an admiral's daughter and a Gold Stick. We came in at almost exactly the same moment – "if it had been a bit worse we couldn't have drunk it and if it had been a bit better we shouldn't have got it . . ." oh, the dim dim jokes.

1 *Clayhanger*, Arnold Bennett's 1910 *Bildungsroman*.
2 Gwen Darwin and Jacques Raverat were to be married on 27 May.
3 An actor and friend of the Stracheys, Charles Charrington Martin (d. 1926) produced the 1909 London version of Ibsen's *The Master Builder*.
4 'The Follies' began its run at the Apollo in August 1910 and continued for 506
   performances.

This afternoon there was a slight relief – a visit to the Zoo with Virginia [Stephen] and Desmond [MacCarthy]. Desmond, in a topper and his queer cutaway coat, became incredibly interested by an Aye-aye – a very small animal halfway between a monkey and a bat, with immense eyes and a very vague face. And Virginia fairly gloated over the usual seal with an erection.

The only other thing has been a visit to Mr Clarkson's to be measured for the Shakespeare Ball. Did you hear I was to go in Mrs Strachey's Quadrille Party? St Loe, of course, will be Othello, and the Registrar General Cassio.[1] Iago will be Dan Macmillan,[2] for whom, at Eton, poor Maynard had so pure a love. The great question is "Cod pieces?"

It's all rather tiresome; but perhaps Beenham'll be mo' [?] amusing.

Do send me an account of your Clothilde [von der Planitz] party. I gather Virginia's to be there.

I suppose you're not coming to The Cherry Orchard by Tchekov[3] on Monday afternoon? or the 4th Symphony conducted by [Arthur] Nikish on Monday evening.   Your
James

Dent rather painfully had me in that evening. That worm Purves[4] was there.

JS, Monday night ['May?' is written in pencil at top. The date is probably 29 May 1911], 67 Belsize Park Gardens

Beenham was purely Scandinavian. Dinner last night, for instance, was at a quarter past eleven – out of doors, in hats & coats, to the light of a couple of chinese lanterns. Janet & Charles [Charrington Martin] are quite nice & very domestic – but lord! the lack of mentality. Ashley, though, is a good deal stupider than the others. The arguments that drifted on all the time between him & Ben [Keeling] & "Charrington" were most trying.

1 John Neville Keynes, the father of Maynard and Geoffrey, had just been elected University Registrar at Cambridge.
2 Daniel Macmillan (1886–1964) was the elder brother of the future Prime Minister, Harold Macmillan. Daniel attended Balliol College and eventually became chairman of the Macmillan publishing house.
3 At the Aldwych. The play was translated into English by Constance Garnett, mother of David Garnett. It is not clear what Brooke thought of Chekhov at the time, but when he reviewed the *Plays of Anton Tchekoff* two years later, he wrote that the playwright was a pathetic child and that 'Tchekoff's world is one of tired children, who hurt each other, but not very much, because they're not very strong' (*Cambridge Magazine*, 26 April 1913; quoted in Rogers, *Brooke* 134–5).
4 Chester Purves (1890–1960) was a King's undergraduate who had a brief affair with Maynard Keynes in the spring of 1912. In later life he worked with the League of Nations, the World Health Organization and UNESCO.

Why *should* dear good people argue? However, after dinner yesterday, *I* began – & succeeded in fairly embittering everybody before bedtime at three. It began about ethics & insensibly verged towards vivisection – always a nervy subject. I incline to believe that Nora[1] intends to stab me for it. Beautiful white Nora!

Hope you've been having a bright week end?

The only news here is that the Coronation will have to be postponed, as Mary's confinement is due for June 20th. Rather too unthoughtful of them last September, what? But George of course, like an honourable Englishman, objects to your douche.

My professional duties will be overwhelming this week. Johnny Atkins will be away, & I shall have to write a leader & subleader. So I shan't have time for a paper, I fear. I'll bring some subjects on Saturday, & write for the week after.

My London phase is drawing to a close. If someone 'ld promise me 200 a year or even 150, I'ld leave for Vienna tomorrow – or the Isle of Purbeck.

The part of my soul that marked all those names in the Union Rules has just finished doing a jigsaw of a thousand pieces. I also abused myself after tea. Mon dieu! Jigsaws & self abuse! Could one imagine anything more horrible? But that's what life's come to – oh, well – amongst other things, perhaps.   Your James

JS, The First of June 1911, The Spectator

You are a rat.

D'you think I'ld have gone all that way if I'd known you were *here*? Don't tell anyone, though. And I did enjoy it awfully. There was a most horrible scene when Maynard buggered poor Justin [Brooke] on the lawn, in the middle of a silent and rather embarrassed crowd of neo-pagans. Pozzo's behaviour was considered mauvais ton. As for me, I was very much in love with Daphne [Olivier] – and she *was* brutal to me.

Lytton's never in his life had such a happy evening.

We went into King's afterwards & visited old Sheppard, who was most frightfully mashed by my legs.[2]

I've just finished my First Leader.

I'll try to write a paper for Saturday & I'm going up tomorrow.

Your
James

I do think Jacques is superb, don't you? Nicer than almost anyone.

1 Nora Darwin, later Nora Barlow, whom Leonard Woolf called 'repulsive beyond belief' (L. Woolf, *Letters* 166).
2 Probably Duncan Grant's portrait of the sprawling Strachey. Brooke referred to it in a letter to Edward Marsh as 'the famous picture of James's legs' (10 December 1909).

JS, Thursday evening at the Office [8 June 1911]

Such a *wonderful* pamphlet has just arrived. It's [sic] title is: –
                           PRIVATE KNOWLEDGE
                                FOR BOYS.
It begins like this: –

                            CHAPTER I.
                            ———

'Self-reverence, self-knowledge, self-control – These three alone lead life
to sovereign power.'

                            ———

You have, I am sure, noticed that, just where your legs join your body,
there is a little bag or purse . . .

_____

But it's full of the most hideous lies. I think of reviewing it for the New
Age. We publish one of our brighter leaders this week called The Adult
Review – the attack that we've so long been expecting upon poor old
Thusten Harrison & Sir A. Mond.[1] I do *hope* they'll bring an action.

Everyone's talking of a dissolution in July.

I saw poor old Clot[h]ilde dance last night & then went on to the
Alhambra, where the contrast was amazing. They have the most efficient
woman I've yet seen – astounding technique – but My God, fifty! &
incredibly hideous. Also a man rather like Donald Robertson[2] in old age
with a hundred chins.   Your
                                                                    James

JS, Friday [16? June 1911]

Will you stay here till Monday? Then you could go up with Ka. You
could easily telegraph to your Aunt, couldn't you? And if you must work,[3]
couldn't I get Rochester[4] for you from the London Library.

It was so dreadful tonight. I knew all the time how bored you were, and
that made it only greyer & so uneasy too.

I know you hate my being there in these days. Why should you? It

_____

1 Alfred Moritz Mond (1868–1930), the industrialist, was a Liberal MP from Swansea
   (1910–23). He had been on the defensive since January 1910 concerning charges of
   poor working conditions at his factories. Now he was under renewed attack as a
   'foreign-born millionaire' who had 'successfully combined Liberal or non-Party
   politics with personal gain' (*Throne*, 19 June 1912; quoted in Searle, *Corruption* 133).
2 Donald Robertson (1885–1961) studied classics at Trinity College, and was later a
   professor of Greek at Cambridge.
3 Brooke was working on his dissertation, *John Webster and the Elizabethan Drama*.
4 John Wilmot, second earl of Rochester (1647–80), the Restoration poet who wrote
   A Satyr against Mankind (1675).

always somehow seems necessary to be doing something when we're together. But why shouldn't it be just quiet? I mean, why shouldn't you do what you want – read or write your poems – and let me just sit, or even read? Is it *impossible* for you not to feel worried one way or another if I'm there? Couldn't I be simply furniture or an animal? It seems to me almost intolerable if it must always be on the jump – If you're always to expect to *get* something (interest or amusement or something) out of it, it's bound to be hopeless after a bit. And it's such an awful strain if I'm supposed always to try to be amusing or interesting – except that I collapse almost at once. I liked it so much in the three minutes after you sat down. But it would have been even better, I daresay, if you'd been reading Rochester. Is all this what you said annoyed you most? – it really isn't meant to be insulting. I do think you're very clever & one of the very few people whom one can have amusing conversations with. But I also like sitting on the floor near you and not talking.

Is this very dim? It's shocking to think of you coldly reading it at breakfast in the morning. But you can understand the kind of things I've been meaning to say – Please don't condemn it, if you can help.

Of course you don't stop here. But I shall crouch all tomorrow morning by the telephone hoping for the usual miracle.   James

RB, [postmarked 10.30 a.m., 19 June 1911] to JS, 67 Belsize Park Gardens, Hampstead

I couldn't possibly come for the week-end. As it is, I've only just clung to the edges of life.

I probably couldn't – except a little – write poems when you were by: – nor when anyone else was by. "Why couldn't I?" Why can't you jump six feet? Why can't Lytton fall in love with Cecil? or Oliver be amusing? or Mr Luce intelligible?

But the rest might be possible, when talking didn't fit in. Only, I'ld have you realize that on Friday, I was extremely tired and highly excited. I'd a lot to say to Ka, and she had promised to be back at 10.15. She was so late.

You see, from your point of view (you make out) you & I are in the centre of the stage, an interesting picture, a moving group. But from other points of view – mine or the stage crowd's – there are moments when I and somebody else, or two quite other people, are central. The artists', or Cambridge philosophers', method of isolation is dangerous. A relationship between A and B in which A is wholly occupied with B, & B with A, and each gesture & mood of each is entirely significant towards the other – that doesn't happen much. If Emilia thought every action of Othello's had sole reference to her, if Laertes had such an idea of Hamlet, they must have made sad mistakes. It wasn't, for the moment, Emilia's or Laertes' tragedy.

And I must plaintively insist that there are moments when – to my eyes – it's my tragedy and not yours, when – to my eyes – I'm being the chief character in my life, not the second one in yours, and that when I laugh it's not always with you, when I swear it's not always at you, when I cry it's not always for you, – even when you're in the room.

It's ignominious to have to confess that boredom's a thing one sometimes brings with one into a room. But no one's really been quite captain of his soul since poor Mr Henley,[1] perhaps. I'm afraid I was a little *staccato* on Friday. But with Geoffrey what I used to be like before a House Match. They used to roar with laughter.

Was Woolf,[2] who seems very nice, ever more than minor? Goldie came to the Society last night, drunk as a lord. Lytton, earlier, was incredibly lively and brilliant about turds. He is going to Becky Falls. I stay here. The End draws round.   R

RB, Monday [19 June 1911, Trumpington] to Lytton Strachey, 12 King's Parade,[3] Cambridge

The rain *did* frighten you then . . ? If it softens a bit by tomorrow, you'll find me at lunch here then: or at tea, if you can bear Goldie drunk or sober. But we'll provide fish and wine & things for lunch for you.   R

JS, Monday evening [19 June 1911]

You're rather a sledge-hammer; you know. – However, everything you say seems to me completely true and unanswerable. But there are one or two things – if you can bear to look for a minute at the dimmest of coryphés.

You're so eager to intellectualize. I don't believe there's ever been a moment when I shouldn't have agreed with you that I'm nowhere near the middle. It'ld really have been too absurd to have thought I was. (I should have thought what I asked for implied that I knew other things – Rochester, or a poem – must often be nearer it.) Anyhow, surely it wasn't because I thought we were together in the limelight that I wrote to you? As a matter of fact, it was because when I got home I was (one needn't go into it) upset. One of the psychological (but not, I think, logical) causes of my being upset was I imagine actually that I vaguely saw that I was further than ever from the middle – but it's all very difficult to make out. And it's

---

1 Brooke refers to William Ernest Henley (1849–1903) and his poem 'Invictus'.
2 Leonard Woolf (1880–1969) had returned to England on 11 June after spending seven years with the Ceylon Civil Service.
3 The new Cambridge address of Oliver and Lytton Strachey.

very difficult also to make out why, being upset, I wrote to you. There were lots of reasons, and causes, – and one of them doubtless was a desire to come on a little from the wings. But, truly, what I wanted – not hoped for – was the dimmest of friendly strokings on the back of a postcard – nothing so elaborate as your account of what a bore and an egoist I am.

Of course it's true that what interests me most in you are your relations with me; but I imagine that's an almost essential part of the disease. But it also occurs to me that I know incredibly little about your other relations. I can even believe that if I'd known you were only just clinging to the edges of life I might not have minded your walking up and down . . . It's very difficult to be interested in the other side of the moon.

I hate all of this. It's all silly and unimportant and dull. I really only want to say I'm very sorry if I made a fuss when you were thinking about other things. I'll try not to again – but I probably shall. – Can you understand that one does things of that sort sometimes? I suppose you never do. – But if I do, please don't be exasperated, Rupert. Just don't do anything, rather than that.

It makes me despair so, if the little terms I'm on with you can't be easy. And it seems as though they never could be unless I say nothing I think. Isn't it delightful to look forward to the Albert Hall tomorrow, and Covent Garden on Wednesday,[1] and Westminster Abbey on Thursday?[2]   James

RB, Tuesday [27 June 1911], The Old V.
to JS, 67 Belsize Park Gardens, Hampstead

Dear old fellow, could you put me up – I have to be in town – Thursday and Friday nights? I should appear on Thursday in the middle of the day, no doubt, but that evening I'm unfortunately engaged. I suppose one couldn't leave at nine on Friday, for Covent Garden?[3] Oh, when shall I see them?

Ma[y]nard appeared this afternoon, looking so nice in grey.   Rupert

We were *all* at the Court last night.[4]

Oh! Oh! The Saturday Matinee. Get some seats can you? Not *too* Dear. Quick! Quick!

---

1 For the opening of the Diaghilev production of *Le Carnaval*, with Nijinsky. Strachey and Brooke also went together to *Le Spectre de la Rose* on 24 June.
2 For the Coronation.
3 To see Diaghilev's *Les Sylphides*.
4 For the Irish National Theatre Society's productions of J. M. Synge's *The Well of the Saints* and Lord Dunsany's *King Argimenes*.

RB [no date, but in original order of Strachey's letter album]

You're, you know,
reading, this
week –
R

Caricature on the envelope of Strachey's letter of 1 July 1911.

JS, July 1st 1911, 67 Belsize Park Gardens
to RB, The Old Vicarage, Grantchester, near Cambridge

I'm sending off your periodical publication.

If you really wanted any money, would you like this? I found on consulting my books that I had exactly fourteen pounds, three shillings in the world. It's most improbable that I shall want more than I've kept before August – when I get more. But if I'm ruined, I'll just ask you for some back. Otherwise, you can send it when you like, or not at all.

I've also found the B[ritish].M[useum].R[eading].R[oom]. rules. It *says* nothing about Fellows – so perhaps that's chimerical. In any case I'm sure her Ladyship[1] would oblige.   Your loving

1 Strachey's mother provided a recommendation for Brooke's Reading Room pass.

RB [postmarked 4? July 1911, Trumpington] to JS, 67 Belsize Park Gardens, Hampstead

He's merely a mulled gump. And as there was a bare quorum, and the weather hot, we sat round and couldn't spend more than £8 out of £15. Oh, they *were* soft, and he, Mr Elliot, worse than any. I wept for Zacch and crumpled *them*. It ended – £2 music, after consultation with Mr Rootham,[1] £5 Select Committee List, and £1 for me to advise German etc.

I thought a little more Schnitzler, a Wedekind, and – a Bahr?[2] what? or what else?

But what I *wanted* was, the French names of Dostoieffsky, in a list. You'd have that almost at hand? Then we'd get what we haven't in English, in French . . . .

Or anything else? *New* French – Tertius [Norton] has been away.

Thanks for the cheque. That + × I'll return some-time. If you run dry demand an instalment.

Yesterday at 8.30 I crossed the fields, back from a bathe. Two youths passed me. They'd also been bathing in an astounding purple twilight, with bats sitting on your head as you emerge, and the world luminous with fishes' eyes. They were talking in low tones. One was saying " . . . . . 'e spent the rest of the day scratching 'is back. *Laugh*! Ho, *my*! y'know, *some* folks say it isn't right to treat a poor blind man so. But 'e doesn't seem to mind, y' know. And they're always putting pepper in his tea, and . . . ."

James dear, what a lot we miss.

Gerald, Jack [Sheppard], & Cecil to tea yesterday. Gerry in great form. Oh, I've just read Jack on the Greeks, – in proof. It's something ponderous. 'The Professor explains.' And then you're supposed to see his nice nature through it all. So simple a fellow; so sincere, & so democratic. "It is, of course, (as the present writer remembers Dr [Walter] Headlam remarking to him) a tendency, in effect, in Greek drama, to represent a *moral* idea, which is, I think, very hard – *chalepon*, (χάλεπον) [sic][3] – for the modern spectator fully to understand." Begotten by Moore out of the Christian Commonwealth.   Damn the flies.[4]

                                                                                    Rupert

---

1 Cyril Rootham, who directed Brooke in Mozart's *The Magic Flute* at the end of the year.
2 Herman Bahr. An adaptation of Bahr's *Daz Konzert* was soon to be performed at the Duke of York's.
3 'difficult'.
4 Brooke seems to have been obsessed with insects during this period. When Jacques Raverat came to visit one evening, he found Brooke on his floor, completely nude, tracking a flea between the floorboards. Raverat suggested flea powder ('It's advertised a lot'), but Brooke replied that it only excited their appetites (*RBB* 266).

JS, Saturday night [8–9 July 1911], TreFeddian Hotel, Aberdovey, North Wales

I've been spending the last two hours on a terrace (that commands a wide panorama of the Gulph of Cardigan) and watching an incredibly elaborate and horribly hideous sunset designed by M. Bakst. All that was needed, I felt, was a pair of tights upon the seat by my side. And then of course came the lightest of footfalls upon the grass behind me. "Are you stopping in this hotel to get a little golf, sir?" queried the etolonel[1] colonel.

Sunday afternoon.

I'm really here, did I tell you?, to see whether Balkan Hill would be likely to suit St Loe for the summer. Tomorrow morning I return. I'll look out Dostoievsky for you then . . But I'm told by M. Baring[2] that the French translations give only one sentence in three. Won't you get the German? I'll also enquire from Mme [Dorothy] Bussy what are the best books of the moment.

Oh la, did you see Mr [Arnold] Bennett's account of the Dinner in this week's Nation. Was he one of the waiters? or Sir H. Wilson?[3] Very bright of him, I thought, to be so up to date.

There was quite a painful scene the other day when I chatted to Ka about the Society. I really don't quite like to think *what* happened. I made an infinitely dim speech, and she seemed almost on the brink of tears or then again perhaps merely rather bored. Anyhow, I'm practically certain that whatever impression I created was hopelessly wrong. The fact is that you atmospheric people can't ever stand up to a strong earthy bit of soul-struggle. I've noticed that time and again. So when I start one with rather a bounce, you somehow succeed in making it all seem either like catching a tennis ball in one's toes, or altogether in bad taste, or just as though one hadn't spoken at all. Perhaps *you* might clear things up with her a little? I find I'm very fond of her when I'm *with* her, anyhow alone. But I admit that I get rather jumpy about it sometimes.

Such a soothing dinner party with G[eoffrey]. Keynes! He showed me all of Blake's pictures. And isn't he a dear?

Oh, are you coming up for Gordon Craig's dinner? Will [Rothenstein] tells me it'll be most frightfully chic. If you send me a postcard I'll get you a ticket. – I suppose you won't put off your week at the Museum till the 29th & then stay at my house. I shall be absolutely alone and very unhappy. Not even servants – just a charwoman. You should have your private suite & key. It would perhaps save you some money . . . . My

1 Read 'eternal'.
2 Maurice Baring (1874–1945), whose book *The Russian People* was published in 1911.
3 Field Marshal Sir Henry Wilson, who was assassinated in 1922.

behaviour would be awfly good, you know, if I knew it was to be for as much as a week . . And I'ld see you very little.   Yours
                                                                          James

Shall I drop in on my way to London tomorrow & call at number 24. Should I find dear Alfred to bugger, or only the Ranee?

JS, July 13th 1911, Hampstead

Do you give me leave to order a seat for you for the Ring[1] & Tristan [*und Isolde*] next October?

Dear Chawner,

I have much pleasure in enclosing her Ladyship's testimonial. She thinks you'd better mention in your letter that she's *Lady* S. – which doesn't appear in her signature. Note also in making your application that they insist upon your giving your exact object in going: – e.g. "with a view to writing a history of eunuchry in England". It won't do merely to say "for research".

A little political gossip today, I think, is all I can manage. You saw that that dreadful paralytic[2] (as St Loe calls him) has arrived in London from Birmingham. You recognised of course that that was the clou[3] of the situation. It's really rather pretty. As far as one can see almost the whole Unionist party in the Commons and the Principal Lords are in favour of giving way. Even violent tariff-reformers such as Steel Maitland and Ridley, as well as Curzon[4] and [Alfred, Lord] Milner and even Midleton [sic] agree. Only two groups want to hold out & force the creation of peers: on the one hand Mr [Joseph] Chamberlain & Austen [Chamberlain] & one or two creatures like Amery – and on the other the Cecil[5] group – Hugh [Cecil] & Robert, Selborne and Salisbury. Well, and what will Arthur [Balfour] & Lord Lansdowne[6] decide? It's known that *Lady* Lansdowne is in favour of surrender, & there's every reason to think his Lordship is too. And Arthur – of course his reason leads him the same way & then he so

---

1 Wagner's *Der Ring des Nibelungen* (Ring Cycle).
2 Lord Halsbury (1823–1921), the former Lord Chancellor, led the 'ditchers' – that faction of the Unionists who were ready to die in the last ditch rather than give in on the Parliament Bill.
3 'crux' (literally, 'nail' or 'stud').
4 George Nathaniel Curzon (1859–1925), the future Viceroy of India.
5 Lord Hugh Cecil (1869–1956), a Unionist and anti-Protectionist who wrote the 1912 Home University Library volume on *Conservatism*.
6 Lord Lansdowne (1845–1927) had continued to resist the Parliament Bill, believing Asquith was bluffing. In the end, he joined the 'hedgers', who were willing to give in under protest.

67 Belsize Park Gardens.

detests Hugh – but no one knows: The fact is no one can even get a sight of him these days. The Archbishop, yesterday morning, tried to catch him – but Arthur dodged . . . . Into it all, then, comes Mr. C[ecil]. It's clear enough that he's come out with his whole weight. He's threatened Arthur that if there's the least sign of yielding he'll bring out the last and most stirring manifesto of his life – and will, in short, split the Party. So Arthur wonders . . .

I told you (didn't I?) that I had it from Lord Knollys that the King *will* create the peers.[1]

Oh dear, you mustn't tell Eddie [Marsh] any of this you know . . that

1   In early July, in the face of opposition to the Parliament Bill from the House of Lords, Asquith had asked King George V to prepare to create a large number of Liberal peers. The government provided a list of 249 names, which included Thomas Hardy, J. M. Barrie and Bertrand Russell. When the Unionists learned of the King's commitment to Asquith, they backed down and the Parliament Bill was passed. Soon afterwards, Balfour resigned as party leader.

last bit especially . . . I should have to go out of Public Life if it were known.

Your
James

Ralph's[1] in the final for the Croquet Amateur Championship.

RB, Thursday [13 July 1911, Trumpington]

The letter's to be to "The Director"
B[ritish]. Museum
it's to be a "written recommendation from a householder" giving her address, with full signature, given *on personal knowledge* of me, & certifying that I shall make proper use of the Reading Room.

Could your office boy run across & find out (a) on which days till the end of their visit the Russians are performing. (b) programmes as far as known (c) If Schéhérazade's going to be at all.

I shall come up sometime perhaps next week. I really can't this week. Justin e.g. is coming here.   R

JS, Friday afternoon [14 July 1911], Wellington Street

Don't imagine, my poor poodle-face, that things are as simple as that – with your a b c s.

Nobody knows what's going to happen at the Opera more than a week ahead, and often less. And with the Ballet they begin by merely announcing "Ballet" and don't give the exact programme till sometimes 3 or even 2 days beforehand. At this moment no one knows more than is to be found in today's *Times*: viz. Tonight, Aïda. – Saturday, Sylph, Cleo., Rose, Igor. – Monday, Sylph, Il Segreto di Susanna, Cleo. – Tuesday, Thaïs – Wednesday, Special Mat. Il Barbiere – Evening, Madama Butterfly.[2] Very well. We may *infer* from this that the Ballet will probably appear on Thursday or Friday, and that there'll possibly be a matinee on Saturday. By tomorrow morning we may know for certain. But in any case it's highly necessary to order seats beforehand – long, long, beforehand. Therefore it's worth while ignoring the question of the *exact* programme. To conclude, Keep your eye on the Press and, if you want me to get you one or more seats, Wire me at once – here if it's in the morning – except

1 Ralph Strachey, James's elder brother by nineteen years.
2 Strachey lists a series of Covent Garden shows. *Les Sylphides, Le Spectre de la Rose, Prince Igor* and *Cleopatra* are all performances by Serge Diaghilev's Ballets Russes, featuring Nijinsky. Other Nijinsky performances not listed here but mentioned in subsequent letters include *Giselle* and *Schéhérazade. Madama Butterfly, Aïda, Il Barbiere di Siviglia, Il Segreto di Susanna* and *Thaïs* are Grand Opera Syndicate productions.

Saturday or Monday. (You will have noted that the *halfpenny* press *never* gives details.) We may add that the last performance of the Opera season takes place on July 31st, that is, on Monday fortnight.

———————

Of course, I'm rather sad about my house not being empty at the right time – as I gathered you might have stayed in it if it had been. – Will you come with me for a week or even a fortnight to Rothiemurchus in August, 1912? I've asked you every year for four years and you've never minded accepting for the year after. – It's very odd: but to go there with you's always been a thing I've wanted perhaps more than anything . . . long before I ever dared to ask you. I suppose it's not sense [sic] to think a place different from everything else in the world.

———————

St Loe thinks Rhythm's an awfly good paper. I wonder if he's in love with Michael.[1]

Kindly glance at Mr Stephen Paget on wild oats. What unscrupulous liars doctors are.[2] In his covering letter Mr Paget wrote: – "I myself sowed no wild oats – for I had none to sow." Help!

Well, good bye. I must spend the next hour and a half writing forty letters.

Your

James

RB, [postcard, postmarked 27 July 1911],
2 Rawlinson Road,[3] Oxford
to JS, 67 Belsize Park Gardens, Hampstead

Just, please, send them[4] here, now. I leave on Friday morning: so post instanter. And if you'll give me a Barclay cheque I'll write £8. I'm frightfully rich.[5] A cheque book's all I lack.

If you're really likely to benefit I'll come to you on Friday night. If not I'll go to Rugby. But it won't be before 9 p.m. More information later. Thanks.

R.

1 *Rhythm* was founded by Michael Sadleir and Middleton Murry while the two were Oxford undergraduates. It was the first English 'little magazine'. Murry was editor, Albert Rothenstein art director, and Brooke joined the editorial committee in 1912, giving him a chance to have frequent lunches with Sadleir at the Cheshire Cheese on Fleet Street, and also giving him the obligation to defend the journal against charges that it displayed 'modernist tendencies' (see *RBB* 375). Brooke contributed articles to both *Rhythm* and its short-lived offshoot, the *Blue Review* (May–July 1913, three issues), with Sadleir his editor.

2 Strachey had recently taken on the medical profession in an article for the *Spectator* titled 'Doctors and Advertising' (10 June 1911, p. 876).

3 The Oliviers' new address.

4 Tickets to see Nijinsky.

5 Sidgwick & Jackson had made an offer to publish Brooke's first volume of poems, promising a commission of 15 per cent on copies sold.

If you don't get this in time: send them to N.L.C.

JS, Thursday [27 July 1911], The Spectator, *London*

Tickets enclosed.

I say, there's something I rather want to talk to you about . . . . I fear I may have committed an indiscretion, in a conversation with Virginia last night[1] – but she was so *STUPID*.

At the moment I feel that nothing could be pleasanter than to be with a person of sense for a little. It'ld be very nice of you if you'ld take the risk – tho' I think I'm rather an opium eater perhaps.

On the other hand, my house is in such turmoil that they won't have you. The family moves on Saturday morning to Prof. Murray's[2] you see. Couldn't we go and spend Friday night at the Star and Garter and take a walk at six next morning in Richmond Park?

If you think it all too fantastic tell me tomorrow. I shall be in the back row somewhere.

If it's Noel that you're going with, may we meet for a moment in an interval? I always imagine her so amazing.[3]

Yours
James

The poor Goat last night fairly 'went it' over you – thought your poems must be so good, as you had such a wonderful Grasp of Things. I suppose you may be trusted to have refused her invitation.

RB, [postcard], Tuesday [22 August 1911],
Clifford Camp, Drewsteignton, Devon
to Lytton Strachey, 82 Woodstock Road, Oxford

I hear you're going to Becky [Falls] soon. Could I come on for a day or two there? Or couldn't you bear it? Say. For I'm utterly offensive and angry. I might come any time between the 1st and the 7th.   RB

His Lordship's[4] hard by –

1 Strachey and Brooke had come across Virginia Stephen and Leonard Woolf at a performance of *Le Spectre de la Rose*.
2 The Oxford house of classical scholar Gilbert Murray (1866-1957) at 82 Woodstock Road, which Strachey's mother had taken for a month.
3 Brooke arranged for himself and Olivier to have dinner with Strachey at one of Brooke's favourite eating places – a vegetarian restaurant in Soho owned by lawn tennis champion Eustace Miles. The dinner took place on 31 July before he and Olivier left to see *Schéhérazade*.
4 Gerald Shove.

RB, [postcard], Friday [1 September 1911],
Clifford Camp, Drewsteignton, Devon
to Lytton Strachey, c/o Mrs Hern, Becky Falls, Manaton, Devon

Not tomorrow, I *think*. Expect me any day – Monday, perhaps . . . .
Don't be disturbed about food. I dare say I shall wire when I come: If
you're full up – with his Lordship & our brother Keynes – I shall pass on.[1]
Probably Tuesday.
Must go [illegible] the blackberries.   R

I expect it'll after all be Monday week.

RB, Wednesday [20 September 1911], The Old Vicarage
to JS, 67 Belsize Park Gardens [on envelope is written:
'Please forward immediately'; letter was forwarded to
Poste Restante, Brussels, Belgium]

The Ranee's at length written. It's all very dim. I shall settle nothing. Mr
BiggWither's presence (*chez* M. Dudley Wallis)[2] confuses, too. But he goes
on the 27th: & anyhow, there's a Room.
Come then as soon as you get tired of the Walloons. If you get ill and
bored soon, you may come immediately (immediately you get ill & bored,
I mean, ... Fuck!). Any how, the latest I shall go to Rugby is the 9th. so
don't come later than the first or second. (The Ranee's away 6th–8th: so I
guess it will be the 9th.)
You may not find me here. Mr Wallis told me late last night (I had
worked 12 hours) that the house was said to have a Ghost.[3] Add to that,
that La Neeve had told me earlier in the day that Mr BiggWither (a doctor)
had diagnosed the kitten's disease as Infantile Paralysis! . . . You may
imagine I had the Horrors all night.
Estrid is a limpet.[4] She assures me however I shall *certainly* get £10 + 25.
So I'm planning a lavish season.

1   Before Brooke left the Clifford Bridge camp, James joined him but 'arrived late one
    night and was discovered in the morning, shivering under a bush with a blanket
    round him' (*SOL* 107). James quickly left Clifford to join Lytton in more comfortable
    surroundings at Manaton, where Brooke soon joined them. Gerald Shove also came,
    then Rupert and James left for London together to hear Beethoven's Fifth
    Symphony and introduce David Garnett to the National Liberal Club.
2   A Labour Exchange official who also had rooms at the Old Vicarage.
3   Peter Underwood's *Gazetteer of British Ghosts* (Souvenir Press, 1971) mentions reports
    of ghosts at the Old Vicarage and says some of the footsteps are believed to be
    Brooke's.
4   Estrid Linder, a Swedish student at Newnham College, had sought Brooke's assist-
    ance in translating two plays by Gustave Collijn (*Dust* and *Bland Vassen*) into English.

Noel Rooke's woodcut of The Old Vicarage, Grantchester.

And now Mr Sidgwick[1] writes that my sonnet entitled *Lust* is not good as poetry and not decent as idea. Do you agree about the first? I'm so despondent about the value of the whole book, that it may have to go – the sonnet. But I'm pretending to be firm. I've written him such a letter.[2]

A card with future addresses (if known) please.

And a wire before you arrive.   Rupert

Oh, will you, as you're coming, kindly promise to do not less than an average of 3½ hours *creative* work a day? (Creative means among other things *not* for the *Spectator*.) Dramatic preferably: but as you like. R

JS, Friday p.m., Sept. 1911, Hotel Russie,
Rue de la Longue Haie, Bruxelles

Yes; it was a damn trick sending me to this place. Oh! dreadful, dreadful. . . . I'm feeling better now . . . there's always the Babylonian Law courts – and your letter. . But on Wednesday – my word! I thought my bottom was coming out. – Those *beastly* middle ages. La! I feel like our poor old Graves turning over a copy of Simplicissimus.[3]

1 Frank Sidgwick, founder of Sidgwick & Jackson publishers. Sidgwick was conscripted in 1917 and killed on 23 September 1917.
2 In the letter to Sidgwick, Brooke defended 'Lust' thus: 'If it's thought to be improper, it must be sadly misunderstood. Its meaning is quite "proper" and so moral as to be almost untrue. [...] My own feeling is that to remove it would be to overbalance the book still more in the direction of unimportant prettiness. There's plenty of that sort of wash in the other pages for the readers who like it. They needn't read the parts which are new and serious. [...] I should like it to stand, as a representative in the book of abortive poetry against literary verse' (20 September 1911). Arthur Lane says this letter 'is a useful corrective to that attitude which would have the "new poetry" of Eliot and Pound born in a literary vacuum' (62). Brooke obviously cared deeply about the poem. If the poem is autobiographical and about a successful seduction, as the most obvious reading of the poem demands, then it could only be about Denham Russell-Smith, Brooke's only conquest at the time it was written. The 'remembered smell' that Sidgwick presumed to be the smell of a woman, and, in his mind, therefore obscene, may in fact be Russell-Smith the night prior to the seduction, when he drifted off to sleep in Brooke's arms. Or it could be the smell of Denham on the hammock at Brockenhurst. Brooke's notebook copy of 'Lust' has a drawing of a figure on a bed at the bottom of the page. The back of the notebook page has a drawing of a short-cropped (and apparently male) head viewed from the back. The opening lines of the poem were originally, 'How could I know? The image of your kin / Drove me cold-eyed on tired and sleepless feet.' If the poem was indeed written for Denham, 'the image of your kin' would refer to Denham's brother Hugh.
   The sonnet stayed in *Poems* 1911, but with the title changed to 'Libido'. In the copies he sent to friends, Brooke crossed through the new title and restored the old.
3 A German magazine edited by Hans Jacob Christoph von Grimmelshausen. Brooke thought it contained 'extraordinarily good and pungent criticism of things Prussian', and during the war suggested that Sidgwick & Jackson publish a selection from it since 'it really does give the evil and ridiculous side of what we're fighting against, better than anyone else' (letter to Frank Sidgwick, 23 October 1914).

Sunday night at fin de saison Ostend[e] was sufficiently depressing. I hoped to be able to make a little by gambling – so I went into the Kursaal – to find only three thousand whores listening to the Ouverture Guillaume Tell. The arrival at Bruges next morning seemed quite a relief. The Panier d'or was *so* delightful – everyone *so* kind & attentive. "What!" as Mrs Basscombe exclaimed, "are you all by your lone lonesome?" And the General and all the dear girls echoed: "All by his lone lonesome!" Then there was the dissenting Minister, whose heart was strained, and who had in consequence to weigh for himself at mealtimes 200 grammes of grapes and 150 grammes of salad. And the contractor from Liverpool who travelled with his mistress, though he pretended it was his daughter and called her 'the youngster' – at least we all hoped it was his pretence when he announced en pleine table d'hôte that they had only one bedroom between them.

But through it all you have to figure, hour by hour, and quarter by quarter, those dreadful bells. Who, I ask you, but a member of the Middle Ages, would have thought of playing the Moonlight Sonata once an hour on the "Chimes" – or Chopin's Valse in B minor? I heard those lovely morceaux rendered 72 times each during my stay at Bruges – not to mention Haydn's Surprise and the Gypsy Rondo (whatever that may be) at the quarter *to* and the quarter *past*. But, Lord-love-a-duck, the worst was to think that they've been playing 'em, playing 'em, over and over again, all through one's life. When first Mr Sandford asked me to hand round slips, they were just winding up the sonata. Or, again, when Watty told me it was as though something beautiful were broken, they were just starting on it . . . But I mustn't give way.

D'you mean to say these pictures don't horrify you? The whole thing is pure saddism [sic]. At least it's mixed up with the beastliest mystik and general fuzziness. I venture to except the Van Eyck man. He was evidently a person of eminence and possibly a cynic. But I can really see next to *nothing* in [Hans] Memling. His pictures, as M. Baedeker informs us, are extremely well finished. – As for the second raters, they fairly make the flesh creep. . . I think on the whole the limit was a party being flayed . . . But there were smaller ones . . oh! yes! especially one set where things had fairly broken out all over. God preserve us! – So I felt pretty mashed after three days. And on Wednesday I caught a severe cold & cough too.

So I determined to strike for Brussells yesterday. I only stopped an hour or so at Ghent – for the Van Eyck. This hotel was recommended by Mr Howse, the saturnine artist, late of Caius College. This morning besides fetching your letter, I looked for a change at Modern Belge Painting. *Not* very bright, I'll allow. Alf. Stevens is rather good. Did I detect some frights by Elizabeth [van Rysselbergh]'s Papa? Now I must go to the old pictures. I rely on there being plenty of Rubenses & Rembrandts – what? – The Churches too are just awful – all painted up in stripes.

I guess that I'll spend Sunday night with Dudley & come on on Monday. If the Musée Wiertz is too attractive I'll wait another day. But I think there's something in going to you then – as I'ld have a week left for a bracing before my return to W[ellington]. Street.

How I *hate* that Frank [Sidgwick]. If you'll withdraw it from him, I'll undertake to do the publishing for you myself far more efficiently.

I think I thought it ['Lust'] was a good one – though obscure, you recollect.

Is Bigwither a man I Know? His name is familiar.

————

Creative Work? Well, I'll do my best. But I only feel creative when I'm listening to some kinds of Light Music.

————

I saw Mr & Mrs Brooke & sons figuring in the Book at the Basket.

> Yours
> James

RB, Saturday night [23 September 1911], The old old Vikkerage to JS, 67 Belsize Park Gardens [On envelope appears 'Immediate. Please forward.' Apparently it wasn't necessary]

I wonder where you are. I suppose this will never reach you.

Come when you like, then. I don't quite know how things will pan out. But all can be arranged. Mr Entwistle-Blenkinsop is here till Wednesday, so till then you'll sleep in an attic, at the Orchard, or in an extra bed in my room. I rather incline to the last: because I want a night's sleep; and at present when I get to bed I'm a mere rag, and – since I was told about the Ghost – I've been able to do nothing but lie awake wet with terror.

The days, though, are incredibly lovely.

And you get your light music all right.

I'm sorry Belgium didn't quite take you. You've such queer tastes.[1]   R

Mr B[elloc]'s latest . . . . .

Estrid [Linder] I've fairly got under now. She crawls.

Have you written Ka?

Frank collapsed, wildly. But I think he despairs. But I'm really very fond of him. I treated him shamefully. He'll never know.

1   Brooke wrote to Cox the same day: 'A note from James. Belgium was too much for him: Life always is. Knocks him down again and again.'

RB, Monday dawn [25 September 1911, in envelope with only 'James Strachey' written on it][1]

The first day of the University Library, I think.

I may come back any time. Probably 4.30.

Mrs N[eeve]. will consult you about your meals.

Paper pen and ink I've ready: so you'll have plenty to do. If you snatch five minutes, there's Mr B[elloc]'s latest about.

My bicycle *goes*, if its pumped up and the mudguard's tied. But I doubt you'll want it.   R.

JS, Saturday morning [7 October 1911], Hampstead

About the Ring.

There are three seats for the 2nd Cycle. Two of them are for Ka and Me. I find, on consideration, that I'm disinclined to have you for the third in that particular party.

On the other hand, there are *two* seats for the 3rd Cycle. It's therefore suggested that you should go with Ka to that, instead. There's the additional gain that none of the performances are on a Saturday; so you'ld get the whole thing.

As the time's so short, I've already disposed of the third seat for the second cycle. If, however, you're for any reason particularly anxious (or even anxious) to go to the 2nd and not the 3rd – or to both – you can have my seat, and I'll make other arrangements.

Telegraph in that case on Monday morning: – a letter on Sunday night would come as soon.

––––––––

Forgive this change. I think it's for the best, or at least better.

––––––––

Give my love to the Society. I hope to appear on the hearthrug today fortnight. Don't let them elect Mr Luce.

Lytton was frightfully excited (and still is) about his Lordship's letter to

––––––––––––––––––––

1 This is a note left for Strachey to read upon his arrival at Grantchester. Brooke had written to Cox: 'James comes tomorrow, Monday, morning. [...] Normally James stays exactly till the following Monday morn.' Following Cox's reply, Brooke wrote again on 1 October: 'Damn you, I am not tired! [...] Nor does James exhaust me. He exhausts you because you try to do him good. I don't try to do him good. I merely make use of him. At present he's gone to take some m.ss. to Estrid, & to buy a Sunday paper. [...] P.P.S. There are a lot of men in such *wonderful* clothes in the kitchen. [...] I admire them *so* much. One is so beautiful, shining . . .' Keynes deleted the post script in *LRB*.

you, that arrived here. He thinks it was either a proposal or a challenge to a duel.

Your loving
James

Do you return on Monday? Could I have tea with you then, if so?
Is Love the same thing as Lust and Affection combined? Surely not.

RB, [postcard], S[unday, 8 October 1911],
24 B[ilton] R[oad] R[ugby]
to JS, 67 Belsize Park Gardens, Hampstead

I've got a seat – *a* seat, said I? – two, at least, 6th row. I suppose I shall never find anyone to take my second one.[1] I hardly care: I'm so excited by proofs.[2] Oh! oh! ee! aah!

Second Ring, though, I'm vacant. But I shall only go thrice.

I have no room

no peace

no God   R

RB, [postcard], M[onday, 9 October 1911],
24 B[ilton]R[oad] R[ugby]
to JS, 67 Belsize Park Gardens, Hampstead

You're not even as good as Lytton on the telephon[e]: – of course you may have been crying. Mother (whose health and spirits are devastating) gave an imitation of you in the drawing room afterwards. It consisted in saying "May I speak with Wupert?" very softly. 'Straordinary woman.

I've since thought, I shall *probably* be in London for the Monday: the first go-off. So we might see Gisel[le] (5/.)? I could give the ticket to Dudley or someone if I couldn't? If you're fixed, it doesn't matter. I shan't go to the Ballet more than once that week.

All my proofs: oh *God*!

Have you heard of an attic anywhere?[3] Gus. Collins[4] has agreed to the £35. I have it in writing. So I'm a made man.

I've even started a paper (on Art) for the C[ambridge]. C[onversa-

---

1 Noel Olivier agreed to go to two performances, but only if she was allowed to pay her own way. She volunteered Bryn for a third performance. In the end, Brooke went to *Die Walküre* with Adrian and Virginia Stephen and Leonard Woolf.
2 Of *Poems*, 1911.
3 Brooke had decided he must move to London in order to work on his dissertation at the British Museum.
4 Gustave Collijn (1880-1943), the Swedish playwright.

zione]. S[ociety].

But my dissertation . . is merely a Corpse. All is lost.   R

JS, Monday night [9 October 1911], Hampstead

You *are* a hard hearted family, damn you. And especially at breakfast, I've always thought. *Your* voice . . but it all fits in wonderfully with the new view of life. As poor Marjorie said this very afternoon, "I'm not surprised people don't fall in love with Rupert: he's so beautiful that he's scarcely human." "Ah, yes yes! Temperamentally, no doubt," I posited in agreement.

Anyhow I shan't send you the Grande Constatation des Affaires Humaines which I've been preparing for the opening of the Autumn Season. You'll have to wait till the close; and things are so fluid just now . .

This must account for my delay in thanking you for my delightful week in old Grantchester – which fairly set my bowels on their legs [drawing of bowels on legs appears here]. I beg your pardon, Wupsie dear, but I'm in rather high spirits tonight.

Speaking seriously though, the world wonderfully widens. Help me a bit, and I'll come through, I'll come through! – Let me add, all the same, that my admiration for you fairly grows. What energy! What multifarious prolixity! Ah! la! – which leads me to your pretty ones,[1] whom I've been going over this afternoon. I *do* think some of those later ones are frightfully good. I wish I could think of things to say about them. And that you hadn't altogether misunderstood what I was trying to say about 'Jealousy' – and finally forced me to say the things I didn't think but that you thought I did and that you despised so. – The earlier ones are very nice too.

Yes. I happen to have 2 seats for the first night. Not 5/. but 4/. – right at the back, but in the middle. I'll hold it for you – & also the one for the 2nd Ring. Doubtless Marjorie 'll like to use it for Götterd[*ämmerung*].

Will you be in Cambridge? I go on Saturday. I hope you will – as I've asked [Leonard] Woolf & Turner[2] to be there – & his lordship [Shove] & I couldn't deal with them alone. And our Harry [Norton] too.

Tomorrow I begin the Office. St Loe writes that I shall have to do a sub leader & a leader this week, as Johnnie Atkins is ill – "bad boils on both his legs". Oh dear.

---

1 Brooke's poems.
2 Saxon Sydney-Turner (1880–1962), Apostle no. 240, who had become an extreme introvert. Lytton wrote to James (October 1912): 'It would never do to become Turnerian, and I feel it's a danger that hangs over all of us' (quoted in Holroyd, *Unknown* 111). Sydney-Turner was a civil servant employed by the Treasury. He lost most of his money gambling on horses.

You seem very vague about your Attic. If I see one on Belsize Parade may I take it?   Yours
                                                                                James

What I wrote in the middle of the last page has had the most awful results. Before I'd written 2 more sentences I was suddenly seized with violent diarrhoea – and I've already 'been' twice. Did you notice the falling spirits? I'm now a regular wreck. Probably it's Ptomaine poisoning or Appendicitis – and before you open this I shall be dead.

JS, [19 or 20? October 1911]

Dearest Rupert, I'm so very sorry if I was unpleasant tonight – letting you in for the corporal [Walter Lamb] like that. I was feeling rather jumpy. I should have liked so much to walk with you. It all made me cry in the tube as I've not for a long time. You know, don't you, that whatever happens in the world I'm very fond of you.   Your loving James.

RB, [postcard, postmarked 2 a.m., 21 October 1911],
21 F[itzroy]. S[quare].[1]
to JS, 67 Belsize Park Gardens, Hampstead

Don't apologise – to *me*, anyhow. Your lookout; and the corporal's. He wasn't really very dreadful. Considering (as I found out after) he'd that very evening been – – – however, not on a postcard. Still, I admire the lad's cheery courage.

Jacques appears to me too disintegrated to be satisfactory –   R

JS, December 4th 1911, Hampstead

As a matter of fact I suddenly cried[2] – but perhaps it's much the same thing.

It's strange how one gets moved by such absurd things. It all seemed to rise up before me – terribly external – and then there was you, wonderful splendid you – and I wanted to say your name very loud (yes, even with the Chawner to laugh at). And I want to write it now, all over the paper, very big. – – – – – -Do you think it was awfly bad for me to be absorbed

---

1 Brooke was staying in the London flat of Maynard Keynes and Duncan Grant while they were away. In a letter to Noel Olivier, Brooke called it 'the dirtiest place in London, and the uncomfortablest' (*SOL* 122).
2 Brooke's *Poems* was published on this day by Sidgwick & Jackson.

in you for five years? Lord! it was pretty complete. No one can really have known how far – certainly not you. – Oh I'll go through Hell – it was superbly worth while – I don't care if you laugh at me. And to think that by an amazing miracle you happened to be a person – really, if you come to look into it, almost the *only* person I knew – worth being absorbed in. That, of course, is why the *effects* too have been so good – on *me* anyhow. Do you know what a horrid creature I was in November, 1906? Why, I was even a member of the Unionist Party. No, no. One might have managed it better in details no doubt – but as a whole I *won't* regret it. What?

The horrors, you know, are connected with the End. I feel far more inclined to commit suicide in these days than ever I felt on Bloody Friday. But if one resolutely faces the facts, one can steer through, can't one? But it does seem to me a tragic flaw in the constitution of the human mind that I should be infinitely shattered by the sound of your voice a thousand and one times, but that the thousand and second time I should be shattered a little less. If one's honest about it one feels mean, if one's dishonest one feels a traitor. And apart from the grey cynicism of all this, there's a dreadful feeling of loneliness.

I'm sorry to bother you with this – but I suppose the truth is that I fell in love with you just now when I opened your book. And you, poor dear, are you just rushing off to Miss Pate with your seventeenth appendix?

It was so sad missing the flute.[1] My cheek became incredibly puffy and Lytton said I looked like Den[n]is Robertson. Pippa[2] tells me you danced the best.

Your
James

Will you have done with your knïtting in time for me to dine with you on Saturday? I should, for *most* sentimental reasons, rather like to. So don't hesitate to refuse. Either in Grantchester or Cambridge. Or if preferable I could get a pair of seats for the last night of the season at C[ovent]. G[arden]. Tell me on a post card.

RB, December ['Dec 19. 1911' written in pencil at top,
probably by Lytton] 24 Bilton Road, Rugby
to Lytton Strachey

Dear Lytton.

There's going to be a reading-party in dear old Lulworth. In January:

---

1 On 1 and 2 December, Brooke had played the Seventh Nubian Slave in Mozart's *The Magic Flute* directed by Cyril Rootham at Cambridge's New Theatre.
2 James's elder sister, Philippa.

3rd or 4th – Norton, I think, is going to be there. And Ka and I. And perhaps his Lordship. And possibly Virginia. Will you come? it will cost you 30/- a week, perhaps. Everybody will be writing plays. I suppose it will be dreadfully Apostolic . . If you came earlier, you'd find a different lot – S[ignor]. [Ferenc] Békássy amongst them.[1] But I recommend the later.

Could you come – a week – or if not, less, even? Rupert

RB, [postcard, postmarked 12.15 a.m., 20 December 1911][2] to JS, 67 Belsize Park Gardens, Hampstead

Dear J. I don't know *how* but a strange aberration seems to have come over me tonight. I asked you to come Thursday but M[argery]. [Olivier] points out that we shall be gone by the evening. And I'm afraid she is quite right. I am so sorry to be such an idiot.[3] I was mostly thinking about B[eachy]. Head. I wanted to come to Ka's, but had'nt [sic] the face to after elaborately pleading tiredness to the Rowntrees and they still hovering round. So we shall never see you any more. N[oel] & I are going to the "Lower depths"[4] tomorrow but you've been already have'nt [sic] you?

Yrs
B[rynhild]. O[livier].

I am really *very* sorry that you won't be able to come here.

JS, [postcard, 25 December 1911], Hampstead to RB, 24 Bilton Road, Rugby

Tod und Hölle![5]
Even in *my* rather advanced set we don't draw attention to our peculations – and with such a *nasty* comment.[6]

1 Brooke had also invited Maynard Keynes for the earlier week and asked him to bring Duncan Grant. This is why he suggested the later week to Strachey, for Strachey had not forgiven Keynes for taking Grant from him.
2 'Heartiest Congratulations dear J.' written on front of card.
3 Aside from the joke of writing this letter in Bryn Olivier's style and signing her initials to it, Brooke is also venting some genuine frustration at Strachey. He wrote to Bill and Eva Hubback the same day: 'I made all arrangements to go to the *Alcestis* on Friday. And that idiot James Strachey, to whom I left negotiations, forgot to post a letter. So I missed it. I'm very angry with James and sorry for myself.'
4 *The Lower Depths* by Maxim Gorki, translated by Laurence Irving ('H. M. Clark'), at the Kingsway. Brooke mentions it, perhaps, for the play on words.
5 'Death and Hell!'
6 The correspondence contains an envelope to Strachey from Rugby postmarked 23 December 1911, but the letter is missing. Whatever Brooke had written may have upset Strachey so much that he destroyed the letter.

And how the –   J.

Weihnachtsfest[1] 1911

[in pencil at bottom: 'Hotel Pavillon, Cannes, Alpes Maritimes']

---

1 Christmas.

1912

Brooke and Strachey began the year at Lulworth Cove – an event that would prove to be Brooke's undoing. The rush to complete his dissertation on John Webster and Elizabethan drama by the end of the term had caused him to suffer severe insomnia. Once finished, he had collapsed for several days and slept, but he was still in a fragile mental state when he joined Katherine Cox, Lytton Strachey and other friends for their party at Lulworth Cove at the end of December. Unknown to Brooke, Cox had suggested to Lytton that he invite Henry Lamb to stay nearby. Lytton, who was in love with Lamb, was happy to oblige. Still not feeling well and confined to bed, Brooke was then informed by Cox that she was in love with Lamb, not with him.

James Strachey arrived in Lulworth shortly thereafter, finding Brooke in a state of mental anguish. Strachey could not stay long, and when it was time for his return to London, Brooke said he would go with him. He changed his mind at the last minute, but nevertheless spent the day walking with Strachey through the downs and the Purbeck Hills. Strachey caught a train at Corfe Castle, and Brooke continued walking until he reached Jacques and Gwen Raverat in Studland. The Raverats decided at once that Brooke's mental condition needed attention and convinced him to see Dr Maurice Craig, a Harley Street neurologist. Dr Craig concluded that Brooke 'was in a state of severe breakdown' and was 'hypersensitive and introspective' (*RBB* 313). His prescription: cease literary activities, perform no exercise, go to bed early and drink plenty of milk and stout (and 'the compressed blood of bullocks', Brooke claimed in a letter to Hugh Dalton). Soon after the consultation, Brooke was on a train to join his mother and Alfred in the south of France.

While Brooke convalesced, he continued to write feverish love letters to Cox and began developing a scheme to meet up with her somewhere on the Continent. He eventually came up with a successful plan, meeting her in Verona. The two went almost immediately from there to Munich, where they stayed through most of February. During this rendezvous, they apparently slept together for the first, and perhaps only, time – after which Cox admitted that she had continued to see Lamb following the incident at Lulworth. The news plunged Brooke deeper into hysteria.

Brooke's letters to both Strachey and Cox show the deep changes in his mood at this time. He and Strachey were at the Mermaid Club in Rye, Sussex, in late March when he wrote to Cox about someone named Dick (probably Richard Aldington), who, he said, 'had been a flame of James' for years'. He then turned his attention to Cox's anatomy: 'Oh my god, I *want* you so tonight. Your nakedness and beauty – your mouth and breast & cunt. – Shall I turn in a frenzy & rape James in the night?' A few days later, from the same place, he wrote: 'James nibbles at the past – oh, the Remote past – & I throw him scraps. [...] I feel myself standing up proud & strong & erect & naked in front of you, with all my sex bursting into flame. I feel you under me & hear your low cries.'

Brooke's mental unbalance soon turned to paranoia: he imagined that all of Bloomsbury had been plotting to wreck his relationship with Cox. He knew that it was Lytton Strachey who had arranged for Lamb to be near by at Lulworth; thus, Lytton became the principal target of his relentless attacks. Brooke wrote in an undated letter to Cox:

> I'm glad Lytton has been having a bad time [...] I loathe him [...] If I can still, at moments, hate you for having, in pitiful sight of a flirtation, invited that creature [Henry Lamb] to Lulworth, & then left the rest of us, to go out walks & out for meals with him, how do you think I hate Lytton, who hadn't even your excuse of ignorance and helplessness, for having worked to get the man down there, & having seen the whole thing being engineered from the beginning, – and obligingly acquiesced in it as one of the creature's whims? You told me – in the first flush of your young romance – of the whole picture – Lytton 'hovering' (your word) with a fond paternal anxiousness in the background, eyeing the two young lovers at their sport: – it was the filthiest filthiest [sic] part of the most unbearable sickening disgusting blinding nightmare – and then one shrieks with the unceasing pain that it was *true*.

Certainly, Brooke was shrieking. Something had snapped, and gradually most of his friends came to see it as Brooke drew them into – and often blamed them for – his pain. For some time his letters to Cox continued in the same fashion as the one quoted above. When he was not blaming her for his problems, he blamed Lytton, whose role in the matter was the opposite of what Brooke imagined. When Cox had confided in him that she was in love with Lamb, Lytton sent a letter to Lamb – who had moved away – telling him of Cox's love for him but also writing, 'Henry I almost believe the best thing she could do now would be to marry Rupert straight off. He is much nicer than I had thought him' (Holroyd, *Achievement* 26). Months later, Lytton wrote to James: 'As for Ka, I believe I ought to have done something; but I didn't realize the position even dimly, until too late' (13 May 1912).

During this period Brooke frequently complains in his letters to Cox of headaches and fatigue. A strong current of self-pity is also present. Lines such as 'You can't hear my sobbing' or 'I'm starting downhill again' appear with regularity. Brooke's letters also begin to exhibit misogyny, with Cox often the object of his insults and tirades. 'Aren't we just "lovers"?' he asks. 'There's still, in a way, an equality – which "mistress" misses: – though you *have* brought me, roughly enough, to see that women are lower, below men' (March 1912).

Another letter to Cox the same month (written while Brooke was in the company of James Strachey, who had joined him in Rugby to go on walks) reflects on Lulworth: 'I was very ill and tortured & mad.' It goes on to recount everything that had happened there, shifting the blame slightly from Lytton to Lamb and Cox. But each of his friends was the target of hostile remarks at one time or another during this year. He attacked Cox and James Strachey in letters to Virginia Stephen, for instance, then insulted Stephen in letters to other friends. Noel Olivier was a target, as well. In April he wrote to Cox: 'Please don't mention Noel in your letters: even *à propos* of James. I hate her & I can't bear to think of her.' But when Cox became interested in possibly marrying him, he told her he was in love with Olivier. Brooke wrote to Olivier on 2 May:

> Ka's done the most evil thing in the world. She has – or she's on the way to have – dirtied good & honour & all high things, & betrayed & degraded love. Think of the filthiest image you can for the fouling of the best things by the worst. Ka is doing that [...] I'd not care if I saw Ka *dying* of some torture I could inflict on her, slowly. (*SOL* 168)

Later the same month, he wrote to Jacques Raverat: 'I go *about* with the woman [Cox], dutifully. [...] Love her? – bless you, no: but I don't love anybody. The bother is I don't really *like* her, at all' (24 May 1912). During this period Brooke often refers to Cox as unclean. It is evident in this same letter to Raverat: 'There is a feeling of staleness, ugliness, trustlessness about her. I don't know. Dirt. [...] I've a sort of hunger for cleanness' (24 May 1912). He also compared having 'Ka in the body' to 'having black-beetles in the house' (*LRB* 337), a comment strikingly similar to D. H. Lawrence's famous remark about Francis Birrell: 'There is something nasty about him, like black-beetles' (quoted in Garnett, *Friends* 88).

In April Brooke learned that he had not been awarded a fellowship at King's College. By May he had returned to Germany. He stayed with Dudley Ward for a while, and was joined by Cox in Berlin for ten days. For the remainder of the year, he tossed about from place to place, most frequently ending up in either Grantchester or Berlin.

Strachey, meanwhile, found himself falling in love with Noel Olivier. He wrote to Lytton on 11 July: 'it's the oldest thing in the world, this new bit of my character that's coming out. We shall end, I daresay, by not being able to speak to one another. As a matter of fact, though, even *you* could see something in Noel.' He also said of Olivier that it was nice to see someone who behaved with decency – 'I'd simply forgotten the possibility.'

Although the repercussions of Brooke's 'nervous collapse' were felt throughout 1912, it was not until the summer that his friendship with Strachey was seriously affected. In June James met Rupert in Cologne then accompanied him to The Hague. They apparently had a good time, for Brooke wrote to Olivier, 'Holland's a flat country: James is very amusing' (*SOL* 185). Strachey also invited him to Scotland again, and for a while Brooke was planning to go. He wrote to Cox, '[James] is a worm. I hope I shan't be beastly to him up North. He gets pretty badly treated by Noel.' Brooke had, in fact, defended Strachey in a letter to Olivier on 30 May, but when he cancelled the trip to Scotland it was Noel's turn to defend James. She wrote to Brooke on 19 August: 'I was so sorry when I heard that you'd let James anoy [sic] you and had discarded his holiday; he should be the last person to be taken offence with' (*SOL* 208). Brooke wrote back on the 28th:

> You are rather mistaken about James I didn't 'take offence with' him. It had been coming inevitably to this, for months & months. It's complicated & bound up with things you don't understand – . It's part of my new view of things, that I find creatures like that, Stracheys & so forth, not only no good but actually dangerous, spots of decay, menaces to all good. Even if one doesn't mind rats *qua* rats, one has to stamp out carriers of typhoid – All that conflicts so violently with my personal affection for James, that being with them for long produces great unrest & explosions. It's impossible. I don't mind seeing him occasionally for short periods. But he doesn't want that – I have been very fond of him. And I miss him more than you'd think. (*SOL* 213)

John Lehmann, who probably got his information first-hand from Strachey, says James visited Brooke in August 1912, at which time they argued heatedly about Lytton's alleged role in the Cox–Lamb affair: 'The more they argued, the more extreme and unreasonable Rupert's attitude became, until all Bloomsbury friends, James himself, Duncan Grant and even Virginia [...] were lumped together among the accused and accursed. Finally James had to leave the house with Rupert's denunciations ringing in his ears' (*Strange* 17).

James could reach no other conclusion except that his best friend had lost his mind. He wrote to Lytton on 17 August:

> I've been going through horrors too, and am pretty well wrecked now. It's all so senseless and unnecessary – but that doesn't prevent it reducing me to tears.

One of the results is that I'm not going away with Rupert. I don't mind telling you that it's now bestimmt [certain] and announced that he's 'abandoned' Ka and 'loves' Noel. The explosion with me, however, has had every motive assigned to it except the obvious one. Oh lord there *have* been scenes. And the dreadful thing is that he's clearly slightly cracked and has now cut himself off from everyone.

'I've cut myself off from James (whom I'm fond of): anyhow for the present,' Brooke wrote to Jacques Raverat at about the same time. 'It's too difficult, when one's tired.'

It began to appear that Brooke was set on destroying every close relationship he had. He went on to say in the same letter to Raverat that Olivier was 'one of these virgin-harlots of modern days', and he wrote to Cox the same month: 'I've had enough. It *hasn't* been splendid, Ka, for me. Some things & moments perhaps. It might have been without the dirt. But there *was* the dirt.' Cox apparently responded by sending him a shirt, which he liked enough to write back: 'The shirt's so *extraordinarily* nice. I've worn it ever since. [...] It is, my dear, *such* a *feminine* shirt!' He was wearing this shirt when Yeats met him and proclaimed, 'He is the handsomest man in England, and he wears the most beautiful shirts' (*RBB* 374).

The shirt softened Brooke's hostility towards Cox, at least temporarily. Late in the year, he was willing to pay her the off-hand compliment: 'you're not a whore, like an Olivier'. But his letters to her had by then taken on a pattern, as he repeatedly mentioned 'dirt' and 'cleanness', sometimes expressing love, sometimes disgust. However, it was in his letters to the Raverats that his hostility towards women was most virulent. He also shared Jacques's anti-Semitism, and both he and Jacques began referring to the Woolfs and the Stracheys as 'the Jews'.

By October, Strachey's mood had changed from despair to hostility. He wrote to Lytton on 3 October, the day of Brynhild Olivier's marriage to Hugh Popham: 'I hear that Ka's to be there; so if they've been clever enough to get Rupert without warning me – a little cyanide of potassium in the oysters would about fix up that gentleman's wishes. [...] I hope Henry [Lamb] will conduct the burial service.' But Brooke had gone into a rage when he heard of Bryn's engagement, and he refused to attend the wedding. It was the same old story of Brooke wanting women most when they were most out of reach. He had courted Bryn sporadically for years, but he never showed any serious interest in her until she became engaged to Popham. Then, he suddenly had to have her. He wrote her a letter pleading with her to break off with Popham and go away with him instead. Bryn, of course, refused.

Later in October, Strachey received news that Brooke's condition was improving. He reported to Lytton on 25 October, 'I hear that Rupert's much better. He wrote to Norton, & Gerald reports the same. He is said to have announced that he felt he'd not been making enough of his male friends in the last few years & would now try to atone for it. Is there a chance for us all yet?' Then Brooke and Strachey ran into each other on 1 November at the National Liberal Club. James wrote later that evening to Lytton:

> The sudden sight of him across the room made my heart fairly *bound*, in quite the old style. But it's no use. He showed not a touch of affection, though I could have forgiven *everything* if he had. [...] I couldn't see that he was any 'better' or different, really. I don't think people know what they're talking about.

Though Brooke and Strachey continued to exchange letters sporadically for the next two years, their friendship was effectively over. In his distress, Brooke had begun to destroy the very things he loved most in the world – his closest friendships. He wanted complete devotion from his friends. In the end, no one could live up to – or was willing to put up with – those expectations, not even James Strachey. Angry, disappointed and uncomprehending, Brooke insulted his friends then pushed them aside, probably hoping to injure them as much as they had, quite innocently, injured him with their lack of total homage. He replaced them with a new set of admirers in London, with Edward Marsh now the principal devotee. His 28 August letter to Noel Olivier had also included the following:

> You are enabled, by initial stupidity and by years of careful and laborious practice, to despise me. There is the extraordinary spectacle of a silly little worm like you thinking me 'unbalanced' and 'pathetic'. So you'll not understand the waste. But I know, & a few more, what I am & can be like. I know how superb my body is, & how great my bodily strength. I know that with my mind I could do anything. I know that I can be the greatest poet and writer in England. (*SOL* 212)

It was on this goal – being the greatest poet in England – that he now set his sights. He began working with Marsh on the first *Georgian Poetry* anthology, and he didn't look back for quite some time. But on 1 December 1913, he wrote to Jacques Raverat:

> I'd once thought it necessary to marry. I *approve* of marriage for the world. I think you're all quite right. So don't be alarmed. But not for me. I'm too old. [...] I know what things are good: friendship and work and conversation. These I shall have. [...] And there is no man who has had such friends as I, so many, so fine, so various, so multiform, so prone to laughter, so strong in affection and so permanent, so trustworthy, so courteous, so stern with vices, and so blind to faults or folly, of such swiftness of mind and strength of body, so polypist and yet

benevolent, and so apt both to make jokes and to understand them. Also, their faces are beautiful, and I love them. I repeat a very long list of their names, every night before I sleep. Friendship is always exciting and yet always safe. There is no lust in it, and therefore no poison. It is cleaner than love, and older; for children and very old people have friends, but they do not love. It gives more and takes less, it is fine in the enjoying, and without pain when absent, and it leaves only good memories. In love all laughter ends with an ache, but laughter is the very garland on the head of friendship. I will not love, and I will not be loved. But I will have friends round me continually, all the days of my life, and in whatever lands I may be. So we shall laugh and eat and sing and go great journeys in boats and on foot and write plays and perform them and pass innumerable laws taking their money from the rich.

RB, [postcard], Sunday [14 January 1912],
Hotel du Pavillon, Cannes [France]
to JS, 67 Belsize Park Gardens, Hampstead

Did Ka ask you to get my letters from the N.L.C. and forward them? Praps they're on the way.

I am temporarily well. What fools nerve-specialists are!

This is mere Morgan, here. "Heute oder Morgan oder uberMorgan – "[1]

dein[2]   R

P.S. Glaub 'es nicht.[3]

JS, Wednesday night January 24th, 1912

It's very wrong to have put off writing this for so long. But there seems to have been rather a flurry these last days.

First of all then: – "The confinement took place in due course on Sunday morning, twins being delivered.[4] While one of the children is doing extremely well, it unfortunately became necessary to employ the forceps in the case of the other. As an inevitable consequence it suffered grave injuries to the head and other parts, and, though the infant cannot be pronounced actually still-born, it is not expected to survive many

---

1   'Today or tomorrow or the day after tomorrow – ' The German for *morning* is *Morgen*, not *Morgan*, but Brooke intends a play on words with the 'Morgan' in the preceding sentence which refers to Morgan Forster.
2   'your' or 'yours'.
3   'Don't believe it.'
4   When newly elected Apostles were inducted, the ceremony was referred to as a 'birth'.

hours. The mother is as well as could be anticipated in the unfavourable circumstances." This bulletin was circulated through the usual channels on Monday afternoon, since when there has been no further news.

Aïe, aïe! Que faire, mon dieu?[1] That *damned* Squitter-squatter![2] . . . However . . . you'll like to have some account of what happened.

Before I went to Cambridge I'd gathered from one or two conversations that all opposition to Mr Békássy and Mr Luce was going to be withdrawn. Gerald had never been altogether in earnest – and the Sq.-sq. isn't very strong minded. The question was as to fathers – and there was a preliminary sort of idea that I should take the foreigner and our little friend [Cecil Taylor] that other man. Though, as I said all along, how he could reconcile it with the line he took last term was a puzzle to an honest man like me. However – Well, I reached Cambridge for luncheon on Saturday. (There was a room for me in his lordship's [Shove's] warren.) I at once became aware of one of the usual intrigues. Pozzo, of course. It happened that things (I'll tell you presently perhaps) were a trifle strained between me and Vulture Minor (as they ca' him); but I'd no notion he'ld proceed to such lengths. The proper person, it seems, to propose the Signor [Békássy] was "Mr" Taylor, who knew him so much better than I did. While in that case Mr Luce would obviously fall to Hove [Shove]. The latter however was luckily firm, and agreed with me that the principal and vital point was the Taylor person's utter incompetence. We saw quite plainly that, as he didn't understand things himself, he'ld be unlikely to be able to explain them to anyone else. We put it – in a simplified way – that he took the Society too seriously. The question was then in what position he'ld do less harm. It seemed *impossible* to prevent his being *someone's* dad. It was from a feverish desire to become it, indeed, that he'd finally ratted. Not that *that* was a good reason, as I said before. But it seemed to us – his lordship and myself – that the only way of knocking him upon the point altogether would be to knock him upon every point. And could we pronounce en plein Société that he just wasn't apostolic? Sheppard's presence alone made it impossible. Whether it was nevertheless our duty you must decide. Since, then, it was premised that he must propose one of them, the question was which. The answer was clear and even now I feel sure correct. Mr Luce was infinitely less important from every aspect. He was at best a freak – and a transitory one at that. Also, there was the excuse of his being so intimate with Cecil. Let them breakfast together then . . . Finally, I nobly offered Gerald the great privilege of taking the Count. And . . Gerald disinterestedly refused it. I needn't explain to you how Pozzo was terrified or cajoled into accepting the position. In any case, it was all settled beforehand; and there was not a single word of argument

1 'Ouch! Ouch! What's to be done, by God?'
2 Cecil Taylor, so nicknamed because he reputedly had three testicles (see James's letter of 6 August 1909 on page 71).

either on the election or the proposers at the Society. We had rather a bright evening at Maynard's. Goldie and Mr Taggart were there, far better than usual, with some stories of their undergraduate days. The principal breakfast for the next day was to be at Sheppard's (with the resident Angels). Cecil would have Mr Luce in his rooms, I Mr Békássy in Gerald's. So we parted – I trembling with terror and a sleepless night before me; Cecil determined, confident, brisk.

– – –

I got down a minute after 9.30, and found him already waiting. I shut the door, and made dim remarks while breakfast was brought in. It was arranged that Gerald should not appear at all. As a matter of fact he characteristically listened at the key hole until he got too nervous of being caught there by his landlady. My whole body shook as I helped him to the eggs à l'aurore, and knew that in another minute his soul would be launched . . . "Er . . I've got some rather important news to break to you . . . er . . I don't know if you've ever heard of a society called the Apostles?." . . you know the rest. My dear, he took it like a fish. He fairly wolfed it down. He just *revelled* in it. It struck him from the first that it was something he'd been looking for all his life; and as every detail was divulged he found the whole thing fitting him more and more incredibly like a glove. Our brother Maine[1] was almost too much for him – but when it came to Clerk-Maxwell[2] the Universe heaved . . "Ach! ach! Clarrrk Maxvell! ach! a *most* rre*marrk*able mann!" and he smacked his thigh once, and again. When he gathered that there was a party waiting at Sheppard's, he was in a desperate hurry to go on to it, and wouldn't by any means have the twenty minutes' reflexion by the fire that seemed so proper to me. So it was barely twenty past ten when I led the way into Sheppard's room. He, of course, hadn't got up. But there were enough of them! There, at the head of the table with his back towards the door, was his Lordship's portentous frame, and on either side of him 'huge masses of angelic flesh banked up' – Dickinson, Moore, Russell, McTaggart – God knows who else. Lord! what a sight to see the whole black congeries stir and rise and wheel heavily round to meet that little naked baby. But Lord, too, it was only with pleasure that the baby blushed . . . . . "Marrrvelous! marrrvelous!"

Oh, everything was very gay; Bertie [Russell] looking frightfully wicked but more brilliant than ever – Sheppard giving a few preliminary imitations of bits of Oedipus Rex. The Book, too, was produced. And our brother Békássy of course found it indescribably witty and lingered with fond enquiries over every division and note. But some of us, after a bit,

1 Sir Henry James Sumner Maine, Apostle no. 111 (elected 1843, d. 1888). Maine had been a British administrator in India and a friend of Strachey's father.
2 James Clerk Maxwell, Apostle no. 128 (elected 1852, d. 1879).

began to look at our watches. An occasional glance of anxiety might be seen upon our faces. As time passed, the anxiety began to turn to alarm. We feared to catch one another's eyes. Mr Taggart at last rose and said he had a committee meeting that he must attend. I began seriously to think of organizing a stretcher-party. But just then the door opened again, and with an ashy face the Squitter-squatter made his way into the room.

[It's midnight and I must go to bed. You shall have some more of this by the next post.   Yours J.]¹

JS, Friday afternoon, January 26th 1912

Rather mean, I know.

However, things weren't at the worst – for he was followed by our brother Luce, looking very wild, with bloodshot eyes and disordered hair. After the usual pénible² ceremony we resumed our seats, and with great presence of mind I ordered Sheppard to perform the whole of Oedipus from beginning to end – which took just ¾ of an hour and rather relieved the strain. Even then, however, it was *most* awful. What kind of state was he in? I could hardly tell. He seemed frightened – but above all angry – or as Pozzo put it later 'surly'. After a bit I showed him the book – but he 'ld have none of it, and just raced over the pages without asking a single question or showing anything but boredom. Everyone else crouched round, longing to remember and discuss every meeting, and to answer the poor Békássy's cross examination – but the Luce wouldn't pause, and in a moment the page was turned. Very soon afterwards the angels began to take flight, and Gordon H[annington Luce]. himself put on his coat and said he had to go out for a walk with Mr Harold Wright.³ Some people thought he should have been allowed to go – but as a matter of fact he was persuaded to stop, and things at last began to improve. Eventually some of us (Sheppard & T[aylor], Gerald & I, and the twins) had lunch in Gerald's rooms, and the fellow brightened up a lot – though only, one had to admit, as the subject of the Society receded. Finally we broke up at tea-time, when Luce announced that he must go for a 2 hours' constitutional. With incredible courage and nobility Békássy said he'ld accompany him. So off they started together. It really seemed quite likely, as Gerald suggested, that they'ld jump hand-in-hand into the mill-race. A good way of winding things up, we thought – as the angels'ld never dare to recommend another birth, if *that* was what it implied. However, they *did* get back – though Luce made no further appearance that day, and started for London early on

1 Strachey's square brackets.
2 'painful'.
3 The president of the Union Society, whom Brooke considered a reactionary.

Monday morning to see his father off to the Holy Land.

The explanation of all this unpleasantness? I really believe just simply that the Squitter-squatter disgraced himself. In the end he admitted as much, and was more reduced than I've ever seen anyone. He was evidently fearfully pompous and (as Sheppard at once remarked) Greeneresque[1] – and the other creature was from the first irritated, *couldn't* see the point of any of it, & was finally furious. He 'resented' the imposition of this Awful Organization upon his private life, and was almost in tears because he realised that all his relations with people had been fraudulent up to then. The little man, when questioned, said: "I impressed upon him the importance and joyful character of the occasion." Is it to be wondered at that the fellow jibbed?

Mr Békássy said that it was almost impossible to get him to say a word about the Society on their walk, and that "he didn't seem at all enthusiastic about it." In fact, the whole situation seemed most black when I left on Monday. I took B. to the Ark that morning – but it was of course felt that Gordon must wait till he quieted down. When I returned here, Lytton suggested and I agreed, that if the man really didn't want to be elected and hated the thought of the Society there was no reason why the egg should be hatched. Nothing, after all, had been written in the book – and everyone would soon forget (at least he and the angels would) that dreadful breakfast. So I wrote to suggest that if things got no better by Thursday Lytton should go down & try to stitch the womb up again. But a telegram from Gerald came yesterday to say "Child doing well" – so (unless he's lying) we may hope for the best.

I'm afraid I've given no idea of how disagre[e]able it's all been. Perhaps the worst feature is that one can hardly doubt that Maynard was right in trying (so long ago) to prevent Mr Taylor's election . . . The horror was that Sheppard saw it, and nearly died, on Sunday night . . . Well, well . . . But the foreigner is certainly a consolation – though I find it hard to believe he can be anything but dim. One hopeful sign – he was questioned about Mr Bliss,[2] and said that he thought him very clever – much cleverer than himself – he also thought that he wasn't apostolic.

They're a queer couple anyway, and I believe they'll fairly *hate* one another. I gather that Lytton's writing a paper for tomorrow night – on "one's relations to oneself" I believe. I hope to God there'll not be a great crush. I haven't heard whether it's yet decided who's to be V.P.

Oh! there was one very fine scene at the Sunday breakfast. As we [were] looking at the book, we got to: –

1 Possibly a reference to the Apostle Leonard Hugh Graham Greenwood, who had introduced Luce – one of his students at Emmanuel College – to the Apostles.
2 Francis Kennard Bliss came to King's in 1911 from Rugby. This is the same Bliss who became Apostle no. 253 and Ferenc Békássy's best friend. Bliss was killed in France in 1916.

"Why is it that one does not like
A monkey on a motor-bike?
Why is it than [sic] one so prefers
Philosophers, philosophers?'

Bertie roared with laughter and asked what it was about; and Gerald in a
moment of vagueness said "Moore or Russell?" Of course everyone carried
it off very well in fits of laughter, especially poor Bertie himself – though
I'm sure he felt it a lot. Moore, too, was red in the face, and I've no doubt
thought that *he* was the monkey.

I'll send you some less ecclesiastical gossip presently.   Your
                                                                       James

I hope you EAT a lot?[1]
Send me any change of address.

_____

I shall despatch today or tomorrow Lytton on Fr. Lit. and Bertie on
Philosophy.[2]

RB, Saturday [27 January 1912], Hotel du Pavillon, Cannes
to JS, 67 Belsize Park Gardens, Hampstead

Pappah dear,
I don't write letters; you know (if ever, indeed, I did) but if you like a
few par[agraph]s . . . . .
[How, indeed, can I write at all with Mrs Fox telling me once more how
she first heard Liszt & had her pocket picked?.][3]
You *are* a Khadd. Leaving me more than thirty hours in suspense: with
that grey figure in the doorway. What *is* going to happen?
I had a telegram – it was *so* difficult explaining to the Ranee about
[Apostles founder Bishop] Tomlinson. But as it came before 10 on
Saturday, I thought it a hoax & wired to Shove for confirmation.

Sunday.
I forget – oh, yes. Shove didn't reply.
Of course, I see why, now. He misconstrued my telegram in the most
beastly way. It's the old story. But I suppose nothing matters.
I'm glad it turned out fairly all right. Though I was so damned uneasy
till 1.15 this morning, that I'm pretty certain the worst happened.

_____

1   Brooke is said to have lost about fifteen pounds during the previous two months.
2   Lytton Strachey's *Landmarks in French Literature* and Bertrand Russell's *The Problems
    of Philosophy* were published this month. This was Strachey's first book.
3   Brooke's brackets.

The Ranee, mixing my Ovaltine, was alarmed to see me get out of bed a few minutes past ten last night & stand, hands folded & head bent, on my lips nothing. ". . . roby [sic], – buzz . . vacuum . . ." they framed. She made no comment. It's part (I've discovered) of the Treatment to pretend that nothing I do is out of the way. Daresay I often get out of bed in the worser moments.

You are a devil. Two nights I haven't slept. That grey little figure has gibbered to me . . But tonight I'll sink to my accustomed stupor.

I barely remember the Society (R.I.P.). But I must say electing those two is the maddest thing I ever heard of. It's just possible Farry [Békássy] might have been the beginning of the new *régime* I so desired, & should so dislike. But Farry & Gordon [Luce] together, January 1912. God! I could so perfectly picture Farry wolfing it all down, and all you wolfing *him* down. It'll be amusing to hear (though I, who alone 'd find it amusing, shan't hear) the gradual dismay, as that delicious Chinee slowly lays his cards down. The lack of taste (worse than even mine was); the distance, the interstellar distance; the iron incomprehension; the Shout; the ever longer speeches from the Rug. By God! with the firelight on his bottom he'll regularly Colonel it over you: And Lucy gibbering; and Squitter squitting.

It's so like a lyric of Fanny's [Frances Cornford]

The Lucy gibbering; the Squitter squitting,
And you upon *il Pozzo's* sofa sitting;
And great brown gutturals rumbling from the Hun;
And Lucy gibbering; and all is done –

Troja fuit: fuimus Troes.[1]

Not – you'll all retort – that it's my business. Oh, quite! In my odd state, I don't for all my egoism even feel aggrieved. I see it all so very clearly, and I'm only – barely – amused. G L Strachey, Keynes, Norton, Shove, Taylor – funny lot of friends you have. The machinery for not having births till I was out of the way, was a bit clumsy. God's great finger gave it a luckier sequel than it deserved. Now they can fairly race ahead. Imagine England aglow with happiness & satisfaction. The gloom of Cannes is a trifle lightened for me by the reflection that *gott sie dank*[2] I've done with all that.

Queerly, yet, your letter gave me a hold on things & a pseudo-return to some sanity. It's one of the chief horrors that at the bottom of the inferae[3] abysses one can't even be, irritably and self-dependently, balmy, in peace.

Oh, yes, my condition. I feel sure I ought to tell you about it. You'll even want to know. But don't spread it to your grinning fellow-countrymen.

1 A variation of Virgil's *'Fuimus Troes, fuit Ilíum'* ('Troy is no more: we Trojans are no more'.
2 'Thank God'.
3 'lower'.

The first week here I put on 6½ pounds, the second week ⅕ lb. I am, indeed, better – but, one gathers, stationary. So, once more, suicide's pointed at. However, I'm sick of this place & this existence. I'm going to try more violent methods. Kill or cure, for me. (My great grandfather – a Curtis – was in the army.). Kindly address all further letters to Rugby, marking them "forward".

Yes, you gave me a sort of lift out of this, for five minutes. Someday – anywhen – if you've time, could you send a short account of the actual births this week? Oh, and if you'd kindly step across to Calais for five minutes one day next week, & tell me when, I shall, with great pleasure, give orders that England is to be wiped out, SUNK, and D E L E T E D.

Was I fairly beastly at Lulworth & in London? I'm very sorry. I really wasn't responsible for my behaviour. I now see in a dim way that I have been infinitely ill for months and more than infinitely ill during this month. I got far far worse after that Swanage journey. I didn't know one could be like that for days & days without intermission – even Jews sleep. You were really well out of that grey hole. I was entirely unpleasant to everybody. The lucky presence of Cox (an admirable nurse) prevented me committing suicide in the drawing room, out of spleen. Here, I've been better. I thought I was mad for two days. But it's now doubtful. I imagine it's merely hanging up, & I shall get a stroke during the summer. But I may recover. It's seems [sic] incredible I should ever be in fair health again; but I suppose it's just possible.

I find it's Monday, & Bertie has arrived. Many thanks for him. Can I bear to read him? The truths & thirty jokes on every page! –

There's a so beautiful lift-boy, here. Literature, I conceive, is at an end for ever (though the doctor says only for three months.). Aberdeen's offer, no doubt, will stay open for me – you'll see me Professor next January. But I employ my time, oh, yes, in light verse. My parodies of *The Everlasting Mercy* are much thought of here

"Dropping bricks & dropping aitches,
Throwing stones at all the Stracheys. – "

Not very amusing.

God be with you

yours (for what it's worth)
Rupert

JS, Monday afternoon [29 January 1912], back in Hampstead

Just some words to say that it all went off with the greatest possible success. Of course Lytton didn't finish a paper but read an old one on why we want to know people (1903). It was a large meeting (twelve altogether); but only Ainsworth from London – so it was quite fairly homely. Luce seems to have come round completely – *most* nice, and with deligh[t]ful feeling tone. Békássy wildly excited and remarkably intelligent. Luce was of course very frightened, especially on the hearthrug – but pulled through without the smallest horror. We were very nervous about the Curse – & Sheppard feared that he'ld rush out of the room in a panic. But nothing visible happened – though no one I think ventured to look. Békássy really seems admirable in every way – for practical purposes too. Lytton & Gerald even wanted to bugger him when he was on the hearthrug. Of course I don't follow that sort of thing – and Alix[1] was at the Heretics on Sunday night.

Lytton finally quarreled with Maynard this morning in a typically sordid way on the question of whether or not Lytton should be given an egg for his breakfast.

I get the dimmest sort of news from Ka. Shall you be seeing her?

Mrs Humphrey Ward's[2] here to tea; so I suppose I must go in.   Yours

James

RB, Feb. 13th, 1912, Obenstrasse 3, Gartenhaus (But not the old rooms;) not that. [Munich][3] to JS, 67 Belsize Park Gardens, Hampstead

It stirs occasionally; flaps. There's so little wind down here. It lifts, and you catch a gleam of white; or, in the sun, it all seems, half a second, reddish . . .

It's very good of you to have gone on giving me news. I can't see why I didn't give you my address. I only know I should do the same again. Secretiveness, I think, grows to a monomania, as the bonds of the body are breaking, and all comes in sight. Poor Dad, towards the end, used to hide little pieces of string. I took the most elaborate pains to prevent anyone knowing where I was. There was no point in it; and anyhow I knew Cox would be here, prattling eight letters a day to England. Like Ovid & his book, you say. Well! Well! One does the queerest things among the

---

1 Alix Sargent-Florence (1892–1973) of Newnham College, James's future wife.
2 Mary Augusta Ward (1851–1920), novelist and social worker. After reviewing Ward's popular novel *Robert Elsmere*, Oscar Wilde wrote to a friend: 'I have blown my trumpet against the gate of dullness, and I hope some shaft has hit *Robert Elsmere* between the joints of his nineteenth edition' (Wilde 237–8). The daughter of Thomas Arnold, Ward had organized the Women's National Anti-Suffrage League in 1908 to oppose extending the vote to women. During the war, she wrote propaganda for America.
3 The fact that Hugh Russell-Smith was in Munich had given Brooke his excuse to go. Had Mrs Brooke known he was going to meet Cox there, she probably would have tried to prevent his going.

crustaceans. I'd rather, though; compare me to a chap at Rugger, kicked in the balls, doubling up and vanishing. I'd rather wriggle into a ballless sleep with out everyone standing round to prevent the spectators seeing where I'm kicked. Bless you, they always *know*.

oh, well –

I lean with all my weight on Cox. It is infinitely wicked, but I'm beyond morals. I really rather believe she's pulled me through. She is stupid enough for me to be lazy and silly enough for me to impose on her. We drift round Mr Hodler's pictures, and in & out of Beethoven. We sit in the [Café] Bauer (ah, but the Stimming's[1] dreadfully changed, my dear.). "Was ists denn, das Leben?" I say, "Das leben – das heisst – "[2] and then anything. The café rocks, and Katherine roars applause. It *is* easy to go down in German. How Oscar 'ld have loved the language. As the flood subsides, I totter around, picking up the jetsam. There is not much that a man may save. A broken blossom I have. There's a blob in the near distance that may turn out to be a ruined rhyme. Oh, but I'm running up a shanty. I'll tell you, Beaumont, authentically and as a not too strict confidence, there's very little doubt now, but that its going to stand. It may be rather a grubby affair in some ways, but it'll possess some surprising features. And if it does come down, by God, you'll hear of it. I'll give you something to chat about. Damn it, one lives only once, one may as well flaunt.

Nikolai Platz[3] gets two letters a day from you: I occasionally am read extracts. I see England queerly, through such a double glass. Your staccato indignancies mellowed by the slow lapse of that melancholy wave. "All is subdued and suffered as by the faint light of a half remembered sorrow of long ago" as Mr [Gustave] Collijn says (Brooke's translation.). It is like hearing Orpheus through the waters of Lethe, or Dostoieffsky in a translation by Sir William Temple.[4]

Have you been to Gadava lately? And did I ask you to convey my congratulations to Békássy & Luce? Do so, if you haven't. Say something tired but witty for me: about the hearthrug you know. In German if you like. I thought of writing one of my posthumous letters to the Hun. But I suppose I shall never have the energy.

Immensity, cloistered in my dear womb, popped a red thumb out the other day. One has to Drive it in: I'm bidden. There's only scraps of the ode to Narcissus: and even they get scattered.

"Should Helen press a candle home
'Twixt either pretty thigh

1 'mood's'.
2 ' "What is it then, life?" I say. "Life – it means – " '
3 Where Cox was staying.
4 British diplomatist and essay-writer (1628–99).

The next line's unfortunately lost; the verse ends, of course,

    Or God eat Pigeon-pie?"

Ah, yes: the Mask.[1] The whole affairs merely this: I want to pay 15/- for my current subscription. Could you send them 15/- Foreign P.O. as from *me*: stating its for subscription. Arena Goldoni, etc.

I'm to say (I was told of your lights on the G-E affair) how much ahead Germany is in the news. Six days ago my letter from Eddie [Marsh] came:

    . . . . "George Mallory, whom I met on a Sunday visit to the Neville-Lyttons. . . . I have rather a grievance about never having seen ['met' is crossed out and replaced with 'seen'] him before. Besides his great beauty of face I think he has enormous charm of mind and character. I have an idea that you don't like him very much, tell me." – He goes off onto Duncan. [Brooke here reproduces the crossed out 'met' replaced with 'seen'] 's good, eh?

Ah, well.

                     deiu

                           Rupert

Cox's luv.

JS, Friday night [16 February 1912], Hampstead

It was very nice to have some more from you, even though so dummy-finned. I shall at all events be glad if you have chosen and clung to the chance they sent you – but it seems rather a shame that I should only hear of your shanty, by God, if it comes down. Mayn't I at least send you an oleograph to hang over the mantlepiece ? . . . But let that pass.

Lumsden Barkway is stopping the night here. Lumsden, you know, is the nonconformist minister with whom Lytton used to share rooms in Liverpool fifteen years back. He is now a popular preacher in Redcar, Yorks.[2] Such a nice fellow.

No. I'm afraid I've not recovered the power of coherent thought. I got rather over excited by a concert on Wednesday, which seems to have jarred the ewer. The night before that, too, was a very thrilling Labour Party meeting at the Albert Hall on the Suffrage. Mr Crooks was positively magistral. What literary power! After the Scotch rhetoric of Mr MacDonald[3] & the palsied blither of Mr K. Hardie,[4] it was too superb when

1 Gordon Craig's theatre magazine.
2 Barkway was later Bishop of St Andrews.
3 Labour Party leader J. Ramsay MacDonald.
4 Keir Hardie, a Labour Party leader whose appearance at Cambridge as a guest of the Fabians caused quite a sensation (see *RBB* 118–19).

that great man sprang to his feet and exclaimed "The Constitootion is in dinger!"

There was a fairly grave scandal over the Friday Club Exhibition – which has finally settled Albert [Rothenstein]'s hash. The hanging committee consisted of Duncan, Nessa [Bell], Roger [Fry], 3 faded more or less reaction[ar]ies, & Albert. The selecting went off quite easily; & among the things unanimously chosen was a set of caricature "statuettes" by a person called Allinson.[1] Next morning, Press day, everything was arranged & various people came & looked round. They all of them said the "statuettes" were too horribly vulgar. Among the complainers was one of the hanging committee who hadn't been there when they were chosen . . . There was a good deal of agitation, & the two other faded members of the committee joined this person in saying that after all these things couldn't be exhibited. "Why, they were actually caricatures of Slade Professors". Albert was not present. Duncan, Nessa & Roger remained perfectly firm, & pointed out that the things had been definitely accepted & couldn't possibly now be sent away, that they weren't the least vulgar (rather dull in fact), & that as Roger himself was one of the people caricatured surely no one else could object. The objectors wavered. Then suddenly there came a telephone message from Albert saying that if the things were exhibited, he'ld not only resign his membership of the club but would remove his pictures from the exhibition. My dear! would you believe it? those cowards gave way. They positively sent them away – on the ground that it would injure the exhibition if Albert took away his pictures. All that D. N. & R. did was very feebly say that they'ld resign at the end of the exhibition – & now it's uncertain whether they'll even do that. But can you *conceive* giving way to such wretched & impertinent bluff – & down a telephone! And the so-called pictures are 6 wretched watercolours. There's pretty strong feeling about it all in London, you may imagine.

This must do for the present.

Gadava? No. I've not been that way for weeks. Lytton goes for a week tomorrow. His difficulty with Henry is smoothed over. *He* thinks (or pretends to) that it's cured. But *my* knowledge of life convinces me that the difficulty 'll get worse & worse. You can't have such a lop-sided relation without explosions – can you?

I fear I wrote injudiciously to Ka this morning. Graves kept on coming in and out in such an awful state. Really! It's too bad! St Loe's entirely given up measuring the front page notes. And today he's not even remembered them right. Sickening! And so on in his staccato way – opening & shutting the door. So naturally I couldn't think or write down what I thought.   Your
                                                                James

1 Adrian Allinson (1890–1959), painter and sculptor.

*RB, [postcard], Cinder Thursday [22 February 1912], Rugby
to JS, 67 Belsize Park Gardens, Hampstead*

You've heard Ka brought me back?[1] Have you seen her? Will you? I was so unpleasant on the journey that she became infinitely tired. Now Hester [Cox] cries all day. I suppose we shall slay that immense woman (K.) before the end of it.

Are you – could you face – coming here ever? With luck you might hit one of my chirpy periods: in one of your week-ends. Not this one though. I'm not ever coming to London. England is inevedibly [sic] beastly. Why has only she good food? I loathe England & being in it. But I am very bright: & shallow as a midge.

I'll write someday. Here I think of doing a very little work. But I feel restless.   R

JS, Saturday evening [24 February 1912], Hampstead

Dear Rupert,

It's very nice to know you're within reach. You all but found me on the platform at Victoria. As a matter of fact I met about four trains that afternoon – and only stopped because I remembered dear Lady Glenconner's witty mot: "If you knock often enough at a door, it is sure to be opened by the devil."

. . . Such a racketty day yesterday – with Mr Philpotts[2] in the afternoon & Mr Lloyd George in the evening. *This* afternoon, too, I went to such a chic Beecham Concert[3] of 18th century French music at the Aeolian Hall. Who should be there, coming out, but Eddie – with *dear* Lady Diana![4] We took tea at Barbellion's – and Eddie brought out of his tail pocket (where it always lies) his review of your poems. He's *most* anxious for a word from you. Such a *nice* man, I thought.

I can't go on, as I've got to dine with those Kave rats.

May I come to Rugby next Friday? I expect it'ld be all right – and I want very much to see you.   Yours
                                                                          James

I've interviewed that Ka woman. She seems as misty and globular as ever.

---

1 Brooke and Cox had gone from Munich to Starnbergersee, where Cox told him she had been seeing Henry Lamb again. Brooke went into a rage and appeared to be having another breakdown; thus Cox took him back to England four days later.
2 Probably the writer Eden Phillpotts (1862–1960).
3 Thomas Beecham (1879–1961), the conductor.
4 Marsh's friend, Lady Diana Cooper.

Lytton was frightfully bucked at the Kingsway yesterday, when an earnest looking young woman shook him by the hand. His eyes must have quivered a bit – for she hurriedly murmured: "It *is* Mr Sturge Moore,[1] isn't it?"

RB, Monday [26 February 1912], 24 B.R.
to JS, 67 Belsize Park Gardens, Hampstead

Right-O.

I say, *did* you ever send the Mask 15/-? It doesn't matter a bit if you didn't: only I'd like to know . . . . . .

Could you, when you come, bring me a copy of Mr Shaw on Munciple Trading?[2] It costs 6d or 1/- at the Revolutionary Bookshop in Charing Cross Road. The Rugby bookshops are *so* stupid.

You'll be here to a latish tea on Friday?

A letter from Miss Barker (to the Ranee). Nothing else very important.

R.

Do you think it my duty to go to Cambridge on the 8th? I'm not certain I could bear it. .

RB, Later [26 February 1912, Rugby]

I now remember what I wanted to write about. It was this. Mr L. Irving is performing his version of *Schuld und Sühne* (by M. Dostoieffsky)[3] here on Thursday & on Saturday nights. If you want to see it we go on Saturday, the Ranee & I; if not, on Thursday.   Answer
Rupert

JS, February 27th, 1912, The Spectator

Fact is, my dear fellow, I *didn't* send that 15 sh. = 15 M = 20 fr. = \$4 to the Arena Goldoni. *So* sorry – but flush is hardly the word just now.

Next, if my taschenwörterbuch[4] tells me true, I *don't* want to see Mons. Dostoevski's play *Zukunft und Selbstbildniss* or whatever it's called. I was

1 Thomas Sturge Moore, the poet and elder brother of G. E. Moore.
2 Bernard Shaw's *The Common Sense of Municipal Trading* (1904).
3 Laurence Irving's *The Unwritten Law*, based on *Crime and Punishment*, was first performed at the Gaiety Theatre in Manchester on 15 August 1910. It had also been staged in London at the Garrick and the Kingsway.
4 'pocket dictionary'.

given *such* an account of it – rewritten by our Lorrie in an a'fu manner.

I shall have much pleasure in visiting Mr Henderson's bombshop[1] and doing your job.

———

Alas! alas! my soul is withered, and loveliness is gone from the world. (By the way, I told you what Whattie [Walter Lamb] said to me when I threw him over. I remembered yesterday what he said to me when I accepted him. We were sitting on the sofa in his attic on letter Q – you recollect? After I'd said what I had to say, *he* said, trembling and émotionné – "then may I kiss you now?" I murmured an assent, and he (as he proceeded to act accordingly) exclaimed: "Oh! come to me with all your beauty." – Good God! Don't repeat that for Christy's sake – don't.) But the tragedy of life's too dark. – You recollect perhaps how, some years ago, I used sometimes to meet about in the tubes a young Girl for whom I conceived a lively affection? It's many months now since I'd seen her. But this morning, rather late for Office, I got into an unusual train at B[elsize]. P[ar]k. There, dear lord, she was – Large, coarse, red, with her hair up and – it's death! – in spurtacles. Götternoth! Götternoth! Die Ende! Die Ende![2]

———

I'm bound to say I found Mr & Mrs Raverat a little unsatisfactory. The slump in intellectualism is complete – really carried too far even for me. The conversation heaved and staggered along, and every vestige of interest was promptly snuffed. The man seemed to me really very nice, & if left to himself would probably even be interesting. But he's wedded to a sheer hulk – whatever that may be.

I'll write as to my arrival later on.

Oh, don't go into that Quogg yet.

Your
James
turn

over[3]

Who the devil's writing were you trying to imitate on the envelope? It was like a cross between McTaggart and Beatrice Chamberlain.

RB, Thursday, [29? February 1912, Rugby]

Dear lad,

I shall have heard what time you'll appear tomorrow?

Be Youth & Gaiety itself.

Will you kindly be Discreet in this house? I'll prepare a list. The most

1 That is, the Revolutionary Bookshop. Arthur Henderson was a Labour Party official.
2 'Plight of the gods! Plight of the gods! The end! The end!'
3 Written on back of paper.

notable recent point is that Ka's existence in Germany & voyage home
with me is not known. O yes, & also you rang me up at 4.15 this afternoon.

R

P.S. No one's handwriting – my own – the mood of the moment. If *you*
ever felt like a mixture of Beatrice & Jack, you wouldn't be so scornful. It's
not at all a nice feeling. But you, you're so damn healthy.[1]

RB, March 12 [1912, Rugby]
to JS, 67 Belsize Park Gardens, Hampstead

Did Ka tell you, – she was to, – that I'd at length broken it to the Ranee?
She quite accepts you: though I gathered you were to sleep apart. But one
of you may have Alfred for a night: & I daresay Madge'll oblige the other.[2]
For me, I inhabit my watch-tower[3] with the Highlander.

I'm leaving Rugby almost immediately. There's an Almond Tree in full
blossom down the Road. That sort of thing a chap can't stand. Is Estrid
[Linder] all that's left?

Jacques came: & surpassed your worst calumnies. Eo vehor?[4] Perhaps
defiles are better than plains.

Do not bring th' Eyewitness.[5] It will be here. Bring me my Shaw. Put on
my boots. I am Not very well. There is no more to say.   ·   R

1 Brooke wrote to Virginia Stephen, who was experiencing mental problems of her
   own, on 9 March: 'I feel drawn to you, in this robust hard world. What tormented
   and crucified figures we literary people are! God! how I hate the healthy
   unimaginative hard shelled dilettanti, like James and Ka.'
2 Madge was a maid. Brooke wrote to Cox during Strachey's visit: 'It's nice having him
   here: though one's skating riskily, at times. Arguments on fucking [...] And there's
   James still in collapse because I said Madge, the second parlour-maid, was so natty.'
   Later, Brooke invited Cox to visit while Strachey was still at Rugby, explaining,
   'Don't mind, anyway, about James. He can have – if he wants it – a tête à têter in
   whatever weekend you're not here.' Still later, he wrote: 'James has been very nice
   & done me a lot of good, I think.' Another letter: 'You, I, she [Mrs Brooke], James:
   what a tangle of cross-motives & dissimulations it'll be! We'll want our clear heads.
   But it'll be fun.' There had also been an argument with his mother about Cox.
   Brooke wrote to her: '. . . and then we were fairly launched on you. I felt the red
   creep slowly up – Damn! It's just as it always was; even from the time when the
   holiday mention, at lunch, of the boy of the moment in the House (with apologies,
   dear!) left me the level red of this blotting-paper, & crying with silent wrath. This
   time, I'd my back to the window.'
3 Brooke is referring to his room at Rugby, but knew that 'The Watch-tower' was the
   name given to Lytton Strachey's former rooms in a turret on the Great Court of
   Trinity College.
4 'In view of that, am I carried?'
5 Hilaire Belloc founded the *Eye Witness* in 1911. Cecil Chesterton became editor in
   1912 and published Brooke's 'By a Lake. A Music for three voices' in the 10 October
   1912 issue.

JS, Wednesday [13 March 1912]

Dear Rupert, It *is* beastly of me never to have sent a Collijns. I found it so very soothing with you.

I'm rather a corpse just now, having had a fit in the night . . . & complications have just supervened. Perhaps it's the result of those stage society plays that I went to with Desmond on Monday.[1]

I've been a good bit on the move. Did you hear of Mr Wells's fancy dress dance? Miss Gilmour and Mr Sydney Waterlow? Mr Francis Meynell and Mr Rudolph Besier? The Countess von Arnim and Mr Henry James? usw[2] . . . I had the usual mild flirtation with Bunny[3] – which culminates tonight in a visit to Mr Bennett's play.[4] What shall we have to say, o lord?

1 Translations of Hermann Bahr's *The Fool and the Wise Man* and August Strindberg's *Creditors* (*Fordringsagare*).
2 '*und so weiter*' ('and so on').
3 David 'Bunny' Garnett (1892–1981). An author and critic and son of the translator Constance Garnett, Bunny was a life-long friend of the Oliviers. He studied at the Royal College of Science, Kensington, and met Brooke in 1909. Four and a half years younger than Brooke, Garnett was only eighteen when in the spring of 1910 Brooke asked Noel Olivier to invite him to Grantchester (Garnett, *Echo* 174). Garnett recalls that during this visit Brooke was free 'from any affectations such as I noticed later. [...] We went about midnight – for I had arrived rather late – to bathe in Byron's pool. We walked out of the garden [...] to bathe naked in the unseen water, smelling of wild peppermint and mud' (175). He also remembers that once when he was at Grantchester an American visitor insisted they join hands in prayer before lunch, whereupon Brooke 'gave me a vicious pinch as we clasped hands' (*Echo* 177).
The next summer Garnett again went to Grantchester at Brooke's invitation, then they joined the Oliviers for a holiday on the Norfolk Broads. Garnett and Brooke shared a cabin, and Garnett remembers:

> I was very happy and was aware that for some reason Rupert liked me. That holiday was the time of my closest friendship with him. His immense charm and intelligence had not yet been spoilt by success and by certain *idées fixes*, which later came to resemble hallucinations. With me, in our midnight cabin talks, he was simple, sincere and intimate, with a certain lazy warmth. It was only later that he was apt to utter warnings about the wickedness of other people. (*Echo* 222)

As Robert Skidelsky points out in his biography of Maynard Keynes, Garnett was remarkable in his social circle because he was neither an Apostle nor even a Cambridge man, nor a Strachey, nor a Stephen (247). Garnett was, however, a handsome boy, with liberal views on sex. James Strachey wrote to Lytton on 10 June 1915: 'I had a long interview with Bunny the other night. He was partly drunk, & poured out a lot of interesting information. He said he was very fond of a great many different people, and enjoyed copulating with all of them, of whatever sex.' Garnett's relationships included Vanessa Bell, Daphne Olivier, Francis Birrell and Duncan Grant, who fell deeply in love with him (Noel Olivier called Garnett and Grant 'the darlings'). Paul Roche, in *With Duncan Grant in Southern Turkey*, says that once when he remarked that he thought Garnett was 'the great heterosexual of all time', Grant responded: 'He was, but he could still make love to me' (19–20).
After the war, Garnett lived with Grant. Soon, Vanessa Bell was also living with them. When Bell and Grant had a daughter, Angelica, in 1918, Garnett said he would marry her when she was older – which, in fact, he did. The best source of information on Garnett is his three-volume autobiography: *The Golden Echo* (1953), *The Flowers of the Forest* (1956) and *The Familiar Faces* (1962).
4 *Milestones*, at the Royalty.

On Friday at the Office I received a visit from our brother C[ecil]. F. Taylor, who was anxious for me to approve of his appointment as private secretary to the Baron de Forest.[1] Chimerical, I suspect. The dear H.C.F.[2] was as ever – and I fear that I was undisguisedly contemptuous. He had something about a very eminent scientist getting your fellowship[3] . . . Chimerical, I fancy. He talked a lot, too, about an easter party with every sort of Trevelyan and Luce and Sanger, as well as the Warlock. Chimerical, no doubt.

The CHIMERICAL, in fact, is the Keynote of the Age.

My arrangements seem to be of such a nature as to forbid my starting by any train earlier than (Euston 5.35 Rugby 7.39). I don't intend to inquire whether it goes or not till I reach the station – & I'll telegraph then if it doesn't & come by the next that does. If you think '7.39' 's too awkward an hour for arrival I'll have some supper at the station before driving on. That's Friday night, bien entendu. Ka, I suppose, follows on Saturday.

Oh dear. Lytton & I have become Suffragettes since I saw you.

Woe to Ariel, to Ariel the city where David dwelt.   Your
                                                                      James

RB, [postmarked 14 March 1912, Rugby] to JS, 67 Belsize Park Gardens, Hampstead

Right: you'll find food on the table & me on my last legs.

Are you bringing the Laudanum?

God damn you. God damn everyone. God burn roast castrate bugger & tear the bowels out of everyone.

Have you heard of Momentum?   R.B.

P.S. You'd better give it up; wash your bloody hands. I'm not sane.

RB, [postcard, postmarked 23 March 1912, Rugby] to JS, 67 Belsize Park Gardens, Hampstead

I seem to have stopped just here for a bit.

---

1 An intimate friend of Winston Churchill who currently represented West Ham North in the House of Commons.
2 Possibly 'Honourable Cecil Francis [Taylor]'.
3 Brooke lost his fellowship to the scientist Hamilton Hartridge (1886-1976), whose thesis asserted that the blood of coal miners requires relatively little oxygen.

I thought of going to the Sea or the Country, perhaps, in five days. Do you still want to join me? Don't if you feel it'd fetch it all up again. Only if you're fairly resigned to the [arrow drawn here pointing to blanks that follow] __ __.

Where, I don't know. Oh, God, where *can* one? R

RB, Tuesday [26? March 1912]
to JS, 67 Belsize Park Gardens, Hampstead

I *can't* find your letter.

I say, I *must* get away from here. My nights average four hours: & that's absurd if one's deferred dissolution. I'm coming to London on *Thursday*. I hope to stay with the Raverats: but that's uncertain & private. Then we'd catch the 2.5 to Marazion on Friday?

Thursday evening I want to see Bryn & Margery – I hear they're off to Wales. I want to see them before the END, eh? – (I had thought as Bryn wanted to come down here she might take me off somewhere – after you'd gone back. But that's no good, I gather.)

Hunstanton seems beastly far, & I *hear* it's rather awful. It'd be bracing though . . . Isn't there anywhere in the South? (Dorsetshire barred).[1] You see after you've left me, I want to be *able* to slip up to London, Woking, Limpsfield[2] unless I get anyone else to take me on. I go abroad in a fortnight. Till then, I *won't* be alone much.

There's also the expense of these Hunstanton Hotels.

But, of course, I abide by your decision. I shall be intolerable anywhere. Don't come if you don't want to. It's absurd to be Quixotic about the Departed. Thine

Rupert

RB, Wednesday [27 March 1912, Rugby]
to JS, 67 Belsize Park Gardens, Hampstead

I'm sorry you're so busy. I can scarcely do any thing. Winchelsea was suggested . . .[3]

I get to London (Euston) at 5.0 tomorrow. I go to Loudoun Road (unless

---

1 For the Apostles' annual Easter reading party.
2 Cox was staying at Woking, the Oliviers at Limpsfield.
3 Strachey accompanied Brooke to Winchelsea to look for a suitable location for the reading party. During this visit together, they tried to call on Henry James at nine in the evening. Brooke reported to Katherine that although they heard sounds in the house (including the loud rattling of chains and bolts at the door) and saw a shadow in the window, the door was never answered.

they reject me there, too) for tea; to Ka for dinner & stay till prayers. Then to Baron's Court, where I sleep.[1]

It seems impossible to see you.[2] You might catch me on a telephone? Friday I'm at present empty: but you aren't. Will you find me in the [National Liberal] Club at 3?

I don't think I'll want to stay Friday night. If you're really ill, perhaps you'd better not come. I shall be a handful – not kicking, but impish.

I've not heard from the Oliviers. But I gather I should only find Noel at Limpsfield the next week – scarcely enough, eh?

(You don't think we could abduct Bryn for Sunday to the Metropole at Brighton – & go shares?)

I slept fragmentarily.

I feel so humble & ashamed to you.   thine
                                                                            Rupert

RB, Wednesday morning [10 April 1912, Brockenhurst]
to JS, 67 Belsize Park Gardens, Hampstead

Of course, a letter had come as we were sweeping under the pleached boughs. She [Bryn Olivier] explained she was staying in Wales in case I'd changed my plans, that she didn't *want* to come, but would . . . if I liked. (Oh, she hadn't received my letter then.). So I wired she was to come *immediately*. No doubt, she won't.[3]

It'll be a comfort to get to the German ladies, who are kept in their place: who are kind & trustable, like a well beaten dog. 'Oh, daughters of dreams' did you know I'd been turning the Poems & Ballads[4] into Deutsch?

Von Gedicht und Geschichte Ihr Mädchen,
    Wie gütig, unmüdevoll wie!
Sophonista und Sara und Gretchen,
    Und Clothilde und Annamarie . . .[5]

Turk[6] sends his love.   R.

1   The Oliviers had a house in St John's Wood: 12 Loudoun Road. Brooke was staying
    with Edward Marsh.
2   Brooke did find the time to see Strachey; they spent three days together at the
    Mermaid Club, Rye, Sussex.
3   Bryn Olivier did eventually join him.
4   Brooke refers to Swinburne's *Poems and Ballads* (1866, 1878).
5   'From poem and story you girls / how generous, how untiring! / Sophonista and
    Sara and Gretchen, / and Clothilde and Annamarie.' As for his reason for returning
    to Germany, Brooke wrote to Hugh Dalton around Easter 1912: 'I go back to
    Germany soon. They are a slow race and will not know I am stupid.'
6   Hugh Russell-Smith.

RB, Sunday [14 April 1912], The Smoking room,
National Liberal Club, Whitehall
to JS, 67 Belsize Park Gardens, Hampstead

Bryn & I are reclining here a moment on our way to The Chart. I say: I've nothing in the Bank (Barclay's). and I've just written a cheque for [Mrs] Primmer[1] for £6-0-6. I'll detail *your* share afterwards. (Her charges are magnificent.). But could you spare a cheque for £7 by return? If not I must hurriedly apply elsewhere –

Bryn was infinitely sympathetic. Did I tell you her remarks about Auntie Helen?

I fancy I leave for Berlin on Thursday – I leave Limpsfield then.

"fond of me" – *wirklich*?[2] – But surely, if you regrettably *were*, you'd have started revolver practice. Perhaps you have. One doesn't live *in vacuo*.

I'll see you on Thursday? I'll write again. You couldn't tell me how to get to Berlein? Rupert

RB, [22 April 1912, on a train]
to JS, 67 Belsize Park Gardens, Hampstead

The Dawn.

Mr D'Aucastre nods opposite. He has followed me like a dog, ever since he got over the shock of those first few minutes when, entering late & finding me in bed, my hair only visible, he thought he'd got into the lady's quarters.

Charming, sterling fellow. He brushed my forehead lightly with his dreamy brown mustache once, & twice, & then skipped aloft to the upper birth [sic]. Uninterestedly and with a brown bag he spent those throbbing dreadful hours in abusing himself. Lucky fellow!

One hour, one gaunt shrieking hour I dozed. You have talked to the Major, abused yourself, & slept, since Victoria. In a few hours you will have a late, bitter breakfast. And I, I have only that one intolerable ghost of an hour between me and yesterday. I hover eternally on the doubtful borderland between today and yesterday: a grayhaired embryo; creature of no world; horrible. A bell clanged us out of delirium at 3.30. We put on our life belts – I snatched the Photos of my Letter of Credit – & went on deck. It was merely Flushing.

---

1 Strachey had rejoined Brooke at Mrs Primmer's cottage in Bank, New Forest. Bryn Olivier was there as well. Brooke wrote to Cox (April 1912) from Bank: 'James left yesterday. He was very freakish – what they call delightful – when he was here. But at the end "a sense of impending doom" seemed to hang over him. [...] "You should see a birch in Autumn, my boy!" he said, rather simply. "I *have*", I said, with some irritation. [...] James hurt himself vaulting a fence.'
2 'truly?'

Flushing – the lewdness! It means when you (else where than at Woking) persuade it to come off. "Always flush the pan" creeps into my mind. *What* pan? χρὴ τὸ πᾶν ἀε φλύδεν[1] our Euripides the human (with his droppings of warm tears) tells you. All Ionia in half a line.

Steady. We're going through the New Forest just now. It is as credible as anything else. Will you be at Lyndhurst Road? Or, if I'm Bryn, will Rupert? . . . . Mr D'Aucastre (my last foot-hold over the abyss) sleeps opposite. He sleeps, always, with one eye, the right, not quite shut. A thin white line gleams, twixt lid and lid. The pupil is tucked away – he's genuinely asleep. It's a trifle like the moon we saw last night. What does it mean?

Two of the others are in the carriage now – the skirty lower ones. They bend their bodies and souls in vague meek inferiority. "If it came to the Straight Thing between us" they continually think, "you'd put us down, drive supremely home, & we'd open our legs, submit, accept mastery, whimper & smirk." Oh! oh! I am touched also to tears for them: because they never *quite* know what's up. Women aren't quite animals, alas! They have twilight[2] souls, like a cat behind a hedge. What can one do? I, at present at least, can only stare at the windmills & sing

"Oh, *is* it my gay Parisian style,
or is it the dimples on my tile,
Or (*Bang*) *IS* it my twenty foot openwork smile
that seems to tickle their fan-cy?"

But how dreadful that the whole world's a-cunt for one. The clouds are but petticoats, swirled so alluringly high . . . For *them*, do you think, are all the trees excitingly waving TR – S-RS?

Leonard[3] (a mixture of H.G. [Wells] & Bonar Law)[4] is awake & glooming at my reflexion in the window & the landscape through it. Now, *which* is he looking at? And which, for that, am I? That spectral melancholy face floats unceasingly between the tulips & me. My Toolips. – Two Lips or Toolips? patented for my next (& last) paper at the Society. [Also, as a choice, "Is it" . . . etc. N.B.][5]

Unter vier Augen,[6] my dear chap. I'm more than a little tired.

Rupert

1 'It is always altogether fitting.'
2 This word is written over another, which appears to be 'shadowy'.
3 Apparently Mr D'Aucastre's Christian name.
4 Andrew Bonar-Law (1858-1923), the Chancellor of the Exchequer, was among the Conservative Party's inner circle. A bitter, defiant man, he violently opposed Home Rule for Ireland.
5 Brooke's brackets.
6 'Just between the two of us.'

Of course, I forgot the Ovaltine, mine & hers. *Would* you be so kind as to send a small tin immediately to Margery, in mediate handwriting? I'd meant to. I'll explain on a card to her. It's *so* important for all of us – ah! for all of *you* – that she should live.

RB, Friday [3 May 1912, Berlin]
to JS, 67 Belsize Park Gardens, Hampstead

My dear chap.

I begin this waiting for my money in the Deutsche Bank. Heaven knows when I shall finish it.

It rains. Does it rain? No. It is raining.

You got the address right. G.H. is, as always, Gartenhaus. Never omit Dudley's name. Underline Ward & Berlin.

The past, – I suppose it's always so in these Indian summers, these curiously pacific lulls before the end, – comes back to me with a vivid & pathetic precision, as I emerge from the Underground or smoke my [Victoria-Café, later.][1]

cigar in the Café des Westens, or roam from Nollendorf Platz down to the Sagen Allee. So incomprehensibly fantastic it seems – and why has it led to this? or, *has* it led to this? and how?

"Habe, habito,

Habita,

Habite, habitote,

Habeunto."[2] I found the old refrains rising – from what tender abysm of the subliminal, who knows? – with all the old rhythm & charm to my lips. "Habitote, habeunte". . . . But there is added now something beyond charm, something of an enorm [sic] and periculose fantasy. What *is* it all? Why should we, incomparably tender & beautiful, have had to insculp that extraordinary rigmarole on our minds? Do you *realise* that we sat in wooden desks, striving to get it *right*, biting the words into our brains so that they've always since more indelibly & subtly & importantly than anything else, than Milton or Mozart or Monticelli, been part of the heart of our mentality? And that if we, imaginatively, shrilled, "habeote, habitanto", Mr Sandford's lower jaw quivered & quivered, & then our starting eyes saw the rhythm caught up & redoubled & flung back by his biceps – more toadlike he grew, & the pulsing more complex & more swift, rising through extraordinary degrees & minor heavens, to the perfect orgasm and ejaculation of his rage? And, no doubt, there was a booming

---

1 Brooke's square brackets.
2 Brooke is conjugating the Latin verb meaning 'to have', with some perhaps deliberate errors.

& swelling & throbbing below his flies, too. But for *that*, I never had the knowledge to look, in those days.

And tickets. I found myself, the other morning, wandering, in unconscious distress, round the pension. I was looking for something, I knew not what; some key to relief, and corridor towards comfort. I only knew, I'd somewhere missed something. It was like a feeling in a dream; dim, forlorn, vaguely discomfiting. Then I found my eyes wandering up along the wall; & I knew I was seeking a little board with eight hooks, & a jangling symbol on each. 'Might I take a ticket, Sir?' I murmured to Frau Ricpel. But she was blank. I slid into the *Abort*[1] with a feeling of guilt. I knew that when I crept out again, even if I'd craftily not pulled the plug – a melancholy military shade would wait me, with "What number were you, Brooke?"

The occult indecency of those horribly yellow jangling tickets. One always shuddered a little in taking them. And it might be warm, too, dreadfully, from some Pale hot little pocket. And that meant that there'd be warmth, or worse, on the *Seat. Gott! was haben wir erlebt!*[2]

Yet, – if you'd a little board put up, & if you went to it, every morning, & unhooked no. 1, and trotted meekly off, mightn't it perhaps, *mein alte*,[3] cure your constipation, and alleviate even the heartache, & the thousand other ills . . . ? I, at least, intend to try it, when I settle down, & if I have money enough.

Old Church,[4] yes, I dropped a tear over the *Times*: & several over your letter. Curious how much he's become part of one's life.

Part II. Friday evening.

Oh, I see it clearly enough: how it's my duty to tell you about my life in Berlin. It's not a very high level. The opportunities, even, aren't so great as you think. The artistic world is highly excited over a new exhibition, just opened, of – The Futurists! – all the old things. A Cézanne exhibition which was in London in November. *Und so weiter*. The Futurists are much admired. It's time we have a weekly 2[d], & a fortnightly 3[d], paper devoted to the Quite New. The former has Picasso, Matisse, Koschovska,[5] & Futurist drawings: & the latter Matisse at least. That's nice, picking up a Pablo for your evening paper. The advanced literature in these papers is

1 'lavatory'.
2 'God! What have we experienced?'
3 'My old one.'
4 Apparently an employee of the *Spectator*. Strachey had written to Brooke on 14 March: 'I rushed upstairs a minute ago and plunged very suddenly into the Forth. And there was poor old Church, standing in the chiaroscuro with his black trousers knotted around his ankles.'
5 Probably Oskar Kokoschka, the Austrian-born British painter.

translations from Clodel,[1] Gide, & Charles-Louis Philippe: & articles on Stenier.

Herr Reinhardt[2] turns out to be quite the dullest kind of fraud: a mere Sir Tree.[3] Midsummer Night's Dream – with the lovers played as farce & a German Puck. *Der Artzt am Scheideweg*[4] with most of the points missed – but tolerably well-act[ed] in the old fashion. (The M[idsummer]. N[ight's].D[ream] was mere His Majesty's.). You know, they're *merely* 1898/9. Only one thing I've seen well done, in their funny way: Frühling's Erwachen,[5] of course. But even poor old München shows up well. – I saw *Der Rosenkavalier* here, – the acting & music were nine times worse.

The Stage Society – oh, no, the Stage Society of 1901 – a *most* advanced & go-ahead body gave its show on Monday. (I read about it.). The plays of the Future, they were called. An anonymous masque: a Wedekind attempt – probably all right – and . . . [Shaw's] Press-Cuttings!

I tell you all this to warn you, once & for all, that no help is to be got from this quarter. Mr Wedekind's got stuff in him, from some points of view. But the *Theatreo* – pah! As Mr [Gordon] Craig said.

I fairly held my breath when the curtains went up on darkness & the lady kept screaming "You're near enough, Melchior!" [?] & at length there was a pop, & he was all too near, in fact, right inside. But when the lights returned the Fraülein all round, bless 'em, hadn't turned a hair. I was the only pink thing in the whole blessed Kreisenerspiele.[6]

Oh, and I had a turn when it came to the Star & Garter at Richmond. They'd a queer idea of the S. & G., the Germans – very new-arty they made it. But they got the *Society* all right. There were the two *schwind-süchtig*[7] brethren, Forster & Shove*: & the Jew, silent; & the strong quiet Ridgeon-Hobber[?]; & B.B. infinitely like Maynard grown old (it was played so.). And the waiters . . . . . I cried to think how lonely I'd be, down in Tripoli, on June 26th.

B'the bye: I've now seen *Gespenster*[8] twice in Germany in Munich & in Berlin. And each time, Oswald was got up *exactly* as Morgan [Forster]. *Was ist's denn?*[9]

* This name is pronounced to rhyme with *grove*, not with *love*.

1 Paul Claudel (1868–1955), the French poet.
2 The Austrian theatrical director Max Reinhardt (1873–1943). His 1905 production of *A Midsummer Night's Dream* at the Deutsches Theater in Berlin used a revolving stage as an essential part of the performance for the first time in Europe.
3 The English actor, director and producer Herbert Beerbohm Tree (1853–1917). He directed *A Midsummer Night's Dream* at His Majesty's Theatre in 1911.
4 Siegfried Trebitsch's German translation of George Bernard Shaw's *The Doctor's Dilemma*.
5 Wedekind's *The Awakening of Spring*.
6 'revolving theatre'.
7 'consumptive'.
8 Henrik Ibsen's *Ghosts*. 'Oswald Alving' is the main character.
9 'What is it then?'

By God, this is dull. I'm very sorry. I'm going to have a bath (my first.).
I'm not very lively. I've discovered God's law. It is, if I work *no* hours in a
day, I sleep *eight* hours that night: if I work *one* hour in a day, I sleep *four*
hours that night: if I work *two* hours in a day, I sleep *no* hours that night.
Simple, & conclusive.

What else? Have you put a bomb in the *Saturday Review* offices? – I say,
you're keeping your mouth shut, aren't you? Even to people you trust so
much as your own kith & kin. Do you see, the circles you move in . . . . .

Rupert

Noel (typically) sent a letter to the N.L.C. that Saturday. It got here
yesterday.

Your last three letters (& others of other people) have been thrown
away by the malicious Anna.[1] Damn. And it'll make the Judgement Day
complicated, Lacunar.

Ah, yes, one thing: Mr Stead[2] has been worrying me a good deal these
last few days. What shall I do?

RB, [May? 1912], Berlin
to JS, 67 Belsize Park Gardens, Hampstead

Pension Riepel
   Kantstrasse 162
      Charlottenburg
        Berlin –
is where I (with Anna) sleep. And on Dudley's going away you can write
to this or that. But don't give anyone else *this*.

I find 4/- in my pocket. It seems singularly useless here. Won't you let
it cover any minor outlay you incur, my dear chap, . . . ?

This bit of paper once belonged to Charlie.

I enclose what I do i' the long hours of the night. I'm so sorry.

And I enclose my bill.

I've given up theatres: & I do nothing. Both in vain.

R. "What do the dead do, Jimmy?"

J.   "Faith, coz, they sleep."

R. "Oh, then I wish to God that I were dead. I have not slept this seven
days."

---

1 Annemarie von der Planitz, who married Dudley Ward the next week, on 11 May.
2 Possibly Henry Wickham Steed (1871-1956), the future editor of *The Times*. Steed
  worked as a foreign correspondent in Berlin and Vienna during this period.

So Fletcherian – but by Webster.

I've had Jacques' account of his relations with you. I wait yours.[1]

I'm, privately, frightfully hurt at not having – officially – received Mr Lawrence's book.

Mr Reynolds[2] – Rothay, we call him – proposed yesterday. He took a lot of pulling up to the mark. I got a tea out of it. But today I lunched alone. The Polish waiter was moved.

My play[3] does not progress. Nor do I.   R

Before Rye

I owed you £2 + a little.
for Rye £1 + a bit.
Sum = £3 – 10. – about

+ various expenses in the New Forest	10/-
+ cheque for £7–[4]	£7
	£11

I lent you £1 on Lyndhurst No. Station.

	£10

your part of the Primmer bill was board at .5/- a day	£1
1/4 of rooms	8/-
baths or something	1/-
	£1-10-0

∴ I owe you £8-10-0

                                                                            R

---

1 Jacques and Gwen Raverat had taken a strong dislike to Strachey and apparently were trying to influence Noel Olivier, who wrote to Brooke that she could not really believe Strachey was 'quite a wicked worm'. Brooke wrote back on 30 May: 'You write rather beastily about James – rather anyhow, as if the position was that one had to make out he wasn't altogether a worm. I suppose Gwen's been telling you he's a worm. It's not true. Lytton is filthy, & for God's sake don't touch him. The rest of the family are pretty slippery. But James is all right. He's unlike you in being sensitive. But he's a very fine person extraordinarily honest and trustworthy, very intelligent, and meaning well (which is important)' (*SOL* 177).
2 Alfred Rothay Reynolds, a writer from Pembroke College, was Dudley Ward's housemate.
3 *Lithuania*.
4 Strachey had financed Brooke's latest trip to Berlin and had also seen him off at the station.

When do you want how much? And is this right?

BALLADE, with Double Refrain.[1]

To J.B.S.

Boys! mine is not a pleasant task today.
 But to the pure everything is pure . . . . .
(Levinstein, do not fidget!) Let us Pray! . . .
 You often must have noticed, I am sure,
 When washing in your tiny tub, or ewer,
Or wondering how Godfashioned you, or, worse,
 Yielding to Curiosity'sbase lure,
– Between your legs there hangs a bag, or purse.

Sir, have you wondered *why* the world is grey,
 Why I amgrim and hollow-cheeked, and you're
Snappy, and She issmiling in a way
 You often must have noticed, I am sure?
 Some say, the higher that we go, the fewer;
Some, there's a Purpose in the Universe . . . . . .
 – Look down, young man! The Thing is not obscure.
Between your legs there hangs a bag, or purse.

Fraülein, (your skirt is rather in the way)
 Your ankle (I'm the merest amateur,
But....may I stroke it?) takes my breath away,
 – You often must have noticed, Iam sure; –
 Your knee! . . . (don't wriggle, we are quite secure!) . . . .
– Fuck! Bugger! Drat it! Blast your vitals! Curse!
 – Für *dies* hab' ich verriegelt meine Thür? –[2]
Between your legs there hangs a bag, or purse.

ENVOY

Prince, there is one fault you can hardly cure,
 Which, I regret, ... which makes me . . . . – to be terse! –
(You *often* must have noticed, I am sure!)
 Between your legs there hangs a Bag, or Purse.

1 Brooke has typed the poem. It is reproduced here exactly as he typed it. Although
 none of Brooke's published verse includes an envoy, many of his unpublished
 poems do. This particular poem was also included in a notebook of poems that
 Brooke left with Edward Marsh, and which Marsh later gave to Geoffrey Keynes.
 However, this poem has been ripped from that notebook. Fortunately, a typescript
 of the notebook exists, and it includes the poem.
2 'For this I have locked my door?'

RB, May 24th [1912, Felberg, Germany][1]
to JS, 67 Belsize Park Gardens, Hampstead

An Inn. Hoo!

Such a day, and I met people on the road.

Ha!

I'm sitting, you know, tired and happy over a fire after such a supper. I saw Rupert in Berlin. He was very nice, I thought. But then –

And this morning I had an Adventure – I met a Horse. Ha!

I had a letter from old Justin [Brooke] yesterday. He seems ever so much better.

The weather, you know – and these German lakes – its very fine – and Berlin. I know all about the German character now. I'll tell you, one day.

How's that old Pernel?[2]   Ka

Goodnight.

RB, May 29 (Dick's birthday) 1912 & ff.[that is, folgende –
*'following'], bei Dudley, Spichernstrasse 16/G[arten].H[aus].,
Charlottenburg, Berlin
– kindly note change of address
to JS, 67 Belsize Park Gardens, Hampstead*

The *Connaught* rooms,[3] James? Is *that* your compromise? And afterward – do we (do *you*) wander through the quiet parterres & shaded groves of Great Queen Street, while Bob Trevy & Roger Fry argue what Art is? Or does Lena entertain us all with recitations? I suppose it's a step up from Campden [sic] Town: but will it be really nice? However, I suppose the ladies are to be allowed in this year. I figure you with Daphne [Olivier] on your arm, – Eddie behind with Lady Di [Cooper], Tovey[4] leading all with Mrs Davidson.

This is the bright style of letter. Oh my God! The degradation! The grey horror! The degradation! The slime! The slime! The slime! You & I, thundering down to Eternity, write these bright letters to each other. James! James!

Well, if you can stand it, it relieves me (how ignobly!) to do it. It's after

---

1 Brooke and Cox left Berlin on 20 May to visit Neu Strelitz, Felberg and Müritz. As he had done before with Bryn Olivier, Brooke here tries to reproduce a letter in Cox's style, using her handwriting. Unlike the first attempt, this one was successful in fooling Strachey.
2 Pernel Strachey, one of James's many sisters.
3 A fashionable dining club on Great Queen Street.
4 Donald Tovey (1875–1940), composer and musician.

all an inch above the general mud-level of my jetzig[1] life. Was fur Eine Ausicht hat man![2] What a view! I may say I very nearly write you a small bright note every day. The falseness! But you're spared.

Look here, I've just had a – "a" – "the" were better – letter from Bryn. Oh, my God. Frightfully nice of her, of course. And an absolute smack in the face for me. Refused – oh, Lord. There are some people (including all women) one should never propose to by letter. Remember that.

The letter, in that well-known hand-writing, begins, in pencil, April 30th. The second half is dated, May 19, and is in ink. It was posted May 20 from Hampstead. It is very long.

"Dear Rupert" it begins. So *that's* something. "R.'" is dropped. The words are well-formed. The letters go stiffly up and down. Not much give and take about *her*, a graphologist would murmur. The spelling is inaccurate enough to be completely vulgar, but not sufficiently to be – like Noel's – insane and rather fascinating. The whole page gives the impression of a thoroughly superior housemaid.

I'd, of course, in the lonely evenings – oh, you know how one *does* it – been wistfully murmuring "Banque" to myself. A hundred times Highland Waters sounded vaguely from beyond the balcony. A hundred times great beeches shadowily obscured the gaunt yellow stove. A hundred times I felt .. oh, but that, I remember, is a secret.

But she – oh, it had all passed from her, like water from a duck's back, or facts from a philosopher. Bank was past, was nothing. I – oh, you're all so fond of me, I hear, in England. Fondness, a genuine, brotherly, fondness – is the keynote of the letter. But the 794 miles is emphasised. What am I saying? Never mind.

"I must say that Berlin, just now, seems like a fussy, exhausting irrelevance." – But earlier than that she's – oh, so painstakingly, so deliberately, – drawn, with precision, the lines, all lines. Did I ever tell you women were vague & sloppy? Not at all, James: not at all. Clear as Euclid. She sizes up & dismisses my letter to her. The emotional one. "All things considered, disingenuous was, I thought, the word for it." So that's at an end. She goes on to the scenery. "The oaks in the weald that were so dull & bare when you were here are a fine rich yellow ochre, and the little wood below the house is full of bluebells. One can smell them going down the path. I wish you were here still." English literature has not been written in vain. Then there's April news. You were there once. "We climbed beech trees – some of us. I don't think James liked it much –" It goes on to be pretty fairly beastly about you. But I mayn't say.

At Ka she gets in a very nice hit or two. (Females are at their best in malice.).

1 'present'.
2 'What a view one has!'

"I met her on the road – a glorious sight in her blue smock." Then a long description of a picnic they all had – descriptions of everybody else, but no word more about Ka. It ends "Oh yes Life is very nice & not for me alone. At least there are moments for everybody."'

That's good. What? I fairly chuckled. Ka winced a bit.

I now think it's perhaps dishonourable to cite all this – it's in a way laughing at what are, after all, perhaps a poor woman's upward struggles. At least, you must never *breathe* a word of this to any of that family: no matter what sudden triumph it'd give you! Swear! Swear old truepenny! You & I can, after all, taste the subtle beauty of it . . . – I say, *won't* you – if I do – chuck it all & join me in the country & write it all out as a Comedy?

To proceed. There's a lot in the new style about psychology. The first half ends a little abruptly with expressions of chastened affection. . . . Three weeks later, & with a stylo[graph], she returned. – I say, there are things I can't copy out, even to you, for very shame: There are some deeps we've yet to plumb (plomb? plum?) together.

It begins – what the devil *had* she been doing, talking to you? or reading me? "So far I got, and then, lamentably, *stuck*." She a little regrets her earlier beastliness, but won't look back to see how beastly it is. [Which, in a way, I grant, has fineness.].[1] ([You'll have gathered, my dear, that after she so heart-warmingly wrote that lovely hurried note in pencil, saying I must stop in England, on principle, because it was my Duty as an English Poet . . . . I, at 1.30 in the morning, and very drunk, wrote a *very* long letter, which said "My dearest, your letter would – if aught could – have saved me from making a hole in the water. *Not*, heart, because of the *general* grounds for living you advance, but (oh God) because your lips (I'm trembling) are like a rosebud, & they curve distractingly. I love you so . . ." And more to the same effect. – Oh, I was young & mad. But, after all, she couldn't have *thought* I'd think she was in earnest with her principles – oh, well.])

She seems pretty rocky, though. The loveliness of summer depresses her "sends one's heart into one's boots" . . . . . "The sweet-sour smells of May-flowers and this fat green sleepy land spread out so blatantly." ("Blatantly"?, James. *Blatantly*??).

It's because, she hints at the end of the letter, she's twenty five ("a quarter of a century" she phrases it.) I'm getting bored. There's some literary & dramatic criticism. One more plum. "I've been reading more sonnets and Mother read 'Fathers & Children' to us. It is an extraordinary book. I think Turgeniev is a very great man. What do you think?"

It is signed, simply, "Brynhild".

I hope I haven't gone too far, anywhere. I've got a bad headache this

---

1 The brackets in this paragraph are Brooke's.

afternoon. And it's difficult to know what "the recipient" is just like – your rid ex [?], I mean.

Oh, there are pieces of playfulness in it, which I've not quoted. Oh James: I think that Life's *just* too beastly to bear. Too utterly foul.

But it's the irresistible, false, fondness of the whole that pins me shrieking down.

I wonder how you are. I look westward to you as to the guardian of civilization. Are you keeping things all right? Do you know you are mere Atlas?

I'm going soon either North or South. If North, to Gustav [Collijn] & the rest – should we meet, one Friday night, at the Hague? Expect a telegram.

I am flat and dead. I'll not give any lay account of this part of the world now. When we meet, perhaps. Victory's precisely as hollow as anything else, to the dead. It's better to be dead than to be what one was: but can't one be hard and yet alive? It must be possible. And I'm almost completely hard now. Do be hard, James. Hard. Hard. HARD. Damn you. Hard as stone. Solidify yourself. Quick. Please do. I wish you good. You've no idea how I wish you good. On this infinitesimal scale on which the dead feel, I'm so frightfully fond of you. Even envy dies. I hope so much you're happy –   Rupert

RB, June 10, 1912, bei Dudley Ward,
Spichernstrasse 16 G.H., Charlottenburg, Berlin.
to JS, 67 Belsize Park Gardens, Hampstead

It's so rarely the case that I'm 3½ to 1: that I'm fairly complacent about it. And I really can't be troubled, anyway, to show any emotion – or do anything but avoid Dudley & read *Der Sturm*.[1] [Oh, and of course I frequent the Wedekind *saison*.[2] What a man! *Naïf*! my dear chap! oh, distinctly naive – in fact *naïve*'s scarcely the word for it! Gnayeef to a degree.][3]

Still, it's – infinitesimally – adding to the flatness, [*can* one add to flatness? – razing the penultimate pimple from the boundless plain of existence, let us say:] to allow me to conclude that you've taken the plunge.[4] Not – indeed – that one couldn't foresee it? But you might have flung me the customary unveracious detail. Where, for instance, is she

---

1 *'The Tempest'*.
2 'season' – the annual Wedekind season was performed at the Deutsches Theater in Berlin 1912-14 with Wedekind directing.
3 The brackets in this and the next paragraph are Brooke's.
4 Brooke refers to Strachey's infatuation with Noel Olivier.

now? And how did Dr Craig[5] take it? And do you *remember* your bromide? And are the keepers nice to you? And what price holes now?

I – to anticipate your all-human retort – have as little as you'll so wittily, in your reply, profess to report. (Is that poetry? or what?) I can give you a too harrowing account of the present and recent anguish of Annemarie. But you'll not care to have it. Of myself, – I smell (transitive) as one with a cold in the head smells. What can I tell you? That I fare well, as the' dead fare? I am infinitely strong and level. I can even work, I believe. Very nice. Oh do not grieve for me when I am dead – The sullen surly [Clive] Bell reminds me that Virginia has married into the Society: they tell me.[6] No doubt you've a heap of funny stories about it. I *thought* the little man 'ld get her. Directly he began saying he was the only man who'd had a woman she knew, & telling tales about prostitutes – oh, you should have seen the love light dance & dawn in her eyes! *That* gets 'em. To him that hath shall be given: from him that hath not shall be taken away even that which he hath. Even that which he *hath*, James: one by one. Two, two for the lily white balls; clothed all in hair, oh! Look out, James, look out: One cometh, with a Knife . . . . .

But I wonder. I only wanted to explain . . . I forget what I wanted. Any how, I am quite well again, in this new world. So cheer up, in as far as you're interested in foreign policy. I've mislaid something . . . . But it'll turn up in the end, like a bad penis.[7] Just let me know if you're dead. Tell me that all's delightful – you know the old delights? – That so & so's elected: that Maynard proposed to X–: that somebody joked: that there was a good concert: that Bryn's delightful & stupid: that Lytton wittily said Shakespeare was not a good writer: that Ka is Kind: that Sheppard gave an amazing imitation of another don: that I am a bad poet: that St Loe is a remarkable character: that—— [scribbles appear here]

If I went to the Hague for a weekend, would you join me? Why shouldn't you? Why should you? I'm going to Copenhagen: but I find that's too far for you. Oh, it is difficult to choose between Stockholm, [illegible], Venice, & Pesth![8]

Do give my love to all the old people, you know.

I often and distinctly desire your presence. This sounds like a proposal from Daddy. But it is not. It is not a proposal. And it is not, in a way, from Daddy. That is in my witty style: you'll recognize. You'll recognize. And

5 Dr. Maurice Craig (1866–1935), the Harley Street neurologist who had prescribed milk, stout, and a conservative lifestyle for Brooke following his breakdown. Vanessa Bell was also his patient for a time after her miscarriage. Brooke mentions Craig (and the bromide and the 'keepers') here to imply that Strachey is crazy for turning his attentions to Olivier.
6 Virginia Stephen and Leonard Woolf became engaged on 29 May, but did not marry until 10 August.
7 Brooke has drawn an up-turned penis in the left-hand margin.
8 A line is drawn from 'Pesth' to the left margin, where is written: 'Buda not N.B.'

you'll know, therefore, that I'm tired. Forgive. Smile upon me. Raise healing hands. That is in my St John style. Oh well, goodbye. I suppose if London breaks you, you can always go to Grantchester? You might find it rather nice..

How nice a good long chat would be, old chap!   Rupert

Are you sending me Mr Belloc's new book "Four Men."—?

JS, Wednesday, June 12th [1912], Hampstead

Dear Rupert, I've just been having tea with Ka at the Civil Service Stores in the Haymarket.

I gather that you now know about the inside of my head these last months – or something about it. I'm very glad you should – if you really do. But perhaps you don't properly, and anyhow it's impossible for me to make out from Ka what you feel. Don't you hate me? It seems so likely, and it's the danger of that that I simply can't face. Don't you still love Noel too much to bear anyone else loving her at all? All that's too horrible. And if you *do* hate me, I don't know if I could go on. You've no idea how alone I am – there's no one I can speak to. But I always love *you*, and if you can be fond of me a little – other horrors matter infinitely less.

This isn't sentimental, is it? I feel desperate. You see, I've not succeeded in getting anything else. If I had, (and of course one's mad enough at moments to think one has) I should I suppose be ready to throw you away. Even so, Heaven would be turned into something of a pis aller.

Apart from you, there isn't much that's tragic about my condition yet. In many way[s] it's been superb for me. I was beginning last autumn to be fairly stuck. Think of the vistas that are opened – think how it's improved my feelings to *you* . . . I believe too that I'm pretty hard – though, as I told you the other day, there have been some shocks lately. She's really rather remarkable, isn't she? What?

I don't know what this letter's like. I want to see you so. Won't you meet me for a week-end in Paris or Brussels soon?

Dearest Rupert. I love you.   James

RB, Friday [14 June 1912], bei Dudley
to JS, 67 Belsize Park Gardens, Hampstead

I suppose, then, you've got the latest from Ka. I didn't write much from my Hochzeits-reise:[1] partly I didn't feel like it: partly, I knew, so well, the feeling solitaries have about people in that position. Oh, yes. It was

---

1 'Honeymoon'.

enough you should be hating & envying & being jealous & feeling, incomprehensibly, inferior and ashamed . . and all the rest of it. Without my appearing to rub it in.

There's not really much in it, you know. It seems to me certainer than ever that it's all a matter of the person, & that *A*, copulating with his most Beloved for the first time, is *miles* below – in intensity of feeling – , *B*, touching a chance little finger. [That is supposing *we* are B . . . you remember my old paper?][1] And, anyway, cohabitation (the whole business of copulation & going off with & all the rest) is merely a factor. If it multiplies you at 10 – you touch 100. If you're only .001 to begin with, just then, it only gets you to .01 – less than a good glass of stout leaves you at in better days. *Nicht wahr*? I assure you. And I assure you that I'm so very dead that you needn't feel – you needn't have felt – envious. I'm dead, dead, dead. Strong, you know, & sane & everything. But if you don't meet me in two months, & bury me, you'll nose me as you go upstairs into the lobby.

Ka let slip your plight, yes. I wrote you an enormous letter promptly. But – if I remember – it was only about Bryn, after all. Still, it was meant well. I felt very fond of you at the moment & extremely anxious all should go well. And that's curious, for I don't feel anything about anybody at all, most of the time. Theridamas (vel Usumcasane libentius audi) it is a glorious thing to be a king.[2] But can't I give you a few tips about the process? I suppose they'll fall on your deaf ear, JAMES.

Hate you? Oh, dear me, no! What *I* say is, Fair play & no favours, & let the best man win! Don't you hear my too honest English voice? Don't you see my English hand too heartily stretched forward. "Shake, Jim."

My dear, you're male & you understand things: and even I want somebody like that I can exchange a sort of love with. After all, *I* have got & probably shall get only good things from my relationship to you: and it'd

---

1 The brackets are, of course, Brooke's. On 13 February 1909, he had read a paper (apparently his second) to the Apostles titled 'A or B', in which he envisioned them all 'attended by dumb naked boys, who ran to and from the pagoda in a constant stream bearing food or drink or toys and practising light lust with one another on the way'.

2 Theridamas and Usumcasane were the kings of Argier and Morocco, respectively, in Christopher Marlowe's *Tamburlaine*. Both men became Tamburlaine's lieutenants. The Latin passage reads, 'Or in this case, Usumcasane might more willingly hear.' The reference to the glory of being a king comes from Part 1, Act 2, Scene 5, in which Tamburlaine begins to reveal his plan to capture the Persian throne:

> Tamburlaine: Is it not brave to be a King, Techelles?—
>   Usumcasane and Theridamas,
>   Is it not passing brave to be a King,
>   And ride in triumph through Persepolis?
> Techelles: O my lord, tis sweet and full of pompe.
> Usumcasane: To be a King is halfe to be a God.
> Theridamas: A God is not as glorious as a King,
>   I thinke the pleasure they enjoy in heaven
>   Cannot compare with kingly joyes in earth.

be rather *too* mad of me, wouldn't it, to sacrifice that for an off chance at a cunt? I'd rather have a brother than a penisholder any day. As long as I stay sane I know that; and sane's the one thing I precisely and permanently am. I'm very sorry for you and contemptuous of you; but I love you and I'm ready to be of any help. – Oh, you'll want it whatever happens. Yur [sic] sure to get let down somewhere.

For myself, by the way, the situation (to use a strong word) is this. I fell (by May) completely out of love with Ka. I've got no emotions worth the name about anybody. I feel an affection for her, in a slight way: mixed with other feelings. I'm ready to flirt with Bryn or anybody else in the world. I *do* love Noel in a dim & distant way: I feel a great deal of gratitude to her, with good reason, and a great (worship/reverence)[1] for her – quite without any ground. I'm going to wait over this summer somewhere (in England a certain amount, anyhow): & see if I get feelings and energy of any kind back. If I can work up enough love for Ka I suppose I shall marry her. But it seems unlikely enough, as I am now. If we don't marry, she or I 'll go off somewhere. So, at least, it's at present arranged. But she's very weak & changeable: no I suppose anything may happen to her: as she's got no one to look after her.

All this is *am strengsten*2 private.

I'm glad I gave you a detail or two of my experience with Noel, ere I went. I *thought* you seemed a little startled. What a joke! "Remarkable" you wrote. So I conclude you're fairly well trapped. "Remarkable" . . ? No: not really, I think. Slightly unusual, perhaps. But not very. – But I'll admit she gives one more chance of pretending to oneself that she's remarkable, if one's in love with her, than most females. Which is as much as one can expect or demand.

I think it's on the whole better to be in love with her than with most women; because she is much harder and rather honester than they. She's a very ordinary person underneath the pink-brown mist, you know. And she's just a female: so she may let you down any moment. As she's unusually unemotional and stony, and as she's backed up by her adamantine family with that loony-man at the head, she *may* be fairly safe. Of course, you'll get let down in lots of ways whatever your position – rejected suitor, accepted, 2nd lovee, sole Romeo, or what not – as long as you're in love at all. (And I'm awfully afraid you mayn't be so hard as you make out – only selfish, & its not at *all* the same thing.) But the fun 'ld *really* begin if she accepted you, dear chap. Then the fact she hasn't any emotions 'll come out. She 'll be *extraordinarily* kind – she's ripening towards that. But she won't look round 20 yards after parting; & you will; you'll see a stupid blank cow-like back of the head, imperturbably moving down the street; and you'll fairly drench the pillow all night. But I expect,

1   One word is written atop the other, both in parenthesis.
2   'strictly'.

really, she won't fall in love with anybody for at least two years. After that there 'll come a day when she'll suddenly feel a sort of collapse & sliding in her womb, & incomprehensible longings. It's when the ova suddenly begin popping out like peas. Then she'll just be ripe for anybody. But not for you, dear boy. Some rather small & very shiny man, probably syphilitic, & certainly a Jew. She'll crawl up to him, will Noel, – to Albert Rothenstein, or Mr Foss (if she has *very* good taste), or M. Picciotto, or (if he's joined us) Mr Applegate – and ask him to have her. And no doubt he will. I need hardly ask you to visualise it. Then you'll have some fun.

Meanwhile keep an eye on England; & protect it from these scandals. Recognize, I mean, the feminine soul: & when you see Albert nosing round, turn him away. When the smash comes telegraph, & I'll bring my little German revolver across (you'll discover by then how difficult it is to buy them in England: as I did on April Xth): & we'll call at Thurloe Square[1] together.

God be with you, & enjoy yourself as much as you can. I'd advise you to cut clear & go entirely back to balls (not mine): if I thought it any use. But I've no doubt you're too incurably romantic.

I'm still in a stupor here. In how much of a stupor is proved by the fact that when from my solitary room I hear these two little mice scuffling away next door, I don't feel the slightest touch of envy or anything else, I just take another sip of bromide[2] & turn over. It's *almost* inconceivable. And when, in the morning, I find a towel in the bathroom bloody that was clean at midnight, I'm not in the least disgusted. This is my haven.

When I'm less in a stupor, I might creep along to Brussels perhaps. I'll let you know. Isn't there an Extradition Treaty with Belgium, though? Give my love to the *Universitäts unterhaltungsverein*,[3] on Wednesday week.

Write. I'm sorry I'm so meagre and grey in trying to mitigate your loneliness. I should so like to – if indulging your necrophilistic leaning would do it. What can I do. I feel immortally strong and wanly affectionate – that I could support you through anything & love you through most things. But I daresay I'm really as useless to other people as I am to myself. *Schade*.[4] Oh, I love you all right, if that's anything. – On the diminished scale, you know: but that's the scale's fault. Live & enjoy yourself.

with love (is how letters are being signed, in these days[*])   Rupert

[*]   Not Bryn's, though.

Did I ask for Mr Belloc.
Send me all important Elizabethan books to review . .

1   Albert Rothenstein's London residence at 5 Thurloe Square, South Kensington. Brooke stayed there while Rothenstein was away in the spring of 1913.
2   Brooke had begun taking strong sedatives for his insomnia. He reported to Cox that he was taking 'anti-erection pills' that 'turn out to excite one *frightfully*' (c. April 1912).
3   'University conversation society' – that is, the Apostles.
4   'Sorry.'

RB, Sunday [16 June 1912, Berlin-Hannover Bahnpost]
to JS, 67 Belsize Park Gardens, Hampstead

I hasten to explain that my last letter but one (3½:1) was written as from an outsider. Eh? At that time, you see, I didn't know *you* knew that *Ka* had told *me* . . . . So my letter was (and rather well done, I think, for that) as from one who modernly *supposed* you were in *some* lap – & jocularly – bitterly – assumed the common course of events. The "she" was – had to be – you fool, entirely impersonal, then. You were mere St John to me – you *know* I'm indistinguishable from M. [John] Buchan – "Poor Strachey: I believe some Woman made havoc of his life . . .". . You were, *ex hypothesi*, distraught. Mine was it, with delicious raillery, out of my ignorance & experience, to murmur "Suchen Sie das Weib!",[1] our old German proverb. Oh, wasn't that all clear? For the Lord's sake, don't suspect me of joking about *individuals* (except Bryn).

3½:1, you gump, was the number of *my* letters to *you* compared with the number of *yours* to *me*. The ½ was the pseudo-Ka – which, I hear, was completely successful. So *she's* exploded . . What a chap I am!

It'd be funny if, a week today, we were breakfasting in the Temple of Peace. If you can get *one* extra day that week, it'd be worth doing. If so, wire; for I may go to Copenhagen on Wednesday.

I say, I rather gather Ka's in a bad way. She's rather ill, you see. And none of her bloody relations is aware that anyone tragically wants help except him- or herself. Only, for once, Ka *does*. *I* could look after her – I know how. Only, as things are, I can't. And as she has cultivated always only takers, and no givers, she's got nowhere to turn. It requires a lot of strength & intuition to be able to support people, & all this Hester [Cox]-"Mar"–Virginia–Justin [Brooke]–Graham-sort of crowd,[2] can't do it. It's personality you know. We can do it. Can't you get hold of her? You needn't argue things *out*. Just sit & smile at her for three days. She fairly "responds" to gentleness, you know. Only she never asks for it . . . She's really so *badly* in need of it: & there's no sensible person in England save you. Damn it, aren't you supreme enough to be able to prop her a bit. She's as lonely as you, & far weaker. I wish to God you might go down for a day or two: or take her a walking tour. Or something. If she gets well in a month or so, she can work things out. But I don't want her to go into the abyss – or what'll happen? I'm so helpless. I only know from her letters how bloody things are with her. Do keep wiring to her. Psychological

---

1 'Look for the woman!'
2 'Mar' is probably Strachey's sister Marjorie, who had become active in the Suffrage Movement. Graham's identity is a mystery, but Virginia Woolf mentioned her in a letter to Cox: 'an awful elongated woman called Graham report[s] that you fed the swans in the Kaisergarten last Tuesday at four' (16 May 1913).

support's the only thing in the world ever worth having. Don't tell her I said she wanted your support.

I'll give you or any body anything: if only you'll give her –

Leb'wohl.[1] Send M. Belloc *straight* out. I'll write you a short review, gratis. Rupert

RB, Sonntag [16 June 1912], bei Dudley to JS, 67 Belsize Park Gardens, Hampstead

On *Thursday* I go to Cologne. Hotel Kölner Hof.

If you come to the Hague – & do, but get an extra day – write or wire or something. It's only a few hours to Cöln from the Haag. I'd get there (ie Hague) at dawn on Saturday. Bring a Baedeker, or learn of a hotel.

There *are* just moments, after all, when these two gaze at each other, & I, who'se privately put both right, and know far more about each than the other, suddenly find myself after all outside bristling walls, palisades, ... oh, oh! Furchtbar peinlich nicht wahr?[2] Oh, one *knows* one's even more intimate with either than the other – understands better – being more intelligent. One *knows* they're children & one's old & wise & kind to them. *But* . . . . . I'm writing this; and they, across the table, have got their hands together, & his other hand's on her neck . . . Wisdom's lonely. So I cry; & swear; & write this to you – that I'm glad I'll perhaps be seeing you in a few days.

If you've not sent Hilary [Belloc]: don't.

Don't let on – except to the Inner Circle – about my movements. I may send a card with the neuesten Nachrichten.[3] At present – I leave here Thurs. noon – get to Cologne Thursday night.[4]

thy
Rupert

RB, Wednesday night, July 10, 1912, The Old Vicarage to JS, 67 Belsize Park Gardens, Hampstead

Solitude is my one unbearable fear. I had escaped it fairly well all day till evening. But when, at 6, Daphne [Olivier] breezily pedalled away to a "coach", I turned desolately to my little table, and saw a certain 14 hours

1 'Live well.'
2 'Terribly embarrassing, isn't it?'
3 'latest news'.
4 Strachey met Brooke in Cologne. They attended a Van Gogh exhibition, which Strachey reviewed for the *Spectator* ('An Expressionist Exhibition at Cologne', 29 June 1912, p. 1037). The two then shared a room at the Hôtel des Indes in the Hague before returning to England.

of loneliness before me. I worked till supper. I ate supper. It was 8.30 & the Worst was visibly beginning, under bushes & behind corners. . . . . I changed into my best grey, & bicycled off to call on Mr [A. C.] Benson. For once, he was out. I draggled round to Trinity. Mr Shanks & Mr G E Moore were *not* up. Mr [Bertrand] Russell & Mr Gow[1] *were*. But again, not in. It was 9.30. Should I try Kings or Johns? . . . . . . John's was nearer. I was utterly indifferent. I asked for Mr [Hugh] R[ussell]-Smith & Mr Benians.[2] They *were* up. I knocked & entered a pied[3] Benians. I had last seen him on the *München Hauptbahnhof*,[4] early in March, 1911 – before, good god!, I'd become really entangled with even Elizabeth! A lot lay between. I felt incredibly smirched as I wrung his hand – .

How things shelve back! History takes you to January 1912 – Archaeology to the end of 1910 – Anthropology to, perhaps, the autumn of 1909. –[5]

The autumn of 1909! We had hugged & kissed & strained, Denham & I, on & off for years – ever since that quiet evening I rubbed him, in the dark, speechlessly, in the smaller of the two Small Dorms. An abortive affair, as I told you. But in the summer holidays of 1906 & 1907 he had often taken me out to the hammock, after dinner, to lie entwined there. – He had vaguely hoped, I fancy, . . . But I lay always thinking Charlie [Lascelles].

Denham was though, to my taste, attractive. So honestly and friendlily lascivious. Charm,[6] not beauty, was his *fate*. He was not unlike Ka, in the allurement of vitality & of physical magic. – oh, but Ka has beauty too. –

1   A. S. F. Gow of Trinity College was a friend of both Brooke and A. E. Housman. He was in the cast of *Faustus* with Brooke.
2   E. A. Benians (1880-1952), the author of *The Cambridge Modern History* (1902) and – later – *The Cambridge History of the British Empire* (1929), taught history at St John's College.
3   'on foot'.
4   'Munich central station'.
5   It is not clear whether Brooke intends for all three dates to relate to Russell-Smith or simply to important times in his own life. The account of seduction in this letter belongs to the last year mentioned, the autumn of 1909. Brooke was trying to recover from his nervous breakdown in January 1912. He might have seen Denham that month in Munich, since Hugh Russell-Smith was also there at the time. At the 'end of 1910', Brooke moved his belongings from the Orchard to the Old Vicarage, went home for Christmas, and then left for Germany. Denham had stayed with Brooke 28–30 October of that year, and certainly might have visited again nearer the end of the year.
6   Brooke wrote a poem in the autumn of 1909 called 'The Charm', a loving testament to a sleeping beloved. Brooke did not often fix his poems with an exact date, but he did so with this one: 8 November 1909. In the poem, Brooke writes of the 'One white hand on the white / Unrumpled sheet', and ends with the language of religion: 'holy joy' and 'holiness upon the deep'. If Brooke was feeling some guilt about seducing his young friend, it is possible he wrote this poem in an attempt to restore Russell-Smith's innocence and absolve himself. 'Beauty and Beauty' (1912) may also have been written for Russell-Smith as a tribute to their night in bed together.

He was lustful, immoral, affectionate, & delightful. As romance faded in me, I began, all unacknowledgedly, to cherish a hope . . . But I was never in the slightest degree in love with him.

In the early autumn of 1909, then, I was glad to get him to come & stay with me, at the Orchard. I came back late that Saturday night. Nothing was formulated in my mind. I found him asleep in front of the fire, at 1.45. I took him up to his bed – he was very like a child when he was sleepy – and lay down on it. We hugged, & my fingers wandered a little. His skin was always very smooth. I had, I remember, a vast erection. He dropped off to sleep in my arms. I stole away to my own room: & lay in bed thinking – my head full of tiredness & my mouth of the taste of tea & whales,[1] as usual. I decided, almost quite consciously, I *would* put the thing through next night. You see, I didn't at all know how he would take it. But I wanted to have some fun, &, still more, to see what it was *like*, and to do away with the shame (as I was taught it was) of being a virgin. At length, I thought, I shall know something of all that James & Norton & Maynard & Lytton know & hold over me.

of course, I *said* nothing.

Next evening, we talked long in front of the sitting room fire. My head was on his knees, after a bit. We discussed Sodomy. He said he, finally, thought it *was* wrong. . . . We got undressed there, as it was warm. Flesh is exciting, in firelight. You must remember that *openly* we were nothing to each other – less even than in 1906. About what one is with Bunny (who so resembles Denham.). Oh, quite distant!

Again we went up to his room. He got into bed. I sat on it & talked. Then I lay on it. Then we put the light out & talked in the dark. I complained of the cold: & so got under the eiderdown. My brain was, I remember, almost all through, absolutely calm & indifferent, observing progress, & mapping out the next step. Of course, I had planned the general scheme beforehand.

I was still cold. He wasn't. "Of course not, you're in bed!" "Well then, you get right in, too." I made him ask me – oh! without difficulty! I got right in. Our arms were round each other. "An adventure!" I kept thinking: And was horribly detached.

We stirred and pressed. The tides seem to wax. . At the right moment I, as planned, said "Come into my room, it's better there. . . ." I suppose he knew what I meant. Anyhow he followed me. In that larger bed it was cold; we clung together. Intentions became plain; but still nothing was said. I broke away a second, as the dance began, to slip my pyjamas. His was the woman's part throughout. I had to make him take his off – do it for him. Then it was purely body to body – my first, you know!

---

1 As tea and sardines were the customary fare at Apostles' meetings, Brooke had probably just returned from one.

I was still a little frightened of his, at any too sudden step, bolting; and he, I suppose, was shy. We kissed very little, as far as I can remember, face to face. And I only rarely handled his penis. Mine he touched once with his fingers; and that made me shiver so much that I think he was frightened. But, with alternate stirrings, and still pressures, we mounted. My right hand got hold of the left half of his bottom, clutched it, and pressed his body into me. The smell of sweat began to be noticeable. At length we took to rolling to & fro over each other, in the excitement. Quite calm things, I remember, were passing though my brain "The Elizabethan joke 'The Dance of the Sheets' has, then, something in it." "I hope his erection is all right" . . . and so on. I thought of him entirely in the third person. At length the waves grew more terrific: my control of the situation was over; I treated him with the utmost violence, to which he more quietly, but incessantly, responded. Half under him & half over, I came off. I *think* he came off at the same time, but of that I have never been sure. A silent moment: & then he slipped away to his room, carrying his pyjamas. We wished each other "Good-night." It was between 4 & 5 in the morning. I lit a candle after he had gone. There was a dreadful mess on the bed. I wiped it as clear as I could, & left the place exposed in the air, to dry. I sat on the lower part of the bed, a blanket round me, & stared at the wall, & thought. I thought of innumerable things, that this was all; that the boasted jump from virginity to Knowledge seemed a very tiny affair, after all; that I hoped Denham, for whom I felt great tenderness, was sleeping. My thoughts went backward & forward. I unexcitedly reviewed my whole life, & indeed the whole universe. I was tired, and rather pleased with myself, and a little bleak. About six it was grayly daylight; I blew the candle out & slept till 8. At 8 Denham had to bicycle in to breakfast with Mr Benians, before catching his train. I bicycled with him, and turned off at the corner of – , is it Grange Road? – . We said scarcely anything to each other. I felt sad at the thought he was perhaps hurt & angry, & wouldn't ever want to see me again. – He did, of course, & was exactly as ever. Only we never referred to it. But that night I looked with some awe at the room – fifty yards away to the West from the bed I'm writing in – in which I Began; in which I "copulated with" Denham; and I felt a curious private tie with Denham himself.

So you'll understand it was – not with a *shock*, for I'm far too dead for that, but with a sort of dreary wonder and dizzy discomfort – that I heard Mr Benians inform me, after we'd greeted, that Denham died at one o'clock on Wednesday morning, – just twenty four hours ago now.

Rupert

JS, Thursday morning [11 July 1912]

I've just seen about Denham in the Times. It's the sort of thing that'll probably make you gloomy – *how* gloomy I can't altogether decide. I suppose you haven't really known him well for rather a long time . . . Still, it's rarely that anyone one's been to bed with dies.   Yours
James

JS, Thursday night [11 July 1912], Hampstead

Don't, don't be too grey.

If you feel too solitary in your garden, send me a telegram tomorrow morning to the office, and I'll come and talk to you. Ka'll really be all right by herself – in fact it may be better for her to be quite alone.

Your letter didn't, as you'll have gathered from mine, give me the shock – but it was very wonderful, I thought. It seemed to give the whole of that sort of copulation so completely. They say there's another sort, that I know nothing about, – with people one's in love with. Is that really quite different? I've always thought it must be. . . . Well, one way or another you've immortalized Denham. And oughtn't he to be satisfied with that? I'ld certainly have chosen his fate, if I could have known it, in the early autumn of 1909.

You *will* get someone to talk to, won't you?   Your
James

I'll be in W[ellington]. St[reet]. till 5 anyway & then here.

RB, [postcard, postmarked 12 July 1912, Cambridge] to JS, 67 Belsize Park Gardens, Hampstead

But I don't see why I should meet father [?] Tanguy [?] on a bicycle in Sidgwick Avenue at 6.50 p.m   R

RB, Friday [12 July 1912], The Old Vicarage to JS, 67 Belsize Park Gardens, Hampstead

No, Denham doesn't make me much more gloomy.[1] Just takes a shade more light from the landscape; that's all. It's really rather nice to have something to think about. Anyway, death's extremely unimportant,

---

1 Brooke wrote to Noel Olivier the same day: 'Denham Russell-Smith is dead. That doesn't mean anything to you? It makes me gloomy' (*SOL* 191).

really: it turns out. I daresay he did it all rather cleverly. I may see his ghost
– I thought there was something last night. It's the only one I'm not afraid
of. That's something perhaps.

I went to sleep on the lawn in the middle of this letter for an hour: and
woke up saying "Family Life. Family Trousers." Is there anything in it?

The Post has come. I don't think you'd better come here. I'm in a bloody
state. I should only torment you & stifle you with gloom. On the other
hand, try not to be absolutely selfish to Ka.

She seems to be all right, in some ways, &, I'm glad to say, to be getting
clear of me. But I suppose she'll soon go to hell. And you won't be of the
slightest use in stopping her, or want to be.

Uncle Trevor's cottage sounds almost too exciting.[1]

I suppose there's no danger of your brother Lytton being in it or
anywhere near? Because I shan't come if there is.

A letter from the Ranee on finance: limiting me to £100 a year, &
making out she's already paid £72. So I live till January on £28. So you
might give me anything in my line that wants receiving. Shillings mean so
much to people on 22/. a week.   Rupert

P.S. When I pumpship, it's bright green. What does that portend?[2] I
bathe in the heat, in the hope of drowning. And Frank[3] has wired for an
interview. No doubt he'll bring a pistol. So there's lots of hope.

RB, Tuesday noon [16 July 1912, Cambridge]
to JS, 67 Belsize Park Gardens, Hampstead

My God, Jimmy, they've begun.

Last night it was awful. There must be between three & four hundred
thousand of them. They emerge, at 10 p.m. punctually, from two caverns
by each window. Their survey of the room is (as the Webbs said of India)
a "stupendous example of British amateurishness". The Old Ones, vast and
potbellied, stay in meditative raptures near the night-air. The babies trot
in and out between their legs. The middle-aged travel. They dizzily climb
the walls: they turn triumphantly along the ceiling – its glades & peaks are
extraordinarily romantic to them – above the bed they become uneasily

1   Strachey's Uncle Trevor Grant had offered his cottage at Rothiemurchus for James
    to use during his annual summer visit.
2   Brooke's 'bright green' semen could have portended a number of illnesses including
    mumps (see RB to JS, 27 April 1911 above) and venereal disease, a hypothesis raised
    by Arthur Stringer but not mentioned in his biography of Brooke.
3   Frank Griffith, whom Brooke thought was in love with Cox.

aware that Something's Up . . . they look down . . they agnisily perceive "There's someone else in the room". They lose their heads invariably. I watch them reel, & totter. With a slight scream they fall: & then there's a new wood-louse chase through the bedclothes for me. Sometimes I hunt the louse. Sometimes W L [wood louse] livid with terror hunts me. Sometimes I burn them with a candle flame on the ceiling. They shriek terribly. But when I awake in the morning, my hair is full of them.

Oh God Oh God.

Yes, it's an open joke in Cambridge. "Ka & James have gone off for the week-end." "Where to?" "Kissedher."[1]

I wish St John'd reply. Will you give me 6d to wire when he does?[2]

I see you've not got the full Noel technique at all yet . . . It's too long for a letter. But I suppose it makes no odds. A letter from her – two points. One, that – it turns out – the infinitely brightest spot in His Excellency's English visit was the moment he met you & me in the Nazional Liberals Verein Gebaüde.[3] He talked of little else that evening & the next day. The one bright spot – we – in the Club in London. ! That final whoop then, was exhilaration? Shall we have to elect him, after all?

Frank, my dear chap, turned out *such* a failure – from *my* point of view. Not a trace of a grievance! – *Am* I wrong in thinking it impossibly feeble & unmanly not to wish to kill any man who dreams of the same cunt as you? He, at any rate – perhaps he thinks it all past – was rather admiring, very cordial, & – of course – delightfully Irish! No stiletto – not a penknife! Has *nobody* my guts? James, James, shall I have to turn to you to find my Brutus? I'm getting so tired.

– Oh, the second point. It's *too* disgusting. A quotation may help – though it only *hints*. "Lord! [it's pretty different & weak in my feminine handwriting][4] Margery is pale as Tallow and her eyes still look suspicious & desperate & affraid [sic]; She has quarreled again *Furiously* with Bryn (B was furious too) and she & her Ladyship are on – au fond – rotten bad terms; [. . . . about her Ladyship].[4] Bryn I – of course – still find very pleasant; but its true she isnt [sic] the best thing in the world

1 Strachey and Cox had visited a 'fun city' (carnival) outside Cirencester.
2 Brooke had asked St John Lucas to come for the weekend – and wanted Strachey to come if Lucas declined.
3 'National Liberal Club building.' 'His Excellency' is Sydney Olivier, Noel's father. Brooke is being kind. What Noel had written was (the spelling and punctuation are hers): 'Did His Excellency show how pleased he was to meet you in the NLC? He said you were the only fresh & pleasant-looking person there, & he seemed really to have been touched by the sight of James too, he admires his phisique so! Theres a little beast, found in Australia, a kind of Lemure or a cross between that & a degenerate monkey, with silky fur & small round face: its eyes are very large for seing in the dark and it goes about by night; the people call it the 'Night Walker'. All this Father compares to James. I expect that its quite a little beast with a rare, shrill cry' (*SOL* 193).
4 Brooke's brackets.

for Mudie."[1] [Brooke's footnote]

Oughtn't we, perhaps, to refuse to speak to Noel or Bryn again?

I hope the tallow woman may come here. If it *is* you, it wouldn't matter if she overlapped.

I wish this could cool you in London.

You *could* really come down every afternoon for the night – Do you like Lice?

in death yours   Rupert

[1] Margery, you recognize: not the bookseller.

JS, Wednesday night [17 July 1912]

Mercy on us! Shall I maïl you some Keating's?[1]

I don't care when you can tell me about St John. If you can't have me I shall go to Goring & Mrs Shove – Gerald 'll be away. For the following week-end I've been asked by Maynard to his inn.[2] There was some talk I seem to remember of *your* being there; also, I gather, the ladies. Am I to go? – Technique? Oh yes, they always say that playing the organ spoils one's touch for the piano – or is it the other way on?

Wonderful literary power, what? Unless *that* was a forgery too. But I've always thought that the only possible explanation of her character was that she was a great creative artist.

Sorry Mr Griffith (or is he plural?) wasn't up to the mark. I'm there at last, you see.

I must work now.

Love.

Your   James

This came yesterday.

RB, Thursday [18 July 1912, Cambridge]
to JS, 67 Belsize Park Gardens, Hampstead

Yes: there's a stage when one believes she's a "great creative genius". It's rather a nice one. It lasted 22 months with me. Conversation with her breaks it down in the end –

St John won't come. If you want to . . . . *I've* got to go out to dinner on

1 Probably an insecticide.
2 Keynes was hosting a house-party at Eversleigh.

Saturday. If Margery appears, & wants to spend Friday night in my arms, you could defer till Saturday morning? Perhaps you want to anyhow. Or perhaps you anyhow want Bertha.[1]

I agree with every word of Mr Analenotos [?]: & – mostly by the unmistakeable jellygraph machine[2] – I recognize the hand of H.P. Harwood.[3]

Oh, Maynard. I gather Justin [Brooke] too 'll be of us. Very painful. Bryn Noel & Daphne on Monday, Self on Thursday or so; N. & D. vanish on Monday week. They'll, of course, ride all day.   Rupert

[Written on back of envelope: 'Hugh [Russell-Smith] appeared: woebegone. Three months they fought it. Frau S[mith]. only once outside the house in that time.']

RB, [postcard showing Henry W. Wellingworth,
Correspondent, and the Seal of the City of San Francisco,
postmarked 19 July 1912, Cambridge]
to JS, 67 Belsize Park Gardens, Hampstead

Why the *Teufel*[4] don't you come & do your work *here*?

I'm sick of Grantchester. I'm going to London on Monday morning: tea with Jack [Shephard].

If you don't want to go to Pozzo's why go?

But Justin's only there till the Saturday.   R

RB, [telegram, 3:50 p.m., 19 July 1912, Cambridge]
to JS, Spectator, *Strand, London*

WHY NOT WORK HERE TONIGHT MY ONLY FREE NIGHT AND I GO MONDAY MORNING RUPERT

1 Brooke refers to Gerald Shove's mother, known in Brooke's circles primarily for her affair with her son's friend Hugh Popham (the same Hugh Popham who was currently Bryn Olivier's fiancé).
2 A primitive duplicating device.
3 A Hillbrow master with a cavalry moustache who once shouted to Strachey and Brooke: 'Back to the changing room, both of you, and part your hair properly! You look like a couple of *girls*!' (*RBB* 30). This paragraph apparently refers to the 'this' that 'came yesterday' in Strachey's last letter.
4 'Devil'.

RB, [postcard], Friday [2 August 1912, East Everleigh]
to JS, 67 Belsize Park Gardens, Hampstead

Schlecht – [1]

No: I'm going to stay with Prof. [Gilbert] Murray on Wednesday for perhaps a week. About the 14th I'll be ready – if you really want it. I don't advise you to, you know. I may give, any time.

I go to Rugby in a few minutes –

Hadn't you better drop me?   R.

RB, Tuesday late afternoon [6 August 1912], Rugby
to JS, 67 Belsize Park Gardens, Hampstead

Dear James,

Is it any good?

You see, I really have come round such a very great deal. I feel most immeasurably and definitely grown up; & I feel as if you very blatantly weren't. The gulf seems almost *too* wide, especially with the hedge of Disapproval making the take-off so difficult. With the ardency of a neophyte, I occupy my mind, I find, entirely with a few ideas. They are all of them entirely incomprehensible to you.

To be a Strachey is to be blind – without a sense – towards good & bad, & clean & dirty; irrelevantly clever about a few things, dangerously infantile about many; to have undescended spiritual testicles; to be a mere bugger; useless as a baby as means; & a little smirched as an end. You have – by heredity & more by environment – a little of the Strachey. Buggery, with its mild irresponsibilities & simple problems, still hangs about you. You can't understand anything being really important – except selfishly – can you? So you'll not understand the possibility of "He that is not with me is against me"[2] being occasionally true. –

Oh, what language can I use? Perhaps if I knew French I could begin to make you understand that you don't understand.

People can't be blind to the difference between cleanness & shine, without, after a bit, getting a touch or two on them. And anyhow they're so frightfully – oh, unwilfully! – untrustworthy – a rotten spot: Disgust –

1 'Bad', 'wicked', 'poor' or 'ill.' The word is an adjective. Hassall says this was 'the worst day he [Brooke] had ever known' (*RBB* 351). Brooke told Cox that their relationship was over and wrote to Frances Cornford in the evening: 'I can't love her, you see. So now it's all at an end.'

2 Brooke used the same line in a paper he wrote in October 1912 titled 'In Xanadu did Kubla Khan': 'I see the world as two armies in mortal combat, & inextricably confused. The word "He that is not with me is against me" has gone out.'

disapproval – creeps round. It becomes possible to see what was meant by the person who said that seeing you & any member of the Olivier family together made them cold & sick. – It was wrong not to be able to distinguish between you & Lytton: but, if one's to believe *you*, not so very wrong. –

But then I suppose you can't understand anyone turning cold & sick to see any body with any body else – except through jealousy, & what [?] makes hot – ; can you? It doesn't happen in buggery.

It's the perception of all this that makes me fear I cannot adopt anything but my dreary flippancy towards you. The thought of that, & of the disapproval & the rest, make me uneasy as to how long, in my moroseness, affection can hold out against them: even in Scotland. Wouldn't mine give very soon? The shorter the trial the better, I feel. I even wonder if reducing it to nil wouldn't be wisest. And I feel, in my grown-up way, as if I shall have to decide. But you may have relevant views, I suppose.   Rupert

JS, Wednesday morning [7 August 1912], Hampstead

Dear Rupert. I'm very sorry that I was beastly the other night. I can't see at all what made it happen – except perhaps my feelings to Ka. It was incredibly stupid of me to talk like that – and especially at that moment. I hope it was all really irrelevant to our relation to one another – I certainly thought so at the time.

After all, is the gulf such a very terrible one? Part of it, at least, seems to me to be merely a difference of intellectual opinion. From my point of view I can see very little else. Do I disapprove of your behaviour and your feelings in this one business? Yes. But I thought perhaps you knew how cold and mental the disapproval was. I've not changed during the last few months either in this or in any other part of my relation to you. And if during the last few months I've ever showed you what I imagined the relation was, I'm sure it was the truth then and now as well.

As for what you think or feel about me, I've even less to say. I simply hope you aren't entirely indifferent and contemptuous. If you are, there certainly seems very little point in going on upon the old terms. If you're not, I can't see why what seems to me merely a painful subject shouldn't just be avoided. I suppose that to you it's the most impor[tant][1] one, and you 'ld think it dishonest perhaps to pretend [it] wasn't there. – But these are questions for yo[u].

Yes. It's you that must decide about Scotland: B[ut] you've had to every year for the last five, haven't you[?] And I'm not sure the reason's so new as you make out.   Your loving
          James

---

1 A stain has made the lower right edge of the letter illegible. Likely possibilities have been inserted in brackets.

RB, Thursday [8 August 1912], Woburn Sands, Gamlingay
[letter is postmarked 12 August]
to JS, 67 Belsize Park Gardens, Hampstead [forwarded to:
c/o Mrs Russell, Ford Place, Arundel, Sussex]¹

Dear James,

There are only two views of the events of the first half of this year. There is the view of the person for whom life is very dim – that Ka was a mixture between a bloody fool & an infinitely-to-be-pitied silly little girl, that the whole thing's one more example that virgins oughtn't to be allowed out loose, & that Ka's "friends", me & the rest, deserve to be kicked for our negligence & indifference (I have been.) That is, in part, Dudley's view, for instance. Then there's the view of people for whom life isn't dim: that the whole thing was too incredibly & bloodily filthy for words. (These are supposing that people know the story & the facts, Ka being one of the facts.).

Of course you don't know the story. But it seems to me you know enough to make your "intellectual opinion" unforgivable.

Listen. Men & women neither "copulate" nor want to "copulate": men have women: women are had by men.

Listen. There is between men & women, sometimes, a thing called love: unknown to you. It has its laws & demands. It can be defiled: poisoned: & killed.

Listen. It is not equally sensible to talk of your friend Lamb having nearly seduced Ka, & of Ka having nearly seduced your friend Lamb.

Listen. Ka wrote to me that if she had done what she once contemplated, & what she was saved from by my love, she would have killed her-self long ago.

— — — — — —

It's no good making a long list, as I could. All these sentences -- there's the point – are *entirely* meaningless to you. I might as well write in Assyrian. You'd just twitter on that your "feelings to Ka" make you "disapprove" of my "behaviour" . . . . Your thin, dirty little feelings to Ka. It's just they that incline to infuriate me. A damned lot of good they'd have been! A damned lot of good they *are*! I have loved Ka: I love her in a way: I know what she's like . . that she's incredibly brave, incredibly honest, & a woman. You find her useful as a sleeping-draught: you have a dim little factitious respect for her as an impossible sexless thing: & on those "feelings" you have the impudence to base – not even an atom of help or kindliness to her – but "disapproval" of me.

1 A note across the top in Strachey's hand reads: '[My long letter, to which this is the reply, is unluckily missing.]'. It seems possible, however, that Strachey may have written this note on the wrong letter. This letter from Brooke appears to be a response to Strachey's letter of 7 August; Brooke's next (13 August) seems to be a response to a missing Strachey letter.

It's past, you feel, & can be "avoided" as a "painful subject". Well, how much it can is partly the point. You see, to a person in my condition, it stretches so into a test.

Wymmih [?] Friday.

For instance, I may be going to Canada or somewhere for a year. Noel stays in London, away [from] all you people: a virgin of 19½ with all the bright little ideas about the identity of the sexes that we 've all had, & that you have. I've an unfortunate trick of staking too much on people. You know, with friends like you & your Bloomsbury acquaintances, she'll go through the same process as Ka. With Virginia buttering her up in order to get her for Adrian, with you, with all the rest, she'll soon be as independent as any man – like Ka. Then any dirty little man could get hold of her – not you, my little friend, for she knows you too well, – but anybody she doesn't know. And what use'd a fool like you be?

This is an instance chosen because though you don't love Noel, it may be time that you want to bugger her so it may appeal to you. It implies, anyhow, generally, that, if I view her acquaintance with you with dismay, I shall do my best to diminish it, doesn't it? So there's another "painful subject to be avoided", — it spreads, that's all I'm trying to point out.

We relapse on our brotherhood, & our common interest in . . journalism & philosophy. An excellent relationship to be on – as one is with Gerald. But not to fall back to. Besides: I don't go away with Gerald.

Your romantically bitter answer that I don't with [sic] you: that if I don't go to Scotland with you in 1912, it'll only make 1912 like 1911, 1910, & 1909, won't hold. I've been with you every week-end for ages. I've not been to Scotland in other years because I don't like Scotland, & because there was Camp, which I preferred. There is no Camp this August. Last year I went to Becky Falls, & you came to Grantchester. This year really *is* very different, my good man: I'm different, & not you.

I suppose I'm ill & irritable.

I shall stay here till Thursday: then go off to the Ouse, till Saturday: I think. I really don't know what to do afterwards. If I could spend only a week with you it might be all right – especially if I'm in today's state of fairly well giving up everything. If I could calculate on going off with Bryn between you & Kircudbright [Scotland] – But I can't: & anyway a week's rather little, to drag you to North Britain for.

In September I go to "Harry", then – perhaps – Camp; Then either with Justin to Canada, or shoot myself. I think the latter more probable.

I'll try a week with you, I *think*, if you dare ask it. But is it worth it? You'd better find something else. Rupert

It seems to me improbable I can be more miserable with you than I am with decent people, like these – [1]

1 Brooke was staying with Professor Gilbert Murray and his family in Norfolk.

RB, [postmarked 13 August 1912],
Beckhythe [Manor, Overstrand, Norfolk]
to JS, 67 Belsize Park Gardens, Hampstead

My dear James,
    The truth is that in my present condition, I don't mind where I am.
    No, I don't hate you, & certainly didn't always. Nor did I (after I got past my youthful & insolent little ignorance) think you had dirty little feelings.
    I explained every thing in my last letter. I've changed, not you. I suppose if I got better; or if you grew up: we could manage it again.
    I don't know where I shall go drift. I shall be within a few hours of London, so if you're vacant, we could spend a weekend somewhere . . . I may go to Justin, or to Mr Masefield,[1] or to Rugby.
    "Try to hurt you" – I'd like to hurt anybody with the ideas you have: only that.
    That's a fault in me: but my disapproval of that part of you, isn't.

                                                                    Rupert

RB, [postcard, postmarked 2 November 1912, Exeter]
to JS, 67 Belsize Park Gardens, Hampstead

I'm very sorry. Unavoidable business came suddenly on, and removed me.[2] I'll be seeing you again some time.   R.B.

JS, Sunday Nov. 11th [1912]

Dear Rupert,
    You may like to know that the Society's once more confined with twins. The confinement began at nine-thirty this morning, and the delivery seems likely to prove unusually painful. But with luck your brothers Wit[t]genstein[3] and Bliss will make their début on the hearthrug next Saturday.

---

1 John Edward Masefield (1878–1967), the poet.
2 Strachey and Brooke had made plans to meet for tea. The 'unavoidable business' might have been a rendezvous with Noel Olivier, who rejected Brooke's latest advances.
3 Ludwig Josef Johann Wittgenstein (1889–1951), the philosopher, was Apostle no. 252. Wittgenstein had come to Cambridge to study under Bertrand Russell at Trinity. Though homosexual, Wittgenstein 'loathed the idea of making homosexuality a cult and absolutely rejected the doctrine of the "Higher Sodomy" (Deacon 65). He did not like either Bliss or Békássy and offered to resign after attending only one meeting. However, after a conversation with Lytton Strachey, he decided to remain a member. Born in Vienna, he fought with the Austrian army during the war.

The crises have been pretty severe. "Békássy" had the Bliss job – which wasn't very hard, really. The poor young man was comprimé, opprimé, and finally supprimé.[1] The edgier task was given to Gerald, whose cynicism melted like a dream, and who became more completely nervous than I've seen him for years. Bertie, mad with jealousy, is trying to wreck the whole thing – but I fancy that all will be well.[2]

Yours James

RB, Tuesday [12 November 1912], bei Dudley, Charlottenburg, Berlinerstrasse 100, Berlin to JS, 67 Belsize Park Gardens, Hampstead

Many thanks. I'm glad, on the whole, it happened. I felt that if I left England, it was sure to happen. An infallible dodge. I'm the Society's Umbilical Cord: no birth complete till I'm away. I feel infinite faith in Wit[t]genstein: the only brother I've never met. But I'm afraid a person of Bliss' *morale* 'll prove the last worm in the trichinotic – we'll shortly out-herod Herod, I mean. *'Macht nichts.*[3]

I shall see 'em once on the rug, I suppose, before the end. I feel doubtful though.

Berlin's full of dramatic triumphs.[4] R.

I suppose I couldn't send *viele Grüsse*[5] to W[ittgenstein].? I hope he'll introduce Beer into the Kneipe.[6]

1 'repressed, oppressed, and finally suppressed'.
2 The Apostles felt that Bertrand Russell had selfishly tried to keep Wittgenstein from them so that he alone might enjoy the young man's company. Various Apostles reported that Russell was furious when they announced plans to elect Wittgenstein, but years later Russell told Michael Holroyd that this had not been the case (Holroyd, *Achievement* 71).
3 'But it doesn't matter.'
4 Brooke went the following evening to Max Reinhardt's production of Strindberg's *The Dance of Death* at the Deutsches Theater. He left the performance feeling that Reinhardt had butchered a work (and a writer) he loved.
5 'many greetings'.
6 'pub'.

1913–1914

Brooke all but disappeared from Strachey's life after August 1912. Noel Olivier wrote to Strachey on 20 January 1913: 'Are you allowed to meet Rupert? I hear that he always has lunch at the Vienna Caffé and has lots of new friends, and hardly likes any of his old ones any more. Your [sic] probably cut out too. Its [sic] pretty fearful; isn't it?'

Strachey's name also began to disappear from Brooke's letters to other friends. By February 1913, He was referring to the 'Stracheys', in the plural, as a disease. His contempt, his anti-feminism and his brutality are all well illustrated in a letter he wrote to Katherine Cox that month:

> I went to King's for the weekend. I hoped to meet Lytton & insult him. But there was only the less dirty little James, who is so defenceless that it is no sport kicking him, after a bit. [...] Geoffrey came here a bit. [...] Jacques & I spent one evening explaining to him about the female question, suffrage etc. He was very much upset, & nearly cried. It was rather unfair on him, of course, for whenever he appealed to what females think or feel, Gwen gave verdict against him.

Brooke's letters to Cox written in March show an increasing self-hatred. In one, he first tells her to 'keep clean', then becomes apologetic: 'I've hurt you so: oh my dear – wasting years of your loveliness. I hate myself.' His self-loathing, however, was coupled with the self-righteousness and egotism he had begun to develop the year before. He wrote to Cox:

> [Now that] I've hardened myself a good deal, & cut off other emotions fairly short, ambition grows & grows in me. It's inordinate, gigantic. It's no use: it doesn't even make me work. I just sit and think ambitious thoughts. As I used to sit and think lustful thoughts. I'm egotistic tonight. Sorry. (25 March 1913)

This was followed the next month by a letter stating: 'my sexual egoism makes me believe that all young women I know are oozing for me.'

Another letter from Brooke to Cox in April 1913 defined once and for all his new relationship with Strachey, which had become no relationship whatsoever:

> James. I'm glad he left off worrying you. He's all right. He always is. He wrote to me, saying he had hated me lately, but loved me again, & always had – a love letter – & would I stay with him in the New Forest? Luckily my Hamlets & things prevented me. I told him it was no good, because he didn't understand about the only important things . . . He replied it was a pity sorrow had made me a prig. . . . There it stands. I see him every three weeks, perhaps. But there's always the nauseating chance of finding Lytton in his rooms. So one doesn't go. But don't worry about him. He's far too selfish & minor to be hurt ever. He's precisely as he always was: with his brilliant sense of humour, & his liking for contemptuous criticism: which keep him happy.

Brooke goes on to talk of how spring had left him 'prostrated', concluding: 'I wish I was a woman and didn't feel things.' His next letter (also written in April) expands upon his reasons for not wanting to see Strachey:

> 'Suicide' – oh, it's not because I've messed things with you. I'm too selfish for that. It's, as far as it goes, not for any rational reason – but because I'm finished. It's merely the feeling – I'm no good; there's despair; – the days bring a sort of pain, & nothing else; I think I'm a little mad. My dear, it's nothing to do with you – I'm somehow rotten. And I guess it'll be better if I don't leave children – , people like me – behind. [...] I find I've finished with James, somehow. I find I can't stand his being a Strachey, & a public danger; when I'm with him. So it's better not to see him.

There is an undated letter in Brooke's papers to Cox that apparently followed the one above: '[I was] noting that sometimes I feel I must be diseased & fundamentally at odds with the world, & that then I know I mustn't have children. Haven't you ever heard that it's bad form for syphilitics to have children – even though they egotistically recognize the fact?'

Throughout this tirade of letter-writing to Cox, Brooke was simultaneously passing up opportunities to see her. One old friend whom he did wish to see was Charles Lascelles. He wrote to Geoffrey Keynes on 26 April 1913, asking, in return for a favour, 'will you send me, on a card, Charlie Lascelles' London address?'

Brooke's relationship with the actress Cathleen Nesbitt near the end of his life was probably the most stable of his several explosive romantic entanglements. Nesbitt says she and Brooke 'never actually became lovers in the sense that he seduced me' (80), although Brooke sometimes fell asleep at night with his head on her bed before returning to his own room (Lehmann, *Strange* 79). Brooke at times appeared to be deeply in love with Nesbitt, but at other times – as with Olivier, Cox and van Rysselbergh – appeared to be running from the relationship. His letters to Nesbitt show nothing but devotion, but his excessive adulation calls his sincerity into question. After first meeting Nesbitt, Brooke wrote: 'I adore you. [...] Why do you look like that? Have you any idea what you look like? I didn't know that human beings could look like that. It's as far beyond beauty as beauty is beyond ugliness.' She did not take the letter seriously, replying that he was in love with his own words (Geoffrey Keynes's editor at Faber and Faber didn't take the letters to Nesbitt seriously either – he wrote on Keynes's typescript: '[Brooke's] letters to Cathleen Nesbitt make me slightly sick – they are so *consciously* shallow'). Brooke was insulted but continued to write in the same effusive style. Sometimes intermingled in his words of devotion is a note of fear and despair:

> It's the one thing I've got, to love you [...] to learn to worship you [...] to lose myself in your kindliness, like a child – It might be that, in the end, it wouldn't do, & we'd find that I didn't love you enough, or you me. [...] Dear love, I *daren't* go wandering. You don't know what a helpless poor fool I am. It's only in love & marriage I can find peace. (April 1913)

As before, Brooke's actions failed to live up to his words. After convincing Nesbitt, who was considering an acting tour of America, to cancel her plans so they could be together, he himself abruptly decided to embark on his journey to America and the Pacific. Years later, Nesbitt confided to Geoffrey Keynes that at first Brooke had wanted a romantic relationship, but she was unsure. Then later, when she wanted romance, she sensed that he did not. She also told Keynes:

> I remember when he sent me the 'Safety' sonnet I found myself weeping bitterly because of some subconscious certainty that I had had the best of what he had to give [...] I always had a feeling – even when he seemed to love me most – that I was too small a vessel for all the richness he had to pour out – that he would in time discover it. (20 February 1956)

Brooke had three other relationships with women. Little is known about Marchesa Copponi, whom he met while in America (shortly after she had lost her son). The evidence suggests that this relationship was more friendship than romance, but two other entanglements may well have been sexual. Lady Eileen Wellesley, the daughter of the fourth Duke of Wellington, claimed in July 1915 that she had been involved in a serious love affair with Brooke (C. Asquith, *Diaries* 50). It is at least interesting that the two women who made this claim – Wellesley and van Rysselbergh – are the same women whose letters Brooke, in his dying hours, asked Dudley Ward to destroy.

A third probable sexual relationship involved the Tahitian woman, Taata Mata, whom Brooke met during his trip through the South Pacific. In a letter to Ward written on his way to Gallipoli, Brooke reports having dreamed that Mata killed herself after he left Tahiti and says he thinks the dream might be true (15 December 1914). This is no doubt his egotism and adolescent sentimentality speaking. But a month later he reported to Ward that he had received a letter from Mata: 'I can't decipher any reference to prospects of a baby. So that dream goes with the rest.' The reference to a possible baby certainly sounds as if Brooke and Mata were lovers, though the letter he mentions – her letter to him – does not read like one a person would send to an ex-lover. She tells him, for instance, what a nice time she has been having with a recently arrived shipload of sailors. But she also writes, 'I get fat all the time sweetheart', a line which some believe is the reference to 'prospects of a baby' that Brooke was looking for and missed. It has been suggested that Mata's daughter, Alice Rapolo, was the daughter of Brooke. The *Sunday Times*, at least, was convinced, running a story on 27 October 1996, under the matter-of-fact headline: 'Secret child of Rupert Brooke found.' It is certainly possible, but it is also possible that Rapolo was the daughter of one of Mata's sailors.

In any case, Mata and Cox are the only women whom Brooke himself suggests were lovers. Cathleen Nesbitt said Cox had a still-born child by Brooke. Several biographers have treated this as fact, though none has offered evidence to support the claim. When Cox died, her son sent to Geoffrey Keynes her box of Brooke letters unopened. It is possible that there was mention of a pregnancy in some of those letters and that the letters were destroyed. However, many (if not all) of these letters – including some that were reserved (and therefore inaccessible) for many years – are now stored at King's College Library, and among these, there is only one possible reference to a pregnancy. Brooke wrote in March 1912, within weeks of first having slept with Cox:

> [James] broke out once that he'd 'never accepted the conventional theory of my breakdown'. But he hardly seemed clear as to the correct theory. [...] I think its splendid for him & very nice for you if he sees you a great deal: as long as it's before 11: and he recognizes your condition.
>
> But Lord! how the man worships you! Worships & loves, rather. I was in agony between killing & kissing him. Either would have been so disastrous!

Cox's 'condition', however, could refer to a number of things besides pregnancy – Brooke refers in several other letters to her being very tired.

Whatever the truth, one can say with some authority that Brooke's relationships with women, and especially those that seemed most important to him and which are most thoroughly chronicled in surviving letters, were always problematic. It is possible that the lack of sexual inhibition in the South Pacific served as an elixir for Brooke – that he had a satisfying sexual relationship with Mata, then returned to London and had other sexual affairs with van Rysselberghe and Wellesley. If so, he was conducting these affairs simultaneously, while at the same time continuing to express his love for Nesbitt – and this, too, raises questions.

Brooke's life in the Pacific with Mata has the problem of verifiability. William Stelling told Geoffrey Keynes that while in Hawaii 'Brooke was detached about people, especially young girls at the time (so I'd heard, then)' (24 November 1968). There is also the problem of his poetry from this period, which, although technically superior to anything he had written previously, is almost completely lacking in passion. Whatever the case, Brooke was presumably more impressed with the women of the South Seas than with those of North America – he wrote to Jacques Raverat in April 1914, from Arizona: 'There is no young woman in America who could, under any circumstances, give a self-respecting penis an erection.'

Toward the end of his life, Brooke repeatedly expressed a desire to marry, as in the letter to Nesbitt quoted above. But when the possibility arose, Brooke was never willing to take the final step. Cecil Degrotte Eby says Brooke 'yearned for marriage but not a wife' (224). A letter Brooke wrote to Jacques Raverat in 1914 supports Eby's assertion: 'I *must* marry soon. And I can't find anyone to marry – oh, I suppose one *could* marry anyone: but, I mean, I can't decide whom to marry.' Still later, as he prepared to go to the front, Brooke wrote again to Raverat: 'should one marry without being particularly in love, before going to the front? How divine to have even a few hours of what the rest of life is a grey pre-existence to – marriage: with, oh! *anybody*. But how dreadful to return from Berlin to a partner for Eternity whom one didn't particularly *want*' (19 January 1915). Brooke had also written to Dudley Ward shortly before:

> I rather feel that if the war *hadn't* happened, I'd have gone on eyeing the brink, hesitating, and deferring [...] until I relapsed into a friendly celibate middle-age, the amiable bachelor, a [E. J.] Dent or livelier [Charles] Sayle, or less distinguished Eddie [Marsh], with my rooms and bedder and hosts of young friends. [...] If it's true the war'll last two years more, there's very little chance of anyone who goes out in January 1915 returning. Now, if I *knew* I'd be shot, I'd marry in a flash, – oh any of two or three ladies – and do my best to leave a son. [...] But, oh, if I came back in a year, and found myself caught. [...] When I feel I'll be killed (which is my general feeling and deepest), I have a revulsion towards marriage. (15 December 1914).

Possibly, Brooke's new obsession with marriage was the result of his not wanting to be left out. He had once penned a 'pact', which he circulated among his friends to little effect, in which they were all encouraged to renounce marriage and promise to stay young for ever. It pained Brooke greatly when these friends began to pair off and marry, and what strikes one about his complaints more than anything is, indeed, his feeling of exclusion. But he apparently left London with all affairs of the heart unresolved; the green locket he was wearing around his neck when he died contained no photograph.

Brooke continued to mention frequent headaches (as well as pains, influenzas and unexplained fevers) in many of his 1913 letters. He had recovered somewhat before leaving for America, reporting in a letter to Cox that he felt good two out of three days, and considered that 'a healthy average'. When he first considered a trip abroad as a possible relief from his anxiety, he went to visit A. C. Benson, who later wrote:

> he spoke of his trouble very seriously, and even with a sort of terror, as if he had for the first time realised that there might be onsets which he could not resist, and wounds which he could not cure. He said gravely that he had made unpleasant discoveries about his constitution, and that it was not so immune, when confronted with a strain, as he had imagined. (*Memories* 330)

The trip to America and the South Pacific was designed, in part, for Brooke to recover his health, both mental and physical. His mother provided much of the money, and he earned a little extra by sending back articles for the *Westminster Gazette*. These, subsequently published as *Letters from America*, were viewed by Marsh as an annoying waste of Brooke's time – and he said as much in his letters. Marsh had a stake in Brooke's poetry because of the Georgian anthology, and wanted Brooke to concentrate on poetry rather than prose. But the travel articles are among Brooke's best work.

Brooke's North American itinerary was set primarily by his letters of introduction. New York and Boston were followed by Montreal, Ottawa, Toronto and Niagara. He then made his way across Canada to British Columbia, then south to San Francisco. Hawaii, Samoa, Fiji, New Zealand and Tahiti followed.

While in Fiji (December 1913), Brooke cut his leg on coral and got a bad case of coral poisoning. His leg became infected in five places, and he was still limping the following March.

Brooke sailed for Tahiti in early January, met Mata – the 'Mamua' of his poem 'Tiare Tahiti' – after arriving there, and put off leaving until 5 April. He then returned to the United States, making his way to New York via the Grand Canyon, Chicago, Pittsburgh and Washington.

While Brooke was in America and the Pacific, Strachey stayed with

Dudley Ward for a while in Berlin, then went to Moscow. His name began to crop up again in Brooke's correspondence with Noel Olivier, beginning with a letter Brooke wrote on 8 October 1913:

> I am very fond of James, though I disapprove of him so strongly that I have to keep away. [...] (Really the unrelieved *sordidness* of that man's career – loving me for nine years & you for the rest of his life! I sometimes think God has been a little *too* hard on him, dreadful as he is.). (*SOL* 255).

Olivier returned to the subject on 3 January 1914:

> I *must* say: that I think you *ridiculous* in your attitude towards Lytton & James. [...] why be afraid of James, if you *do* like him? You can so easily understand him. And if you understand & love the fellow, it's only silly & unkind to run away. This fear of 'contamination' is surely only a phase.

Brooke responded on 25 April:

> I was so touched by your plea for James; & your dropping out that he was going abroad for six months, that I wrote to him. I was alarmed for his health & happiness. After all, the poor creature is lonely: & he's not the sort that can stand loneliness. And he does, in his fashion, attempt spasmodically to protest against the more obvious nastiness of Lyttonism. He has been brought up not to know what good is. But he *means* well. And that's something. And in the last seventeen years I've grown to like him. Well, I shall see him, just as I shall see you and everybody else – some day. Meanwhile, I hope he's fairly well. (267)

Upon returning to England, Brooke took a train to London and was met at the station by Edward Marsh, Cathleen Nesbitt and Denis Browne, who eventually would bury him on Skyros. Marsh, who was Winston Churchill's private secretary, introduced Brooke to Churchill, Anthony Asquith, and Sir Ian Hamilton. Ironically – or perhaps not – it was the members of this powerful group who seemed to take Brooke most seriously as a poet. They tried to talk him into giving up his military commission for health reasons, but Brooke refused. They tried to rescue him from the Gallipoli campaign by offering him an appointment on Hamilton's staff, but Brooke was ready to die.

Brooke's circle of acquaintances had altered so much that Virginia Woolf was under the impression that he was giving up literature for a career in politics. However, although Brooke came to think of them as his friends, it is obvious from their private diaries that – aside from Marsh – Rupert did not figure heavily in their lives. He receives scant mention in any of the Asquith diaries, and when he does appear, there never seems to be much genuine concern for him, as exemplified in Margot Asquith's detached contemplations on 25 February 1915: 'Rupert told Oc [Arthur Asquith] he was quite certain he would never come back [from the war] but would be killed – it didn't depress him at all but he was just convinced – I shall be curious to see if this turns out to be a true instinct.' Churchill, too, had more important things on his mind than Brooke. Although he was reportedly upset that Marsh had not introduced Brooke to him earlier (see Gilbert, *Challenge* 401), the posthumous tribute to Brooke bearing his name was actually written by Marsh.

However, the acquaintances in high places – and the appearance of the *Georgian Poetry* anthology – certainly did no harm to Brooke's literary career. His first reading of poetry at Harold Munro's Poetry Bookshop in London on 28 January 1913 – when he read from Swinburne and Donne – had been attended by six people. But when Brooke made his second appearance in July 1914, he read his own work to a packed house (Grant 81).

This same month – July 1914 – there was a reunion of the Apostles in London at the Connaught Rooms. Brooke went with Marsh and saw again his old friends James Strachey, Maynard Keynes, Gerald Shove, John Sheppard and Harry Norton. This may have been the same evening after which Brooke wrote his last letter to Strachey. If so, that final letter was written on the day when Brooke met D. H. Lawrence and the two were observed 'in lively talk and roaring with laughter' (*RBB* 450).

During the war, James and Lytton Strachey, Duncan Grant, Maynard Keynes, Henry Lamb, David Garnett, Gerald Shove and Harry Norton did not enlist. Alfred Brooke, George Mallory, Francis Birrell, Geoffrey Keynes and Hugh Russell-Smith did.

Noel Olivier persuaded Brooke to attend a Bloomsbury gathering while he was on leave recuperating from conjunctivitis, which he had come down with at Antwerp. David Garnett, recalling the event, said Brooke tried to talk him into joining his division but that 'the moment had passed and Rupert's marked hostility to James and Frankie [Birrell] antagonised me. Later the patriotism of his famous sonnets seemed to me to ring false and to be mixed up with an almost insane repudiation of many of his oldest friends' (*Flowers* 7).

> *RB, Monday, [13 January] 1913, Rugby*
> *to JS, 67 Belsize Park Gardens, Hampstead*
> *[forwarded to 5 Clement's Inn, E.C.]*

Dear James,

Sudden, inevitable, & irrelevant entanglements prevented me coming to that arranged tea meeting, last time – in November? My conscience pricked, though; & bid me tell you that I'm going to stay with Eddie [Marsh] on

Wednesday for three days, & perhaps six. I'm generally free at tea-time still. So I leave it there. I say nothing more definite. You know what you want to do. You may have a thousand good reasons for wanting to see me, & a thousand for not wanting to: or none either way. You know what I'm like. I've any how counteracted, to myself, any impression of rudeness my November's behaviour may have given. Why should I want to do more?

Have you seen Ben [Keeling]? he seemed to want to see you. And I met two old friends of yours who were asking after you, Ashley Dukes & a Miss Charrington.[1]   Rupert

RB, Tuesday [25 February 1913], c/o E[dward].M[arsh]., Raymond Buildings [London] to JS, 5 & 6 Clements Inn, Strand, London

My dear Boy,

I'm very crowded, I find. I'm not doing anything tomorrow (*Wednesday* night). So I could show you *Hullo Ragtime*[2] then? But I'm, unfortunately, dining with Fraülein So & So.[3] If you like, could we meet in the Hippodrome Vestibule, at 8.45 – it begins at 9–? You might ring me up, tomorrow, perhaps? – But not before ten, I beg –[4]   Rupert

JS, Saturday [8 March 1913], 5 Clement's Inn

Dear Rupert

May one congratulate?[5]

Your   James

JS, Monday [24 March 1913], 5 Clement's Inn, Strand

Dear Rupert,

Will you come and stay a few days with me at Mrs Primmer's? I'm going to have next week off, and I've taken her rooms from this Thursday (27th) till the following Tuesday week (8th). Pernel [Strachey]'s going to be with

1 Ashley Dukes was drama critic for the *Star* in 1913. Miss Charrington may have been a relative of Charles Charrington Martin, the actor and friend of the Strachey family.
2 Brooke saw *Hullo, Ragtime* ten times.
3 Probably the actress Cathleen Nesbitt, whom Brooke was now seeing.
4 In a letter to Katherine Cox from this period, Brooke writes: '[Norton] stayed a week-end with Ottoline so I could scarcely stand seeing him. I probably shan't much. He lectured me about James. I had a dutiful tea with James but no more.'
5 Brooke received word on 8 March that he had been elected a Fellow of King's College.

me at first; but she can't stay to the end. So I thought perhaps you might come one day next week (Wednesday or Thursday) and stop till I return to London.

Perhaps it'ld be very unpleasant or irritating for you. No doubt there may be some real objection. I can only be as honest as I can, and say that however deep I go *I* can't see one. But of course it's all a question of feeling, and it's likely enough *you* feel different. As for me, I hated you, dear, a good deal a few months ago, one way and another. But that's gone now, I think. I love you (and I don't care if you laugh at me for saying so) and I believe I've loved you all the time.[1]

Do come.

Your
James

RB, Tuesday evening [25 March 1913], 24 Bilton Road, Rugby
to JS, 5 & 6 Clement's Inn, Strand, London

My dear James,

As I'm averse, by temper, to worrying decisions: so I'm rather meanly glad that I've promised to go to Hamlet next Wednesday (the 2nd, I mean) or Friday, to dine on the Thursday, & to see people on the Friday, & to walk in the country on Sunday. So the decision's taken from me by my pre-arrangements.

(There'd also have been the difficulty of facing Mrs P[rimmer]. after my last departure from her, with Brynhild Popham.)

You'd better go on hating me, I expect.

My good James, I know you're different from a creature like Lytton, & that you're becoming more different. Still, there *is* the immense gulf between us still, I suppose, that you have no sense of what are to me the most important things in the world. Perhaps one day you'll grow up: or I shall have got down to your level. No doubt, both motions are in process.

But I wish you well.

By this point you will have got influenza from this letter; for I am still infectious, I suppose.

I send my cheque for 10/6 – . I have written you a good many: & lost them all. But no doubt *somebody*'s cashed them.

One must pay for one's pleasant evenings.

Rupert

I've discovered the most wonderful embryo since Tomlinson [*was* T. an embryo? – a difficult point.].[2] My life will be devoted to making him come to Cambridge. Aetat. 16.

---

1 Brooke's reaction, in a letter to Cox written on 25 March: 'I've had a dreadful note from James.'
2 Brooke's brackets.

JS, Thursday [27 March 1913]

Dear Rupert,

Many thanks for the ten and six. It's a comfort to think that *someone* enjoyed that party enough to consider it worth paying for.

It seems rather a pity that your sorrows should have turned you into a prig. And aren't you a bit uncharitable too? But I suppose that usually goes with self-righteousness.

Well, well. I hope you'll have a good time next week with Mr Arundel del Re and that he'll go on displaying his sense of what are to you the most important things in the world.

— — — — — —

You may notice that the stimmung[1] of your last has been making me foam a good deal. But like all the troubles of babyhood, ça passe, ça passe. I feel, and always felt, infinitely benevolent towards the mysterious worries of these perplexed grown ups at whose feet I crawl – I'm placid even when they tread on my fingers. My good Rupert, I've got one great advantage over you. You can't prevent my being fonder of you than of – well, of almost anyone else in the world.

Your loving   James

I wish you could have come, though.

RB, [postcard of RMS Cedric, *White Star Line,*
postmarked 23 May 1913, Queenstown]
to JS, The Spectator

Did you mean it about that Introduction? For it would fairly complete the list.[2]

Never mind, if you didn't.

Among my fellow passengers are Mr Le Gallienne

Mrs Le Gallienne
and, oh, Miss Le Gallienne.[3]
Rupert

1 'mood'.
2 Brooke was sailing to America armed with a stack of letters from various friends introducing him to their acquaintances in North America. Even Hugh Dalton's father, 'the Canon', wrote a letter – to the Canadian Premier, Sir Wilfrid Laurier.
3 Richard Thomas Le Gallienne (1866–1947) was author of *The Quest of the Golden Girl,* and was known as the 'Golden Boy' in the 1890s. Brooke held him in low regard and made no attempt to meet him on the ship (Stringer 143). Le Gallienne had settled in America in 1901. In 1913, he would have been married to Irma, his third wife (the former wife of American sculptor Roland Hinton Perry). Gwen, their daughter, became a portrait artist, but the 'Miss Le Gallienne' referred to here might have been Eva, a daughter from his second marriage who became an actress. He had a daughter from his first marriage as well.

JS, *August 3, 1913, 5 Clement's Inn*

Dear Rupert. I'd meant to telegraph today;[1] but I don't know your address. Perhaps you won't even get this. But if you do, it's just to give you my love.　　　　　　　　　　　　　　　　　　　　　　　　　　Your James

RB, *Midnight August 18 [1913], A train, in the Rockies [Banff, Alberta] to JS, The* Spectator *[forwarded to Milton Cottage, Rothiemurchus, Aviemore, Scotland]*

My dear Boy,

I wonder how the world is treating you. I sometimes see the old *Spectator*; & I often think of the old days. I saw, by the way, in a number I picked up in the Indian agent's hut at Morley, Al[ber]ta, that Br[other] James had inserted Br Barney's[2] attack on Br Eddy's florilege[3] from Br Rupert. So it's all in the family anyway.

Lots of things happen to me, of the kind you used to laugh at, I remember. I'm awfully healthy & strong. But the process you saw dawning has run its atrocious path. Poetry, even, has gone by the bawd. I'm relapsed comfortably onto the mattress of second class. Good.[4] Perhaps my children . . . .

I only write to hope that you are becoming good or wise. You needed it.　　　　　　　　　　　　　　　　　　　　　　　　　　　　　Rupert

RB, *October [postmarked 2 October 1913], 'Frisco [Hotel Carlton, Berkeley, California] to JS, The* Spectator

My dear James,

Thank you for your birthday letter: my only one. It blew in sometime in the middle of September – at Nanaimo [British Columbia], was it? or way back at Field [BC]? I forget.

---

1 Brooke's birthday.
2 Possibly the Apostle Bernard Holland.
3 The first anthology of Georgian poetry.
4 This sentiment was nothing new. In an address to Rugby's Eranos Society in 1906, the nineteen-year-old Brooke quoted from several poems by 'minor poets' whom he admired, then admonished his audience: 'Do not listen to my quotations with a sneer in your souls because they are "minor poetry". People who speak disparagingly of minor poetry are either stockbrokers and lawyers and rich practical people who don't understand, or reviewers in the Press, who are always young men fresh from a university with souls so stuffed full of intellectual pride that they might as lightly speak of minor roses or minor sunsets' (quoted in Lane 58). Though Brooke was not speaking of himself directly, it is not difficult to believe that he had his future self in mind. His egotism was often balanced by a self-awareness of his limitations as a scholar and poet.

I hope you got my enclosures from T'ronto.[1] They weren't meant to distress you. Only to show you how frightfully life's everywhere the same.

I hope you're fairly well, fairly good, & fairly happy.   Rupert

RB, [postcard of Dragon's Mouth, Wairakei, New Zealand],
Dec. 25. 1913
to JS, The Spectator *[forwarded to chez Madame Voronoff,*
Teply per., g.18, kb.3, Subovo, Moscow, Russia]

Who'd have thought I should be keeping the Day in Wairakei? You in London no doubt – or have you commenced your annual Xmas vacation on the South Coast? In any case, another Glad New Year.   R.B.

JS, February 7th 1914 (O[ld].S[tyle].) [20 February 1914], chez
Madame Voronoff, Teply per., g.18, kb.3, Zubovo, Moscow, Russia

My dear Rupert,

I've been thinking about you more than usual lately, and been on the brink of writing to you for some time, and then yesterday evening your Christmas postcard arrived. You see from the address that after all things aren't *quite* flat even in my life.

The second letter you sent me before this came some time in September. It got to me while I was in Scotland at a place you may remember the name of, and I read it sitting in the parlour of Milton Cottage, with Noel on one side of me and Lytton on the other. The next one I got all right at 1 Wellington Street, Strand, London, W.C. But this last time I'm in Moscow. Perhaps however to an impartial observer situated in Wairakei there's no very obvious distinction between Cairn Gorm and Crockham Hill, or between Morskaia Ulitsa and Marlborough Road.

Well, there it is anyway. And I need only add that for a month before I came here – all through January in fact – my address was "bei Herrn Dudley Ward, Berlinerstrasse 100, *Berlin-Charlottenburg*".

What I really wanted to say though was: if you ever get this, won't you call here on your way home? I'm only ten days from Nagasaki, you know. Do just start off as soon as you've done reading this. Send me a telegram so that I don't move on. I can't imagine anything much nicer than seeing you again. – It's really quite tolerable here (if one's not too far gone), with the ballet & theatre (you must hurry up because they stop after Easter), and even fashionable among our Great Men: – H. G. [Wells] was here the

---

1 On 20 July, Brooke had sent Strachey two newspaper articles on tapeworms.

week before last; Mr [Harley Granville-]Barker arrives today. I can give you the entrée; – indeed, Lykiardopoulos is one of your admirers.

I do hope, my dear, that you're still a human being and alive. I still go on loving you, you know; and wish in my sentimental way that we could know one another as I used to think we did. I suppose you won't live in some rooms with me when we get back? I've given up Clement's Inn; & have said I'd take on a flat in Regent Square that some friends of mine are leaving in June. There are two large sitting rooms & 2 bedrooms: total rent £65, which divided in half seems cheap. But your damn theories about privacy make it out of the question probably. I think it 'ld be very good for both of us myself. Do at all events consider it; & if you're back in London before me (I may not be till August) I give you complete power to turn those other people out & install yourself.

But perhaps you'll go to Cambridge? No. I fancy that place has finally shaken us off its boots. My God! it does seem queer to think of them oozing away over there in their ditches. I heard last week from Norton, who'd heard from Dickinson, that they'd recently elected a person called – well, now, what was it? Phillips? Gordon? – *I* don't remember. In any case I'm sure that we all (Dickinson, Norton, Brooke, & J.B. Strachey) rejoice to think that the Society is still flourishing, though I must say I think they seem a great deal more fastidious about their elections than we used to be. What the Society wants is *numbers* . . .

It makes me uneasy to be able to imagine where you'll be when you read this. In Calcutta (call on my brother Ralph, a dear man, Chief Engineer, East Indian Railway, Howrah, Calcutta)? In Pietermaritzburg (do *not* call on my cousin Arthur Plowden)? Do you stick to the All Red Route?

But wherever it is I embrace you and want very much to see you again.
Your loving   James

RB, May 24, 1914, Hotel McAlpin, Greeley Square, New York City
to JS, The Spectator *[forwarded to*
67 Belsize Park Gardens, Hampstead]

My dear James,
Yesterday I got your letter from Moscow. Is Russia really still the mode? I thought it was wearing a bit thin even by May 22, 1913.[1] But I suppose Russia is even more – and certainly more interestingly – unlike "Russia" than America's unlike "America". D'y' get me? I expect its less dirty than

1 The date Brooke left England for America.

Lytton hopes, & less reactionary than Mr Baring¹ pretends.

I wonder if, when you get this, you'd send a line to me at Rugby saying when theatrical things in Russia open up. Some people who run a Kleines Theater² in Chicago are making a theatrical pilgrimage – Florence, Hellerau,³ Paris, Budapesth –

Russia, from June to September: & I'm arranging it.

I'd a letter from Noel this morning. She said Bryn had a baby, & you a beard. I cried nearly half an hour over the baby. I'm nervous about the beard.

No: I don't think I'll take half Regents' Squarr (Regent Square? Regents Quhair?) One thing is, I'm not going to live in London. How the devil do you think a clean man can live in London? I've grown hard in the Antipodes; but damme! I've not grown tolerant.

Another thing is, Lytton would always be crawling in.

No, you must come down & stay with me in King's, when you feel anti-feminist enough. And we'll go & have a smoke & a chat with some jolly fellows on Saturday night.

Have you chucked the Spectator? I hope so/not. 'not', . . I think. Or perhaps, 'so'.

I want to build a *kleines Theater* at Cambridge. There's a garage the right shape already there – So I shall spend next year collecting money. Will you be *Regisseur*?⁴ Five dollars a week —

Aufwiedersehen – at the dinner?   Rupert

JS, [after 7? June 1914], 6 Belsize Park Gardens, Hampstead ['Kindly note' is written at top, with arrow drawn to the '6' in the address]

Cher Monsieur. I met our brother Marsh last night, and heard from him that you'd reached London just four hours after me. Your letter was waiting for me here.

The only part of it that seems to deserve an answer is about your poor Pilgrims. June to September isn't at all a bright time for theatres. The Moscow Artistic Th[eatre]. for instance only opens in October or even November (it varies) & closes at Easter. In fact there'll certainly be nothing of any sort at Moscow in the summer, & I should think the same's true of

---

1 Maurice Baring's *Mainsprings of Russia* was published in 1914. Rupert read one of Baring's books on Russia (probably this one) in July of this year.
2 'Little Theater' – the persons referred to are Maurice Browne, director of the Chicago Little Theater, and his wife Ellen Van Volkenburg, an actress.
3 A town near Dresden where in 1912 the French-Swiss designer Adolphe Appia had teamed with modern dance instructor Jaques Dalcroze to launch the Hellerau Festivals.
4 'stage manager'.

Buda Pest and most other towns. Even at Hellerau they'll only find a vacation course & probably no Jaques [Dalcroze]. This summer the people from the Düsseldorf Schauspielhaus[1] are to be at the Munich Künstlertheater,[2] I hear, doing Shakespeare among other things (d. badly). Also some time in July (15th I think) Jaques is giving a Festspiel[3] in Geneva. Also at Cologne in the Exhibition there's a section of "the theatre" including some models etc of Teddy's[4] & of [Adolphe] Appia's. (They've come on from the theatrical exhibition that's just closed at Zürich.) . . . Well, of course there's always Teddy, from whom I parted in mutual tears at the Arena Goldoni only a week ago.

Lord! I've been to between 50 & 60 plays operas & ballets in these last few months. Paris, Düsseldorf, Cologne, Berlin, Dresden, Warsaw, Moscow, Vienna, Buda Pest, Florence.

By the way, your friends of course know about the Thèâtre [sic] du Vieux Colombier,[5] in Paris, run by M. Coppeau? They've lately done 12th night with scenery etc by Duncan. – But that too's shut for the summer. – Don't let them miss the Svobodny Teatr (Free Theatre) in Moscow, which does interesting things. Also they've just started at Warsaw a theatre supposed to be on the lines of the Moscow Artistic Theatre. It's called the Polish National Th[eatre], or something of the sort. I suspect Hevesy & Buda-P of being frauds.

I don't know if these scraps are any use. Probably you know all about it.

If you're in London, will you send a p.c. here, or ring me up? But I may be going to the country. Yours James

> *RB, Saturday. 1.a.m. [Strachey has written at top of page:*
> *'[July? 1914] (After an apparently very friendly evening*
> *at the Hippodrome etc.)]' c/o E[ddie].M[arsh].*
> *to JS, 6 Belsize Park Gardens, Hampstead*

My dear James,

I have realized that, in the excitement of the evening, I may not have explained to you how much I was grieved at your opinions. I had hoped you had got rid of them. They seem to me not only eunuch & shocking, but also damned silly & slightly dangerous.   R.B.

———————

[Strachey has written at the bottom of the page: 'My last letter from him.']

1 'Playhouse'.
2 'Artists' Theater'.
3 'festival'.
4 Edward Gordon Craig, the designer.
5 'Theatre of the Old Dovecote'.

Afterword

In her posthumous review of *The Collected Poems of Rupert Brooke* in *Poetry* magazine, Harriet Monroe said, 'Brooke ran toward death as toward the consummation which life had not given, perhaps could not have given to one of his temperament.' Indeed, in letters written to several friends while he was preparing for war, Brooke hinted that his reason for wanting to go was his wish to die. He wrote to Katherine Cox: 'I've only one remedy for anything. I'm afraid you'll guess it' (10 January 1915). He obviously meant either enlistment or death or – most likely – both. He remarked that some men of England apparently did not want to die ('and this I cannot understand') and that 'large numbers of male people don't want to die; which is odd' (*LRB* 637). He wrote to Andrew Gow: 'My brother & Frank Birch are each signing a similar document and want to die with me' (24 August 1914). After enlisting he wrote to John Drinkwater: 'I'd not be able to exist, for torment, if I weren't doing it. Not a bad place and time to die, Belgium, 1915? [...] Come and die. It'll be great fun' (January 1915), which both shows his immature attitude towards the matter and also reminds one not only of *Peter Pan* ('to die will be an awfully big adventure') but also of Jenny Wren exhorting Riah to 'Come up and be Dead' in Dickens's *Our Mutual Friend* (or even of the melancholy retainer's imagined invitation to 'Come down and be poisoned, ye unhappy children of men,' from the same book).

There is a second reason Brooke wished to enlist: he wanted to share the experience of a great campaign. Like his death-wish, this, too, was a desire to escape his present life. But it was more than that; it was a longing to return to the camaraderie of his Rugby days. Just as Brooke had felt left behind as friend after friend got married, he began to feel left behind as friend after friend joined the ranks. Geoffrey Keynes says that when he happened to come across Brooke in Bloomsbury on 18 August 1914, 'He gazed at my uniform with envy and almost with despair' (*Gates* 124).

At first, Brooke was unsure what to do. He wrote to Eileen Wellesley: 'One grows introspective. I find in myself two natures – not necessarily conflicting, but – different. There's half my heart which is normal &

English – what's the word, not quite "good" or "honourable" – "*straight*", I think. But the other half is a wanderer' (15 August 1914). In the past, Brooke generally liked his country more when he was in another. 'Grantchester', for instance, was written in a café in Germany when he had been away from England several months and was feeling homesick (the poem's original title was 'The Sentimental Exile'). Nevertheless, it was not long before Brooke was rebuffing his former friends for their pacifism, stating that his purpose in life, 'the aim and end of it, now, the thing God wants of me is to get good at beating Germans. That's sure' (*RBB* 471). Still, even after writing his war sonnets, Brooke continued to criticize his home country. He wrote to Jacques Raverat on 3 December 1914 that he was 'largely dissatisfied with the English, just now' and that he had been 'praying for a German raid' on England.

Brooke enlisted in the first branch that would take him, though he found his first assignment less than satisfactory. Douglas Jerrold recalls that there was some excitement among the men in his battalion when they learned that Brooke was to join them, but that enthusiasm soon vanished after Brooke arrived and told Jerrold 'that he had insisted on being transferred from my battalion because there was no one in it to whom he could possibly talk' (*Georgian* 120). No doubt Beatrice Webb would have smiled. Edward Marsh managed to pull enough strings for Brooke to be transferred to a unit containing several friends, including Denis Browne and Arthur Asquith, and soon Brooke was writing to John Drinkwater of the 'great feeling of fellowship' he had found among the soldiers (January 1915). He wrote to Cathleen Nesbitt, 'I'm rather happy, really, in this new battalion.' He went on to give a description of each soldier in his unit, ending with, 'there's a *very* charming and beautiful American youth, infinitely industrious and simple beyond belief. And finally there's a very hard bitter man, a poet, very strong and silent, called Rupert Brooke' (5 December 1914).

Across the Channel, other writers were also supporting involvement in the war. Both Charles Péguy (1873–1914) and Ernest Psichari (1883–1914), for instance, believed the war would revitalize France. Brooke knew this, and, in fact, just before writing his war sonnets, he received word of Péguy's death at the Battle of the Marne. At the time Brooke wrote the sonnets, he had seen very little action (though it was all he would ever see). He had taken part in Churchill's failed Antwerp expedition but had arrived at the front just in time to retreat, spending less than seventy-four hours in the Belgian war zone (Eby 227). The wounded Belgians he encountered, and the Belgian women struggling to survive, heightened his romantic belief that he was part of a noble campaign – though Strachey wondered exactly how much of an impact the Belgians' suffering had truly made on him. James wrote to Lytton: 'You'll be glad to know that Rupert appeared in London this morning. His account of Antwerp was of interest, though nothing much seems to have happened there. The Horrors of War haven't in the least got inside *his* head yet, as far as I can make out' (15 October 1914).

Once back in England, Brooke wrote the sonnets and immediately sent them to *New Numbers* for publication. These poems – 'Peace', 'Safety', 'The Dead (I)', 'The Dead (II)', and 'The Soldier' – do not simply show death as a patriotic sacrifice. Instead, each – and especially 'Peace' – suggests that death is not a sacrifice at all, for the world is a miserable place, gladly left behind. Knowing the words he was using at the time to insult Lytton Strachey, one cannot help but think that Brooke had him in mind when he writes of 'half-men' in 'Peace'.' But the 'half-men' in the poem write 'dirty songs' – and Lytton was famous for his 'dirty' poems. Eby says that 'by [Brooke's] definition men are those who fight; those who refuse are half-men with nothing better to do than to make dirty love poems. The poem reflects Brooke's self-hatred, for what has he been but a maker of love poems?' (228).

Brooke himself did not much care for the sonnets. He wrote to Sybil Pye: 'Did you like them? I'm glad. I thought 4 and 5 good: the rest poor, but not worthless' (21 March 1915). The two he liked are 'The Dead (II)' and 'The Soldier'. It is reassuring that he did not think much of the two that his future detractors would use to murder his reputation: 'Peace', with its 'Now, God be thanked Who has matched us with His hour', and its 'sick hearts that honour could not move', and 'The Dead (I)', with its 'red / Sweet wine of youth'. The other poem not listed as a favourite, 'Safety', was written for Cathleen Nesbitt. Rupert asked her forgiveness for including it with the war sonnets, but added as justification, 'It seems to belong to them'. Nesbitt says that she and Brooke agreed that the fourth sonnet was the best. 'I was always surprised,' she wrote, 'that the fifth was the one that became famous.' But whether Brooke liked the poems or not – he wrote them. And they are certainly a departure from the verse of the youthful Brooke who once asked in his 'To a Cadet Officer', what the most ridiculous thing about the officer might be, and answered:

'Tis naught wherewith the mere civilians taunt you.
     'Tis not your frown, more mocked, alas, than feared –
Not even your ghastly hat (though that, I grant you,
     Is more than weird).

It is ironic for a man who spent much of life at odds with religion and especially the Church of England, that Brooke's legend was first made by Dean Inge of St Paul's in an Easter sermon, when he read aloud 'The Soldier' and then told his congregation that 'the enthusiasm of a pure and elevated patriotism had never found a nobler expression' (*RBB* 502).

In preparation for the Gallipoli campaign, Brooke was inoculated against typhoid on 4 December 1914. He immediately fell ill and was still bedridden on the 16th when he sent Cox a detailed description of the design for curtains he wanted her to send: 'the stuff should be such that it can get wet often: & of a bright hue, which'll go with planks & khaki: scarlet perhaps. It should be not too light; so that it won't blow about.' He also included a floor plan of his quarters – complete with dimensions – and requested a carpet and chair. But not long after obtaining these items Brooke no longer had need for them, for he was sailing to Gallipoli. An entry from his journal reveals something of his frame of mind as he made his way across the Aegean, and also shows his skill – exhibited earlier in his articles on North America – as a travel writer:

> There are moments – there have been several, especially in the Aegean – when, through some beauty of sky and air and earth, and some harmony with the mind, peace is complete and completely satisfying. One is at rest from the world, and with it, entirely content, drinking to the full of the placidity of the loveliness. Every second seems divine and sufficient. And there are men and women who seem to do what one so terribly can't, and so terribly at these moments, *aches* to do – store up reservoirs of this calm and content, fill and seal great jars or pitchers during these half-hours, and draw on them at later moments, when the source isn't there, but the need is very great. I wish there were more people of that character about on this expedition.

Brooke received more shots aboard ship. Whether he relapsed into serious illness or whether he was just being morbid is uncertain, but a day later his letter to Marsh presupposed his death, containing instructions regarding the posthumous dispersal of his personal items. A letter to Cox dated 10 March begins: 'I suppose you're about the best I can do in the way of a widow. I'm telling the Ranee that after she's dead, you're to have my papers. They may want to write a biography! How am I to know if I shant be eminent?' Brooke concludes with 'You were the best thing I found in life. [...] It's a good thing I die. Goodbye, child.   Rupert.'

Brooke recovered enough to enjoy a few days' shore leave in Egypt, but by the time General Hamilton visited him in early April and proffered a safe position on his staff (which Brooke refused), he was ill again. Brooke's biographers attribute this illness to sunstroke, food poisoning, an insect bite or some combination of the three. There is also the possibility that he was suffering still from a reaction to his inoculations. Some have further speculated that the inoculations, or perhaps an insect bite, triggered a recurrence of the coral poisoning he suffered in the Pacific. Back on ship, he went to bed and his lip began to swell. Arthur Gaskell, the fleet surgeon, says Brooke was ill for three days, 'but was seized on the night of the 21st with sudden severe Pneumococcic Septicaemia, as proved by a most thorough bacteriological examination'. E. G. Schlesinger, medical officer of the 2nd Brigade, adds that the sore on Brooke's upper lip was swollen on the morning of the 22nd. 'Bacteriological examination of the pus from the sore showed the presence of Pneumococci in large numbers. The swelling spread to include the side of the neck, temp rose to 104.' Dr McCracken, the battalion surgeon, wrote to Mrs Brooke that the 'infection proved to be due to a diplococcus, morphologically resembling the Pneumococcus'.

When General Hamilton received word that Brooke was dying, he wrote in his diary, 'The first-born of the intellect must die. Is *That* the answer to the riddle?' (*RBB* 510).

Brooke's death certificate says he died at 4.46 p.m. on 23 April – England's day, the day of Shakespeare and St George – on the French hospital ship *Duguay-Trouin* off the coast of Skyros from 'oedéme malin et septicémie foudroyante' – that is, malignant oedema and rapid septicaemia.

Henry James, upon hearing the news that Brooke had died, said simply, 'Of course, of course,' then lowered his head and began to weep (*RBB* 515). Edward Marsh wrote twenty-four years later: 'Rupert Brooke's death in April 1915, was the worst blow I have ever had, and it changed everything for me' (*Number* 247). In Bloomsbury, Brooke's former friends, for the most part, seemed too shocked by the news to put much of their feelings in writing. But a few did write letters to each other. James Strachey wrote to Harry Norton on 3 May:

> Yes. It's horrible.
>
> But somehow I haven't personally felt as much as I should have expected. There are various reasons, I suppose. Chiefly, I've seen hardly anything of him in the last three years – and that softens things. It's more like losing the possible chance of making friends with him again than an actual loss. I cried a lot more over him when he went off in 1912 than last week.
>
> Other people feel it shockingly. Poor Eddie, whom I interviewed at the Admiralty the other day, seemed almost done for. And Ka one doesn't like to think of. Then there's Mrs B. – Alfred being in France.
>
> The only actual collapse I've heard of is most unexpected and queer. – Daphne Olivier went quite mad last night.

Lytton Strachey and Maynard Keynes both wrote to Duncan Grant on 25 April, the day the news hit the London papers. Strachey's letter said, 'It was impossible not to like him, impossible not to hope that he might like one again.' Keynes wrote, 'And to-day Rupert's death. In spite of all one has ever said, I find myself crying for him. It is too horrible.'

Katherine Cox wrote to James Strachey on 28 April (this is the entire letter):

> Tuesday.
> My dear. There really isn't anything. Give my love to Noel.
>   Ka
> Presently come. I'll write.

Less then two months later, Mrs Brooke received word concerning Alfred, the last of her sons. James wrote to Lytton: 'Dudley's just telephoned to say that Mrs. Brooke's heard that Alfred's been killed' (17 June 1915). Before his death, Alfred had written a letter to his mother entreating her not to believe Rupert's last poems. War, he said, was horrible.

On his deathbed, Brooke had sent letters asking both Jacques Raverat and Dudley Ward to name a son after him. Neither was able to fulfil the request, but his old friend Frances Cornford did. Rupert John Cornford (1915–36) grew up to write poetry, and his stunning good looks won him much of the same attention at Cambridge that Brooke had enjoyed. An avid communist, John was the first Englishman to join the Loyalist forces in the Spanish Civil War. He was killed in Spain on his twenty-first birthday, his body never recovered. William Russell-Smith, the elder brother of Hugh and Denham, also named a child after Brooke – Rupert Russell-Smith.

Brooke was buried by his friends under twelve olive trees that he had earlier noticed were especially beautiful, on a hillside location known as Mesadhi, on Skyros. His fellow soldiers placed rocks and an inscribed wooden cross on his grave, but these were later replaced by a more traditional memorial at Mrs Brooke's request.

Brooke's battalion lost eleven of fifteen officers in the Gallipoli campaign. As the situation deteriorated on the shores of Turkey, Denis Browne, Brooke's friend from Rugby schooldays, wrote: 'I've gone now too; not too badly I hope. I'm luckier than Rupert, because I've fought. But there's no one to bury me as I buried him, so perhaps he's better off in the long run.' Browne was killed in the trenches on 7 June. Of the group who buried Brooke, only Bernard Freyberg and Arthur Asquith survived the war. Freyberg proved himself a hero in battle and later became Governor-General of New Zealand.

The canonization and simplification of Brooke into a national symbol began with Dean Inge's sermon and continued with Winston Churchill's Marsh-penned eulogy in *The Times*. Recollections of a more personal nature followed from D. H. Lawrence, Henry James, Edward Thomas, Sybil Pye and Edward Marsh – this time writing under his own name. Gwen Raverat said the articles 'might have been written about King David, or Lord Byron, or Sophocles, or any other young man that wrote verse and was good-looking. [...] They never got the faintest feeling of his being a human being at all' (*RBB* 521). In this way Rupert Brooke, the national hero, was born.

While Brooke was becoming more and more conservative in the years leading up to the war, James Strachey was becoming more and more liberal. He became, in fact, too liberal for the liberals, withdrawing his membership of the National Liberal Club on 31 December 1913 due to what he perceived as their 'oppressive' handling of the women's enfranchisement issue. He worked alongside his sister Margery in both the Suffrage Movement and, during the war, in the anti-conscription campaign.

James had written a lengthy letter to Lytton on 31 July 1914, detailing sensible reasons why England should stay out of the war. Once the war began, St Loe fired him from his position at the *Spectator* on account of his opinions. James was able to obtain conscientious objector status and spent his national service time working with Quaker Relief. After the war, he was drama critic for the *Athenium* in the years 1919 and 1920.

During these years Strachey continued to court Noel Olivier, but Noel said after Brooke's death that she now knew she would never marry for love, and Strachey eventually gave up (though his lingering affection for her eventually manifested itself in a ten-year affair beginning in 1932, when both he and she were happily married to others).

Strachey, meanwhile, was being courted by Alix Sargant-Florence (1892–1973), whom he had first met at the Fabian Summer School in 1910. At the time, Brooke had written to Noel Olivier saying he thought Alix 'rather fine, for four reasons (1) she had a large, sensible head (2) she always sat or stood absolutely still. (3) She displayed a right judgement about you [...] (4) She understood what one said and answered exactly sufficiently, always to the point, & always with an appearance of thought' (*SOL* 48–49). Strachey and Sargant-Florence married in 1920. Fredegond Shove, the wife of Gerald Shove, wrote to Strachey when she heard news of the engagement:

> I feel I must just write you a line to say how glad I am that you are going to marry Alix. I've found it such a comfort to be married and I don't think it can make any difference to ones [sic] feelings. I can't help thinking that you and she will find it convenient [...] Gerald sends his love and is glad. (12 May 1920)

The couple spent their honeymoon in Vienna, where they were the first couple to be analyzed by Freud. Strachey had first become interested in psychoanalysis when he heard a paper by Freud read at a meeting of the Society for Psychical Research. Later, he and Alix became the foremost English translators of Freud's work. It is likely that Strachey's desire to understand both his own sexuality and Brooke's strange behaviour partially accounts for his being drawn to Freud. The letters between James and Alix written during this period were published in 1985 under the title *Bloomsbury/Freud: The Letters of James and Alix Strachey 1924–1925*.

Just as James's conversion to Fabianism had influenced Lytton, James's interest in Freud had a notable impact on his brother as well. When Lytton published *Elizabeth and Essex* in 1928, he dedicated it to James and Alix for good reason: Freud's theories show up frequently in its pages. Indeed, Lytton sent a copy of the book to Freud, who wrote back that he thought

Lytton's account of Elizabeth was 'quite correct' (J. Strachey, *American Imago* 359).

James entered into private practice as a psychoanalyst, and also enjoyed a reputation as a musicologist. He was a founding member of the Glyndebourne Opera.

Although Strachey's letters in the years after Brooke's death seldom mention Brooke, it is evident that he continued to think of his old friend, though perhaps not altogether kindly. The first evidence of lingering bitterness occurs in Virginia Woolf's diary in an entry written after she and Strachey had met in 1918 to discuss Marsh's *Memoir*, which Woolf was about to review. According to Woolf, she and Strachey 'couldn't say much about Rupert, save that he was jealous, moody, ill-balanced, all of which I knew, but can hardly say in writing' (V. Woolf, *Diary* 172). Further evidence appears years later. Frances Cornford wrote to Geoffrey Keynes in 1954 saying that Strachey was visiting for the weekend. She says Strachey 'was born knowing a lot about people without wanting to judge them – with, I must admit, a *marked* exception in the case of Naval Officers' (22 March 1954). Strachey never wrote anything on Brooke himself but co-operated fully with many who did.[1] His last printed word on Brooke was his unattributed quotation in Raymond Mortimer's review ('The Mixed-up World of Adonis') of Hassall's Brooke biography: 'Rupert wasn't nearly so nice as people now imagine; but he was a great deal cleverer.'[2]

Strachey was awarded the Schlegel-Tieck Prize by the Society of Authors in 1967 for his translations of Freud (particularly the *Standard Edition*), but died prior to the ceremony. Although *The Times* ignored his death, Leonard Woolf wrote an obituary appreciation.

1 Strachey provided perhaps too much co-operation for Christopher Hassall's liking: Hassall reported to Geoffrey Keynes that Strachey had written expressing his desire that Hassall would use the 'right' illustrations of Brooke in his book (Hassall to Keynes, 12 October 1962).
2 Mortimer revealed the source in a 15 May 1964 letter to Geoffrey Keynes, written in response to Keynes's complaint about his review.

Works Consulted

Abercrombie, Lascelles. *Emblems of Love: Designed in Several Discourses*. London: John Lane, 1912.

——. 'A Friend's Tribute'. *Morning Post*. 27 April 1915.

Allen, Peter. *The Cambridge Apostles: The Early Years*. Cambridge: Cambridge University Press, 1978.

Anderson, Patrick. Review of *The Letters of Rupert Brooke*, ed. Geoffrey Keynes. *Spectator* 14 June 1968.

Anscombe, Isabelle. *Omega and After*. London: Thames & Hudson, 1981.

Archer, Mary. *Rupert Brooke and The Old Vicarage, Grantchester*. Cambridge: Silent Books, 1989.

Asquith, Lady Cynthia. *Diaries 1915–1918*. New York: Knopf, 1969.

——. *Portrait of Barrie*. London: James Barrie, 1954.

Asquith, Margot. *The Autobiography of Margot Asquith*. Ed. Mark Bonham Carter. 1962. Boston: Houghton, 1963.

Badley, J. H. *A Schoolmaster's Testament*. Oxford: Basil Blackwell, 1937.

Banerjee, A. *Spirit above Wars: A Study of the English Poetry of the Two World Wars*. New Delhi: Macmillan, 1976.

Barrie, J. M. *Peter Pan*. 1911. New York: Scribner's, 1980.

Baynes, Ken. *War*. Boston: Boston Book and Art, 1970.

Bell, Clive. *Old Friends: Personal Recollections*. London: Chatto & Windus, 1956.

Bell, Quentin. *Bloomsbury*. New York: Basic Books, 1968.

——. *Virginia Woolf: A Biography*. New York: Harcourt, 1972.

Bell, Vanessa. *Vanessa Bell's Family Album*. Comp. Quentin Bell and Angelica Garnett. London: Jill Norman & Hobhouse, 1981.

Benkovitz, Miriam J. *Ronald Firbank: A Biography*. New York: Knopf, 1969.

Benson, A. C. *Memories and Friends*. London: John Murray, 1924.

Bergonzi, Bernard. *Heroes' Twilight: A Study of the Literature of the Great War*. London: Constable, 1965.

Birkin, Andrew. *J. M. Barrie and the Lost Boys: The Love Story that Gave Birth to Peter Pan*. New York: Potter, 1979.

Bonham Carter, Violet. *Winston Churchill: An Intimate Portrait*. New York: Harcourt, 1965.

Brooke, Rupert. *The Authorship of the Later 'Appius and Virginia'*. Cambridge: Cambridge University Press, 1913.

——. *The Collected Poems of Rupert Brooke: With a Memoir*. 1918. London: Sidgwick & Jackson, 1931.

——. *The Complete Poems of Rupert Brooke*. London: Sidgwick & Jackson, 1932.

——. *Democracy and the Arts*. London: Rupert Hart-Davis, 1946.

——. *John Webster and Elizabethan Drama*. 1916. New York: Russell-Atheneum, 1967.

——. *A Letter to the Editor of the* Poetry Review. Peekskill: Watch Hill, 1929.

——. *Letters from America*. 1916. New York: Beaufort, 1988.

——. *The Letters of Rupert Brooke*. Ed. Geoffrey Keynes. New York: Harcourt, 1968.

——. *Lithuania*. London: Sidgwick & Jackson, 1935.

——. *1914 and Other Poems*. London: Sidgwick & Jackson, 1915.

——. *The Poetical Works*. Ed. Geoffrey Keynes. 1946. London: Faber & Faber, 1988.

——. *The Prose of Rupert Brooke*. Ed. Christopher Hassall. London: Sidgwick & Jackson, 1956.

——. *Rupert Brooke in Canada*. Ed. Sandra Martin and Roger Hall. Toronto: Peter Martin, 1978.

——. *Song of Love: The Letters of Rupert Brooke and Noel Olivier*. Ed. Pippa Harris. New York: Crown, 1991.

'The Brooke Legend'. *Literary Digest* 2 September 1916.

Browne, Maurice. *Recollections of Rupert Brooke*. 510 copies printed. Chicago: Alexander Greene, 1927.

Bullough, Geoffrey. *The Trend of Modern Poetry*. 1934. Edinburgh: Oliver & Boyd, 1941.

Buxton, Richard. 'Two Cambridge Poets'. *Cambridge Magazine* 20 January 1912: 19.

Caesar, Adrian. *Taking It Like a Man: Suffering, Sexuality and the War Poets: Brooke, Sassoon, Owen, Graves*. Manchester: Manchester University Press, 1993.

Chainey, Graham. *A Literary History of Cambridge*. Ann Arbor: University of Michigan Press, 1986.

Cheason, Denis. *The Cambridgeshire of Rupert Brooke: An Illustrated Guide*. Waterbeach: D. Cheason, [c. 1980].

Clark, Keith. *The Muse Colony: Rupert Brooke, Edward Thomas, Robert Frost, and Friends: Dymock, 1914*. Bristol: Redcliffe Press, 1992.

Clements, Keith. *Henry Lamb*. London: Redcliffe Press, 1984.

Cole, Margaret. 'H. G. Wells and the Fabian Society'. *Edwardian Radicalism*. Ed. A. J. A. Morris. 97-113.

Connolly, Cyril. *Enemies of Promise*. Boston: Little, Brown, 1939.

Cornford, Frances. 'The Poet of Eternal Youth'. *Daily Telegraph* 23 April 1953.

Cox, C. B. and A. E. Dyson, eds. *The Twentieth Century Mind 1: 1900–1918: History, Ideas, and Literature in Britain*. London: Oxford University Press, 1972.

Cross, Tim, ed. *The Lost Voices of World War I: An International Anthology of Writers, Poets & Playwrights*. Iowa City: University of Iowa Press, 1988.

Dalton, Hugh. *Call Back Yesterday*. London: Frederick Muller, 1953.

Dangerfield, George. 'Epilogue: The Lofty Shade'. *The Strange Death of Liberal England 1910-1914*. 1935. New York: Capricorn, 1961. 426–42.

Deacon, Richard. *The Cambridge Apostles: A History of Cambridge University's Élite Intellectual Secret Society*. 1985. New York: Farrar, 1986.

'Death of Mr Rupert Brooke: Sunstroke at Lemnos'.' *The Times* 26 April 1915.

De la Mare, Walter. *Pleasures and Speculations*. Freeport, NY: Books for Libraries Press, 1969.

——. *Rupert Brooke and the Intellectual Imagination*. Limited edition. New York: Harcourt, 1920.

Delany, Paul. *D. H. Lawrence's Nightmare: The Writer and his Circle in the Years of the Great War*. New York: Basic Books, 1978.

——. *The Neo-pagans: Rupert Brooke and the Ordeal of Youth*. New York: Free Press, 1987.

Dent, Edward. 'Rupert Brooke'. *Cambridge Magazine* 8 May 1915.

Dickinson, G. Lowes. *The Autobiography of G. Lowes Dickinson and Other Unpublished Writings*. Ed. Dennis Proctor. London: Duckworth, 1973.

Drinkwater, John. *Discovery: Being the Second Book of an Autobiography 1897–1913*. London: Ernest Benn, 1932.

——. *The Muse in Council: Being Essays on Poets and Poetry*. Boston: Houghton Mifflin, 1925.

——. 'Rupert Brooke' and 'Rupert Brooke on John Webster'. *Prose Papers*. London: Elkin Mathews, 1918. 174–98.

Duncan, Joseph E. *The Revival of Metaphysical Poetry: The History of a Style, 1800 to the Present*. Minneapolis: University of Minnesota Press, 1959.

Dunn, Jane. *A Very Close Conspiracy: Vanessa Bell and Virginia Woolf*. London: Jonathan Cape, 1990.

Eby, Cecil Degrotte. *The Road to Armageddon: The Martial Spirit in English Popular Literature, 1870–1914*. Durham, NC: Duke University Press, 1987.

Eliot, T. S. *The Letters of T. S. Eliot*. Ed. Valerie Eliot. Vol. 1. San Diego: Harcourt, 1988.

Elliot, Michael. 'Cathleen Nesbitt Talks to Michael Elliot about Rupert Brooke'. *Listener* 20 January 1972: 83–5.

Fairchild, Hoxie Neale. *Religious Trends in English Poetry*. Vol. V: *1880–1920*. New York: Columbia University Press, 1962.

Farjeon, Eleanor. *Edward Thomas: The Last Four Years*. 1958. Oxford: Oxford University Press, 1979.

Fergusson, James. Review of *Song of Love: The Letters of Rupert Brooke and Noel Olivier*, ed. Pippa Harris. *Charleston Magazine* 5 (Summer/Autumn 1992): 43–5.

Field, Frank. *British and French Writers of the First World War: Comparative Studies in Cultural History*. Cambridge: Cambridge University Press, 1991.

Flory, Wendy Stallard. *The American Ezra Pound*. New Haven: Yale University Press, 1989.

Forster, E. M. *Goldsworthy Lowes Dickinson*. New York: Harcourt, 1934.

Furbank, P. N. *E. M. Forster: A Life*. 2 vols. London: Secker & Warburg, 1977, 1978.

Fussell, Paul. *The Great War and Modern Memory*. New York: Oxford University

Press, 1975.

——. *The Norton Book of Modern War*. New York: Norton, 1991.

Garnett, Angelica. *Deceived with Kindness: A Bloomsbury Childhood*. 1984. San Diego: Harcourt, 1985.

Garnett, David. *The Golden Echo*. 1953. London: Chatto & Windus, 1954.

——. *The Flowers of the Forest*. New York: Harcourt Brace, 1956.

——. *The Familiar Faces*. 1962. New York: Harcourt Brace, 1963.

——. *Great Friends: Portraits of Seventeen Writers*. 1979. New York: Atheneum, 1980.

Garnett, Richard. *Constance Garnett: A Heroic Life*. London: Sinclair Stevenson, 1991.

Garrod, H. W. 'Rupert Brooke'. *The Profession of Poetry and Other Lectures*. Oxford: Clarendon Press, 1929. 160–78.

Gathorne-Hardy, Jonathan. *The Old School Tie: The Phenomenon of the English Public Schools*. New York: Viking, 1978. (UK: *The Public School Phenomenon*)

Georgian Poetry, 1911–1912. Ed. Edward Marsh. *Times Literary Supplement* 27 February 1913: 1-2.

Gerhardie, William. *God's Fifth Column: A Biography of the Age 1890–1940*. New York: Simon & Schuster, 1981.

Gilbert, Martin. *Winston S. Churchill*. Companion vol. II, Part I: *July 1914–April 1915*. Boston: Houghton, 1973.

——. *Winston S. Churchill*. Vol. III, *1914–1916, The Challenge of War*. Boston: Houghton, 1971.

Gordon, John D. *Letters to an Editor: Georgian Poetry, 1912–1922: An Exhibition from the Berg Collection*. New York: NY Public Library, 1967.

Grant, Joy. *Harold Munro and the Poetry Bookshop*. Berkeley: University of California Press, 1967.

Graves, Robert. *But It Still Goes On*. London: Jonathan Cape, 1930.

——. *Good-bye to All That*. 1929. London: Cassell, 1958.

Halliburton, Richard. *The Royal Road to Romance*. Garden City, NY: Bobbs-Merrill, 1925.

Harrod, Roy F. *The Life of John Maynard Keynes*. London: Macmillan, 1951.

Harvey, C. J. D. *A Complete Guide to T. S. Eliot's* The Waste Land. Cape Town: Juta, 1978.

Hassall, Christopher. *Edward Marsh: Patron of the Arts*. London: Longmans, 1959.

——. *Rupert Brooke: A Biography*. 1964. London: Faber Paperbacks, 1972.

Hastings, Michael. *Rupert Brooke: The Handsomest Young Man in England*. London: Michael Joseph, 1967.

Henderson, James L. *Irregularly Bold: A Study of Bedales School*. London: André Deutsch, 1978.

Hibberd, Dominic. *Owen the Poet*. Athens, GA: University of Georgia Press, 1986.

——. *The First World War*. Basingstoke: Macmillan, 1990.

Higgins, Trumbull. *Winston Churchill and the Dardanelles: A Dialogue in Ends and Means*. New York: Macmillan, 1963.

Hiscock, Eric. *The Bells of Hell Go Ting-A-Ling-A-Ling: An Autobiographical Fragment without Maps*. London: Arlington, 1976.

Holroyd, Michael. *Augustus John: A Biography*. London: William Heinemann, 1974.

——. *Bernard Shaw*. Vol. I: *1856–1898, The Search for Love*. New York: Random, 1988.

——. *Bernard Shaw*. Vol. II: *1898–1918, The Pursuit of Power*. New York: Random, 1989.

——. *Lytton Strachey: A Critical Biography*. Vol. I: *The Unknown Years 1880–1910*. New York: Holt, 1968.

——. *Lytton Strachey: A Critical Biography*. Vol. II: *The Years of Achievement 1910–1932*. New York: Holt, 1968.

Housman, Laurence. *War Letters of Fallen Englishmen*. London: Victor Gollancz, 1930.

Hynes, Samuel. *The Edwardian Turn of Mind*. Princeton: Princeton University Press, 1968.

——. *Edwardian Occasions: Essays on English Writing in the Early Twentieth Century*. London: Routledge, 1972.

——. *A War Imagined: The First World War and English Culture*. New York: Atheneum, 1991.

James, Henry. *Letters*. Vol. II. Ed. Percy Lubbock. New York: Scribner's, 1920.

——. Preface. *Letters from America*. By Rupert Brooke. 1916. New York: Beaufort, 1988.

Jebb, Julian. 'Rupert Brooke: The Blond Beastliness'. Review of *The Letters of Rupert Brooke*, ed. Geoffrey Keynes. *The Times* 8 June 1968.

Jerrold, Douglas. *Georgian Adventure*. London: Collins, 1937.

——. *The Royal Naval Division*. London: Hutchinson, 1923.

John, Augustus. *Autobiography*. London: Jonathan Cape, 1975.

Johnston, John H. *English Poetry of the First World War: A Study in the Evolution of Lyric and Narrative Form*. Princeton: Princeton University Press, 1964.

Jones, Alun R. *The Life and Opinions of T. E. Hulme*. London: Victor Gollancz, 1960.

Kains-Jackson, Charles. 'Antinous'. Trans. Ernest Raymond. *Artist* 1 October 1891.

Kallich, Martin. *The Psychological Milieu of Lytton Strachey*. New York: Bookman, 1961.

Keynes, Geoffrey. *A Bibliography of Rupert Brooke*. London: Rupert Hart-Davis, 1954.

——. *The Gates of Memory*. 1981. Oxford: Oxford University Press, 1983.

——. *Henry James in Cambridge*. London: Heffer, 1967.

Keynes, John Maynard. *Two Memoirs*. London: Macmillan, 1949.

Knox, Ronald. *Patrick Shaw-Stewart*. London: Collins, 1920.

Lambert, Royston. *Beloved and God: The Story of Hadrian and Antinous*. Secausus, NJ: Meadowland, 1988.

Lane, Arthur E. *An Adequate Response: The War Poetry of Wilfred Owen and Siegfried Sassoon*. Detroit: Wayne State University Press, 1972.

Larkin, Philip. 'The Apollo Bit'. Review of *The Letters of Rupert Brooke*. Ed. Geoffrey Keynes. *New Statesman* 14 June 1968.

'The Late Rupert Brooke: England's Poet Soldier'. *Morning Post* 27 April 1915.

Lawrence, D. H. 'The Georgian Renaissance'. *Rhythm* March 1913: xvii–xx.

——. *Letters*. Ed. Aldous Huxley. London: William Heinemann, 1932.

Lawrence, T. E. *The Letters of T. E. Lawrence*. Ed. David Garnett. London: Jonathan Cape, 1938.

Leavis, F. R. *New Bearings in English Poetry: A Study of the Contemporary Situation*.

London: Chatto & Windus, 1932.

Lee, Francis. *Fabianism and Colonialism: The Life & Political Thought of Lord Sydney Olivier.* London: Defiant Books, 1988.

Lehmann, John. *The English Poets of the First World War.* London: Thames & Hudson, 1982.

——. *The Strange Destiny of Rupert Brooke.* New York: Holt, 1980. (UK: *Rupert Brooke: His Life and his Legend.*)

Leslie, Shane. *The End of a Chapter.* London: Constable, 1916.

Levy, Paul. *Moore: G. E. Moore and the Cambridge Apostles.* 1979. New York: Holt, 1980.

Lucas, John. *Modern English Poetry from Hardy to Hughes: A Critical Survey.* Totowa, NJ: Barnes, 1986.

MacKail, Denis. *The Story of J. M. B.: A Biography.* London: Peter Davies, 1941.

MacKendrick, L. K. Review of *Taking It Like a Man*, by Adrian Caesar. *Choice* 31 (1993): 452.

Mackenzie, Norman and Jeanne Mackenzie. *The First Fabians.* London: Weidenfeld & Nicolson, 1977.

——. *The Time Traveller: A Biography of H. G. Wells.* London: Weidenfeld & Nicolson, 1973.

Mais, S. P. B. 'Rupert Brooke'. *From Shakespeare to O. Henry: Studies in Literature.* 1923. Freeport, NY: Books for Libraries Press, 1968.

Marsh, Edward, ed. *Georgian Poetry 1911–1912.* London: Poetry Bookshop, 1912.

——. *Georgian Poetry 1913–1915.* London: Poetry Bookshop, 1915.

——. *Georgian Poetry 1916–1917.* London: Poetry Bookshop, 1917.

——. *Georgian Poetry 1918–1919.* London: Poetry Bookshop, 1919.

——. *Georgian Poetry 1920–1922.* London: Poetry Bookshop, 1922.

——. Memoir. *The Collected Poems of Rupert Brooke.* 1918. New York: Dodd, 1931.

——. *A Number of People: A Book of Reminiscences.* London: William Heinemann and Hamish Hamilton, 1939.

Martin, Sandra. *Rupert Brooke in Canada.* Toronto: PMA Books, 1978.

Masefield, John. *Gallipoli.* New York: Macmillan, 1916.

——. *Poems.* London: Macmillan, 1930.

Mason, Geoffrey. *Newer Numbers: Four Georgian Parodies.* Upton-upon-Severn: G. Mason, 1988.

Menand, Louis. *Discovering Modernism: T. S. Eliot and his Context.* New York: Oxford University Press, 1987.

Meyers, Jeffrey. *Homosexuality and Literature, 1890–1930.* Montreal: McGill University Press, 1977.

Millard, Kenneth. *Edwardian Poetry.* Oxford: Clarendon Press, 1991.

Miller, Peter. *Rupert Brooke: A Brief Biography.* Warwick: Warwickshire County Council, 1987.

——. comp. *The Rugby Centenary Brooke: An Anthology Selected and Compiled by Peter Miller.* Rugby: Rupert Brooke Centenary Association, 1987.

'Mr. Brooke's Poems'. *Cambridge Review* 8 February 1912.

'Mr. Rupert Brooke: The Poet and Sub-Lieutenant Killed by Sunstroke'. *Westminster Gazette* 26 April 1915.

Monro, Harold. 'Some Thoughts on the Poetry of Rupert Brooke'. *Cambridge Magazine* 22 May 1915: 424.

Monroe, Harriet. Review of *The Collected Poems of Rupert Brooke*, ed. Edward Marsh. *Poetry* February 1916: 263.

Moore, John. *Edward Thomas*. London: William Heinemann, 1939.

Moore, T. Sturge. 'Rupert Brooke'. *Some Soldier Poets*. London: Grant Richards, 1919. 21–6.

Moorehead, Alan. *Gallipoli*. New York: Harper, 1956.

Morley, Christopher. 'To Rupert Brooke (England 1913)'. *Chimneysmoke*. New York: George H. Doran, 1921.

Morris, A. J. A. *Edwardian Radicalism 1900–1914: Some Aspects of British Radicalism*. London: Routledge, 1974.

Mortimer, Raymond. 'The Mixed-up World of Adonis'. Review of *Rupert Brooke: A Biography*, by Christopher Hassall. *Sunday Times* 10 May 1964.

Moult, Thomas. *Barrie*. New York: Scribner's, 1928.

Murray, Gilbert. *A Biography of Francis Macdonald Cornford 1874–1943*. Oxford: Oxford University Press, 1944.

Murry, John Middleton. *Between Two Worlds: An Autobiography*. London: Jonathan Cape, 1935.

Nesbitt, Cathleen. *A Little Love and Good Company*. London: Faber & Faber, 1975.

Nevinson, Henry W. *The Dardanelles Campaign*. London: Nisbet, 1918.

——. 'Rupert Brooke'. *Nation* 1 May 1915.

Newbolt, Henry. *The Later Life and Letters of Sir Henry Newbolt*. Ed. Margaret Newbolt. London: Faber and Faber, 1942.

——. *A New Study of English Poetry*. London: Constable, 1917.

——. 'Rupert Brooke'. *The English Poets: Selections with Critical Introductions by Various Writers and a General Introduction by Matthew Arnold*. Vol. V: *Browning to Rupert Brooke*. Ed. Thomas Humphry Ward. London: Macmillan, 1918. 628–31.

New Numbers. A quarterly publication of the poems of Rupert Brooke, John Drinkwater, Wilfrid Wilson Gibson and Lascelles Abercrombie. 1.1–1.4 (February, April, August, December 1914). Ryton, Dymock, Gloucester: Crypt House, 1914.

Review of *New Numbers*, by Rupert Brooke et al. *Times Literary Supplement* 11 March 1915.

Olivier, Sydney. *Letters and Selected Writings*. London: George Allen, 1948.

Ollivant, Alfred. 'The Cost'. *Atlantic Monthly* February 1916.

Orwell, George. *The Road to Wigan Pier*. London: Victor Gollancz, 1937.

Owen, Wilfred. *Collected Letters*. Ed. Harold Owen and John Bell. London: Oxford University Press, 1967.

Palmer, Alan and Veronica. *Who's Who in Bloomsbury*. New York: St Martin's Press, 1987.

Palmer, Herbert. *Post-Victorian Poetry*. London: Dent, 1938.

Parker, Peter. *The Old Lie: The Great War and the Public-School Ethos*. London: Constable, 1987.

Parkman, Mary Rosetta. 'A Poet-Soldier: Rupert Brooke'. *Heroes of Today*. New York: Century, 1917. 263–94.

Partridge, Frances. *A Pacifist's War*. London: Hogarth Press, 1978.

——. *Memories*. London: Victor Gollancz, 1981.

'Patriotism Was Not Enough'. Review of *Rupert Brooke: A Biography*, by Christopher Hassall. *Times Literary Supplement* 28 May 1964: 445–7.

Patterson, Michael. *The Revolution in German Theatre: 1900–1933*. Boston: Routledge & Kegan Paul, 1981.

Pearsall, Robert Brainard. *Rupert Brooke: The Man and Poet*. Amsterdam: Rodopi, 1974.

Perdriel-Vaissiéres, Jeanne. *Rupert Brooke's Death and Burial: Based on the Log of the French Hospital Ship* Duguay-Trouin. Trans. Vincent O'Sullivan. New Haven: W. A. Bradley, Yale University Press, 1917. London: Imperial War Museum Dept of Printed Books, 1992.

Phelps, William Lyon. *The Advance of English Poetry in the Twentieth Century*. New York: Dodd, 1918.

Pimlott, Ben. *Hugh Dalton*. London: Jonathan Cape, 1985.

Pinto, Vivian de Solo. *Crisis in English Poetry: 1880-1940*. London: Hutchinson 1951.

Platnauer, M. 'Variants in the Manuscripts of the Poems of Rupert Brooke and A. E. Housman'. *Review of English Studies* xix, 76 (1943).

Review of *Poems*, 1911, by Rupert Brooke. *English Review* February 1912.

Potter, Richard Montgomery Gilchrist. *Rupert Brooke: A Bibliographical Note on his Works Published in Book Form 1911-1919*. 52 copies printed. Hartford, CT: Potter, 1923.

Pound, Reginald. *The Lost Generation*. London: Constable, 1964.

Press, John. *A Map of Modern English Verse*. London: Oxford University Press, 1969.

Prince, F[rank]. T[empleton]. *Afterword on Rupert Brooke*. London: Menard Press, 1976.

Raverat, Gwen. *Period Piece: A Cambridge Childhood*. New York: Norton, 1952.

Reade, Brian, ed. *Sexual Heretics: Male Homosexuality in English Literature from 1850 to 1900*. New York: Coward-McCann, 1970.

Richardson, Elizabeth P. *A Bloomsbury Iconography*. Winchester: St Paul's Bibliographies, 1989.

Richardson, Frank M. *Mars without Venus: A Study of Some Homosexual Generals*. Edinburgh: William Blackwood, 1981.

Riding, Laura, and Robert Graves. *A Survey of Modernist Poetry*. 1927. Garden City, NY: Doubleday, 1928.

Robertson, David. *George Mallory*. London: Faber & Faber, 1969.

Robson, W. W. *Modern English Literature*. London: Oxford University Press, 1970.

Roche, Paul. *With Duncan Grant in Southern Turkey*. [London]: Honeyglen, 1982.

Rogers, Timothy, ed. *Georgian Poetry 1911–1922: The Critical Heritage*. London: Routledge, 1977.

——. 'Rupert Brooke: Man and Monument'. Review of *The Letters of Rupert*

Brooke, ed. Geoffrey Keynes. *English* xvii, 99 (Autumn 1968): 79–84.

——. *Rupert Brooke: A Reappraisal and Selection from his Writings, Some Hitherto Unpublished*. New York: Barnes & Noble, 1971.

Rose, Jonathan. *The Edwardian Temperament 1895–1919*. Athens, OH: Ohio University Press, 1986.

Rosenbaum, S. P. *Victorian Bloomsbury: The Early Literary History of the Bloomsbury Group*. Vol. I. New York: St Martin's Press, 1987.

Ross, Robert. *The Georgian Revolt: 1910–1922, Rise and Fall of a Poetic Ideal*. Carbondale: Southern Illinois University Press, 1965.

Roy, James A. *James Matthew Barrie: An Appreciation*. London: Jarrolds, 1937.

'Rupert Brooke'. *Saturday Westminster Gazette* 1 May 1915.

'Rupert Brooke'. *Spectator* 1 May 1915.

'Rupert Brooke: The Poet Whom the War Made and Killed'. *American Review of Reviews* October 1915: 499.

Russell-Smith, Hugh Francis. *Harrington and his Oceana: A Study of a 17th Century Utopia and its Influence in America*. 1914. New York: Octagon-Farrar, 1971.

Sadleir, Michael. *Forlorn Sunset*. London: Constable, 1947.

——. *Passages from the Autobiography of a Bibliomaniac*. Los Angeles: University of California Library, 1962.

Sanders, Charles Richard. *The Strachey Family, 1488–1932: Their Writings and Literary Associations*. Durham, NC: Duke University Press, 1953.

Sassoon, Siegfried. *Siegfried's Journey, 1916-1920*. London: Faber and Faber, 1945.

——. *The War Poems of Siegfried Sassoon*. London: Faber and Faber, 1983.

——. *The Weald of Youth*. New York: Viking, 1942.

Schell, Sherril. 'The Story of a Photograph'. *Bookman* 63.6 (1926).

Schroder, John. *Catalogue of Books and Manuscripts by Rupert Brooke, Edward Marsh and Christopher Hassall*. Cambridge: Rampant Lions Press, 1970.

Searle, G. R. *Corruption in British Politics: 1895–1930*. Oxford: Clarendon Press, 1987.

——. *The Quest for National Efficiency: A Study in British Politics and Political Thought, 1899–1914*. 1971. London: Ashfield, 1990.

Sedgwick, Ellery. *The Happy Profession*. Boston: Little, 1946.

Shaw, George Bernard. *Bernard Shaw: Collected Letters 1911–1925* (vol. III). Ed. Dan H. Laurence. New York: Viking, 1985.

S[hepard]., J[ohn]. T[ressider]. 'In Memoriam. Rupert Brooke'. *Cambridge Review* 5 May 1915.

Shone, Richard. *Bloomsbury Portraits: Vanessa Bell, Duncan Grant and their Circle*. Oxford: Phaidon Press, 1976.

Silkin, Jon. *Out of Battle: The Poetry of the Great War*. London: Oxford University Press, 1972.

Sillars, Stuart. *Art and Survival in First World War Britain*. New York: St Martin's Press, 1987.

Simpson, John Hope. *Rugby since Arnold: A History of Rugby School from 1842*. London: Macmillan, 1967.

Sitwell, Edith. *Aspects of Modern Poetry*. London: Duckworth, 1934.

Skidelsky, Robert. *John Maynard Keynes.* Vol. I: *Hopes Betrayed 1883–1920.* London: Macmillan, 1983.

Smith, Timothy d'Arch. *Love in Earnest: Some Notes on the Lives and Writings of English 'Uranian' Poets from 1889 to 1930.* London: Routledge, 1970.

'Some Recent Verse'. Review of *Poems,* by Rupert Brooke. *Times Literary Supplement* 29 August 1912.

Spalding, Frances. *British Art since 1900.* London: Thames & Hudson, 1986.

Spender, Stephen. 'Hidden Passion of the Neglected Poet'. Review of *A. E. Housman: The Scholar–Poet,* by Richard Perceval Graves. *NOW!* 9 November 1979: 94–5.

——. *The Struggle of the Modern.* London: Hamish Hamilton, 1963.

Spurling, Hilary. *Paul Scott: A Life of the Author of* The Raj Quartet. New York: Norton, 1991.

Stallworthy, Jon. 'Who Was Rupert Brooke?' *Critical Survey* 2.2: 185–93.

——. *Wilfred Owen.* London: Oxford University Press, 1974.

Stead, C. K. *The New Poetic.* London: Hutchinson University Library, 1964.

Strachey, James. Letter to Martin Kallich. *American Imago* XV (Winter 1958): 359.

Strachey, James and Alix Strachey. *Bloomsbury/Freud: The Letters of James and Alix Strachey 1924–1925.* Ed. Perry Meisel and Walter Kendrick. New York: Basic Books, 1985.

Strachey, Lytton. *Lytton Strachey by Himself: A Self-Portrait.* Ed. Michael Holroyd. New York: Holt, 1971.

——. *The Really Interesting Question.* Ed. Paul Levy. New York: Coward, 1973.

——. *Virginia Woolf and Lytton Strachey Letters.* Ed. Leonard Woolf and James Strachey. New York: Harcourt Brace, 1956.

Stringer, Arthur. *Red Wine of Youth: A Life of Rupert Brooke.* Indianapolis: Bobbs-Merrill, 1948.

Sturgeon, Mary C. 'Rupert Brooke'. *Studies of Contemporary Poets.* New York: Dodd, 1916. 36–52.

Swinnerton, Frank. *The Georgian Scene: A Literary Panorama.* New York: Farrar & Rinehart, 1934.

Symons, Julian. *Makers of the New: The Revolution in Literature, 1912–1939.* New York: Random, 1987.

Review of *Taking It Like a Man* by Adrian Caesar. *Times Literary Supplement* 1 October 1993: 18.

Toynbee, Philip. 'The Myth of Rupert Brooke'. *Observer Weekend Review* 10 May 1964.

Trevelyan, R[obert]. C. *Selected Poems.* London: MacGibbon, 1953.

Turner, John Frayn. *Splendour and the Pain: Rupert Brooke.* London: Breese, 1992.

Tylee, Claire. *The Great War and Women's Consciousness: Images of Militarism and Womanhood in Women's Writings, 1914–64.* Iowa City: University of Iowa Press, 1990.

Walter, Natasha. 'Rupert the Bare Soul'. Review of *Song of Love: The Letters of*

Rupert Brooke and Noel Olivier, ed. Pippa Harris. *Independent on Sunday* 15 December 1991: 45.

Walters, Lettice D'Oyly. *The Years at the Spring: An Anthology of Recent Poetry.* New York: Brentano's, 1920.

Waugh, Arthur. *Tradition and Change: Studies in Contemporary Literature.* London: Chapman, 1919.

Wearing, J. P. *The London Stage 1900–1909: A Calendar of Plays and Players.* 2 vols. Metuchen, NJ: Scarecrow, 1981.

———. *The London Stage 1910–1919: A Calendar of Plays and Players.* 2 vols. Metuchen, NJ: Scarecrow, 1982.

Webb, Beatrice. *Our Partnership.* Ed. B. Drake and M. I. Cole. New York: Longmans Green, 1975.

———. *The Diary of Beatrice Webb.* Vol. III. London: Virago, 1984.

Webb, Sidney and Beatrice. *The Letters of Sidney and Beatrice Webb.* Vol. II: *Partnership, 1892–1912.* Ed. Norman Mackenzie. Cambridge: Cambridge University Press, 1978.

Wells, H. G. *Wells in Love: Postscript to an Experiment in Autobiography.* Ed. G. P. Wells. London: Faber & Faber, 1984.

Wilde, Oscar. *The Letters of Oscar Wilde.* Ed. Rupert Hart-Davis. New York: Harcourt Brace, 1962.

Wilson, Colin. *Poetry and Mysticism.* London: Hutchinson, 1970.

Wohl, Robert. *The Generation of 1914.* Cambridge, MA: Harvard University Press, 1979.

Woolf, Leonard. *Beginning Again: An Autobiography of the Years 1911 to 1918.* New York: Harcourt Brace, 1964.

———. *Letters of Leonard Woolf.* Ed. Frederic Spotts. San Diego: Harcourt, 1989.

Woolf, Virginia. *Books and Portraits.* Ed. Mary Lyon. London: Hogarth, 1977.

———. *The Diary of Virginia Woolf.* Vol. I: *1915–1919.* Ed. Anne Olivier Bell. New York: Harcourt, 1977.

———. *Moments of Being: Unpublished Autobiographical Writings.* Ed. Jeanne Schulkind. New York: Harcourt, 1976.

———. *The Question of Things Happening: The Letters of Virginia Woolf.* Vol. II, *1912–1922.* Ed. Nigel Nicolson. London: Hogarth Press, 1976.

———. Review of *The Collected Poems of Rupert Brooke*, ed. Edward Marsh. *Times Literary Supplement* 8 August 1918: 371.

———. *A Room of One's Own.* 1929. London: Hogarth Press, 1931.

———. *Virginia Woolf and Lytton Strachey Letters.* Ed. Leonard Woolf and James Strachey. New York: Harcourt, 1956.

———. *A Writer's Diary: Being Extracts from the Diary of Virginia Woolf.* Ed. Leonard Woolf. 1953. London: Hogarth Press, 1954.

Wright, Kenneth W., ed. *Milton's Minor Poems, with Descriptive Poetry of the 18th, 19th and 20th Centuries.* New York: Noble & Noble, [c. 1934].

Young, Ian. *Male Homosexuality in Literature: A Bibliography.* Metuchen, NJ: Scarecrow, 1975.

Index of Names